Discipleship and Imagination

For Catherine
Matri meae D. D. D.

Discipleship and Imagination

Christian Tradition and Truth

DAVID BROWN

OXFORD
UNIVERSITY PRESS

OXFORD
UNIVERSITY PRESS

Great Clarendon Street, Oxford OX2 6DP

Oxford University Press is a department of the University of Oxford.
It furthers the University's objective of excellence in research, scholarship,
and education by publishing worldwide in

Oxford   New York

Athens Auckland Bangkok Bogotá Buenos Aires Calcutta
Cape Town Chennai Dar es Salaam Delhi Florence Hong Kong Istanbul
Karachi Kuala Lumpur Madrid Melbourne Mexico City Mumbai
Nairobi Paris São Paulo Singapore Taipei Tokyo Toronto Warsaw

with associated companies in Berlin Ibadan

Oxford is a registered trade mark of Oxford University Press
in the UK and in certain other countries

Published in the United States
by Oxford University Press Inc., New York

British Library Cataloguing in Publication Data

Data available

Library of Congress Cataloging in Publication Data

Tradition and imagination: revelation and change
David Brown.
Includes bibliographical references.
1. Revelation.   2. Tradition (Theology)   3. Bible—Evidences.
authority, etc.   I. Title.
BT127.2.B76   2000   231.7′4—dc21   99–12411

ISBN 0–19–827018–6

1 3 5 7 9 10 8 6 4 2

Typeset in Bembo by
Cambrian Typesetters, Frimley, Surrey
Printed in Great Britain
on acid-free paper by
Biddles Ltd., Guildford and King's Lynn

PREFACE

As with its earlier companion volume *Tradition and Imagination*, this is a work that has relied heavily on the encouragement, advice and support of colleagues and friends. Jeff Astley, Stephen Barton, Sarah Boss, Thomas Hummel, Michael Ipgrave, Penny Minney, Peter Robinson, Walter Moberly, and Clare Stancliffe read and commented on one or more chapters, while David Fuller and Ann Loades gave detailed attention to the work in its entirety. Both of them did much to widen my horizons. As the narratives of two women, Mary Magdalene and the Mother of Jesus, figure prominently in what follows, I am particularly grateful to Ann for the care she took to try to ensure that, in my eagerness to make the nature of their discipleship equally available to both sexes, I did not discount the importance of feminist issues. As the work was reaching its completion, I was fortunate in being invited to give a week's course of lectures and seminars at the Free University in Amsterdam. I am most grateful for the stimulus provided by Henk Vroom, Aard van Egmond and the students who participated. The following week I spent as a guest of the Redemptorists in Poland. To the outsider the Reformed church in the Netherlands and the Catholic church in Poland can appear to have little in common. It was a particular pleasure therefore to find myself learning from both.

Integral to the discussion that follows is my belief that discipleship is made possible only by community. So, while in no way discounting the influence on me of other individuals, not least the example of my mother, Catherine, I must also thank God for my present context, set as I am in the worshipping community of Durham Cathedral. Joint posts are not the current fashion, but personally I regard myself as singularly fortunate in being both a professor in such a university as Durham and a residentiary canon of the city's splendid Romanesque cathedral. What is required of lecture and sermon is of course quite different. Nonetheless, the measurement of one against the other does generate a rich and lively internal dialogue that I have found hugely beneficial to my own life of discipleship and prayer. Some of the theses in this book and its predecessor have already percolated into sermons and prayers. Encouraging comments from members of the cathedral's various congregations have played no small part in pursuing what at times seemed a daunting task to its completion.

Durham Cathedral

ABBREVIATIONS

AV   Authorized Version
RSV   Revised Standard Version
JB   Jerusalem Bible
NEB New English Bible
PG   Migne, *Patrologia Graeca*
PL   Migne, *Patrologia Latina*

CONTENTS

LIST OF PLATES

INTRODUCTION

ALTHOUGH this is the second of two books on the role of trad-ition, it has been written in such a way that it can easily be read as a self-contained volume, with a somewhat different theme: dis-cipleship. In its predecessor, *Tradition and Imagination*, I worked on a rather larger canvass.[1] Current debates between modernism and postmodernism, the significance of other religions, the function of myth in the classical world, and changing attitudes to revelation, all played their part in shaping how I suggested we perceive the relation between the Bible and the Church's subsequent history. So far from setting them in opposition to one another, I argued that a developing tradition needed to be seen as the motor that kept both engines running, and thus granted the Church the potential to respond effectively to changing social conditions. Revelatory insights were thus by no means to be confined to the canonical dispensation, but instead God must be seen as continu-ing to speak equally across the subsequent two millennia.

This was not intended to suggest inevitable progress. There is no escaping the admission that, from the perspective of the later community, both Bible and Church can alike be seen at times to err. Not infrequently, it will be insights from the biblical period that provide the most effective critique of what comes later. That aspect, however, has received little mention here, not because I deem the matter unimportant but because it is already a well-worn theme in the writings of numerous theologians. Instead, I have chosen to focus on the less familiar implication, the ability of the developing tradition to modify and sometimes even 'correct' its biblical roots. Because Christianity lays claim to an historical reve-lation, the temptation is to suppose that only what is firmly grounded in its historical past could be relevant or true, whereas it is precisely the contention of this volume and its predecessor that,

---

[1] Oxford: Oxford University Press, 1999.

while it remains important to identify what the original perspectives were, trajectories have been opened up which have the inherent power to turn back upon the tradition from which they come and force a new reading of its implications. In *Tradition and Imagination* detailed consideration was given to some examples from the patriarchal narratives in the Old Testament and from the life of Christ in the New, and in particular due note was taken of how this brought about changes in Christian doctrine and self-understanding. Here our focus will be subtly different. Although doctrinal issues will still sometimes be allowed to emerge, our main concern will now be with how such change affects the practice of Christian discipleship.

To that end, this volume is divided into three parts. The opening chapter of Part One uses changing attitudes to the status of women as a mean of focusing the question. I argue that relating neither to Christ as human example nor Christ as Lord is best mediated through the New Testament alone. Chapter 2 then finds confirmation of this from the history of Christianity in some of the factors that help explain the rise of the cult of the saints, as also, more recently, in some of the uses to which the novel has been put. The third chapter of this part of the work then considers how these discoveries relate to the social dimension of discipleship, and argues that, so far from the notion of the communion of saints in heaven being an optional extra, it must be seen as integral to Christianity's conceptual frame, if adequate sense is to be made of the social shaping of human discipleship.

If Part One was concerned with the general structure of discipleship as imitation and relationship within a community, Part Two then tackles the specifics of change by considering in some detail two key types of transformation that have occurred over the centuries, attitudes to suffering, and to family and sexuality, as these have been mediated through the Book of Job and the cult of the Virgin Mary respectively. In both cases, I shall be concerned to illustrate how the Church has much to learn from what happened at almost all the various stages in the story of these developments. So my argument is certainly not that all that matters is where we have now reached, but equally it is important to insist that, while Scripture is entitled to the first word, it is not necessarily to be given the last.

That kind of verdict does, of course, raise acute questions about authority and truth. So, although the relevance of the latter issue in particular is noted throughout this work, detailed attention is given to both questions in Part Three. While Chapter 3 speaks of the unity of the community in heaven, Chapter 6 addresses the Church's present reality but, so far from finding its divisions a subject for inevitable condemnation, argues that conflict is integral to the growth of the community's self-understanding. Heresy is thus indispensable to the growth of orthodoxy, and so, though the ultimate aim should still be a common mind, there remains danger in supposing any issue completely resolved or closed. That might seem to make all religious truth provisional, and in one sense it clearly does, but no more so, I think, than what happens with scientific or historical truth. What I regard as the more fundamental issue of types of truth is addressed in the final chapter, in particular the question of how truth can be said to attach to the non-historical or fictional. Early chapters will have already amply demonstrated the indispensable role of fiction, as the lives of Christ and of his saints were rewritten or redrawn to ensure continuing imaginative engagement. Since such later versions cannot possibly provide one-to-one mapping onto any factual reality, the temptation is to suppose that they can therefore mediate, if truth at all, only an inferior form, but, the final chapter will suggest, so far is this from being so, fiction can sometimes embody the greater and more profound truth. It is thus the imagination that best preserves the continuing tradition's grasp on divine reality and our subjective appropriation of it in our own discipleship.

No bibliography is provided. Instead, complete bibliographical details are to be found at the first mention *within* any chapter of the particular work concerned.

PART ONE
Appropriating Christ for the present

In the earlier volume I sought to draw attention to two implications of the way in which I believe modern historical research now requires us to regard the life of Jesus.[1] The first concerned the radical nature of the kenosis that took place in the incarnation. God in entering into the human condition did not exempt himself from the normal rules of historical conditioning that apply to us all, and so the significance of Jesus' life for us today lies not in him standing apart from the particular culture and assumptions into which he was born but in bringing them to the fullest and best expression that that particular context allowed. Then, secondly, precisely because later contexts have often been very different, what was then initiated was not the appropriation of an unchanging past but its development as new contexts made possible the building of fresh insights upon those initial foundations. The process had begun with Paul's different attitude to the Law, but continued well beyond the closure of the canon in numerous ways, not least in attitudes to art, as the chapter on 'Art as revelation' sought to illustrate. Not only was the incarnation seen as legitimating the violation of the second commandment forbidding images of the divine, that violation eventually made possible a much deeper sense of God's identification with us in all our humanness, especially in our suffering.

In establishing a connection with this volume, one of my main contentions in *Tradition and Imagination* needs to be put bluntly and starkly: were Christ only a figure in the history of first-century Palestine, then much, if not most, of what was later developed in

---

[1] *Tradition and Imagination*, ch. 6 for first implication, *passim* for second.

his name would have been permanently incomprehensible to him. The only way that conclusion can be resisted is if one believes, as I do, that Christ was very much more, and in particular with his resurrection and ascension now enjoys a humanity in heaven that is available to every age and time. Ironically, sometimes a pre-critical age perceived the truth of this observation more clearly than our own day. So, for instance, the modern funeral service of the Church of England opens with the priest declaring: 'Jesus said, I am the resurrection, and I am the life.' By contrast, the Book of Common Prayer offers us: 'I am the resurrection and the life, *saith* the Lord.' Therein lies considerable irony, in that almost certainly the modern version records an historical falsehood, whereas the Prayer Book provides, to my mind, a profound truth: that, though Jesus made no such specific claim in his own lifetime, it is indeed precisely through him that we can discover eternal life and of that fact he himself is now fully aware in his continuing present existence.[2]

Yet, whether we think of Christians living prior or subsequent to critical readings of the New Testament, appeals to the now resurrected Christ can hardly be expected to solve all the problems generated by later contexts quite different from that of the historical Jesus, central though Christ's resurrection is to Christian self-understanding. The problem is twofold. First, we do not have definitive, independent access to the mind of Christ as it now is, and so the question of continuity with that original life has still constantly to be raised, and some answer given. That is where the whole issue of trajectories and their subsequent modification raises itself. In the three chapters that follow a number of trajectories will therefore be identified, and their status ascertained. Life would have been much simpler had every biblical trajectory been allowed to follow its natural path to a conclusion, but what in fact we find is some doing so, while others are either modified or radically undermined by the impact of new perspectives given by fresh cultural contexts; not that these contexts achieve automatic priority over the biblical witness, but they can require alterations, both

---

[2] Funeral Service in *Alternative Service Book* of 1980; Order for the Burial of the Dead in *Book of Common Prayer* of 1662. The modern service has treated the original scriptural text more literally, by using the same past tense as the original narrative: John 11: 25.

small and large, as the pronouncements of Scripture are seen in a new light. As subsequent chapters will illustrate, this can come about as a result of quite a wide range of different factors: sometimes, for instance, because of new empirical data (Chapter 1); at other times, the drawing out of implications from Scripture that turn back on the text to cast doubt on some of the Bible's other emphases (Chapter 3). There is no simple pattern, and that is why close attention to the details of my argument is required.

But, secondly and more directly relevant to the question of discipleship, there is also the issue of what it means to relate to Christ in our own quite different context, no longer the world of first-century Judaism. Chapter 1, 'Prostituting and valuing women', indicates the nature of that problem by linking two apparently unrelated issues—modern attempts to establish the equality of the sexes from Scripture and attacks on the later Church's use of the composite figure of a penitent Mary Magdalene. The second half of the chapter will argue that, despite repeated assertions that her image was used only to malign women, Mary did in fact function successfully as a means of establishing *any* penitent disciple in intimate relation with the risen Lord. In effect, the fictional elements in the way in which she was identified allowed sinners in general, both male and female, to locate themselves within the narrative of Jesus' story and so appropriate for themselves the same forgiveness and relationship. Relating to the risen Lord is one thing, however; quite another, trying to imitate the human Jesus. This is far from as simple an issue as many an exegete or preacher seems to suppose. To illustrate this, the first half of the chapter contends that there is insufficient evidence to justify treating the sexes as equal on the basis of Christ's explicit example or teaching. Rather, an underlying trajectory from that example and teaching needs first to be identified, to explain why the Church of today might be justified in jettisoning aspects even of Jesus' own behaviour and attitudes. In the earlier volume I suggested that this is what in effect happened at an earlier stage in Christian history when Paul adopted a different attitude to law from Jesus. Here, though, it would be a matter of a post-biblical transformation.

In that first chapter I talk of two competing principles, equality of status and equality of regard, with the former reinterpreted in the light of the latter. To express matters this way helps, I believe,

with the clarity of the argument. The danger, though, is that I am
interpreted as claiming that Jesus' life is only relevant in yielding
general principles. That is not at all my point, and I try to indicate
why meditating on the details of Christ's life still remains essential
in giving shape to a life of discipleship. Even so, I do believe that
the search for exact parallels is mistaken, and there is need therefore to identify a more complex type of relation between the original example and the often quite different shape its imitation will
take in a different cultural milieu. Why that is so is clarified in my
second chapter, 'Pattern and particular: Saint and novel'. There it
is noted that, whereas in the early history of Christianity the lives
of saints were made to conform as closely as possible to Christ's
own actions, later history perceived the considerable problems that
confronted any such methodology and so sought a more indirect
correspondence, in effect one of analogy. The first experiments
with this latter type of approach, it will be suggested, are in some
fictional lives, such as those of Catherine of Alexandria and
Margaret of Antioch. Not only shall I argue for their intrinsic
importance and the truth of some of the values they contain, but
also I shall indicate why in some ways they may be seen as an
anticipation of the characteristic modern pattern for such exploration: through the novel. Discipleship is thus both a matter of
locating ourselves within Jesus' story and acknowledging the way
in which our own situation differs significantly from his. Christian
discipleship needs to be aware of these differences if it is not to
make impossible demands upon the Scriptures or judge later
developments by the wrong criteria.

But discipleship is not simply a matter of individual relationship
to Christ as Lord or even of following his example, however indirectly, wherever it might lead. It also has a strong social dimension.
In contemporary theology this is pursued overwhelmingly
through reflection on eschatology, the realization of Christ's kingdom within this world 'at the end of the age', and our present
contribution towards that goal. While in no way decrying the
importance of such reflections, this emphasis has in my view led to
the neglect of other important elements in the history of
Christianity. It is those neglected aspects that will be the focus of
the final chapter of this part of the work, ' Heaven and the defeat
of the Beast'. Its first half will contend that the modern tendency
to deny any importance to an already existing heavenly reality

populated with 'saints' (however understood) in actual fact undermines the social stress that is rightly sought elsewhere. Quite a
number of arguments are offered to this effect, but, to clarify my
meaning, perhaps one will suffice at this stage: that it is hard to see
what all this current talk of social interdependence could amount
to if the present existence of Christ's humanity in heaven is itself
robbed of any effective social dimension. But it is not only the
present existence of the communion of saints that is adversely
affected by current preoccupations, no less affected is understanding of the kind of impact exercised by the more negative aspects
of traditional eschatology. It is easy to treat the doctrine of hell as
a place of eternal punishment as pure aberration, but much can be
learnt, in my view, from the history of its use. I shall argue that
imaginative engagement in the battle to ensure that 'the Beast' did
not triumph helped generate within the Church a powerful sense
of mutual interdependence that is not reducible simply to dependence on Christ. A rich notion of community was thus an incidental result. Throughout I shall draw attention to the way in
which the biblical picture was modified, and what justification for
this might be given.

Such a brief résumé inevitably highlights argumentative and
doctrinal themes. Although these are important, the reader should
not lose sight of the wider context. My overall aim is to defend the
legitimacy of changing patterns of discipleship and to draw attention to the indispensable role that the imagination has played in
bringing about such changes. So far from regarding these as
optional extras, they seem to me integral to the continuing health
of the Christian faith. The Bible remains indispensable for
Christian discipleship, but the danger is that too great a burden is
placed on it. Like everything else in our world it emerged within
a specific context, and that could not help but create tensions as
the Church faced new situations. Although the Christian imagination came to the rescue, often its new responses were simply
projected back into Scripture. The rise of biblical criticism forces
us to be more honest, and face those tensions between biblical past
and our own present. It is to consideration of some of these that I
now turn, beginning with attitudes to women then and now.

I
Valuing and prostituting women: Equality and Mary Magdalene

WE begin then with consideration of what continuities and discontinuities it is important to affirm or deny in respect of the history of Christian attitudes to the status of women. It is only one of a number of possible examples which might have been considered. My reason for making this choice is less its importance or topicality, greatly relevant though these are, more that it illustrates so well what I perceive to be the two most common hermeneutical faults of our own day— how both too much can be claimed for Scripture and too little for subsequent tradition. On the one hand, I shall reject the view that Scripture offers in itself an adequate treatment of how the question of the equality of the two sexes should nowadays be appropriated. On the other, I shall contend that the much maligned treatment of Mary Magdalene in later tradition, so far from denigrating women, actually offers an indispensable model for human discipleship, both male and female. What unites both questions is the exercise of the imagination, the need to acknowledge its capacity to operate with quite different agendas from our own immediate, analytic concerns. At the same time, both illustrate well how revelation operates through the particularities of our human situation, not despite them. The way in which the legend of Mary Magdalene has been treated over the centuries is the topic of the second half of the chapter. We begin, though, with the question of how Christian support for the equality of the sexes might most satisfactorily be maintained.

Valuing women and sexual equality

Here I shall argue against the view that equality of status between women and men can be justified on the basis of New Testament precedent alone. At most what may be deduced is equality of regard, something entirely compatible with hierarchical assumptions. Biblical attitudes were in fact less advanced than pagan, and it was really only the latter's interaction with Christian views on celibacy which generated the first major change in perspective, with a new sense of independence on the part of women. Thereafter in many ways there is regression until the changes consequent on industrial society helped to generate our own present understandings. In attributing the key impetus for change to non-biblical factors, I intend thereby no denigration of the Bible. Its authors operated within a particular set of cultural assumptions that were plausible in their own day, and it needed fresh input from the wider culture before the Bible's more basic principle of equality of regard could be given a fresh, and very different application. An unsympathetic critic might respond that, in making such a distinction between equality of status and equality of regard, I have already abandoned a biblical or imaginative frame of reference for the language and terminology of the Enlightenment. The reasons why I do not believe this to be so will be given in due course, but first let me indicate in more general terms the significance I see in the contrast.

The New Testament principle: equality of regard

Because of the dominance of concern for the status of women in contemporary culture, it is a natural, but, I believe, dangerously seductive temptation for Christians to desire to establish the direct relevance of the Bible to the issue. History then becomes rewritten as the failure of successive generations to take its message with sufficient seriousness, all neatly encapsulated in Paul's famous declaration in Galatians that 'there is neither Jew nor Greek, there is neither slave nor free, there is neither male nor female, for you are all one in Christ Jesus' (Gal. 3: 28 RSV).[1] But that to my mind is to make the theologian's task all too easy.

---

[1] Most modern commentators still fail to give due attention to the difficulties behind any radical, egalitarian reading: cf. e.g. F. F. Bruce, *The Epistle to the Galatians* (Exeter: Paternoster Press, 1982), 187–91; J. D. G. Dunn, *Galatians* (Edinburgh: A & A Black, 1993), 205–8. My own view has been much influenced by Johannes Munck, *Paul and the Salvation of Mankind* (London: SCM Press, 1959), esp. ch. 2, whose general approach has been followed by many scholars since.

Consider first that very verse. Pulled out of context, it does of course sound as though Paul is giving an unequivocal endorsement to equality of race, class, and sex, together with all that that might imply. But, if one examines what he says elsewhere on these matters, such a contention becomes increasingly implausible. Thus in Romans 11 he leaves us in no doubt about the continued privileged position of the Jew; the Gentile wild olive shoot has been grafted on to the cultivated olive tree that is the Jew, and we are not to boast since it is not we who support the Jewish root but the Jewish root which supports us (cf. vv. 17–18). Again, so far as the specific issue of women is concerned, though much contemporary scholarship argues that neither of the two most obviously subordinationist passages in the Pauline corpus—1 Timothy 2 and 1 Corinthians 14—come from his actual hand, that still leaves 1 Corinthians 11 where Paul uses J's creation story (with the man created first) to argue for a prioritizing of male over female, with the woman consequently required to have her head veiled in church.[2] But in any case can it really be maintained that the relation of men and women was at the forefront of Paul's consciousness when not only does he fail even to mention the women witnesses to the resurrection in 1 Corinthians 15, but also in his parallel uses of a Galatians-style argument women likewise fail to reappear, though Jew and Greek, slave and free do? (1 Cor. 12: 13; Col. 3: 11)

So it would seem to me certain that we must look elsewhere for the right interpretation. Perhaps the easiest way of rendering Paul consistent is to say that what he means in Galatians 3 is not that

---

[2] It is possible that Paul here is reinforcing existing Corinthian social practice (cf. Dio Cocceianus, *Speeches* 33.48) with religious argument, just as the leading role of women in some Pauline congregations (Acts 15: 14–15; Phil. 4: 2–3) may have no higher explanation than the more liberal attitudes that Macedonia had inherited from some of its princesses: E. Ferguson, *Backgrounds of Early Christianity* (Grand Rapids, Michigan: Eerdmans, 1987), 58. Although I find them forced, more positive readings are of course possible: e.g. A. Padgett, 'Paul on women in the church', in *Journal of the Society of New Testament Studies* 20 (1984), 69–86. Equally, there are some pointers to suggest that the original J passage carried no such negative implications: e. g. M.-S. Heister, *Frauen in der biblischen Glaubensgeschichte* (Göttingen: Vandenhoeck & Ruprecht, 1984), 135–59, esp. 138–43. But it is hard to discount altogether the notion of inferiority implied by the taking of a part from a whole, rather than, say, an equal division of what was once a single body, as in the Greek version of the myth.

Christ brings absolute equality in everything but rather, and more fundamentally, equality of access to the most important thing of all—salvation. One might compare a modern politician declaring that we are all equal as British citizens; that certainly would not carry with it any automatic commitment to equality in all respects, for instance, equality of incomes. Significantly, both Luther and Calvin in their commentaries on the passage adopt just such an interpretation. Luther, for instance, speaks of the distinctions as 'divinely ordained' and then goes on to comment: 'in the world and according to the flesh there is a great difference and inequality of persons, and these must be diligently observed. For were a woman to wish to be a man . . . there should be chaotic confounding of all estates and things. In Christ, on the other hand . . . there is but one body, one spirit, one hope of vocation for all.'[3]

Such an interpretation would bring Paul's position more closely in line with what I think we may legitimately infer from the actions and teachings of Jesus. Here also it is all too easy to be beguiled by our desire to make Jesus say what we want him to say. Certainly, women were numbered among his followers and he had close relations with some of them, but that in itself hardly shows that he regarded them in every respect as equals of men, any more than does his openness to children or Gentiles. In my earlier volume I argued that the recognition of the value and legitimacy of a Gentile mission was almost certainly subsequent to Jesus' earthly ministry, while his remark about food given to the dogs could well be taken to indicate that he held a very similar, if not still more exalted, view of the privileged status of the Jew to what Paul offers us in Romans.[4] Likewise, then, with women, we need to bear in mind that, in Jesus' selection for positions of leadership, only men are to be found among the Twelve, with consequently only men spoken of as sitting on thrones, 'judging the twelve

---

[3] My trans. of his 1535 *Commentary on Galatians: Luthers Werke* (Weimar edn, 1911), vol. 40.1, 542 and 544–5. Calvin likewise insists that the verse must be read in a way which does not abolish a law that God the Father has himself established: 'il y au mesnage l'homme qui est le chef, et la femme qui luy doit estre suiete'. Quoted with the old French spellings from his *Twenty-third Sermon on Galatians: Calvini Opera* (Brunswick edn, 1893), 568.

[4] Mark 7: 27 for 'the children's bread . . . thrown to dogs'; Matt. 10: 5–6 for the priority of the Jewish mission; cf. also *Tradition and Imagination*, ch. 6, esp. 302–13.

tribes of Israel' (Matt. 19: 28; cf. Luke 22: 30). The Pauline communities are often said to have adopted a different attitude, but single verse allusions to a female 'deacon' and a female 'apostle' need to be approached with caution, since we have no precise information as to what these terms implied while any extensive description of leadership roles that we do have is always ascribed to men.[5] Again, however we interpret it now, the presence of women at the tomb would not have indicated any particular importance for Jesus' ministry but merely their customary role as principal mourners.[6]

Yet, none of this should be taken to deny a key role to Christ in providing an example that would eventually strike the axe against the assumptions upon which such hierarchy was based. For what most certainly can be deduced from his life and teaching is what I called earlier equality of regard, as distinct from equality of status: a unique and irreplaceable value assigned to each and every human being, with everyone he encountered valued and affirmed, his critics included, since reasoned argument is itself a form of affirmation. As friend of 'publicans and sinners' he certainly valued and affirmed the despised in society, but once again it needs to be emphasized that there is no necessary connection between such behaviour and insisting that they should, for instance, serve on the Sanhedrin, any more than today valuing and affirming those with severe learning disabilities or the mentally disturbed carries with it any entailment about the appropriateness of regarding them as potential Members of Parliament or managers of a large industrial concern.

In the latter case what makes the difference is what we believe, rightly or wrongly, the empirical facts to be and the way in which they condition possibilities.[7] In a similar way, then, was

---

[5] Phoebe and Junia: Romans 16: 1 and 6. At 1 Cor. 15: 9 'apostle' appears to mean someone commissioned by a resurrection appearance, but it would be dangerous to infer from this verse alone that identity of function and status in other respects was thereby also envisaged.

[6] As in Jeremiah 9: 17–22. As we shall see later, there are difficulties in regarding Mary Magdalene as the first witness to the resurrection.

[7] One might compare recent arguments within the English charity Mencap over whether some of those for whom they care ought also to be represented on the charity's governing body. The decision has been taken that with sufficient education this is indeed both possible and appropriate.

this so in first-century Palestine, with regard to women. Nowadays, of course, we would wish to question the nature of the 'evidence', but that should not blind us to the fact that it was taken seriously at the time, and not always implausibly so. Most obviously, there was simply the lack of experience of women in positions of power or with education. It is easy to believe a negative, if there is no opportunity of experiencing examples to the contrary; indeed it becomes self-fulfilling. But added to that were, of course, further contributing factors. Unfortunately, we do not possess accounts of Jewish understandings of physiology comparable to those on offer in the classical world,[8] but it is possible to infer similar assumptions. Thus J's version of the creation myth (Gen. 2: 18 ff.) surely suggests dependency of the rib on the source from which it has come, while much Jewish purity legislation seems to assume, for whatever reason, the inferiority of women.

So, for example, in Leviticus 15: 16–24 menstrual impurity takes seven days to purge as against one day for comparable male pollution, and that disparity seems further accentuated in the rule that double the time was required to purge the birth of a female child as against a male. It is of course possible that such legislation was intended to emphasize the holiness of child-bearing, with the woman seen as joining in God's work of creation (Lev. 12: 1–5),[9] but such an explanation loses plausibility when set against so much other evidence of negative attitudes. Equally problematic is the attempt to locate an explanation in a post-exilic assertion of the priority of culture (circumcision) over nature (menstruation),[10] since suspicion of the latter was already widespread throughout the ancient world. Though positive attitudes are found, much more common is the notion that menstruation represents some form of

---

[8] For a good exposition of pagan understandings of female anatomy and their impact upon questions of equality, L. Dean-Jones, 'Medicine: The Proof of Anatomy' in E. Fantham et al. (eds.), *Women in the Classical World* (New York: Oxford University Press, 1994), 183–215.

[9] For such an interpretation: Grace Emmerson, 'Women in Ancient Israel' in R. E. Clements (ed.), *World of Ancient Israel* (Cambridge: Cambridge University Press, 1989), 379.

[10] L. J. Archer, 'Bound by blood: circumcision and menstrual taboo' in J. M. Soskice (ed.), *After Eve* (London: Collins, 1990), 38–61.

instability in the female constitution.[11] Almost certainly such
suspicions and the consequent fear of pollution were also a factor
in the exclusion of women from the annual Jewish festivals, a
phenomenon that itself led to the well-known Mishnah prayer for
men which thanked God 'for not making me a woman'. In generating such attitudes, sexual intercourse itself probably also had an
influence, since it would be very easy to move from assumptions
of receptivity in that sphere to a general endorsement of female
passivity and inferiority.[12]

In noting such attitudes it has been no part of my intention to
imply cultural determinism, as though this were the only way
history could have gone. Though problems of adequate interpretation are complex, some early civilizations may have been more
egalitarian in their attitude to the two sexes,[13] while, as we shall
see, it is incontestable that Jewish attitudes lagged behind those in
many another ancient society. My point rather is that once a
certain pattern of thought is established it can so deeply imbed

[11]   In some Greek writing menstruation appears to have been viewed wholly
positively. So, for instance, some early Hippocratic writings equated it with a
return to order after the instability of virginity: H. King, 'Bound to bleed:
Artemis and Greek women' in A. Cameron and A. Kuhrt (eds.), *Images of Women
in Antiquity* (London: Croom Helm, 1983), 109–27. But the most common image
seems to have been that of purgation, which could easily be taken to suggest a
balance that has gone wrong, and indeed in some writers menstruation came to
be associated with death because its absence in later life meant an end to conception and new life: J. Delaney, *A Cultural History of Menstruation* (New York:
Dutton, 1976); P. Shuttle and P. Redgrove, *The Wise Wound* (London: Gollancz,
1978). This is the key which Rachel Biale uses to unlock Jewish attitudes: *Women
and Jewish Law* (New York: Schoken Books, 1984), ch. 6. Herself a Jew, she calls
for a rabbinical revolution of a kind which has happened in the past: 264–5.
[12]   Thus, for example, it is surely plausible to detect behind Philo's justification for the sacrificial whole-offering being male an implicit allusion to a particular view of sexual intercourse: 'The sacrifice used as a whole burnt offering
should be male because the male is more complete and more dominant than the
female, as well as more akin to an active cause, for the female is incomplete and
in subjection and more to be accounted among what is passive rather than active'
(*De Specialibus Legibus* I, 200 (my trans.)).
[13]   For Spartan attitudes compared favourably with Athenian, and Etruscan
with early Roman: Fantham et al., *Classical World*, chs. 2 and 8. The 'evidence'
needs, however, to be read with care, as the authors in question (e.g. Plato) are
often more concerned with making points against their own society. Equally,
Egypt may not have been as egalitarian in this respect as is sometimes claimed: for
the positive claim, J. Tydesley, *Daughters of Isis* (London: Penguin, 1994).

itself in a particular society, that to talk of 'prejudice' is in fact totally to misunderstand the extent to which its rationale now functions as internalized 'reasons'; it has become an ingrained assumption. The paucity of evidence offered on the other side fails to convince me that either Jesus or Paul escaped from such cultural conditioning, and it seems best therefore to think of their attitude in similar terms to how we now regard some of their assumptions about the Hebrew Scriptures, as plausible in terms of the thought-forms of their own day but not requiring any endorsement on our own part.[14] What Jesus indicated by his practice (and Paul endorsed) is a far more fundamental insight: that, irrespective of any empirical differences, we are all of equal value in the eyes of God, and must therefore be treated accordingly.

That idea may already have been present in Old Testament times but, if so, not only is it nowhere made explicit but also there is much that runs counter to any such notion, not least attitudes to those of different cultures.[15] Where the life of Jesus has a unique contribution to make is, if I may put it like this, in its character as a worked example. The Gospels portray Jesus encountering a great range of different individuals, and him valuing each in their own unique particularity without regard to their worldly standing. It was thus possible to see clearly for the first time what such valuing might mean. But of itself that did not entail that, for instance, differences between child and adult or between centurion and criminal ceased to be relevant, but only that in principle at least such customary differences in treatment could founder, were the conventional perceived reasons for drawing the distinctions ever found to lack justification. In my view women do themselves a great disservice whenever they insist that Jesus must have made that further inference. For it suggests to me an insight that could have been won without too much difficulty, whereas in fact the assumptions behind the prejudice have run deep through almost every aspect of the history of Western civilization.

This in part explains why I want to resist the accusation of

[14] Note, for instance, Paul's (to us) strange use of the Sarah/ Hagar analogy in Galatians or Jesus' appeal to Psalm 110: 1 in his arguments about the nature of the Messiah: Gal. 4: 21 ff; Mark 12: 35–7.

[15] It is easy to forget how seldom other peoples are valued in their own right. Even the eschatological imagery in Isaiah more often than not leaves other peoples in a firmly subordinate role, e.g. 40: 17; 60: 5–7.

introducing irrelevant Enlightenment distinctions. For even Enlightenment thinkers were as deeply imbued with such assumptions about the weaker or more dependent character of women as were the rest of their contemporaries. That women are by nature less rational than men is a notion that one finds in intellectuals as otherwise varied as Bacon, Descartes, Kant, Rousseau, Hegel, and Freud.[16] It is not, therefore, our reason on its own that is likely to defend us from such pitfalls. Nor is it a matter even of getting the right general principles, for 'equality of regard' or even love itself only gain adequate definition through careful contextualization. Notoriously, for example, both Kant and Mill alike thought that their fundamental principles were a variant on Christ's love commandment.[17] Following Christ is thus not just a matter of abstracting the right principles from the narrative. It is more a matter of meditating on that life in a way that takes seriously how the particularity of Jesus' love was expressed in all its specificity. Even so, though, there seems to me nothing in and of itself in the narrative to suggest a further inference to equality of status. For that some further general shocks to the culture as a whole were required, and these were not as yet forthcoming.

Revelation interacting with culture

The full implications for women of Jesus' underlying example were thus to take centuries even to begin to reach their proper application. Even so, some progress was already being made in the more immediate post-biblical period. Tempting though it is to ascribe this exclusively to Christianity, once again caution is necessary. For the status of women in the pagan world was already in advance of Jewish understanding, and what therefore appears to have happened is that further progress was made possible by a

[16] For a survey and some pertinent examples, G. Lloyd, *The Man of Reason: 'Male' and 'Female' in Western Philosophy* (London: Routledge, 1984), esp. 11, 44, 63, 69, 75–6, 82.

[17] For Kant, *Religion within the Limits of Reason Alone,* 4, 1, ed. T. M. Greene and H. H. Hudson (New York: Harper, 1934), 148. For Mill, *Utilitarianism,* ch. 2, ed. M. Warnock (London: Collins, 1962), 268. For an attempt to set matters in a wider context, S. Heine, *Wiederbelebung der Göttinnen?* (Göttingen: Vandenhoeck & Ruprecht, 2nd edn, 1989), esp. 'Enttäuscht von der Auflärung', 127–33.

healthy interaction between the new religion and alternative (pagan) cultural conventions.

That paganism was in advance of the Jewish world is well illustrated by the different attitudes to divorce and property rights. In the Jewish case divorce remained a male prerogative, and while it would probably be unfair to observe that the Hebrew for 'husband' literally means 'owner', it is true that under Old Testament law a wife had no independent property rights, and inherited nothing on her husband's death (Num. 27: 7–11).[18] By contrast, in the Code of Hammurabi and in Assyrian laws the widow not only had automatic right to part of the estate, she could even regain control over her dowry.[19] Some scholars have argued that early Israel had also once displayed a similar degree of liberality,[20] but, while it is plausible to contend that later treatments of the issue show greater negativity, it is very hard to establish any period at which Israel was truly as positive as Assyria. Likewise, though the sexes were probably not yet segregated in the synagogues of Jesus' day and there is also clear evidence to suggest that women acted as benefactors of them, it would be rash to jump from such facts to any suggestion that women sometimes acted as their leaders,[21] when we lack all evidence of any corresponding change in legal status.

Though Greek and early Roman society was in many ways as oppressive as Jewish,[22] by the time of Jesus significant advances had

[18]   Though this passage does speak of the daughter inheriting, even this could only happen in the absence of any male children. Job 42: 13–15 is out of keeping with what Scripture says elsewhere, and perhaps originates in the author's desire to demonstrate Job's enormous wealth; so R. De Vaux, *Ancient Israel* (London: Darton, Longman & Todd, 2nd edn., 1965), 53–5.

[19]   L. Epsztein, *Social Justice in the Ancient Near East* (London: SCM Press, 1986), 113–14.

[20]   Carol Meyers, for example, seeks to give a non-hierarchical interpretation of J in Genesis 3: 16: *Discovering Eve: Ancient Israelite Women in Context* (New York: Oxford University Press, 1988), esp. 117–21 for her revised translation. But the element of dominion seems to remain, and thus by implication the property rules.

[21]   As B. Brooton argues: *Women Leaders in the Ancient Synagogue* (Chico, Cal.: Scholars Press, 1982).

[22]   Eva Keuls in *The Reign of the Phallus* (Berkeley, Cal.: University of California Press, 1995) describes classical Athens as more repressive of women than any other culture in Western history, with them kept firmly behind doors (108–10) and valued only for sex and its resultant product, heirs, together with their labour (229–66). Though this estimate of the situation is exaggerated, Greece and early Rome were clearly in some ways considerably worse than ancient Israel.

in fact taken place in Roman law. In early Roman law, as in Greek, the wife's dowry and any other property came under the husband's full ownership, but by the late Republic this practice (*cum manu*) had been abandoned, the woman became the primary heir of her father, and upon his death an independent property owner. With that right also went very much greater freedom generally, partly perhaps under the impact of male absence during the protracted Second Punic War (218–202 BC), when Italy was occupied for more than fifteen years;[23] certainly Greeks were shocked at the results.[24] Then, with the Emperor Augustus, women no longer had to await the death of their father for independence, as all mothers of three or more children were now automatically exempted from guardianship, while under one of his successors, Claudius (d. AD 54), even this limited guardianship was abolished.[25] As a result it is not surprising that we find plenty of examples in the later imperial period of women freely dispensing their own wealth in public benefactions.[26] One other important point to note is that Roman, unlike Jewish, law allowed the wife to divorce her husband.[27] Even so, a number of factors inhibiting equality remained, among them the fact that girls seem generally to have been much younger than their partners when they married.

It was, then, into just such an environment that Christianity emerged, with pagan attitudes to women in certain important

---

[23] E. Fantham, 'Republican Rome II' in Fantham et al., *Classical World*, 260 ff. [24] Nepos, *De Viris Illustribus*, preface 6.

[25] P. Garnsey and R. Saller, *The Roman Empire* (London: Duckworth, 1987), 130–6; or for a more detailed survey of the changing situation: J. A. Crook, 'Women in Roman Succession' in B. Rawson (ed.), *The Family in Ancient Rome* (London: Routledge, 1992), 58–82.

[26] Fantham et al., *Classical World*, 331–4, 360–6.

[27] Though the Herodian princesses, Salome and Herodias, seem to have got rid of their husbands on their own initiative, and much earlier (in the fifth century BC) there is evidence of Jewish women having the right to initiate divorce, such cases occur in very special circumstances, such as in the Jewish community at Elephantine in Egypt, and so the view continues to prevail that Jewish women were at a disadvantage as against Roman: for references, M. Goodman, *The Ruling Class of Judaea* (Cambridge: Cambridge University Press, 1987), 70. Even up to modern times Orthodox Judaism has refused to allow divorce for desertion, or even the presumption of death, except on the evidence of witnesses.

respects significantly in advance of the Jewish society from which the new religion had emerged. In seeking to determine the precise nature of its contribution, it is necessary to guard against any simplistic projection back of the assumptions most of us would hold today, for, as we saw earlier, most of the evidence seems to point in a rather different direction. Where Christianity had a marked impact was in insisting on the basis of Christ's example upon equality of regard. Even if it was only many centuries later that this was reinforced by a claim to equality of status, new possibilities were already being opened up by that underlying conviction. But it would be a mistake to suggest that Christ's example worked this change alone. For it was precisely because pagan women already enjoyed a greater degree of freedom that upon conversion to this new faith they could perceive where its doctrine of spiritual equality might lead, in generating fresh possibilities of freedom. Recently, the Christian cult of virginity in the patristic period has been plausibly reinterpreted, and it is no longer seen purely negatively as a rejection of the world, but rather as a means of significantly advancing the freedom of women: their choices ceased to be controlled by larger family concerns.[28] The case seems to me a convincing one, but it would be hard to explain the change entirely in terms of Christianity's Jewish inheritance, for that offered no significant precedents for female monasticism. Was it not more a case of some female Gentile converts allowing their own classical culture to interact with Scripture and in consequence being seized by the promptings of the Spirit to go one stage further in terms of personal liberty for women? They already had some control over property; now they hoped for the right to determine their own spiritual formation.

As a matter of fact such freedoms were eventually to be severely curtailed. Under Christian emperors divorce legislation was introduced that worked to the disadvantage of women.[29] The dual

---

[28] P. Brown, *The Body and Society* (New York: Columbia University Press, 1988), where celibacy as liberation is argued in some detail. G. Cloke, *This Female Man of God* (London: Routledge, 1995) agrees, but adds the caveat that it was always on the assumption that such women transcended their sex, becoming in effect surrogate men.

[29] G. Clark, *Women in Late Antiquity* (Oxford: Clarendon Press, 1993), 21–7, though she warns against interpretation in terms of an exclusively Christian motivation.

monasteries that allowed for an abbess to be in overall charge were eventually to disappear, while the role of the male priesthood came to be given greater and greater prominence, with all sacramental acts eventually reserved to them and to them alone.[30] Again, the difficulty of projecting such freedoms beyond the convent is well illustrated by the opposition which was encountered by attempts to found female educational orders, most notably the Ursulines.[31] Nevertheless, something did survive. Women were seen as competent as men to give spiritual advice, as relevant literature surviving from the Middle Ages clearly indicates. So at least the question could now be raised: if spiritually as competent, why not in other ways as well?

It took one set of social circumstances to generate this change; it took another to produce the more radical transformation that is with us today. In pre-industrial society women were of course often expected to perform heavy agricultural work, sometimes even when pregnant. Even so, there is an important sense in which their inferiority in physical strength mattered in a way which became less and less important as industrialization advanced. In societies without a proper police force women remained dependent for everyday protection upon the men in their family, while in societies where war and brigandage were more common than they are in the modern world, again it fell exclusively to the male to exercise the necessary degree of brute force. Industrialization, however, brought in its train a number of changes, many of which could be expected to change perceptions of the role and status of women. An effect of populations congregating in towns was that the primary use of power ceased to lie exclusively with the male head of the family, while an effect of women working in factories was that they were given some perception of themselves as also wage earners, even if

[30] Lay confession continued even as late as the fourteenth century.

[31] If we take Jerome as illustrative of patristic attitudes to female education, he can veer between extreme suspicion (e.g. Letter 228) and very positive encouragement (e.g. Letter 107), though this must still be under a man as teacher ('doctus vir'). Even as late as the sixteenth century, women were still being regarded as unsuitable instructors, as the initial reaction to the first teaching order (the Ursulines) well illustrates, with even the founder's father doubting a woman's competence: M. Monica, *Angela Merici and her Teaching Idea 1474–1540* (New York: Longmans, Green & Co, 1927).

initially the husband continued to try to exercise control. The computer revolution has in fact only accelerated a process that has been going on for several centuries, whereby the physical superiority of the male has become less relevant to the structuring of society, and so with that has gone any sense that such physical superiority is also indicative of other, more insidious forms of supposed superiority. Also relevant in bringing about new attitudes is the very quantity and speed of change in modern society, for, inevitably, it has opened eyes to the possibilities of change elsewhere, as did also the development of a cheap press and other modern forms of mass communication. The rise of female education also helped, as did increasing professionalism in medicine which, long before contraception became an issue, brought with it the realization that women could do something themselves, substantially to better their living conditions. Even with this number of factors mentioned, I hasten to add that this is unlikely to be the complete tally; historical change is immeasurably more complex.[32]

My point is simply that with so many other factors at work it would be naïve to claim that biblical insight was the principal medium in bringing about such change. Indeed, it is arguable that the Bible acted as a restraint, because sufficient care was seldom taken to distinguish between its application to a particular cultural milieu and what might more properly be regarded as its foundational teaching. This is well illustrated by the regression which took place within the history of Christianity on the subject of women's property rights, where the Bible was used, quite plausibly, to argue for a more negative view.[33] On the other side, however, must be set the key role played by some Christian women in moving society towards equality of status, conspicuous among whom were Josephine Butler and Maude Royden. Even

[32] To give but one other relevant factor, note the discovery of the ovum in 1826 and the resultant acknowledgement required of a more active role for the woman in shaping the identity of her children.

[33] For a brief outline of the various changes in English law in the latter half of the nineteenth century, see A. Loades, *Searching for Lost Coins* (London: SPCK, 1987), 6–7; for a detailed presentation of how iniquitous the previous situation was, see H. N. Mozley, 'The Property Disabilities of a Married Woman' in Josephine Butler (ed.), *Woman's Work and Woman's Culture* (London: Macmillan, 1869), 186–245.

here, though, there is a certain irony in that it was partly the Victorian exaltation of women as preservers of the sanctity of the home which first led many a woman beyond its confines in order to further its defence.[34]

Those early advocates of women's rights, like many of their twentieth-century counterparts, frequently read back into the Bible the position they wished to advocate. Some Muslim feminists are now attempting a similar task on Islam's behalf.[35] Both strategies, however, seem to me misguided. To my mind the evidence is insufficient to speak of the presence in either Old Testament or New of anything approaching what we would now mean by movements for sexual equality.[36] Certainly, much of what followed in the later history of the two religions was much worse,[37] but we do our understanding of revelation and God's action in the world a disservice if we ignore the effects of social conditioning. In the patristic period it took contact with the larger rights of women under paganism to precipitate a fresh application of Jesus' example and teaching, and it was to take the huge changes of modern times before Christians could see that this also carried with it full equality of status. The most promising analysis is to suggest that our understanding of revelation becomes deepened as the Bible interacts with each fresh social matrix and we try to draw from each such interaction a fresh account of what revelation should mean for our own day.

[34] As with Josephine Butler herself, over the Contagious Diseases Acts of 1864, 1866 and 1869. For a helpful general survey, B. Heeney, *The Women's Movement in the Church of England 1850–1950* (Oxford: Clarendon Press, 1988).

[35] E.g. F. Mernissi, *Women and Islam* (Oxford: Blackwell, 1991).

[36] Less well known than Elisabeth Schüssler Fiorenza's attempts to detect an original Jesus movement along these lines is the work of Carol Meyers in arguing for similar presuppositions in early Israel (1200–1000 BC): *Discovering Eve: Ancient Israelite Women in Context* (New York: Oxford University Press, 1988). My rejection of that aspect of their work is in no way intended to decry their insistence in detecting the role of women hidden behind the text.

[37] Complementary imagery is perhaps the most insidious because of its pretence at equality. So, for example, Augustine insists that men and women possess both male and female aspects to their minds, but significantly Christ loses the feminine aspect (*scientia*) when he leaves this earth. For a discussion, K. Power, *Veiled Desire: Augustine's Writing on Women* (London: Darton, Longman & Todd, 1995), 131–57, esp. 155 ff.

Scripture's continuing relevance

Though in all I have said thus far there has been a consistent concern to apply the example and teaching of Christ, it may be objected that the style of discipleship implied suggests a certain distance and perhaps even some lack of engagement. The text is allowed to speak, but only in its historically conditioned original context, and thereafter greater interest is shown in contemporary society. At one level, I would reject the criticism, for it seems to me that it is only by taking the past seriously as past that we can properly allow its impact upon the present; otherwise, the danger is that we simply project on to Scripture our own present concerns. However, once that caution has been fully endorsed, I would then have no objection to using Galatians 3: 28 in its new modern sense as a ringing endorsement of the equality of the sexes, for pulled out of context it does admirably express what seems to me the legitimate implication that the Church should draw in our own day from New Testament teaching. Revelation interacting with culture has legitimated the new way of reading the text.

Yet that may still sound as though all the work is being done by changes in the wider culture rather than through Scripture, but this, it seems to me, has not been true of the past, nor need it be true of the future. Consider first the past. The New Testament may not have accorded women what we now mean by equality of status, but Jesus' example did open up the possibility of new claims for women that would in the end help with the undermining of factors alleged to legitimate subordination. Jesus' relations with Mary and Martha, for instance, were soon being used to argue for equality in religious instruction, reading, and prayer, and these could be used as springboards for wider claims.[38] Again, if we turn to our modern context, the awareness of two quite different senses to the Galatians verse, instead of encouraging retreat from Scripture as a model for practice, could be used to encourage a more lively engagement in deeper awareness of the inevitable pitfalls to which all human thinking is subject. Hearing God's address to us through the Bible would then cease to be a simple 'reading off' of surface

[38] As, for example, in double monasteries, with a female abbot over a joint community of both men and women. Apart from other examples mentioned in this chapter, more are given in the chapter on Mary, Ch. 5.

meaning; instead, prayerful readiness would be required to confront the extent to which the experience of women alluded to in the text still lies hidden from our immediate understanding and so requires effort if it is to be brought to consciousness.

A number of women are doing excellent work in this field. Luise Schottroff, for instance, has done much to highlight hitherto ignored aspects of women's work experience and its impact on Jesus' parables and teaching.[39] Some have carried the argument one stage further, and sought to identify a transformation in Jesus' consciousness as a result of some key experiences with women.[40] Perhaps this did happen to some degree, but more plausible in my view are those feminist theologians willing to accept an ambiguous, complex history.[41] It is natural to want to enrol Jesus in support of a position one endorses, but the incarnation inevitably must have involved limitations. If Jesus' attitude to privileges of race was one of them, I fail to see why gender issues might not also have been another.[42] Equally, at the other extreme, it is tempting to place all the blame for what happened on men, but a resultant danger is that we end up with what one writer has labelled a 'deadly innocence', the inability of women to accept any form of self-critique.[43] This is in no way to exempt

[39] L. Schottroff, 'Das geschundene Volk und die Arbeit in der Ernte Gottes' in L. and W. Schottroff (eds.), *Mitarbeiter der Schöpfung* (Munich: Kaiser, 1983), 149–206, esp. 185–7; idem, *Lydia's Impatient Sisters* (London: SCM Press, 1995), e. g. 79–80, 92–6, 194–6. Less satisfactory is her insistence on subsuming the evils of capitalism under patriarchy (19).

[40] C. Mulack, *Jesus—der Gesalbte der Frauen* (Stuttgart: Kreuz Verlag, 1987), esp. 80–90 (for effect of encounter with the Syro-Phoenician woman), 104–28 (for anointing by women as determinative of messianic status).

[41] E. g. S. Heine, *Frauen der frühen Christenheit* (Göttingen: Vandenhoeck & Ruprecht, 1986). Note one of her opening comments: 'Ohne Zweifel läßt sich eine Geschichte christlicher Frauenfreundlichkeit schreiben, aber auch eine Geschichte christlicher Frauenfeindlichkeit' (12). Numerous examples of both then follow.

[42] For Jesus' attitude to his Jewish identity and in particular to the law, Ch. 6 of the earlier volume, Ch. 6 also of this one.

[43] Finely argued by A. West, *Deadly Innocence: Feminism and the Mythology of Sin* (London: Cassell, 1995). She questions whether it is either true or advantageous for women to believe themselves less sinful than men, noting, for instance, the extent of female support for Hitler (30–7), as also the way in which a good image for white women in the southern United States was bought at the expense of their black sisters (38–48, esp. 41 ff.).

men from condemnation for past injustices, but it is to protest against parody and over-simplistic histories.

Take the history of art. It is true that the female is often represented as temptress and thus as implicitly the real culprit, but that is by no means always so. Even where convention demanded a strongly erotic element, such as paintings of the incident of Susanna and the Elders, examples are not wanting where the male voyeurs are indisputably made the guilty party, while even with the fall there are famous examples, not least from Michelangelo, of the primary responsibility being laid at Adam's door.[44] Nor is it true that women have always been trapped by the prejudices of men into debilitating forms of self-perception. Narratives from Christine de Pisan onwards provide obvious literary examples to the contrary, but so sometimes also, perhaps surprisingly, do convents. The recent discovery of a series of late medieval coloured drawings from St Walburg's near Eichstätt provides fascinating insight into women successfully defining themselves apart from men even in a context often thought to be the most male dominated of them all.[45] One finds women replacing the Magi, joining in prayer at Gethsemane, enjoying a eucharistic banquet with the Trinity, and even present in the very heart of Jesus.[46] Again, much the same point could be made of the greatest female painter of whom we are aware until modern times, Artemisia Gentileschi, working in the early seventeenth century. If the

[44] Margaret Miles has argued that 'in Christianity the body scorned, the naked body, is the female body': M. R. Miles, *Carnal Knowing: Female Nakedness and Religious Meaning in the Christian West* (Boston, Mass.: Beacon, 1989), 185. Paintings of Susanna are one of her artistic examples, in which even Rembrandt does not remain immune from critique: 124–5. She strengthens her general case by making extensive use of an atypical artist like Hans Baldung (seven out of thirty-one illustrations), whereas even with Susanna the distorted faces of the lewd elders in Jacob Jordaens' version is not altogether untypical: illustrated in D. Sölle, J. H. Kircheberger, H. Haag (eds.), *Great Women of the Bible* (Grand Rapids, Michigan: Eerdmans, 1994), 237. On the ceiling of the Sistine Chapel, Michelangelo's Adam reaches eagerly for the forbidden fruit, quite independently of Eve, who in fact shows more hesitation.

[45] In the sense of wholly dependent on male priests for Mass and confession, and also subject to their decisions as controlling external 'Visitors'.

[46] J. F. Hamburger, *Nuns as Artists* (Berkeley, Cal.: University of California Press, 1997). For Magi, 14, 56–9; for Gethsemane, 92–4; for trinitarian banquet, 140, 144–5; for heart, 102–6.

nature of the commissions she received from men frequently required her to paint seductive looking representations of her own sex, she did so in a way that not only preserved her own integrity but also implicitly asserted a female identity that refused to be defined by the dominant male culture of her own day.[47] Of Gentileschi's piety or otherwise, we have no knowledge, but matters are quite otherwise with the anonymous nuns and Michelangelo. Religious belief, context and personal experience, all combined to force, however implicitly, new ways of approaching the biblical text.

One way in which that process might be expressed, and which I utilized in the earlier volume, is to speak of a trajectory from the Bible turning back on itself and requiring a new reading of the scriptural text as a whole. Not all will be happy with that way of putting things. Perhaps the most obvious advantage it provides is the stress thereby given to the new frames of references that are periodically thrown up which force upon us new ways of reading Scripture. So, for example, in *Tradition and Imagination* I noted the way in which the trajectory that eventually led to a full-blown doctrine of incarnation necessitated a re-examination of scriptural hostility to images, and that despite the fact that nowhere within the New Testament are Old Testament attitudes challenged. In the case before us here, particularly worthy of note is the fact that not only is a re-examination of the often hidden references to women required but also continuing reflection on the more basic practical principle of equality of regard. For, if the acceptance of 'relevant' empirical differences where there are none is one way in which things can go wrong, another and perhaps even more worrying is the supposition that empirical difference necessarily legitimates radical difference of treatment. Christ may have shared the cultural assumptions of his day, but he consistently treated women with dignity and respect. The same cannot always be said

---

[47] For a detailed analysis of her paintings, M. D. Garrard, *Artemisia Gentileschi* (Princeton, N. J.: Princeton University Press, 1989). Although occasionally her detection of a hidden agenda stretches the bounds of probability, particularly her identification of an Isis theme in the *Cleopatra* paintings (244–77, esp. 266 ff.), Garrard in general establishes her case well. To my mind convincing is her suggestion that *Lucretia's* pose is intended to question the traditional assumption of the necessity of suicide (228 ff.), while *Judith* is meant to assert readiness in the face of fresh danger (278–336, esp. 315, 328).

of the Church in our own day, nor that it emulates Christ where relevant empirical differences would still be widely admitted. One need only think of those with physical handicap or severe learning difficulties, or again of those suffering from mental illness, to see the extent of the problem. Of course, some forms of contribution may be precluded, but that hardly legitimates the slowness of the Church in ensuring some kind of access and role. Jean Vanier's L'Arche communities or the earlier experiments at the shrine of the legendary St Dympna at Gheel remain rare illustrations of a better way of doing things.[48] So I would emphatically reject any contention that my argument precludes a key continuing role for reflection on the example of Christ. It remains pertinent in two key ways. First, as the case of those with learning difficulties indicates, Christ's underlying principle of equality of regard is still far from receiving universal application. Secondly, Jesus' valuing of all irrespective of empirical difference provides a salutary caution against supposing that equality of status, however legitimate and important it is in correcting biblical attitudes to women, is all that matters.

In this particular case imitating the example of Jesus has become more a matter of pursuing where reflection on the details of his life might lead rather than literally copying his mind-set, and for that some degree of imagination is clearly required. But of itself that can hardly take us the whole way in reconceiving the relevance of Christ to the status of women, for Christianity has only ever been secondarily a religion of a book. Its engagement is primarily with the person of Christ, and it is to the question of how the historical and temporal distance which I have been so emphasizing can be overcome in respect of our relation with him that I now want to turn. Much has been written in recent years hostile to what was done in Christian history to the figure of Mary Magdalene. What, however, I would invite the reader to consider is the possibility that her story was developed and retold precisely in order that

---

[48] For the work of Jean Vanier, *The Challenge of L'Arche* (London: Darton, Longman & Todd, 1979); *Man and Woman He Made Them* (London: Darton, Longman & Todd, 1985). The shrine of St Dympna near Antwerp became a great pilgrimage centre for the mentally ill. Already by the fourteenth century a system of boarding them in the local community had been established, and with the formalization of this practice in 1850 this early system of 'care in the community' became one of the most famous and effective in the world.

both women and men might engage more effectively with their risen Lord. Imaginative closeness, not imaginative distance, will thus now be our concern.

Discipleship and Mary Magdalene

In my earlier volume I was much concerned to underline the way in which the imagination has functioned in the history of religion, and within Christianity in particular, as a means of generating new insights, insights which the Christian may legitimately regard as revelation, not merely human responses but divinely motivated. Change is effected not so much by explicit logical argument as by the biblical text in effect being rewritten. Imagination builds upon history to say something rather different from what the original human authors intended. Thus in the chapter on the incarnation I argued that the later Church rightly made explicit a commitment to Christ's divinity that would not have been acknowledged at the time, while in an earlier chapter I drew attention to the various ways in which the stories of the patriarchs were modified in Islam and Judaism no less than in Christianity, in order to function more effectively for a later age.

My analysis was necessarily somewhat complex, since in outlining the history of such developments I also wanted to emphasize three further points. The patriarchal narratives may be used by way of example. First, tradition does not develop in a single straight line but by exploring a range of possibilities, some of which are rightly subsequently discarded. So, for instance, the attempt to blame someone other than God for the sacrifice of Isaac was eventually recognized to be a false trail. Secondly, triggers for change play a crucial, if not indispensable, role. Even if unfairly ascribed to the Pharisees as a group, the way in which the model of obedient action could degenerate into self-righteousness identifies one major incentive towards the retelling of the story of Abraham in terms of faithful trust. Finally, so far as the justification of change is concerned, we cannot escape the messiness of history. Though it is tempting to look for a single criterion, such as a christological one, change occurs against a particular backdrop, and that is essential to assessing legitimacy. Tenuous though the parallels in the life of Joseph were to what happened with Christ, they were sufficient to inhibit any fruitful use of the story of Joseph within Christianity, and he became a cardboard 'type' or anticipation of what was to come. In this case Christology thus actually inhibited rather than encouraged reflection.

As we shall see, all these points can be illustrated from developments in respect of the story of Mary Magdalene. Had the person responsible for the conflated figure not been as historically significant a personage as Pope Gregory the Great, it is doubtful whether there would have been a sufficient trigger to generate the wealth of reflection that was to follow. Even then, it was not without its false avenues, not least in its detours into an obsession with sexuality. Yet ironically it was precisely the presence of that feature that ensured the absence of any cardboard copy of Christ as in the treatment of Joseph, and instead generated extensive reflection on what it might mean to grow into identification with Christ from something quite different. Yet so deeply entrenched is the notion that historical fact must remain the final arbiter of truth that for many it is hard to envisage what could justify giving the greater weight to the imaginative construct. Nonetheless, that is what I wish to argue for here. For my contention is that, though what emerged was less than loyal to history, it embodied the more important truth, one which has very effectively engaged the imagination of believers over the centuries in establishing and deepening their relation with Christ and one which we will now lose at our peril: what is involved in the dialectics of discipleship, in the growth of the disciple from sin and misunderstanding through forgiveness to intimacy and empowerment. I realize in advocating such an approach I go against the great weight of contemporary opinion on the significance of Mary's legend. That is why I ask readers to suspend judgement until they have read this particular section as a whole.

The contemporary context

Another way of putting my present concern is to ask: is there any level of reflection at which an appropriate justification can be found for the decisive stimulus Pope Gregory the Great gave towards the Western tradition's conflation of Mary Magdalene (the witness of the resurrection), Mary of Bethany (the sister of Martha and Lazarus), and the unnamed penitent sinner (who washes Jesus' feet with her tears)?[49] Biblical scholars have been trying to unravel that integrated figure since at least 1517 with Jacques Lefèvre d'Étaples' influential essay,[50] but in recent years such attempts have received powerful reinforcement from feminist theologians, who see later theology producing in Mary Magdalene negative images of woman as the great temptress while at the same time robbing her of her full and proper historical dignity as the first disciple to be charged with preaching the good news of the resurrection.

That she was an historical figure seems certain. Luke mentions her as someone from whom Jesus cast out 'seven devils' and who later accompanied him on his itinerant ministry; Mark, that she was one of the women who stood 'looking on afar off' at the crucifixion; while to John is reserved the longest reference with Christ's appearance and dialogue with her at his tomb, apparently briefly alluded to also in Matthew and in the appendix to Mark's Gospel.[51] The common modern view, therefore, is that we should confine ourselves to this historical core, especially as otherwise we present a picture which is fundamentally deleterious to the status of women.

Frequent is the complaint that later tradition not merely altered but actually perverted Mary Magdalene both as a person and in her role. In attacking that earlier tradition much is made of its unhealthy attitude to sexuality. The most recent major study, for instance, speaks of 'wilful misrepresentation, to suit the purposes of an ascetic Church'.[52] Again, a major German feminist theologian describes herself as 'very angry' at what the tradition has done: 'At the expense of women, a provocative imaginary picture had been created in the patriarchal church. What is left of the great

---

[49] For Mary of Bethany as anointer, John 12:1–8; for anonymous penitent sinner as anointer, Luke 7: 37–50; neither is identified with Mary Magdalene. For Gregory's identification, e.g. *Homilies on the Gospels* 2.25 (*PL* 76. 1188–96, esp. 1189); 2.33 (ibid., 1238–46, esp. 1239).

[50] *De Maria Magdalena et triduo Christi disceptatio* (Paris, 1517), written under the Latin version of his name, Jacobus Faber Stapulensis.

[51] For resurrection, John 20: 1–18 and Matt. 28: 1, 9 with Mark 16: 9; for seven demons and itinerant preaching, Luke 8: 1–3; for her presence at crucifixion, Mark 15: 40.

[52] S. Haskins, *Mary Magdalen* (London: HarperCollins, 1993), 97; cf. 11 'to serve the purposes of the ecclesiastical hierarchy'.

male sinner? . . . What would our tradition look like if it had made Peter a converted pimp?'[53] Without doubt such charges need to be addressed. But, as I shall attempt to demonstrate shortly, they are greatly exaggerated, in large part because they fail to address the question of how the imagery in fact functioned. In the meantime, we may note how reaction against such a reading of history can generate accounts that are no less short on historical justification.

Two illustrations of this may be given. The first and more obvious concerns the question of sexuality itself. Although some modern writers seek to retain a strong erotic component in Mary's relations with Jesus,[54] it is often assumed that any mention of a sexual sin must automatically partake of the generally negative attitude to sexuality in the patristic and medieval period.[55] But in fact one has to wait until the sixteenth century for the visual image to become strongly sensual, and it was to take until the nineteenth before it became an excuse for photographic pornography, with a similar development to be detected in presentations in literature and film.[56] Again, in rightly locating bad motives in the past it is no less important to acknowledge the presence of bad (as well good) reasons in the contemporary desire to extricate Mary Magdalene from such a sexual reputation. With one modern commentator the argument appears to be that, thus released, she is the superior of Peter and Paul since unlike them she committed no great wrong in either betrayal (Peter) or persecution (Paul).[57] A famous scholar of an earlier generation even concludes his discussion by declaring that she now emerges 'with unblemished reputation', having earlier argued the implausibility of the alternative case partly on the grounds that Joanna, the wife of Herod's

[53] E. Moltmann-Wendel, *The Women Around Jesus* (New York: Crossroad, 1990), 64, 66–7.   [54] Ibid., 87–90.

[55] E. g. Haskins, *Magdalen*, 386.

[56] So Haskins herself, 229–400. As examples of the modern trend in literature and film, Michele Roberts' novel *Wild Girl* (London: Methuen, 1984) and Martin Scorcese's film *The Last Temptation of Christ* (1988), or D. H. Lawrence's short story of 1929, 'The man who died' in *Love Among the Haystacks and Other Stories* (Harmondsworth: Penguin, 1960), 125–73.

[57] S. M. Schneiders, 'Women in the Fourth Gospel and the Role of Women in the Contemporary Church' in M. W. G. Stibbe (ed.), *The Gospel of John as Literature* (Leiden: E. J. Brill, 1993), 141.

steward, would hardly have consented to be 'travelling about Galilee with a notorious courtesan'.[58] Such assessments are far removed from the radical inclusiveness promised by the Christian doctrine of forgiveness. The tradition, as we shall see, exalted Mary Magdalene because of a past which forgiveness had put behind her, whereas much contemporary thought seems some-times only able to think of any such past merely pulling her down.

My second example concerns the nature of the 'demons' which afflicted her. So concerned are some exegetes to avoid any of the traditional connections with sexual sin that specific alternative expla-nations are offered. Thus for one commentator the 'seven demons' refer to the sort of mental insecurity from which many of us suffer today,[59] while for another the cause was in the suffocating life-style imposed on women at the time.[60] But the truth surely is that we do not know. The fact that Mary Magdalene is picked out by this desig-nation despite the fact that earlier in the same verse we had already been told that all the women who accompanied Jesus 'had been healed of evil spirits and infirmities' does suggest that her condition was more severe than others, though not so severe as that of 'Legion' described later in the same chapter. None of this of course argues for sexual sin, but again can we really be quite so certain that it must be excluded?[61] Guilt and/or rejection is one of the most common sources of mental breakdown, and first-century treatment of a loose woman might well generate both guilt and rejection.[62] In saying this my intention has *not* been to argue that the tradition was right after all, but only to observe that modern expansions are really no more secure than their earlier rivals. As one biblical scholar has wisely observed, for all we know to the contrary, she may have been 'eighty-six, childless, and keen to mother unkempt young men'.[63]

[58] F. C. Burkitt, 'Mary Magdalene and Mary, Sister of Martha', *Expository Times* 52 (1930–1), 157–9, cf. Luke 8: 3.

[59] M. Hebblethwaite, *Six New Gospels* (London: Geoffrey Chapman, 1994), 121.

[60] C. Ricci, *Mary Magdalene and Many Others* (London: Burns & Oates, 1994), 135–7.

[61] Haskins, *Magdalen*, 14; statement in text ironically contradicted by relevant footnote, 405, n. 32.

[62] Indeed, one might argue that it is essential to 'demythologize' at this point, since without such an attempt much will be lost from Luke, so prominent a feature in that Gospel is struggle with the demonic.

[63] E. P. Sanders, *The Historical Figure of Jesus* (London: Penguin, 1993), 75.

Due caution is therefore required before we too readily endorse the common modern perception that, once we take from Mary her tears and her ointment jar and let her shine in all the glory of her role on that first resurrection morning, she can unqualifiedly be used to bolster arguments for a new status and dignity for women. Our own age, like all its predecessors, has also its characteristic prejudices and distortions. What therefore I want to suggest in what follows is that a fresh, sympathetic look at the composite figure, so far from undermining the dignity of women, can actually add significantly to it. Not only that, we will find that in creating that composite figure the later Church was building on similar imaginative concerns already present within the New Testament itself. I shall proceed by two stages, examining first the relevant biblical texts, and then the further expansions and employment of Mary's story in later church tradition.

Rebuilding the tradition: the biblical imagination

My sub-heading here will to many seem itself a misnomer, since so often is the contrast drawn between the historical factuality of the scriptural portrait and later 'invention'. To illustrate why matters are not that simple, I want to begin with the alleged historical core of Jesus' resurrection appearance to Mary. While in no way wishing to deny that she was among those who had a resurrection appearance and that this was probably at the tomb, it does seem to me that not only are there serious historical grounds for doubting that it was the first, but, more importantly, that to put the stress there is to distort the main point of John's narrative. John was already using the appearance for other purposes, and we shall find that matters are not significantly different when we turn to the anointings.

Resurrection appearance   Though many distinguished biblical scholars endorse the view that this was the first resurrection appearance,[64] we need to take seriously not only contrary indications, but also the weakness of some of the apparently supporting evidence. None of the Synoptics offer strong support. Luke

---

[64] So e.g. R. E. Brown, 'Roles of women in the Fourth Gospel', *Theological Studies* 36 (1975), 688–99, esp. 692, n. 12: 'has a good chance of being historical'.

makes no mention of the incident at all. This is particularly puzzling, for, as the evangelist most sympathetically disposed to women, one would have expected him to have recorded such a strong acknowledgement of the role of women, had he known of it.[65] Again, the reference in Mark is to be found in the concluding section of the Gospel upon which there is general agreement that it does not derive directly from the original evangelist's own work, but through dependence on the other Gospels. Moreover, the verses immediately prior to Mark 16: 9 ff. seem to imply the contrary, that the first appearances were in Galilee. That leaves us with Matthew, where the evidence also turns out to be problematic. One female scholar, commenting on the appearance to Mary Magdalene and another Mary, expresses the difficulties well:

The subsequent appearance of Jesus cutting them off at the pass as they ran (28: 9–10) is the most difficult part of the narrative and may be an addition. It adds nothing to the angel's message to go to Galilee. Moreover, it seemingly contradicts the angel, who has just told them to deliver the message that 'you will see him in Galilee'.[66]

Indeed, as a piece of writing it seems somewhat crass, since it makes the greater theophany the appearance of the angel rather than that of Christ himself: unlike Jesus of whom no description is offered, the angel's 'appearance was like lightning, and his raiment white as snow' (Matt. 28: 3 RSV). It looks therefore as though the evidence of John stands rather insecurely on its own, with some significant indicators actually pulling us in the opposite direction. For on the other side must be placed not only the assumption of our earliest Gospel that the first appearances were in Galilee but also Mary's absence from Paul's list of resurrection appearances. The common attempt to explain the latter by Jewish attitudes to female witnesses is not nearly as well founded as is often believed, while confirmation of Paul's acceptance of precedence for Peter's resurrection appearance may well be indicated by Luke's quotation of what reads suspiciously like an early confessional formula to the

---

[65] Cf. N. M. Flanagan, 'The position of women in the writings of St Luke', *Marianum* 40 (1978), 288–304, esp. 292–3.

[66] C. Osiek, 'The women at the tomb: what are they doing there?', *Ex Auditu* 9 (1993), 97–107, esp. 99.

same effect: 'The Lord has risen indeed, and has appeared to Simon' (Luke 24: 34 RSV; cf. Mark 16: 7; 1 Cor. 15: 5).[67]

Then we need also to consider the narrative intentions of John himself. Modern biblical scholarship has increasingly come to recognize the degree to which reactions of Jesus' disciples towards him have been moulded in the Gospels to make theological points about our own discipleship. So, for instance, it has been suggested that the strength of the contrast between the behaviour of Jesus' disciples in the first and in the second half of Mark's Gospel has a deliberate narrative purpose: the reader is led initially to identify with them, only to experience all the more powerfully the critique of inadequate discipleship which then follows.[68] If that is so in Mark, the case would seem even stronger for John, with his introduction of the mysterious 'beloved disciple'. Attempts continue to be made to give him a definite historic identity. Apart from the most popular candidate, the apostle John, suggestions have included Lazarus and, most recently, doubting Thomas.[69] The absence of any obviously equivalent figure in the Synoptics, however, argues against historicity, but even if he were historical, we miss the point of his introduction unless we acknowledge how he functions in John's narrative which is to represent 'the ideal follower of Jesus'.[70] It is his seeing and believing at the empty tomb without needing to await a personal appearance of Christ which is intended as paradigmatic for our own discipleship (John 20: 8–9).[71]

By contrast, therefore, Mary Magdalene's encounter is intended (like Peter's) to be read as less than perfect. Like the beloved dis-

[67] That Jewish laws of evidence could have led to her omission by Paul is challenged by Osiek, 'Woman at the tomb', 103–4.

[68] R. C. Tannehill, 'The disciples in Mark: the function of a narrative role' in W. Telford (ed.), *The Interpretation of Mark* (London: SPCK, 1985), 134–57, esp. 145.

[69] For Lazarus, J. N. Sanders, 'Those whom Jesus loved', *New Testament Studies* 1 (1954–5), 29–41, esp. 33–6; for Thomas, J. H. Charlesworth, *Beloved Disciple* (Valley Force, Pa.: Trinity Press, International, 1996).

[70] R. E. Brown, *The Gospel According To John XIII–XXI* (New York: Doubleday, 1970), 1005.

[71] Contrast Mary's unbelieving response to the empty tomb at 20: 1–2. The question of how 'seeing' and 'believing' relate is an issue that runs through John's Gospel, and is among those features unique to him: J. Marsh, *Saint John* (Harmondsworth: Penguin, 1968), 625–30.

ciple, Mary shows the eagerness of love to continue in some sort of relationship with Christ, but Christ has to come further towards her before she can believe, and even then she misunderstands the nature of his presence. She tries to cling to him as though his presence were still a purely earthly one. Jesus has therefore to reprimand her (in much the same way as later he chides Thomas): 'Touch me not' or, more accurately, 'Do not keep clinging'.[72] There was thus a good catechetical reason why the evangelist should have placed this resurrection story first: it sets the context for the further accounts that are to follow by indicating how they are *not* to be appropriated. But there is also a further reason in the logic of the narrative. In *Tradition and Imagination* I noted that the natural development of the story as a whole requires the experience of Christ as ascended to follow more intimate and material resurrection experiences even if the historical order had been quite different. Similarly, in this particular case it would have made little narrative sense, even if appearances at the tomb had occurred later than those in Galilee, to return to the tomb for descriptions of them, since the entire narrative structure requires us to move away from the tomb and towards heaven. If we compare John with the Synoptics, we find him elsewhere making major changes in chronology for symbolic purposes, as with the cleansing of the Temple or the precise time when Jesus was crucified (John 2: 13–23, cf. Mark 11: 15–18; John 19: 4, cf. Mark 14: 12); so it would not be out of character to find a similar change here.

In raising such doubts let me stress once more that my concern is not to deny a resurrection appearance to Mary; only to question whether we can be quite so confident, as so many modern writers apparently are, of when precisely it occurred. It could have been simultaneous with other experiences, or even subsequent to them. Where we can be more confident is that she was the first to report the empty tomb, but even then we need to note that what interested John more was her ability to say something about our discipleship in the here and now. In contemporary society individual identity is an ultimate value, but for most of history this has not been so, and therefore we ought not to judge such adaptation of

---

[72] The former is the AV translation of John 20: 17, the latter my own attempt to bring out more forcefully the sense of the present imperative; for Thomas, 20: 29.

historical fact to teach theological truth by modern standards. In any case, Mary is far from being left with the purely negative contrast upon which I have hitherto focused. For, significantly, as a result of the reprimand, she is enabled to see Christ in a new light. No longer simply 'Rabboni' (Master), it is as 'Lord' that she reports the new form of his existence to the disciples. Though the harder-won understanding, it corresponds, I suspect, much more closely to the experience of the great mass of Christians than the ideal pattern proposed by John in his 'beloved disciple'. He is too perfect, his love too unqualified, his perceptions too easily achieved.

Anointings   Once the nature of discipleship is thus seen as the main point of the resurrection narrative, the linkage with the various anointing passages then begins to become comprehensible, even if still altogether lacking in historical justification. For what they do at least share with John 20 is a similarity of theme, in this question of discipleship. To see why such a concern might be sufficient to override the issue of historicity, in conveying some more fundamental truth, we need to look with some care at each of the incidents. Since Matthew follows Mark closely, in effect there are only three anointings that need our attention: the one in Luke (7: 36–50) which takes place in the house of Simon the Pharisee, where the washing of feet with tears is quickly followed by anointing, all done by an anonymous sinner; the one in Mark (14: 3–9) this time in the house of Simon the leper, and performed on Jesus' head by an anonymous woman from Bethany; and, finally, John's version (12: 1–8) where we move once more to the feet and the use of the woman's hair, though this time the woman is named as Mary of Bethany.

When we carefully compare the three, it is hard to resist the conclusion that Luke's and John's tellings have been affected by that of Mark. Historical reconstructions have been attempted, which argue that the primary point had once been a prophetic declaration of Jesus' messiahship.[73] If so, Mark has suborned the

---

[73] A woman acting prophetically and dangerously would then have been usurped for other purposes; so E. Schüssler Fiorenza, *In Memory of Her* (London: SCM Press, 1983), xiii–xiv. For suggestions of how that alternative image might be appropriated liturgically, M. Proctor-Smith, 'Liturgical anamnesis and women's memory', *Worship* 61 (1987), 405–24.

extravagant use of the perfume to other purposes. The anonymous woman is found to be anointing Jesus 'for burial' (v. 8).[74] More importantly for the long-term use of the passage, he also seems concerned to say something about love, that our love should be reckless in its giving, totally uncalculating, like this woman's.[75] Presumably implicit is the idea that God in Christ gave his all for us, and so should we in turn as his disciples. If so, it is a theme which Luke will make explicit.

Though in his case what were once two distinct incidents may have been combined,[76] as his version stands, it has clearly been influenced by Mark, if only because it is inherently unlikely that such an expensive gesture could have occurred twice in Jesus' lifetime.[77] However, it is the issue of discipleship that now dominates, as Luke seeks to illustrate how our love of Christ functions in response to Christ's own. Significantly, in expounding this idea he highlights love as the yearning, not as in the Marcan version to give, but to receive, for Jesus observes: 'He who is forgiven little, loves little' (v. 47 RSV). It is precisely because this woman has yearned to be accepted, longed to be forgiven, that she could now be forgiven. The foolish lover wants only to give and never to receive, whereas the true lover wants to receive as much as to give, to be dependent as much as dependable. The woman's tears spoke of that longing for dependence on Christ's forgiving love that every true disciple of Christ must also have.

Now turn to John. Though any explicit reference to sin is gone, his account (12: 1–8) appears to combine elements from both Mark and Luke. Parallel with Mark is the sum involved, and

[74] The reference to anointing for burial at this stage may, like the implausible anointing two days after death (16: 1), have been apologetically motivated by the desire to avoid the stigma of Jesus not having been so anointed: so J. K. Elliott, 'The Anointing of Jesus', *Expository Times* 85 (1973–4), 105–7.

[75] Characterized as 'the strange economy of love' in S. Barton, *People of the Passion* (London: SPCK, 1994), 9.

[76] For a defence of there being two distinct incidents, A. Legault, 'An application of the form-critique method to the anointings in Galilee and Bethany', *Catholic Biblical Quarterly* 16 (1954), 131–41; for Luke's version as more primitive than Mark, and tears omitted by Mark for theological reasons, R. Holst, 'The anointing of Jesus: another application of the form-critical method', *Journal of Biblical Literature* 95 (1976), 435–46.

[77] Already in Mark the equivalent of a year's salary for a labourer, Luke even increases the amount involved from three hundred to five hundred denarii.

the reference to burial, as well as the complaint of the disciples, though this time specifically identified with Judas Iscariot. However, parallel with Luke is the fact that the anointing is of the feet and not of the head, and that she dries Jesus' feet with her hair. The fact that the incident is, as with Mark, once more explicitly set in Bethany and the woman even named (as Mary, sister of Martha and Lazarus) may seem to stack the cards decisively in favour of Mark, but once again one needs to note carefully the role which theology is playing.[78] In the preceding chapter Mary had just seen her brother, Lazarus, raised from the dead. Has not John borrowed the image of anointing the feet to carry further that theme?[79] Certainly, Jesus is anointed for burial, but her action also says something about discipleship. She desires to be buried with Christ, wholly identified with him in his self-giving, so that she can rise with him to new life, the new life that she had already seen in Christ when her brother was raised by him from the dead.

Yet one vital feature of the Lucan narrative is missing. Mary of Bethany in anointing Jesus sheds no tears. But a woman's tears do appear prominently in this Gospel, and at a point indicated by none of the other three. Someone called Mary Magdalene cries profusely at the empty tomb, and as with the penitent sinner of Luke's version of the anointing is plenteously rewarded. This may not be entirely coincidence, since the failure to take advantage of the emotionally charged setting of Luke's anointing did allow freer rein when it came to the incident at the empty tomb.[80] Indeed, it is not altogether impossible that John explicitly warns us of such a connection, since at 12: 7 Jesus declares: 'Leave her alone; let her keep it till the day when she prepares for my burial.'[81] But unless

[78]   For a similar advocacy of the composite origin of the text, though a different suggested motivation for the anointing: C. K. Barrett, *The Gospel According To St. John* (London: SPCK, 2nd edn., 1978), 408–15, esp. 409.

[79]   We are carried out 'feet first' for our burial. Later tradition was to identify the feet with Jesus' humanity and his head with his divinity: e.g. Bede, *Homilies on the Gospels* 2.4.

[80]   Mary of Bethany does, however, cry at another tomb, that of Lazarus, in the chapter prior to the anointing: 11.31–3. Again, this may not be unconnected, since the events surrounding Lazarus' death and resurrection are of course intended to anticipate and comment on Christ's own.

[81]   NEB, using restored modern text. Yet because of the absence of any future fulfilment, many modern commentators assume that the meaning must still be the same as the different text used by the AV: 'against the day of my burial she has

Mary of Bethany is there hidden in the text of 19: 40 which provides the context for the appearance to Mary Magdalene, the earlier verse will have been one that lacks all fulfilment. This is not to say that John identified Mary of Bethany and Mary Magdalene; only that he may have seen them both as exercising primarily an essentially imaginative rather than historical role: they are both there to tell us about discipleship.

Whether John intended such a link or not, it was this imaginative connection that in effect justified the linking of anointings and resurrection appearance.[82] For in both instances it was not just discipleship in general that was at stake, but a very specific pattern of growth and development that applies to us all. That was why, despite equating the various figures involved, the tradition still often continued to speak of two anointings, one with tears that spoke of penitence and the reception of forgiveness and the other which spoke of response in a generous, uncalculating love.[83] The resurrection events then indicated a deepening of that dialectic, where tears this time indicated another level of longing, again transformed through Christ's love. As we now explore how this basic structure was developed, we shall observe how it was utilized to enable at times a more effective identification with Christ than even the Gospels themselves provide,[84] though essentially the same tactics are employed with history firmly subordinate to theology.

The model disciple of later tradition

At first sight the Eastern tradition might seem more loyal to the Bible and thus more consonant with modern biblical scholarship

---

kept this' (the anointing associated with death is being done now instead of later). For a contrary view, J. H. Bernard, *Gospel According To John* (Edinburgh: T. & T. Clark, 1928), II, 421.

[82] Helped of course by yet another anointing accomplished by Mary Magdalene at the tomb: Mark 16: 1.

[83] For such a pattern in Ambrose and other Latin fathers and its rationale, M.-J. Lagrange, 'Jésus a-t-il été oint plusieurs fois et par plusieurs femmes?', *Revue biblique* 9 (1912), 504–32, esp. 517 ff. and 531.

[84] One suspects that most later writers would have preferred the expensive ointment only to have been used in the second anointing, with the first employing tears alone. Instead, as in *The Golden Legend*, the contrast is more usually drawn between feet and head.

than the Western, in that Mary Magdalene, Mary of Bethany and the woman sinner are all kept distinct.[85] Yet, it would be a mistake to suppose that the primary influence was the biblical text. Part of the reason was probably the existence of separate shrines as places of pilgrimage (at Bethany and Ephesus),[86] while an early restraining influence may well have been Tatian's *Diatessaron*, since this attempted harmonization of the Gospels avoids conflating the figures concerned.[87] A very different pattern, however, established itself in Western Christendom, thanks largely to the influence of Gregory the Great whose acceptance of the identification in a number of his sermons seemed to have carried the day, largely because of the accessibility of his presentation and style.[88] I want to consider that pattern of discipleship under three heads: Mary's example as model penitent, her role as contemplative and preacher, and finally its culminating form in her as image of a restored creation.

The searching penitent To the modern mind it is of course intensely irritating that the precise chronicle of history cannot be recovered, but, as I have sought to argue, the more important issue for the evangelists in speaking of the anointings and resurrection appearance was the nature of discipleship, and so in effect that is what the issue also became for the later Church. Instead of receiving the text at the level of historical muddle, which is in effect what we have in the three versions of the anointing and the conflicting accounts of the ordering of the resurrection appearances, the several women involved were integrated into one symbolic figure of discipleship. That way the new figure of Mary Magdalene came to function as the supreme symbol of the dialectic of Christian discipleship: the receiving of forgiveness (in the acceptance of the use of her hair to dry feet wet by tears) that demands in turn the generous giving of the ointment jar (thus

---

[85] V. Saxer, 'Les saintes Marie Madeleine et Marie de Béthanie dans la tradition liturgique et homilétique orientale', *Revue des sciences religieuses* 32 (1958), 1–37. The author provides a detailed history of the development of the Western tradition in *Le Culte de Marie-Madeleine en Occident* (Paris: Cahiers d'archéologie de d'historie, 1959).   [86] Ibid., 35.

[87] M.-J. Lagrange, 'Jésus', 530–32, esp. 531.

[88] Cf. P. A. DeLeeuw, 'Gregory the Great's *Homilies on the Gospels* in the early Middle Ages', *Studi Medievali* 26 (1985), 855–69.

confirming the new relationship); then, secondly, the searching faith (in her case at the resurrection) that finds its expected object transformed within the process of encounter. Because Mary (with her presence at the crucifixion added) is thus allowed to appear at all the major stages in Christ's ministry, in reading Jesus' story one was also thereby allowed in effect to read what could also be one's own story, in a growing discipleship. In combining what had once almost certainly been three distinct historical personages, the later Church therefore not only continued the New Testament pattern of those figures mediating reflection on discipleship, but in the story of the now composite figure it also effectively created the most powerful vehicle available for probing such issues further. In so doing, men as well as women were to find in her one of the principal means of developing their own discipleship, and so women in general were honoured by her cult.

Yet so used are contemporary writers to assuming a uniform pattern of hostility to female sexuality everywhere throughout Christian history that in effect this has become the customary lens through which, unreflectively, every reference to Mary has also been interpreted. Yet close reading of the meditative texts, poems, and paintings which are on offer, I would contend, suggests a quite other view: that she became the model for every penitent, the model for every disciple, men no less than women. As one medieval historian comments, 'almost every normal human being came under her jurisdiction and sought her intercession at one time or another'.[89]

Medieval hymns, for instance, focus not only on the example and encouragement she provides to all sinners but also upon the exalted status which forgiveness through Christ has brought to her. So, as well as frequent use of the term 'apostle', we also find her described as the bride of Christ (*sponsa*) and most beloved of God (*Deo dilectissima*).[90] Indeed, when one examines in detail the art and literature, one soon discovers that the extent to which stress is

[89] H. M. Garth, 'St. Mary Magdalene in Medieval Literature', *Johns Hopkins University Studies in Historical and Political Science* 67, (1950), 9–114, esp. 105; cf. also 93–7. She also stresses the medieval love of extreme contrast as part of the explanation of why Mary's story was told in the way it was: e. g. 106.

[90] J. Szövérffy, 'Peccatrix quondam femina: a survey of the Mary Magdalene hymns', *Traditio* XIX (1963), 79–146; for her role as patron, 117, 119; for her as bride and beloved of God, 92–3.

laid upon her sexual sin has been greatly exaggerated. That feature only really becomes prominent from the sixteenth century onwards, and even then not universally. Passing allusion rather than specific reference is more characteristic of an earlier age, and in any case what clearly matters more is her identity as a fellow-sinner who has been forgiven. So, for instance, Anselm of Canterbury prays:

Most blessed lady, I the most wicked of men do not touch once more upon your sins as a taunt or reproach but seek to grasp the boundless mercy by which they were blotted out . . . Draw for me from the well where I may wash my sins; Hasten to me from him who can satisfy my thirst; pour over me his waters that my dry land may be made fruitful. For it is not difficult for you to obtain whatever you wish from so loving and so kind a Lord, who is your friend living and reigning.[91]

Almost two centuries earlier, Odo of Cluny had not hesitated to identify her as the mystical symbol for the Church, forgiven and committed, while in 1500 she became for Botticelli, now under the influence of Savonarola's preaching, the symbol of all penitent Christians in Florence, seeking forgiveness at the foot of Christ's Cross.[92]

Particularly moving is the twelfth-century *Life*, once attributed to Rabanus Maurus. Not only is attention carefully drawn to extenuating circumstances—'outward beauty' and 'affluence of possessions'—readers are also reminded of how probable it is that they will have fallen in a similar way in their own lives: 'as is usual at that age' is how the anonymous Cistercian puts it. Here is how

[91] My trans.: *Oratio* 16.10–12 and 22–6 in F. S. Schmitt (ed.), *Opera Omnia* (Edinburgh: Nelson, 1946), 3. 64–5. Notable in the Latin is the close conjunction 'ego sceleratissimus peccata tua' and the way in which the whole passage is made to culminate in the reference to Mary as Christ's friend. The principal literary influences on the prayer, apart from the Bible, were Pope Gregory and Odo of Cluny: V. Saxer, 'Anselme et la Madeleine' in *Les mutations socio-culturelles au tournant des XI–XIIe siècles* (Paris: Editions du CNRS, 1984), 365–82.

[92] Sermon 2 (PL 133, 715). In the East Mary was not identified with the sinful woman, but writers still identified themselves with the latter, as does Romanos the Melodist: *Kontakia*, ed. E. Lash (London: Harper Collins, 1996), 77–84. For a colour illustration of the 'Mystical Crucifixion', B. Deimling, *Botticelli* (Cologne: Taschen, 1994), 80; for further commentary, Plate 1 at the end of this book.

he introduces the issue: 'Because outward beauty is rarely allied to chastity, and an affluence of possessions may often be an enemy of continence, when she became a young woman, abounding in delights and rejoicing in a noble heart, she, as is usual at that age, followed after the pleasures of the flesh.'[93] But still not content with such special pleading, he continues: 'But why linger any longer over this? The soul of youth is a pilgrim; she dwelt in earthly love only for a time.'[94] So instead the focus is upon what new powers her conversion brought and the example they can give to us. When all twelve male disciples proved inadequate 'there still was found in Mary Magdalene the courage of the Redeemer', and so she is the equal of John the Baptist, greater than any other disciple and surpassed only by Christ and his Mother.[95] Consonant with that interpretation, during the Counter-Reformation St Francis de Sales did not hesitate to describe her as queen over all penitent sinners.[96]

It was also that presumed fact of sinfulness which enabled her to function so effectively in literally thousands of devotional writings and works of art that depict the crucifixion. It is a serious mistake to read such sculptures and paintings that include Mary Magdalene with her ointment jar as though the intention were simply to make an historical point, with the jar merely there to identify her presence, and thus their opting for John's account rather than the Synoptic Gospels 'from afar'. Rather, what is at stake is *our* presence, *our* ability to appropriate the fruits of the crucifixion. The representative sinner was there, and so, however sinful we are or feel ourselves to be, we can, like her, appropriate Christ's forgiveness and respond with a similar love. No doubt that is why on some alabaster carvings she wipes the blood off the dead Christ with her hair.[97] As if to underline her complete identification with

[93] *The Life of Saint Mary Magdalene and her Sister Martha*, tr. D. Mycoff (Kalamazoo: Cistercian Publications, 1989), 30. The work has a remarkably modern feel in the relative absence of miracles, though some are ascribed to Martha: 99–105, cf. 98.

[94] 31; contrast the very different estimate of the same passage in Haskins, 158.

[95] 60, 84–5. This surely adequately compensates for the occasional reference to 'a man's soul in a woman's breast' (29, 64).

[96] 'Regina confitentium peccatorum'; *PL* 141.1326.

[97] W. L. Hildburgh, 'English alabaster carvings as records of medieval English drama', *Archaeologia* XCIII (1947), 51–101, esp. 88.

us, Grünewald in the famous Isenheim Altarpiece makes her (unlike the other figures) the traditional smaller size of a donor: Mary has become wholly one of us.[98]

Equal care needs to be taken in apprehending how her resurrection appearance was understood. The numerous representations of *Noli me tangere* again very much make her one of us, either through her ointment jar or in her kneeling, stretching towards Christ's feet. Christ's new status is normally indicated either by a banner or by him pointing heavenwards. Though his other hand seems to push Mary away from him, various devices are used to indicate that he is also drawing her towards him in some new sense. Particularly powerful is the way Giotto represents this in the Scrovegni Chapel in Padua. The eyes of Mary and Christ meet at the rejecting hand, which is itself at the intersection of two strong diagonals that together give the shape of a cross. It is, we are being told, through identification with his crucifixion that Mary will come to experience him as resurrection, a process Giotto indicates has already begun by placing the only garden vegetation in the picture in the space between them.[99]

None of this is to deny a negative side to the tradition, but it is to insist that it is far less prominent than is commonly claimed. In an otherwise excellent study the sole comment on that twelfth-century *Life* from which I quoted earlier is that it 'reflects the clerical equation of physical beauty with evil'.[100] That physical beauty makes it more likely that one will be subject to temptations of this kind I would have thought an obvious truth about human nature, rather than anything to do with the clergy. But even if it were, the author's comments still wholly ignore the *Life's* obvious sympathy with those who fall under such temptation. Again, many a remark that sounds initially rather contemptuous needs its wider context to be supplied before it can be appropriately assessed. So, for instance, when we find Peter Damian asking 'Who needs despair when such a sinner as Mary Magdalene received not only pardon, but glory?' we need also to observe how the very next sentence

---

[98] The power of the image is demonstrated by its influence on Picasso and Sutherland: J. Hayes, *The Art of Graham Sutherland* (Oxford: Phaidon, 1980), 108–9.

[99] Illus. 36 in *Giotto: The Scrovegni Chapel* (New York: George Braziller, 1993).   [100] Haskins, *Magdalen*, 158.

continues: 'She will intercede for our sins today, and will bring back to us our judge and her bridegroom, even God who is blessed for ever.'[101] Even where her 'once notorious' status is juxtaposed with her new role as 'apostle', it still lacks the demeaning tones of Calvin who, while separating Mary from the penitent sinner, insists that the only reason for allowing her to make the announcement of the resurrection was not so that she might function as an apostle but as a 'reproach' to the male disciples.[102] Indeed, in marked contrast to Calvin some writers show willingness to retain a sensual element in the resurrection encounter, but in a manner which gives it a wholly positive evaluation.[103] Admittedly, the fact that Thomas was allowed to touch the resurrected Christ whereas Mary was reprimanded for doing so gave opportunity for the worst sort of sexism.[104] But even here this never became the norm, with most following Chrysostom in speaking only of a temporary reprimand, caused by 'an excess in her affection' and 'a defect in her judgement'. In other words, the suggestion was that it was precisely because she loved her Lord so much that she had been led to call him by his earthly title 'Rabboni' rather than his heavenly, 'My Lord and my God', and in any case the capacity for touch was restored shortly thereafter.[105]

But if it is objected that I am still missing the point of modern feminist criticism since it is a woman rather than a man that is chosen as representative sinner,[106] my response would still be that her prominent status was achieved through all Christians, men as

---

[101] Sermon 39 (my trans.); *PL* 144. 666.

[102] Contrast last line of Marbod of Rennes' poem, 'Hymnus primus de Magdalena' with its 'infamem quondam . . . apostolam' and Calvin's pre-occupation with preventing women from baptising: Marbod, in *PL*, 171.1647; Calvin, *John* (Wheaton, Ill.: Crossway, 1994), 449.

[103] With her body respected, no less than mind; cf. D. K. Shuger, *The Renaissance Bible* (Berkeley, Cal.: University of California Press, 1994), 167–91. Note her conclusion: 'even up to the middle of the eighteenth century . . . the voice of the soul is always soprano.'

[104] Though it is not altogether clear whether John intended the reader to infer that Thomas had actually touched Jesus. Did his confession intervene, making touch unnecessary? Cf. John 20: 27–8.

[105] L. Andrewes, Sermon for Easter Day, 1621 in *The Sermons of Lancelot Andrewes*, ed. M. Dorman (Edinburgh: Pentland Press, 1993), 159–60. A difference of sex is explicitly excluded as an explanation (159).

[106] So Haskins, *Magdalen,* 141.

much as women, being willing to identify with her, and not as a contrast to their own state. It was the gospel theme of loving discipleship as receiving and giving, as searching and finding that was being deepened as her cult grew, not contempt for the female sex. Indeed, there are some grounds for believing that it legitimated female assertiveness, since Mary was in no way portrayed as 'bland' or 'restrained' after her conversion.[107] Two major factors inhibited such a role for the most obvious rival candidates, Peter and Paul. Mary's sin was a common human failure which we all share; much fewer of us sink to the levels of Peter and Paul, either in betraying our friends or in being accessories to judicial murder. Secondly, in neither case was their repentance as dramatic as Mary's. Paul even boasted his perfect observance of the law, while, though Peter wept, he lacked the beautiful, dramatic gesture which Mary offered.

Indeed, it is fascinating to observe how Peter begins increasingly to take over Mary's role at the Counter-Reformation, and that for two reasons, neither discreditable to the Church's attitude to this particular woman. The first was the Renaissance attack, beginning with Jacques Lefévre d'Étaples essay of 1517, on the identification of Mary Magdalene with other aspects of the composite tradition; for clearly, if the penitent sinner had no further story to tell, her capacity to move and influence was effectively undermined. Then, secondly, as we have already noted, Mary from the sixteenth century onwards was given an increasingly secular image as seductive, fallen woman, and as such could not usefully serve as the best example for the Church's defence of the sacrament of penance. The problem is already evident with Titian,[108] but becomes more

---

[107] M. R. Miles, *Image as Insight* (Boston, Mass.: Beacon Press, 1985), 81. For a splendid twentieth-century example of a woman having no difficulty in identifying with the expanded version of Mary's story at its most sensual as well as most religious, M. Yourcenar, 'Mary Magdalene or salvation' in *Fires* (London: Aidan Ellis, 1962), 63–77.

[108] In his highly sensual 'Penitent Magdalene' of *c.* 1530, though the motivation may not have been entirely secular, as the theories of Marsilio Ficino on the connection between love and beauty may also have played their part: E. Philpot, 'Mary Magdalene—saint or sinner?—the visual image' in A. E. Jasper and A. G. Hunter (eds.), *Perspectives on Women and Religion* (Glasgow: Trinity St Mungo, 1996), 52–79, esp. 63–5.

pronounced in the seventeenth century.[109] So, beginning with the writings of Robert Bellarmine,[110] Peter begins to be given the more prominent place. A musical illustration of this comes almost immediately with Lassus' *Lagrimi di San Pietro* of 1595,[111] while artistic examples follow not long after, early in the following century. Thus, though the Spanish painters, Zurburán and Ribera, continue to paint the penitent Magdalene, in both cases their presentation of the crying Peter is better known, in Ribera's case existing in no less than four versions.[112] Even where she remains central, as in Poussin's two series of paintings of the seven sacraments, one notes increasing care to avoid any hint of sensuality that might be misunderstood,[113] and so such works remains in marked contrast to frankly secular compositions such as those of Lely and Kneller where she has become little more than an excuse for painting Charles II's mistresses. Though Martin Scorcese's film *The Last Temptation of Christ* can be interpreted as an attempt to take with equal seriousness both his divinity and humanity, its heavy stress on Mary's sensuality well illustrates the extent to which it is secularism that has manipulated her image rather than the Christian tradition as such.[114]

Contemplative and preacher Once that modern obsession with sexuality as such is laid aside, and her story is allowed once more

[109] To call the seventeenth century 'the Magdalen's century' therefore needs qualification: J. Dillinger, 'The Magdalen: reflections on the image of the saint and sinner in Christian art' in Y. Y. Haddad and E. B. Findly (eds.), *Women, Religion and Social Change* (Albany, N. Y.: SUNY, 1985), 115–45, esp. 135.

[110] Particularly through his *Disputationes de Controversiis Christianae* of 1586–93. There was, however, also some ecclesiastical pressure in the opposite direction through the liturgy, with the post-Tridentine adoption as the reading for her day, Songs of Songs 3: 1–3 in place of Proverbs 31: 10 ff., with its image of her as ideal housewife; D. J. O'Connor, 'The stone the builders rejected', *Irish Theological Quarterly* 61 (1951), 6–8.

[111] Though cantatas and oratorios devoted to Mary continued to be written, as with the fine early eighteenth-century *Maddalena ai piedi di Cristo* of Antonio Caldara.

[112] M. Grigori, *L'opera completa di Zurburán* (Milan: Rizzoli, 1973), n. 485; A. P. Sánchez, *L'opera completa del Ribera* (Milan: Rizzoli, 1978), n. 333–6.

[113] A. Blunt, *Poussin* (London: Pallas Athene, 1995), illus. 132, 157 and author's comments, 251.

[114] Though Eric Gill's 'The Nuptials of God' would be a case of a Christian artist similarly exaggerating the sensual side. For illustration and hostile 1923 reaction, M. Yorke, *Eric Gill* (London: Constable, 1981), 122–3.

to function imaginatively as a way of mediating to us as disciples of Christ the dialectic of forgiveness and the possibility of a deepening relation with Christ, two further elements in the tradition can also be more effectively restored to her story: her role as contemplative and as preacher. The former comes from her identification with Mary of Bethany and the resultant contrast with the over-busy Martha (Luke 10: 38–42), the latter from Jesus' injunction to her to go and tell the other disciples what she has seen. But both were to receive considerable expansion from later legends that spoke of her journeying to the south of France, and then, after many years preaching and meditating there, dying and her body being eventually translated to the north, to Vézelay. Though in generating this legend confusion with an actual historical figure who was a bishop in the south and called Lazarus may have played its part,[115] less honourable motives undoubtedly also had a role, in particular the desire to generate or protect income from pilgrims, particularly at Vézelay. Yet even so, despite the absence of all historical foundation, one must not discount too quickly the more positive contribution made by this further expansion of her story.

Consider first her role as contemplative. Though argument went back and forth over whether the contemplative life could be lived apart from the active (or any rate without prior preparation through it), as one historian of the Middle Ages observes, at no point in considering the developed story of Mary and Martha was there any 'hesitation in applying their roles to men'. Mary Magdalene had become the hero of the contemplative life as much for men as for women.[116] But she became so through detailed expansion of her legend where contemplation and its benefits are highlighted, not least in desert-like experiences, far more so than ever would have been possible had allusion been confined to a single biblical incident. The extent to which that expansion was the product of yet another confusion, this time with the ascetical Mary of Egypt, need not concern us here.[117] History was in any case not the primary motiva-

---

[115] H. Thurston, 'St. Mary Magdalene and the early saints of Provence', *Month* 93 (1989), 75–81, esp. 77.

[116] Cf. G. Constable, 'The interpretation of Mary and Martha' in G. Constable, *Three Studies in Medieval Religious and Social Thought* (Cambridge: Cambridge University Press, 1995), 3–141, esp. 107.

[117] Though protests against such an identification are made even by those who firmly endorse her French retreat; e.g.. in the twelfth century *Life*, 98.

tion, but rather the desire to tell a story of her which could more fully engage the imagination and so enable those who heard it themselves to engage more effectively in the practice of contemplation. One incidental result of such a stress on her contemplative role was that it also helped to secure a more prominent place for women in the monastic tradition. As one illustration of this, consider the famous eighth-century Anglo-Saxon Ruthwell Cross in south-west Scotland, where she is given two representations to Anthony of Egypt's one;[118] further legitimation was thereby afforded to the practice of dual monasteries which allowed female abbesses to exercise sway over men. In short, far from contributing to the suppression of women, it looks as though Mary ensured for them a higher profile, as men and women alike used her story as a means of furthering their own path under God to salvation. It was from this aspect of the tradition that there also derives what is perhaps the most evocative representation of Mary ever produced, that of Donatello.[119]

Similarly, the legends of her preaching in the south of France ought not to be dismissed entirely, simply because they are unhistorical. Earlier, I gave reasons for doubting whether the resurrection appearance to Mary was necessarily the first. Even if it were, it would be unwise to base any major historical claims about Mary's commission to preach on a single verse (John 20: 18),[120] still more so to use this as an historical foundation for justifying the ordination of women, as some feminists do.[121] Yet it can be so used imaginatively, and that is in effect what happened in the legends of Mary preaching in France. Here the tradition of her preaching is very firmly rooted.[122] She is credited with the conversion of numerous

---

[118] P. Meyvaert, 'A new perspective on the Ruthwell Cross: ecclesia and vita monastica' in B. Cassidy (ed.), *The Ruthwell Cross* (Princeton, N. J.: Princeton University Press, 1992), 95–166, esp. 110–12, 131–5 and 138–140.

[119] F. Hartt, *History of Italian Renaissance* (London: Thames & Hudson, 4th edn, 1994), 291, 297. For a poetic example, Henry Constable's 'To St Mary Magdalen'.

[120] For all we know to the contrary from Scripture that report may have been her last public word on Christ's behalf.

[121] E.g. Haskins, *Magdalen*, 392–400.

[122] Widely disseminated through J. de Voragine, *The Golden Legend* (Princeton, N. J. : Princeton University Press, 1993), Vol. I, 377. For a wide range of references, including some fine illustrations from Psalter and Gospel books, K. Ludwig Jansen, 'Maria Magdalena: *Apostola apostolorum*' in B. Mayne Kienzle and P. J. Walker (eds.), *Women Preachers and Prophets* (Berkeley, Cal.: University of California Press, 1998), 57–96.

pagans at Aix; in the twelfth century we find her described as 'a glorious preacher', while in the fourteenth it is argued that she must have been present at the Last Supper, since she was pre-eminently 'the apostle and guardian of the Gospel'.[123]

In confining Mary's historical role to first witness of the empty tomb, it may seem that I have undermined her right to be called *apostola apostolorum*, a title at least as old as Hippolytus.[124] But such an objection seems to me to place the emphasis in the wrong place. Historically, Mary will for ever remain a shadowy figure about whom we know little: no more than that she was a wealthy woman whom Jesus cured of an unknown malady and who, though a faithful follower, left only one incident behind her to be associated uniquely with her, an appearance at the tomb. All else comes from the imagination, yet in a way that allows her to be, in my view, far more significant, since in effect she became the principal symbol for understanding what our own discipleship and commitment entail, in particular how these might be worked out in the dialectic of forgiveness from, and devotion to, Christ.

As image of restored creation   The composite figure allowed a story to be told of progress in the disciple's relation to Christ through sin and misunderstanding to something beyond. Progress, though, demands some sense of eventual completion, and so, as a way of encouraging hope, writers were not slow in identifying Mary's now exalted state in heaven: that could also be our own final destiny, we are in effect being told, however impossible that prospect might seem at the moment. Sometimes, however, we find her goal as representative disciple made still more explicit. So I want to end by observing the way in which in seventeenth- century England her composite character was rounded off, as it were, by her being identified as the image for us of humanity renewed and creation restored.

[123] In the twelfth century, Geoffrey of Vendome speaks of her 'gladly undertaking exile' and 'de propriis egressa finibus, Dominum Jesum Christum Deum verum *assidue* predicans (my italics, *PL* 157.273–4); in the fourteenth, another anonymous *Life of Saint Mary Magdalene*, trans. V. Hawtrey (London: Bodley Head, 1944), 159.

[124] A version already exists in Hippolytus, cf. Haskins, *Magdalen*, 65; clearly used by Bernard of Clairvaux, *Sermons on the Song of Songs*, 75, III, 8 (though applied to all the women at the tomb); title soon to be included in the revised Alternative Service Book of the Church of England.

Despite the Renaissance attack on the historicity of her composite image, in that century she in fact continued to act powerfully as a symbol in both sermon and poetry. Almost every major poet of the period has a poem with her as its theme,[125] and in almost every case the effectiveness of the imagery derives from the fusion of the different biblical accounts. So, for instance, Henry Vaughan ends his poem with a poignant combination of Simon the Pharisee and Simon the Leper:

> Self-boasting Pharisee! How blind
> A judge wert thou, and how unkind!
> .   .   .   .
> This woman (say'st thou) is a sinner;
> And sate there none such at thy dinner?
> Go, leper, go; wash till thy flesh
> Comes like a child's, spotless and fresh;
> He is still leprous, that still paints:
> Who saint themselves, they are no saints.[126]

Again Andrew Marvell talks of

> those captivating eyes,
> Whose liquid chains could flowing meet
> To fetter her Redeemer's feet.[127]

while George Herbert links the washing of the feet directly with the crucifixion:

> Dear soul, she knew who did vouchsafe and deign
> To bear her filth, and that her sins did dash
> Ev'n God himself.[128]

[125] Apart from those poets quoted in the text, Crashaw and Constable also employ their talents in a similar way. In the previous century, we find two impressive examples from Southwell, though it is important to note that one of them, 'Mary Magdalene's Blush', is a deliberate parody of secular love poetry: L. L. Martz, *The Poetry of Meditation* (New Haven: Yale University Press, 1962), 184–93.

[126] 'St Mary Magdalen' in Henry Vaughan, *The Complete Poems* (Harmondsworth: Penguin, 1976), 273–5.

[127] 'Eyes and Tears' in *George Herbert and the Seventeenth Century Religious Poets* ed. M. A. Di Cesare (New York: Norton, 1978), 97–9, esp. 98.

[128] 'Mary Magdalene' in George Herbert, *The Complete Poems* (Penguin, 1991), 163–4,. esp. 163.

Nor were the poets slow in identifying her now exalted state. Vaughan, for instance, opens by addressing her as 'Dear, beauteous Saint!' and declares of those eyes that had once wept so profusely that they

> now are fixed stars, whose light
> Helps such dark stragglers to their sight.

It is particularly to one strand of imagery for such transformation that I want to draw attention here, a good illustration of which is to be found in the sermons of Lancelot Andrewes. In his 1620 Easter sermon Mary has become the symbol of the new resurrection life that Christ brings and the place that he appears to her is already a new Eden, identified as 'the fairest garden that ever was, Paradise', while of Mary he declares that, though 'her spirits were as good as dead . . . the gardener had done his part, made her all green on the sudden'.[129] Two years later, in speaking of her as *apostola apostolorom*, he justifies the title thus: 'That to woman first—it agrees well, for in a garden they came both.'[130] Though in such passages Andrewes assumes that Mary's resurrection experience was the first, what clearly matters more to him is that she constitutes the new Eve, the symbol of the new humanity that Christ has brought to both men and women.

In so describing her, Andrewes was following a long tradition of exegesis. Gregory the Great makes great play of Christ offering himself as a spiritual gardener to Mary, with his love making her virtue grow.[131] It is a theme which is taken up by Odo of Cluny in his insistence that Mary made no mistake of identification since it is always as gardener that Christ comes to his Church.[132] One also finds similar sentiments in a poem of Philip the Chancellor (d. 1236), which begins:

> O Mary, do not weep, there is no need to seek any further;
> truly the gardener and cultivator of souls is here.[133]

---

[129] *Sermons*, II, 145–56, esp. 152, 155. There is an excellent discussion of this sermon by Stanley Fish, *Is There a Text in This Class?* (Cambridge, Mass.: Harvard University Press, 1980), 182–96.

[130] Easter sermon of 1622; ibid. II, 167–78, esp. 169.

[131] *Homilies on the Gospels* 2.25 (PL 76.1192).

[132] Sermon 2 (*PL* 133, 720).

[133] Trans. J. Blakesley in idem (ed.), *Paths of the Heart* (London: SPCK, 1993), 40.

Distinguished scholars of the past, as well as some more recent writers,[134] have all suggested that such symbolism goes back to John himself. Only John places betrayal, crucifixion and resurrection in a garden.[135] Though a different Greek word is used from the Septuagint,[136] the fact that John is alone in this cannot but raise the possibility that a symbolic reason motivates its mention. Jesus would then be presented as the restorer of Eden and Mary Magdalene as its new Eve who meets the Lord of the Garden in the cool of the early morning (Gen. 3: 8 and John 20: 1).[137] Certainly later in the same chapter Jesus breathing over the disciples hints at the idea of a new creation.

However, whether John's intention or not, it is important to observe the way in which within such a reading it is a woman who has become the principal model for all humanity's appropriation of salvation, men no less than women. However far we go along the path of *imitatio Christi*, the new Adam remains someone with whom we can never completely identify. For it is from his divinity that we seek forgiveness, while his humanity has a perfection that makes him necessarily different from any of us. By contrast, we can wholly identify with Mary's story as we seek to appropriate that forgiveness and seek to pattern ourselves, however inadequately, after Christ himself.

> O wit of love! That thus could place
> Fountain and garden in one face.[138]

Her story thus declares the inauguration of a new order that brings new life alike to both sexes. Some may find troubling in itself the notion of a new Eve, but, if so, it needs to be asked whether it is any more inadequate than that of the new Adam. Yet, if it is unusable, let us by all means discard it, and speak instead of her as the

---

[134] E. C. Hoskyns, 'Genesis I–III and St. John's Gospel', *Journal of Theological Studies* 21 (1921), 210–18. Lightfoot takes a similar view, as does, more recently, Clare Amos: 'Love's Labour Unlost', *The Way* 72 (1991), 48–59.

[135] Repeatedly emphasized, at 18: 1 and 26; 19: 41 and 20: 15.

[136] Hoskyns offers some evidence to suggest that the two were equated: 214.

[137] For breath and creation, Gen. 1: 2 and John 20: 22.

[138] *The Poems of Richard Crashaw* ed. L. C. Martin (Oxford: Clarendon Press, 1957), 311, from 'The Weeper', stanza XV. The 'fountain' speaks of penitence, the 'garden' of her transformation.

image of restored humanity. Such restoration at least is the need of us all, men as much, if not more so, than women.

Conclusions

What conclusions, then, may we reach? Though the effectiveness of Mary's story will survive without such links, I have been concerned to detect a trajectory from the New Testament of shared concerns about discipleship that make it legitimate to speak of the central core of that later development as a more powerful expression of what Christian discipleship is about than anything we find in the New Testament itself.[139] Already Luke and John were adapting incidents in the lives of various women to make theological points about discipleship. The later Church not only carried that process a stage further, but in some ways, I suggest, made a better job of it, by developing a continuous narrative of the potential progress available to the Christian disciple. That a woman was chosen was in some ways an accident. The two main alternatives both had their problems. John as the beloved disciple was too perfect; Peter was usurped to make claims about ecclesiastical authority. The result was that Mary Magdalene came to function as the central symbol of the meaning of Christian discipleship throughout most of Christian history, the equivalent of Joseph in the Jewish tradition.[140]

We could of course return to the biblical picture or even try to get beyond it and wrestle with the uncertainties of history, but that way lies a tremendous loss of imaginative engagement with how the Gospel stories might have been developed and their point deepened. Of course, great value will remain in meditating on the individual, isolated incidents, but what is thereby lost if pursued without regard to what came later is a story intended to have universal significance for the nature of discipleship as a whole: one in which its continuing struggle with sin and uncertainty is highlighted, as also the continuing dialectic involved between receiv-

---

[139] The obvious possible exception is the story of Peter, but not only was he, as I note below, usurped for another role, there was also the added disadvantage that, though failures are noted, they are those of someone who is already an intimate of Jesus.

[140] At least where character development is the central theme; cf. *Tradition and Imagination*, ch. 5, 260–71.

ing and giving, between searching and a transformed finding. For some it may seem offensive that such a comparative assessment should even be attempted in relation of the Bible, but, if so, the reader is asked to pause and reflect whether God is really contained by the scriptural text or whether he might not use creative developments of it to continue to speak to subsequent generations. A pattern established within Scripture itself would then simply continue beyond it. This is certainly not to give unqualified endorsement to all that follows, but it is to take with full seriousness the impact of the fictitious portrait of Mary Magdalene, in particular the way in which it enables each one of us to place ourselves within the narrative as we perceive our own struggles with discipleship reflected in the story of her own developing relationship with Christ. Moreover, so far from always demeaning women, there are even key aspects of her legend (such as her later preaching career) that already carry us further than Scripture in helping to promote a new status for women.

But what entitlement, the reader may object, have we to play so fast and loose with the real person, with how someone actually lived? This is a question which one might answer at different levels. Historically, as I have already noted, respect for individuality is very much a modern obsession, and so in one clear sense the question is anachronistic. Even if one takes John's narrative of the resurrection appearance at its face value and attempts to read it from the inside as it were, it has been suggested that Mary would have experienced what led to the positive description of her as the first apostle as uncertain and ambiguous.[141] She is given a message to proclaim but in a context where her own understanding of it is chided and challenged (John 20: 11–18). But a more theological response is also possible. The historical Mary Magdalene may well have committed no great sin. The seven demons expelled from her, mentioned in Luke's Gospel, could well refer exclusively to some physical malady. Even so, unless either in life or death she herself identified with the sort of dialectic of discipleship which the Church made out of her life, her discipleship would have remained less than adequate. For like each one of us, she had to admit that, like the unknown woman sinner of Luke's Gospel, she

---

[141] Cf. A. Jasper, 'Interpretative Approaches to John 20.1–18', *Studia Theologica* 47 (1993), 107–18.

stood in need of Christ's forgiveness. Again, like that other woman with the alabaster box and like each of us, she too must have yearned to express her gratitude and love towards Christ as her Saviour. Might she therefore not now be smiling benignly from Heaven—with some pride—at the use to which her legend has been put? For it is in her as symbolic ideal that there is embodied the deeper, the more profound truth.

In saying this I also thereby indicate why it matters deeply that the tradition developed in one way rather than another. Opting for the fictional by no means legitimates indifferently all forms of fiction. So, for instance, the numerous modern attempts to make her Christ's lover may have something to tell us about secular understandings of sexuality but have little, if anything, to say about growth in Christian discipleship.[142] Those who appeal to her treatment within Gnosticism at least continue to search for a suitable religious frame, but, somewhat surprisingly in view of Gnosticism's basic message, this is often combined with the residual desire to establish historical precedents that too easily make Mary Magdalene a figure of our own day.[143] What for me makes the tradition's development more convincing is the way in which it at once speaks of values not immediately echoed in our own culture (e.g. penitence and transformation) and of resources that had the potential to open up new avenues of thought (e.g. her preaching career). There are thus present in the expanded legend a significant range of truths about the nature of Christian discipleship.

[142] As in D. H. Lawrence's short story, *The Man Who Died* (available in *Love among the Haystacks*, Penguin, 1960), or, more recently, with Michèle Roberts' *The Wild Girl* (London: Methuen, 1985) or Lilian Faschinger's *Magdalena the Sinner* (London: Hodder, 1995).

[143] Perhaps most clearly in Esther de Boer's *Mary Magdalene: Beyond the Myth* (London: SCM Press, 1997), where she argues for an historical core to the *Gospel of Mary*. But almost all the Gnostic texts are more ambiguous than initial impressions suggest: A. Marjanen, *The Woman Jesus Loved: Mary Magdalene in the Nag Hammadi Library* (Leiden: E. J. Brill, 1996). So, for example, the *Gospel of Peter* talks of Jesus loving Mary most, yet assigns her no special authority (163,169); again, *Pistis Sophia* gives her a special eschatological status but no preaching authority (178); while negative sexual imagery is regularly used, most obviously in the *Gospel of Thomas* (41, 49). Even the *Gospel of Mary* seems to assume that she will not be among the itinerant preachers: section 9; de Boer, *Mary Magdalene* 83.

Were this the only case where truths of the imagination require us to go beyond truths of history, the issue would perhaps not be a particularly momentous one. But as a matter of fact, the same question raises itself with almost every Life of a saint which we possess until modern times. Imagination set to work in improving their stories, and sometimes even in inventing them from scratch. In those latter cases quite different explanations and justifications are required from what I have sought to offer in the case of Mary Magdalene. But the same issue of the appropriate role of the imagination in grasping truth pertains. To the saints of the post-biblical Church I therefore next turn.

2

Pattern and particular: Saint and novel

THE developing role assigned to Mary Magdalene which we examined in the previous chapter is of course part of a much larger development in the history of Christianity: making saints more prominent or visible within its conceptual scheme (and with relics and miracles part of that scheme, 'visible' seems a particularly apt description). So what I want to do now is examine more closely the significance of that wider, post-biblical development, though not simply for its own sake. The expanded, composite figure of Mary Magdalene was only one way in which the attempt was made imaginatively to appropriate the relevance of Christ for the believer's own life. In effect, she functioned by allowing believers to place themselves in Jesus' own story, and experience their responses from within. The reader, as it were, became part of the narrative. A more common strategy, however, was to seek to identify Christ's continuing impact in the present, and that is where post-biblical saints were of particular relevance, as they helped demonstrate that conformity to the narrative or example of Christ's life remained a real possibility for the believer's own day. Those sympathetic to narrative theology often write as though discipleship were essentially a matter of direct imitation, of conforming the narrative of our lives to the structure underlying that of Christ's; we are told, for instance, that 'the story of Jesus is the story of each one of us'.[1] But what I hope to illustrate is the

[1] G. Loughlin, *Telling God's Story: Bible, Church, and Narrative Theology* (Cambridge: Cambridge University Press, 1996), 216. A few pages later he describes the relation of the saints to Christ as one of 'repeating his life in their own' (218). Cf. N. Lash, *The Road To Emmaeus* (London: SCM Press, 1986), 42: 'these texts are most appropriately read as the story of Jesus, the story of everyone else, and the story of God,' and so the aim is that they 'may be *performed*, in the following of Christ' (46).

way in which, even in respect of the saints, attempts at direct patterning were eventually to yield to something more complex, and that the reasons for this change are no less applicable in our own day.

This is not necessarily to claim the direct relevance of any of the particular examples which we shall consider. Behind the precise form of these new narratives often lie reasons which can no longer apply today. Their exploration will, however, have its value, I hope, both in encouraging more sympathy for the Church's past and in generating a useful contrast to what I shall suggest is the main question for today. Very roughly, whereas the concern was once to apply indifferently a universal pattern, now we are confronted starkly with issues of particularity. What is meant by that contrast will emerge in due course. For the moment, suffice it to note one fine piece of irony which we shall discover—that the modern concern with particularity was effectively anticipated by the now despised cult of two mythical saints, Catherine of Alexandria and Margaret of Antioch.

My reason for giving such prominence to legendary examples is not based on a misplaced desire to defend every aspect of a growing tradition, but because such a focus enables me to highlight a number of key issues, most notably that developments in tradition are often misjudged because the wrong questions are put to them. Inevitably, legend must fail if history is thought to be the only relevant criterion, but quite another answer *may* emerge if the question becomes one of spirituality, of how Christ's life, significance, and example can be appropriated for our own day. Equally, historicity can never be sufficient justification in itself for accepting the Church's pronouncement of sanctity. An obvious case in point is St Jerome. Partly because of his responsibility for the Vulgate, partly because in the Middle Ages he was often regarded as the real founder of monasticism rather than Benedict or any of his Egyptian or Cappadocian predecessors, and partly because of the support of some fanatical humanists such as Giovanni di Andrea (d. 1348),[2] he came to acquire a major position in Christian piety and art until at least the eighteenth century, but there seems no doubt that, whatever reputation he deserved as a

---

[2] H. van Os, *The Art of Devotion* (London: Merrell Holberton, 1995), 34, 36, 39.

scholar, that of a saint cannot be sustained. Indeed, even the common depiction of him in the desert derives from an untypical and quite short period of his life.[3]

However, it is not with the purely fictional that I wish to begin. Instead, my initial focus will be upon the way in which in so many early lives of the saints fact and fiction are intricately interwoven to produce a single narrative, with one definite object in view, to secure a pattern that continues to reflect the original, normative example of Christ's own life. Thereafter, we shall use more purely fictional lives to illustrate how the Church was eventually to find such an approach unsatisfactory, and so anticipated the problems of our own day, where a precise patterning seems no longer feasible and instead the issue becomes how one form of particularity (the life of Jesus) can be mediated into a very different context with its own equally specific demands and challenges. We begin our examination, though, with consideration of why it was that saints became so popular in the early Church, and why that popularity continued to grow in the early Middle Ages.

Bridging distance: the search for pattern

One distinguished historian of the patristic period is rightly concerned to differentiate sharply the origins of the cults of the saints from any putative parallel with the hero cults of classical religion or some supposed reversion to polytheism.[4] Instead, it is suggested that what emerges is a radically new understanding of the relation between the living and the dead. No longer relegated to cemeteries on the outskirts of cities, the saintly dead now become the very definition of the new Christian city, a place of equality of access for all, even those 'two unaccustomed and potentially disruptive categories, the women and the poor'.[5] Though there had been attempts to keep access to the saints for a privileged few, the actions of bishops like Ambrose in insisting on their tombs as public possessions secured a quite different perspec-

---

[3] J. N. D. Kelly, *Jerome* (London: Duckworth, 1975), esp. 46–56, 333–6. Jerome's desert sojourn lasted at most two years.
[4] P. Brown, *The Cult of the Saints* (London: SCM Press, 1981), 5–6, 15–20.
[5] Ibid., 41–2, 45.

tive.[6] All had equal opportunity of securing from them their patronage and friendship (*patrocinium* and *amicitia*); with such language we do of course enter once more the conventional categories of the classical world, but even so it seems that they were at least no longer based on the same structures of power.

Important though such specific elements were, here I want to draw attention to some more general influences which underlay such changes of attitude, and which can plausibly be argued, at least in part, to lie behind similar changes of practice in later Judaism and Islam. These may conveniently be grouped under three headings, all concerned with the attempt to bridge types of distance: what may be characterized as metaphysical, spatial, and temporal distance. Most basic of all is the question of God's metaphysical distance: his power and perfection came to be perceived as so awesome that some kind of bridge was needed to mediate between the deity and us. Put that way, it sounds as though already we have a denial of the efficacy of the incarnation, and in its most obvious reading that is exactly so. Saints did indeed often function as substitute intercessors and friends in place of Christ. Yet we should not too quickly condemn. The underlying problem was not saints as such but the way in which Christ's divinity came to be characterized, as too awesome to admit of easy access. Moreover, as we shall see, even when in the modern period the focus moves in the opposite direction, to stress the humanity of Jesus, it is not true that the issue then dissolves. The very particularities of what was entailed by humanity in a first-century context are found to generate not dissimilar problems of alienation to those once caused by the remoteness of deity. With regard to the other two forms of distance mentioned above, not only is an intermediate agent (the saint) supplied but very specific forms of bridging. Relics become part of the response to the question of how God could be seen to be active not only somewhere else but also in *my* own particular space. Similarly, miracles declare God to be active not merely in biblical time, but also in my own. As our investigation proceeds, we shall discover more and more the attempt to replicate the pattern of Christ's own life, with the saints exhibiting the same powers and even performing the very same actions. In short, the distance is bridged by the pattern of Jesus' own narrative

[6] Ibid., 31–7.

being repeated in subsequent centuries, often even down to the finest details.[7]

Metaphysical distance

This is a topic to which not enough attention is paid.[8] Yet, if we take Augustine as our example, it is difficult to see his later interest in saints and their miracles as anything other than intimately related to his increasingly stern view of God. Though he never entirely lost the lively sense of personal communion with God which he displays in his *Confessions*, that work breathes a very different spirit from later writings such as *The City of God*, begun about ten to fifteen years later. Here the unique mediatorial role of Christ is still stressed, but sits somewhat uneasily with his picture of the martyrs battling with the supernatural powers of the air, and now called 'our heroes'.[9] Although he is still concerned to insist that none of the tribute associated with pagan demi-gods is offered to the saints,[10] a decade later one late work leaves us in no doubt that we can be certain of their interventions on our behalf, even if the precise mechanism remains in doubt.[11] Might we not see Augustine struggling with himself to solve a problem that was in part self-generated, as he increasingly despaired both of his social world, with the Roman Empire collapsing around him, and in some sense of his own personal world, in his strident and total rejection of the more co-operative view of human destiny offered by Pelagianism? God had become a more arbitrary and distant figure; and so there was now a greater metaphysical distance to be bridged.[12] Thus, though he never expressed himself quite so bluntly as one of his contemporaries, his final position may not

[7] This is intended as a general, not universal claim. For examples of some very different factors operating in Ireland, C. Stancliffe, 'The miracles stories in seventh century Irish saints' Lives' in J. Fontaine and J. N. Hillgarth (eds.), *The Seventh Century: Change and Continuity* (London: Warburg Institute, 1992), 87–112.

[8] Surprisingly, Peter Brown gives the general issue only brief attention: *Cult*, 60–5. [9] *City of God*, 10.21–2.

[10] Ibid., 8.27; 22.10.

[11] *De cura pro mortuis gerenda* 15–16, written *c.* 424; *PL* 40, 605–7.

[12] For pagan, no less than Christian, pessimism in late antiquity about the accessibility of the divine, R. Kirschner, 'The vocation of holiness in late antiquity', *Vigiliae Christianae* 38 (1984), 105–24, esp. 119–20.

have been all that far removed from that of the author of what was to prove the most influential of saintly biographies, that of St Martin of Tours. Significantly, in one of his letters that biographer (Sulpicius) writes, on hearing of Martin's death, that he has sent his patron on in advance to plead his case.[13]

In his study of the Frankish church at the turn of the first millennium Denis Nineham makes this bridging notion decisive to his explanation of why the saints had come to occupy such a central place: 'given a Godhead so remote, unapproachable and threatening, there was bound to be a longing for more kindly intermediaries.'[14] However, he appears to think that this amounts to little more than an alternative technology: 'the attitude is essentially pragmatic . . . What people were interested in was the results the saints and their relics produced . . . Who shall blame them in an age when they had virtually no other resource to help them deal with an unpredictable but always threatening and dangerous environment?'[15] But even from the evidence gathered in his own book, such a heavy emphasis on fear (in the face of anticipated suffering either in this world or the next), when accounting for the position assigned to the saints, seems misconceived. No doubt it played its part, but, as Nineham himself admits, expectation of an imminent end to the world was by no means universal[16] and it is easy to exaggerate the effect of what are seen as distant consequences, or to misread iconography as purely threatening whereas the location chosen for it may suggest a quite other view: placing the Last Judgement at the church's portal surely implied that one could pass beyond into the safety of the Church as one's ark of salvation.

Other features of the cultural landscape that helped to create such a need for a bridging concept also need to be given due weight. Two in particular added to this sense of an enormous distance set between humanity and God. On the one hand, there was the heavy stress on the contrast drawn between the great

---

[13] Sulpicius Severus, *Epistles* 2 'Praemisi patronum (2.8) . . . benedictione nos proteget. (2.16) . . . Spes tamen superest illa sola, illa suprema, ut quod per nos obtinere non possumus, saltim pro nobis orante Martino mereamur' (2.18): *Sources Chrétiennes*, 133 (Paris: Éditions du Cerf, 1967), 325 ff. The date of Sulpicius' death is not known, but his second letter can be dated precisely to 397.

[14] D. Nineham, *Christianity Medieval and Modern* (London: SCM Press, 1993), 80–104.   [15] Ibid., 103.   [16] Ibid., 127–9.

weight of human sin and God as the summit of perfection and on the other, the related contrast between the very different functions assigned to Christ and to the believer in the by then dominant Christus Victor theory of the atonement. On the latter view Christ has already won the victory, and so to human beings was left the much more limited task of demonstrating by obedience that the victory had been accepted. In other words, only a passive, and not any contributing role was assigned to ordinary humanity. Such sharp differentiation of roles is indeed what one might have expected in any case in a strongly hierarchical society where each group is assigned its own distinctive function in contributing to the whole. But the point to note here is how from such a perspective the incarnation becomes part of the problem and not itself the solution. For so successful was the Church in arguing for an exalted role for Christ that in effect he became just as metaphysically distant as God the Father.[17] He now stood apart from human beings, rather than alongside them, with a perfection that stands in marked contrast to human wickedness; and performing a role in virtue of his divine powers to which no other human being could possibly even begin to aspire. It is only against such a wider background, and not on grounds of fear alone, that Sir Richard Southern's judgement on the period becomes fully explicable: 'It is scarcely too much to say that the popular religion of these centuries was centred not on the sacraments, not on God or the life of Christ, but on the saints and their relics.'[18]

Significantly, similar trends are to be detected in the other two major monotheistic religions.[19] Perhaps because of the very exalted role assigned to Muhammad as unique mediator of the perfect revelation, a cult of saints quickly grew up throughout the Moslem

---

[17] In addition to the factors noted in the text, the desire to provide an adequate response to Arianism may well have played a significant role in exaggerating stress on Christ's divinity, since Arianism continued to pose a threat in the west even as late as the sixth and seventh centuries: J. N. Hillgarth, *Christianity and Paganism, 350–750: The Conversion of Western Europe* (Philadelphia: University of Pennsylvania Press, 2nd edn, 1986), 2–3, 72–5, 81–3, 90–3, 137.

[18] 'The Church of the Dark Ages' in S. C. Neill and H. R. Weber (eds.), *The Layman in Christian History* (London: SCM Press, 1963), 88–110, esp. 89.

[19] For some comparative discussions, J. Maux (ed.), 'Sainteté et martyre dans les religions du livre', in the relevant volume of *Problèmes d'histoire du Christianisme* 17–19 (1987–9).

world after his death, with some even acquiring the status of national saints such as Mulay Idris I in Morocco or Abu Madyan in Algeria.[20] Commonly called 'friends of God' (*wali Allah*),[21] the very structure of their tombs came to symbolize a bridging of the metaphysical distance with which we are here concerned. The base is a cube, symbolizing the earth, and the roof a dome, symbolizing heaven, while in between there is an octagonal drum, its eight sides, as in many a baptismal font, emphasizing the transition from one realm to another. Judaism has of course no figure comparable in status to Jesus or even Mohammad. Not even Moses quite functions in this way. Nonetheless, because of a growing sense of the transcendence of God, perhaps in part influenced by the fact that the promised land was no longer directly under Jewish control, increasingly a similar movement was to be observed within Judaism also. Thus we find Joseph transformed into the chief exemplar of a *tzaddik* or righteous man,[22] and in fact both this term and *hasid* are used in later Judaism to identify what Christianity would call a saint. Almost all formal characteristics are shared in common, including miracles, exotic behaviour and the right to receive requests for intercessory prayer. The only major difference lay in Judaism's continuing stress on the need for rabbinical knowledge as a necessary prerequisite for sanctity.[23] Perhaps in implicit recognition of the shared concept, even today Muslims are sometimes to be found praying at the shrine of a Christian saint.[24]

However faulty the logic upon which such attitudes were based, the existence of saints did at least provide some reassurance for the Christian and Muslim that the narratives of lives more like our own could acquire a similar pattern of grace and divine presence to the more metaphysically distant examples from which they were ultimately derived, while soon, even within Judaism, movements arose that sought to emulate earlier holy figures.

[20] The tomb of Ahmad al-Badawi at Tanta in Egypt currently draws over a million pilgrims each year.

[21] The title was derived from the Qur'an: 10.63.

[22] For a discussion of the process, *Tradition and Imagination*, ch. 5.

[23] Yet, how much knowledge was required remained a source of tension: L. Jacobs, *Saints and Saintliness in Judaism* (Northvale, N. J.: Jason Aronson, 1990), esp. 23–32.

[24] For some examples, W. Dalrymple, *From The Holy Mountain* (London: Harper Collins, 1998), e. g. 45–6, 101–4, 167, 187–8, 339–40.

Spatial distance

A second kind of bridging required was that of spatial distance, and it is here that relics came into their own.[25] Though eventually this problem was to be 'solved' in terms of Christ's presence in the Eucharist, it would be a mistake to see that solution as also operative in the 'dark' or earlier Middle Ages. For in effect, apart from its distinctive sacrificial role, the Eucharist seems for a significant segment of Christian history to have been treated as little more than yet another relic rather than in a category entirely by itself.[26] For example, sacramentaries regularly call for hosts to be deposited in altar stones at the time of church dedications,[27] while the Council of Chelsea of 816 makes the identification explicit when at the consecration it speaks of the host being deposited 'along with the other relics'.[28] The use of relics was ubiquitous, from processions to encourage the crops to their placement in royal crowns, while 'even the pope, whatever theoretical claims were made for him, in practice owed most of his authority to the fact that he was the guardian of the body of St. Peter'.[29] In understanding how such attitudes came about, we need to bear at least two factors in mind, the way in which Christianity might be said in general to bring about a dislocation of space and time,[30] but also more specifically the experience of dislocation caused by the break-up of the Roman empire. Though a few travelled far, most were now seldom aware of much more than their own immediate area where they often lay at the mercy of feuding local chieftains.

[25] R. Markus draws an effective contrast between Augustine's insistence that God's presence is entirely spiritual and the increasing stress on martyrs to give a sense of God's identification with particular places: *The End of Ancient Christianity* (Cambridge: Cambridge University Press, 1990), 139–55, especially quotations on pp. 139–40.

[26] Roughly, during the period AD 600–1100.

[27] N. Herrmann-Mascard, *Les reliques des saints* (Paris: Klincksieck, 1975), 159–60.

[28] *Cum aliis reliquiis*; A. W. Haddam and W. Stubbs (eds.), *Councils and Ecclesiastical Documents Relating to Great Britain and Ireland* (Oxford, 1872), III, 580.

[29] R. W. Southern, *Western Society and the Church in the Middle Ages* (Harmondsworth: Penguin, 1970), 30–1.

[30] Cf. D. Brown and A. Loades (eds.), *The Sense of the Sacramental* (London: SPCK, 1995), 1–100, esp. 3–6, 62–6, 90–100.

Religious power had to be localized or it would not be felt at all: the spatial distance of God acting in Palestine, a far distant land beyond most people's imagination, had somehow to be overcome. Even the next valley could seem an altogether different world.

It is against such a backdrop that what seems to us among the most alien of medieval practices needs to be understood: the official endorsement of the theft of holy relics. To some extent Rome herself set the example in the eighth and ninth centuries by moving relics from the catacombs into the city churches, but thieves (Deusdona is the best-known) greatly advanced the process by selling some of them beyond the Alps.[31] In those more distant parts of Western Europe booty raids and gift-giving were in effect normal means of exchange, and so it is this highly unusual context that provides part of the explanation for what came to be known as 'holy thefts' or *furta sacra*.[32] The practice appears to have existed in southern France from the ninth to the thirteenth century.[33] An early instance was the carefully managed theft of the relics of the child martyr, St Faith, from Agen in 866.[34] She was wanted by the monks of Conques not only in her own right but also to ward off any attempt to subordinate them to the nearby, new foundation of Figeac, which makes it nicely ironic that in the official account of the translation her body is brought to the monastery via Figeac.[35] Thereafter numerous other thefts followed, not only by monks but also by townspeople, as was the case with the relics of St Nicholas brought from Myra in Asia Minor to Bari in southern Italy in 1087, itself in part a consequence of rivalry with Venice, which

[31] P. J. Geary, *Furta Sacra: Thefts of Relics in the Central Middle Ages* (Princeton, N. J.: Princeton University Press, 2nd edn, 1990), 44–55. Such sales ironically added to Rome's prestige as the original locus of the saint's activity.

[32] Ibid., x, 128. Despite the oddness of these forms of exchange, though, the economy was not in as bad a state as is sometimes suggested: G. Duby, *The Early Growth of the European Economy* (London: Weidenfeld & Nicholson, 1974), 48–72; R. Hodges, 'The rebirth of towns in the early middle ages' in R. Hodges and B. Hobley (eds.), *The Rebirth of Towns in the West AD 700–1050* (Council for British Archaeology Research Report 68, 1988), 1–7.

[33] P. Sheingorn, *The Book of Sainte Foy* (Philadelphia: University of Pennsylvania Press, 1995), 13.

[34] Geary, *Furta Sacra*, 58–63. There is a fine medieval chapel dedicated to St Faith in Westminster Abbey.

[35] 'Through a village called Figeac'; 'The Translation of Sainte Foy' in Sheingorn, *Sainte Foy*, 270.

had acquired relics of Mark from Alexandria by similar means, perhaps as early as 827.[36]

Yet the very obvious presence of secular motives such as desire for prestige or increased income from pilgrims should not blind us to an underlying religious motivation, no matter how different it may be from our own. Some recurring features of the accounts of translations bring this out well. Frequent reference, for example, is made to the inadequacy of the honour being paid to the saint in his or her existing location, while the fact that the body can be moved at all, it was argued, shows willingness on the part of the saint to endorse the subterfuge. To understand that latter point, one needs to enter into a thought-world in which symbol and reality have become inextricably fused, with the relic in effect wholly identified with the saint.[37] The relic could be moved, it was argued, because the saint expected to be more useful elsewhere and therefore also to be better treated. Indeed, so persuasive did that argument become that it has even been suggested that, so far from Vézelay actually engaging in such a theft of Mary Magdalene's relics from southern France, the growth of the legend actually went the other way. No theft had occurred, but one was invented to explain the already existing cult at Vézelay.[38]

Although what happened at Vézelay, if this is true, is an extreme version of what was already extreme conduct, the reader should not lose sight of the more general, underlying desire to which it bears witness: the wish to relocate the divine power and presence found in the narrative of Christ's life into one's own immediate vicinity. Distant sites were not enough, and so the space that was Palestine or other ancient places of martyrdom continued to be moved into one's own locality until the Crusades from 1095 onwards opened up alternative possibilities. Even then, more often than not, instead of pilgrims going eastward, more relics came westward, as with Venice's treatment of Constantinople in 1204.

Temporal distance

Time, no less than space, needed to be bridged. It is here that miracles came into their own, and in two related ways. First, the

[36] Geary, *Furta Sacra*, 87–107.
[37] Geary, *Furta Sacra*, 34; Sheingorn, *Sainte Foy*, 17.
[38] Geary, *Furta Sacra*, 74–6.

very fact of their performance suggested a connection with the biblical world; but then also secondly, and perhaps more importantly, there was a parallelism of detail which hinted at an even deeper continuity. Miracles demonstrated that the veil between heaven and earth could be breached in present time no less than in the events of the Bible. This is not, however, to say that miracles were sought everywhere; as with the Bible itself, they needed to be mediated through those who walked closely with God, and in the present context that means the saints. Even so it was not the major sites of Christendom which generated such an attitude—the Holy Land, Compostela or Rome (astonishingly, there is no book of miracles associated with St Peter's in Rome)—but the more local shrines.[39] Part of the reason may be the stamina required to go on pilgrimage to more distant lands,[40] but also operative was the need to perceive God active in local time no less than in local space. Recall the months involved in pilgrimage to Rome or Palestine, and the impossibility for most of the population of leaving the land for that length of time.

So concerned has it been to defend the uniqueness of the biblical revelation that a common Protestant mindset has always been reluctant to concede the occurrence of such miracles, assigning the record of them to medieval gullibility. But while, as we shall see, there is good reason to think some invented and others exaggerated, there is little to prevent even the non-believer from endorsing the verdict that they were 'for the most part true accounts of occurrences'.[41] The point is that, given the state of medieval medicine, it is relatively easy to see how much, perhaps most, of what is presented as miracle admits of natural explanation. For instance, some types of temporary food shortage could induce loss of sight that with the restoration of the relevant vitamin would then return; again, temporary remissions were seen as cures and relapses explained through loss of faith; even accounts of return to life may often be due to misreading the signs of death in the first place, so superficial were the indicators available at this time.[42] Even as late as the nineteenth century the Royal Navy still required the last

[39] B. Ward, *Miracles and the Medieval Mind* (Aldershot: Wildwood House, 1987), 117–26.　　[40] Ibid., 125.
[41] R. C. Finucane, *Miracles and Pilgrims* (London: Dent, 1977), 59–82, esp. 82.　　[42] Ibid., 106–7, 75–8, 73–4.

thread of the body-bag to be stitched through the sailor's nose as the only sure-fire way of determining that he was really dead; so, when St Godric of Finchale (near Durham) tells of a girl left by her parents for dead in his cell recovering after two days we need not think that the only two possibilities are either that he is a liar or that a miraculous intervention occurred.[43] Equally, however, we must resist an excessive rationalism that discounts faith as a factor altogether. In many cases belief in the possibility of a cure will have been the decisive element, with God using that belief to effect a transformation that defies immediate categorization into either of our two modern but facile alternatives of miracle or non-miracle. In the more 'open' universe of which contemporary science now speaks, why should it not be more like a sliding scale between the two, along a range of possibilities?

Equally, we need to rid our minds of the stark alternative, manipulation or non-manipulation on the part of the shrine authorities. This is particularly pertinent in considering records of miracles from the earlier medieval period. At this period what dominates in the records is the saint's concern to protect his or her shrine, with cures only later predominating, and along with them (from 1200) a formal canonization process that insisted upon the miracles also being edifying.[44] Some historians urge distrust of the clerical version of how the shrines grew: 'Did the audience generate the cults, as the clergy claimed, or did the cults, enshrined in luxurious art and orchestrated by the clergy, produce the audience?'[45] Instead, for some, economic factors should be brought very much to the fore, and this they find reflected not only in the use to which miracle stories are put but also in the tensions between shrine and local townsmen as also in underlying iconographical themes.[46] But on the other side needs to be set the complicated dynamic that is so often present in the human mind, where more spiritual motivation is inextricably linked with such

---

[43] Reginald of Durham, *Libellus de Vita et Miraculis S. Godrici*, ed. J. Stevenson (Surtees Soc., Vol. 20, 1847), 132–4.

[44] Ward, *Miracles*, 67, 184–6.

[45] B. Abou-El-Haj, *The Medieval Cult of Saints* (Cambridge: Cambridge University Press, 1994), 17.

[46] Ibid., e.g. 13, 20, 23 and 133. Much of her case is based on a detailed study of the iconography produced at St Amand d'Elnone—near Tournai in modern Belgium—between 1066 and 1180.

baser impulses. A good example of this is Gregory of Tours' promotion of the cult of St Martin, where self-interest is matched by a relation comparable to that between the beloved disciple and Christ and in which Martin has become for Gregory a substitute for the father he had lost in childhood.[47]

Gregory of Tours was writing in the sixth century (d. 594). The change that was effected by the late twelfth century is well observed by comparing what happened to the miracles of Cuthbert as Reginald of Durham records them and the approach of one of his predecessors as a monk at Durham, Symeon, at the end of the previous century.[48] For the latter, Cuthbert's power is overwhelmingly used to protect the monastery, whereas in Reginald the dominant theme is the saint's mercy and compassion.[49] Yet questions of power have not disappeared altogether. This is attested, for example, by Reginald's implicit arguments for the superiority of Cuthbert's shrine to Becket's new focus in the south. A similar motivation can be detected in the eulogizing language he uses to describe Cuthbert; this can occasionally even come perilously close to the blasphemous, as when he speaks of Cuthbert as 'father of the world to come'.[50] But to judge either or both in terms of manipulation would be a huge mistake. Local pride clearly played its part, as also the conviction that God would protect his own. In a period of chaos it would be natural to focus more narrowly on self-protection, and in that conviction the earlier preoccupations to be found in Symeon surely do not differ markedly from some parts of the Old Testament, from which indeed his own models may have been drawn.[51]

---

[47] R. Van Dam, *Saints and their Miracles in Late Antique Gaul* (Princeton, N. J.: Princeton University Press, 1993), 50–81, esp. 80–1.

[48] Reginald, *Libellus de admirandis beati Cuthberti virtutibus*; Symeon, *Historia de sancto Cuthberto* as well as his more famous *Historia Dunelmensis ecclesiae*.

[49] V. Tudor, 'The cult of St. Cuthbert in the twelfth century: the evidence of Reginald of Durham' in G. Bonner, D. Rollason, C. Stancliffe (eds.), *St. Cuthbert, His Cult and his Community to AD 1200* (Woodbridge: Boydell Press, 1989), 447–67. For some examples of blatant territorial claims in respect of Bridget and Patrick: J. Stevenson, 'Early Irish saints: some uses of hagiography' in C. Binfield (ed.), *Sainthood Revisioned* (Sheffield: Sheffield Academic Press, 1995), 17–26, esp. 19, 22.   [50] *Libellus*, 145, sec. 71.

[51] Any of the numerous miracles in the Old Testament that speak of God's protection of Israel would provide parallels, but most obvious perhaps are those concerned with the Exodus from Egypt.

But much more was at stake than a protective role. As in the New Testament, often the main reason that comes to the fore for recording miracles is to provide signs that God's salvation has indeed dawned, that the present no less than the biblical past is participating in God's transforming work. This is not always immediately apparent, because it is all too easy to be side-tracked by other ideas that may be present in the narrative, biblical or otherwise. An obvious difficulty is the connection commonly drawn between illness and punishment, and health and divine blessing or salvation. Even as great a mind as Bede did not hesitate to make such a connection. Commenting on why a healing girdle had been allowed by God to disappear, he observes by way of explanation that 'when perhaps one of the sick did not deserve to be healed of his infirmity, he would disparage its power, because it did not heal him, when really he was not worthy of being healed'.[52] Physical health is thus given an intimate connection with being right in God's eyes. Most Christians now read John 9: 1–3 as revoking any such link,[53] but with what justification? The passage, as indeed New Testament teaching in general on the matter, is much less clear than commonly assumed.[54] But, even if the healing miracles in the New Testament only ever intended a symbolic link between health and salvation, it would still be the case that, as for the biblical mind, so also for the medieval, the coming of health indicated a drawing near of salvation, and thus later miracles could be seen as a dissolving of the temporal distance between their own day and the first dawning of that salvation in the New Testament.

However, not content with these general parallels, writers also resorted to more specific indicators, and not just with respect to miracles. In a sense the trend is already there with Luke, who ascribes to Stephen, the first Christian martyr, two very similar

[52]   Bede, 'Life of St. Cuthbert', ch. 23 in B. Colgrave (ed.) *Two Lives of St. Cuthbert* (Cambridge: Cambridge University Press, 1940), 233; for parallels in Gregory of Tours' attitude, Van Dam, *Saints*, 87, 103.

[53]   The modern view of this passage, as of Gal. 3: 28, is taken in D. Nineham, *Christianity Medieval and Modern*, 20, 161.

[54]   Strictly speaking, it only allows the inference that 'not all sickness could be ascribed to sin': C. K. Barrett, *Gospel according to St. John* (London: SPCK, 2nd edn, 1978), 356. So, though supported by Luke 13: 1–5, the possibility of a connection seems re-affirmed at Mark 2: 1–12. We return to the issue in Chapter 5.

sentences to those which Jesus uttered on the cross (Acts 7: 59–60; Luke 23: 34 and 46). One or other (sometimes both) will become the frequent, perhaps even normal, pattern of death for the saints in subsequent eras. Margaret of Antioch, for instance is made to pray: 'O blessed Jesus, forgive the trespass of those who persecute me', while Catherine of Alexandria commends her spirit into God's hands.[55] Both lives are fictitious, but even when we are dealing with historical figures, there remains doubt as to whether the words quoted were in fact the words said or have been subsequently attributed. One instance of this is Walter Daniel's *Vita Aelredi Sancti*, where Daniel has his close friend Aelred of Rievaulx (d. 1167) utter Christ's final words at his own death: 'Into your hands, I commend my spirit.'[56] Despite the closeness of saint and biographer, one is still left wondering whether the words are there to establish the relation with Christ—to bring them into the same time—rather than necessarily to record what actually happened. But of course that question also applies to both uses in Luke. Stephen is clearly repeating the pattern of Christ, and while Paul may have passed on his actual words,[57] it is more natural to think of Luke, as elsewhere in his narrative, following the normal practice of ancient historians, where precise information was lacking: 'my method has been . . . to make the speakers say what, in my opinion, was called for by each occasion.'[58] Even in the case of Christ himself, it seems likely that Luke is expressing what he believes Jesus' final thought to have been rather than necessarily his actual words. He resorts to a psalm that displays confidence in the face of affliction, as indeed also eventually proves the case with the psalm from which the cry of dereliction had been taken. Did Luke perhaps toy with the idea of a quotation from the concluding verses of Psalm 22 only to decide that his own choice better encapsulated Jesus' presumed or actual final state of mind?[59]

[55] E.g. O. Bokenham, *A Legend of Holy Women*, trans. S. Delany (Notre Dame, Indiana: University of Notre Dame Press, 1992), 18 and 139.

[56] *Life of Aelred*, ed. F. M. Powicke (London: Nelson, 1950), 61.

[57] Acts 7: 58 for Paul's presence. Significantly, Luke substitutes the 'Lord Jesus' for the Father as Stephen's final addressee (7: 59).

[58] Thucydides, *The Peloponnesian War*, I, 22, trans. R. Warner (Harmondsworth: Penguin, 1954), 24.

[59] Luke quotes from Ps. 31: 5; The cry of dereliction opens a psalm which concludes very differently: contrast Ps. 22: 1 and 22 ff.

To anyone desirous of knowing what exactly happened all of this is of course extremely irritating, especially as it opens up the possibility of the wrong deductions having been drawn, where 'ought' and 'is' did not coincide. One suspects that this kind of argument may well have misled the biographers of saints to presuppose a greater range of miracle than was in fact the case. Certainly, in Sulpicius Severus' *Life* of Martin of Tours there is a significant number of biblical parallels, while in the case of Gregory the Great's biography of Benedict many of the more spectacular biblical miracles recur within his text.[60] A further complication is that Sulpicius' *Life*, like Athanasius' of Antony, itself eventually became a model for future Lives. For instance, the anonymous *Life of Cuthbert* borrows verbatim the first chapter of Sulpicius and describes Cuthbert in language drawn straight from Athanasius.[61] Likewise, Walter Daniel not only, as we have noted, draws Aelred's last words from the Bible, but the beauty of his body in death from Sulpicius. Yet, as one very illuminating discussion of that *Life* has observed, to treat this as simple deception is to use the wrong category of judgement.[62] The hyperbole was a way both of conveying what Aelred had meant to his community and of firmly setting him within a tradition. It was one means of abolishing temporal distance, just as Bernard of Angers' was another. In his account of the miracles at St Faith's shrine, not only does he offer us biblical parallels where these exist, but where they do not a retrospective biblical justification is offered. For example, a story of sight restored despite eyes being gouged out is justified on the grounds that Christ promised even greater miracles for his followers, while animals being raised to life is given the rationale that this is the only life they have, unlike human beings who long for the resurrection.[63] In short, every possible attempt was made to integrate the reader's world with its source in the earlier, revelatory norm, and in this it surely differs in no substantial way from the

[60] For a listing of the parallels in Severus, C. Stancliffe, *St Martin and his Hagiographer* (Oxford: Clarendon Press, 1983), 363–71; for those in Gregory, Ward, *Miracles*, 168.

[61] P. Hunter Blair, *The World of Bede* (Cambridge: Cambridge University Press, 1970), 275.

[62] T. J. Heffernan, *Sacred Biography* (New York: Oxford University Press, 1988), 72–122, esp. 101 ff.

[63] Sheingorn, *Sainte Foy*, 51, 65.

way in which, within the canon, the crossing of the Jordan is made to parallel that of the Red Sea, or Jesus' own flight to and return from Egypt parallels an earlier such peregrination (Exod. 14: 21–2 and Josh. 3.14–17; Gen. 39: 1 and Matt. 2: 13).

In assessing the significance of such phenomena, we seriously err if we suppose that it was all just a matter of filling up the gaps where no reliable historical evidence was available. Walter Daniel almost certainly knew how his friend Aelred had died, just as the anonymous author of the *Life of Cuthbert*, writing a mere ten years after his death in 687, could almost certainly have used original living memories where instead he chose to resort to descriptions drawn from the more distant past. They wrote differently, not because the historical option was unavailable, but because they wished to say something which they regarded as more important: that Christ had made his impact on the immediate past no less decisively than on time's far horizon. The particularities of the individual life are thus firmly subordinated to a higher purpose, the imaging or echoing of a common pattern. This is, emphatically, not to say that Cuthbert or Aelred (or Stephen for that matter) may have failed to conform to that pattern; rather, my point is that the standard way of indicating such conformity was by a scheme of symbolic reference rather than necessarily by telling what actually happened. Pope Gregory in his life of Benedict even tried to ensure that every miracle of Christ had its parallel in the life of his more immediate, near contemporary, while this pattern of assimilation of one saint's life to another's and ultimately to Christ's led Gregory of Tours to reflect at one point whether he should more properly speak of the 'life' of the saints rather than of 'lives' in the plural.[64]

Bridging distance: imagination and particularity

To all this it may be objected that I have now established too much. For in the process of attempting to explain why saints assumed so much importance for medieval Christianity, I seem to have made them dispensable for our own age. The metaphysical

---

[64] *Liber Vitae Patrum*, preface; for further discussion and commentary, *Life of the Fathers*, trans. E. James, (Liverpool: Liverpool University Press, 1985).

distance of which I spoke is for us no longer a problem, in that we have returned to a much more human picture of Christ and so he can stand by himself once more alongside us. Likewise, spatial and temporal distance cannot present the same problem. It is a commonplace to observe that modern communications place us in a shrinking world, while we are conscious as never before of the interconnectedness of the long march of history that has brought us to where we are. But that would be a superficial judgement.

Consider first the issue of spatial and temporal distance. While it is true that in many ways our world has grown smaller, there is also another highly significant sense in which the life of Jesus has become more remote. Biblical scholarship has forced him back into a world that is not only hugely different from our own but also highly particularized. We know numerous facts about first-century Palestine and about Jesus' thought-world that make them unique, different not only from our own world but also from those that are interposed between. Later generations of Christians tried to generalize, and for most of Christian history the Church has found no difficulty in discovering its own world reflected within the pages of the Bible. But in our more historically conscious age this has become much more difficult. If we are to be honest in the face of historical contingency, then we must allow Jesus first to be placed back into his own world, before we contemplate anew how his life and teaching might still be made to relate to our own present-day concerns.

Surprisingly, the question of metaphysical distance is also not without force. The original form of the problem lay in the fact that Christ had become so exalted that he no longer stood alongside us; he had, as it were, been moved to the other side of the divide between divine and human. Others were needed to help bridge the distance generated by such uniqueness. But that same problem is still with us today, though in a very different form. For the more Jesus' life becomes particularized, the harder does it become to bridge the gap between his humanity and ours. The humanity itself becomes the problem. One can see this happening in a number of ways in contemporary theology, with women for instance asking whether a male Christ can save, or homosexuals whether his orientation ought not to reflect their own.[65]

[65] R. Radford Ruether, *Sexism and God-Talk* (London: SCM Press, 1983), 116–38. The influential article which inaugurated the debate is V. Saiving, 'The human situation: a feminine view', *Journal of Religion* 40 (1960), 100–12.

Yet this kind of dilemma could so easily be resolved if Christ were seen as the head of a body of examples, and not as himself having to carry in his humanity the impossible burden of representing every range of human experience and problem. It is often forgotten that for most of Christian history Christ was envisaged as bearing only a universal humanity, with all personhood and characterization provided by his divine nature.[66] In theory, therefore, when stress moved to the humanity, this should have brought a universal type of humanity, easily applicable to each and every one of us, whereas what in fact happened was the discovery that the incarnation had entailed precisely the same sort of particularity to which we are all subject. It looks, therefore, as though, whereas prior to the modern period Christ's universal humanity was the pattern towards which the particulars of the lives of the saints were made to conform, now the only way for us to generate an analogous relationship is by comparing one particular, the life of Jesus, with that of other such particulars. In other words, the pattern has to be thought through rather than assumed; explicit identity is replaced by a more indirect continuity.

However, we should not think this an entirely modern perception. Already, the medieval period, in its recognition of where sanctity was to be found, was struggling with the possibility of what it might look like in lives very different from Christ's own, such as among the married, in trade, on the battlefield, or in government, though it is interesting to observe how seldom such canonizations came from above, from the clerical hierarchy, rather than spontaneously from below.[67] An example may be given from among those whom we have already mentioned; despite being a layman and a self-made ship captain at that, Godric of Finchale

[66] For the difficulties in 'the impersonal humanity of Christ', whether one takes Cyril of Alexandria's anhypostatic union, or the more moderate enhypostatic union of Leontius and John of Damascus: D. M. Baillie, *God Was In Christ* (London: Faber & Faber, 1961), 85–93.

[67] The degree of spontaneity, though, can be exaggerated. If we turn to the first millennium, a significant number of female saints does emerge, but debate continues about the extent to which their cult was promoted by their families rather than simply because of their intrinsic qualities: M. Lawers, 'Sainteté royale et sainteté féminine dans l'Occident médiéval', *Revue d'historoire ecclesiastique* 83 (1988), 56–69; J. A. McNamara and J. E. Halborg (eds.), *Sainted Women of the Dark Ages* (Durham, N. C.: Duke University Press, 1992), e.g. 7.

secured canonization by popular acclaim on his death in 1170. Even a century later this was still happening, though there was by then a formal procedure for canonization.[68] A good instance is Louis IX of France who was made a saint by popular acclaim, and that despite the fact that he was a king, a warrior, and a husband.[69] Such victories, though, were more limited than they might initially appear. For, though the laity may have wished for more, the official view remained that Louis was really only of value for what he did specifically in the service of the Church, while Godric's life before he became a hermit was likewise declared of no intrinsic worth.[70]

In fact, it was only really where there were no historical restraints that the issue was faced head on and so, surprisingly perhaps, the closest parallel to the questions of our own day are in the struggles of a pre-critical generation with the lives of non-existent saints. Their legends grew—at least in some cases—precisely because they were a way of working out what Christ-like sanctity might be like in what had hitherto been uncharted waters, under conditions of life quite different from Jesus' own. Lest the reader too quickly dismiss the notion, perhaps a reminder is necessary of how often resort was had within the Bible itself to entirely fictional narratives as a way of theological reflection; cases in point

[68] Increasing referral to Rome seems to have happened more by accident than by deliberate design. Though the first documented papal canonization dates from the end of the tenth century, even Gregory VII did not try once to exercise his power in this way. For the factors that were relevant: A. H. Bredero, *Christendom and Christianity in the Middle Ages* (Grand Rapids, Michigan: Eerdmans, 1994), 158–81.

[69] For favourable views of his sanctity from professional historians, J. Richard, *Saint Louis* (Cambridge: Cambridge University Press, English trans., 1992), esp. 237–56; J. Le Goff, *Saint Louis* (Paris: Gallimard, 1996), *passim*. By this time a formal canonization procedure was required, but like Godric and unlike so many other royal elevations this was hardly necessary in this case because of the degree of popular acclaim: cf. M. Goodich, 'The politics of canonisation in the 13th century: lay and mendicant saints', *Church History*, 44 (1975), 294–307, esp., 296.

[70] Although André Vauchez notes an increasing trend towards female canonizations, particularly under the influence of the Mendicant orders (268–9), at the same time he observes that even in contexts where the majority were wives or mothers, 'the processes of canonization portray the marriage as simply an accident in their life or, at most, a stage soon put behind them': *Sainthood in the Later Middle Ages* (Cambridge: Cambridge University Press, 1997), 381.

include the books of Daniel, Esther, Jonah, and Ruth. To illustrate how this worked, I want to consider the lives of two fictitious saints, now largely forgotten but once of enormous importance and influence, Catherine of Alexandria and Margaret of Antioch. If we can grasp why their popularity in the later Middle Ages and at the Renaissance fell only a little short of that of the Virgin Mary and Mary Magdalene, we will come much closer to comprehending why any simple patterning answer to the question of sanctity must be deemed inadequate. Thereafter, we shall consider what the nearest parallel to such reflection might be in our own day.

Truth and value in medieval legend

Probably the best known connection between Margaret and Catherine and historical fact lies in the life of Joan of Arc. For in her defence at her trial Joan mentioned three voices as absolutely decisive in guiding her conduct, the archangel Michael on the battlefield, and Margaret of Antioch and Catherine of Alexandria in her more everyday actions, including her decision to wear male clothing.[71] This is but one indication of the enormous prestige the two female saints had acquired by the time Joan was sent to the stake in 1431, a prestige that was to continue for several centuries more, as the frequency of their representation in art until the seventeenth century amply demonstrates. The fact that almost certainly neither existed does nothing to lessen the reality of the ready endorsement of the relevance of their legend.[72] Nor indeed should it do anything to weaken the reality of Joan's own experience or the Church's assertion of her sanctity, any more than this should be allowed to happen for the nineteenth century

[71] T. D. Murray, *Jeanne d'Arc, Maid of Orleans, 1429–31* (New York, 1902), 366–71; the complete transcript of the trial is available in P. Tisset and Y. Lanhers (eds.), *Jeanne d'Arc: Proces de condamnation* (3 vols., Paris: Klincksieck, 1960–71). For a possible parallel development in the life of Catherine of Siena, the influence on her of the legend of Euphrosyne who was reputed to have worn male clothing, R. Albrecht, 'Kleider machen Leute' in M.-T. Wacker (ed.), *Theologie feministische* (Düsseldorf: Patmos, 1988), 80–114.

[72] For a very positive interpretation, S. Tanz, *Jeanne d'Arc* (Weimar: Hermann Böhlaus, 1991), 123–37 and 239–51, esp.131–2 and 242. Only a little less sympathetic is M. Warner, *Joan of Arc* (Harmondsworth: Penguin, 1983), 126–63, where their specific identification is seen as a later development, though still by Joan (138).

with St Jean-Marie-Baptiste Vianney (the Curé d'Ars) and his equally intimate relation with a non-existent saint, St Philomena, generated through the creative misreading (by others) of a deliberately jumbled inscription in the Roman catacombs.[73] Both instances demonstrate the high degree to which religious experience, like everything else, is affected by the particular social and cultural background against which it is set, but to suppose that it undermines the validity of the experience as a whole would be as absurd as supposing that because Christ believed in the devil and may well have seen him that therefore his entire experience becomes invalidated if we no longer subscribe to the individual existence of such a being.[74] However, there is this contrast with the Curé d'Ars and Philomena, that it was an innovating identity on Joan's part that the two fictitious saints helped to shape, one small indication of which was that decision of hers to wear male clothing.

In understanding the innovatory character of their legends, we must first rid ourselves of the idea of a single version; in particular, of the practice of so many modern scholars in quoting Jacobus de Voragine's *Golden Legend* of 1260 as their main source of how particular saints were regarded in the Middle Ages. What we need to bear in mind is that this work was intended primarily as a 'legendary' and not a 'lectionary', that is as a reference book and not as something to be read devotionally.[75] Significantly, Caxton thought it necessary to add prayers to his own translation, in order to lighten its rather terse and dry style.[76] There is also a rather pedantic concern with history which, while commendable at one level, at another can throw the effectiveness of an entire narrative into question, as with his rejection of the dragon element in Margaret's tale. We are told

[73] L. Sheppard, *The Curé d'Ars* (London: Burns & Oates, 1958), 90–2.

[74] For some observations on this point, *Tradition and Imagination*, 281–2, 308–13, esp. 311.

[75] Some legendaries were intended to be read devotionally, but perhaps the ultimate accolade was to be used liturgically as one of the readings in the third nocturn of the night office.

[76] Helpful for putting the work in context is E. B. Vitz, 'From the oral to the written in saints' lives' in R. Blumenfeld-Kosinski and T. Szell, *Images of Sainthood in Medieval Europe* (Ithaca: Cornell University Press, 1991), 97–114, esp. 101 ff.

that 'what is said here about the beast swallowing the maiden and bursting asunder is considered apocryphal and not to be taken seriously'.[77] We must turn elsewhere, therefore, if we are to discover why it was that these two saints achieved such prominence. We shall consider Catherine's legend first, then that of Margaret.

Catherine of Alexandria   Our earliest certain reference comes from the ninth century in a collection of legends compiled for the Byzantine emperor, Basil I. It is, however, only a brief paragraph, and neither the famous wheel nor the mystical marriage are as yet present.[78] Some scholars suggest that the bare bones of the origins of her tale lie in the transferral to a Christian context of elements in the life of Hypatia, the pagan philosopher who was murdered in Alexandria in 415.[79] Whether so or not, it is certainly Catherine's role as educated, independent woman that becomes decisive in her subsequent popularity. Among the earliest features to emerge is her defeat of fifty pagan philosophers in argument. The famous wheel on which her persecutors try unsuccessfully to break her spirit comes later; still later her mystical marriage to Christ.

But it is not the historical developments as such upon which I wish to dwell, but how these are used in the numerous devotional Lives of her which are written as the centuries advance. One can compare, for instance, an anonymous Latin *Life* from the middle of the twelfth century with the vernacular versions in English and French which emerge in the following century, of which an English adaptation from the earlier part of that century is a particularly fine

---

[77] J. de Voragine, *The Golden Legend*, trans. W. G. Ryan (Princeton, N. J.: Princeton University Press, 1993): 1, 368–70 for Margaret; 2, 334–41 for Catherine; for the dragon quotation, 1, 369.

[78] The original Greek is most easily available in E. Einenkel (ed.), *The Life of Saint Katherine* (Early English Text Society, 1884), viii. The link with Hypatia is made, xi–xii.

[79] Though treated by Toland, Voltaire and Gibbon as a great act of Christian wickedness, modern research suggests a more complicated picture. Despite the fact that her murder took place in a church, the motivation seems to have been political, while there appears even to have been a Christian faction working on her side: M. Dzielska, *Hypatia of Alexandria* (Cambridge, Mass.: Harvard University Press, 1995), 66 ff., esp. 94.

example.[80] At one level, the alterations are what one might expect of an author putting a less educated readership and audience at its ease,[81] with the substitution of 'Franclond' for 'Gaul' or 'maumez' for pagan gods.[82] But there are also many more substantial changes in both style and content. The English version is less formal and didactic, and often large chunks of the Latin speeches are omitted.[83] Indeed, there is so little sympathy with the style of the Latin *Life* that the modern editors suggest a frustrated outburst at one point in the English narrative.[84] Significant additions, however, are also made, including a fine description of the heavenly Jerusalem.

More important is the general change of tone, something that also affects French Lives of this time. Though the Latin does contain the mystical marriage,[85] it lacks the warmth of the English expansion, where the author has Catherine speak of her real intimacy with Christ: 'My sweet life, so sweetly doth he taste and smell to me, that all seems to me delicious and soft that he sends me.' It may not sound particularly significant, but this notion of mystical marriage was one way of giving a new dignity and visibility to women. A direct relationship with Christ, not mediated through men, was what was being claimed. Thus it is not without significance that the person most influential in healing the Great Schism in the medieval church, St Catherine of Siena, had a mystical experience of herself similarly commissioned by Christ in a mystical marriage.[86] The

[80] These are the dates suggested by S. R. d'Ardenne & E. J. Dobson in the most recent scholarly edition, *Seinte Katerine* (Oxford: Oxford University Press for Early English Text Society, 1981), xxi and xxxviii. Einenkel, however, remains useful both for direct comparison of the two texts on the same page, and for his translation of the Middle English.

[81] 'Audience' is relevant because such a work would also have been read to the illiterate.

[82] The medieval way of parodying Islam as the worship of pagan deities: for its implications, *Tradition and Imagination*, 362–4.

[83] E.g. Einenkel, *Katherine* 52–3.

[84] D'Ardenne & Dobson, *Seinte Katerine* xxxvi; for a description of the heavenly Jerusalem, lines 1642 ff.

[85] 'Christus me sibi sponsam adoptavit'; Einenkel, *Katherine* 70–2.

[86] There may be some parallels to be drawn with the way in which a couple of centuries earlier Hildegard of Bingen was inspired towards mystical experiences and expressions by an apparently equally unpromising saint, Ursula: cf. the relevant poem in her *Symphonia* and the comments in P. Dronke, *Poetic Individuality in the Middle Ages* (Oxford: Clarendon Press, 1970), 150–92, esp. 153–65.

painter, Ambrogio Bergognone, captures the link nicely by bringing together the two marriages in his painting of 1490.[87] The reason
why the claim had to be made in this indirect way was because male
clerics were deliberately trying to inhibit the role of women. One
example of this was the continued papal insistence that convents be
strictly enclosed. In the city of Parma in the early sixteenth century
one mother superior successfully resisted over seventeen years until
twenty days before her death.[88] As part of that resistance not only
did she herself commission a painting of Catherine of Alexandria for
her own private chamber, but we find Catherine's popularity at the
time was such that one of the mother superior's contemporaries in
Parma, the painter Correggio, executed no less than four fine studies of Catherine.[89] In other words, her fictitious life was being used
to work out a very different way of applying Christ's example, one
not always mediated through the control of men.

Even more significant, though, than mystical marriage was the
theme of education. The Life of the fictitious Catherine declared
that women also could aspire to wisdom. In a twelfth-century *Life*
of her by a Benedictine nun of Barking Abbey it was even implied
that the real victor over the pagan emperor Maxentius in ensuring
the triumph of Christianity was not Constantine, but Catherine
herself through both her intellect and her courage.[90] Again, the
widowed Christine de Pizan, writing in 1405, declares Catherine
second among the saints in dignity only to the Virgin Mary,
adding that she has been placed with others in heaven 'to demonstrate God's approval of the feminine sex . . . and as excellent
examples for every woman above all other wisdom'.[91] Nor, it

[87] Now in the National Gallery, London. Also there is another important
painting of Catherine of Alexandria's mystic marriage, by Parmigianino; for
discussion, see Plate 2 at end of this book.

[88] Giovanna da Piacenza, who headed the nunnery of San Paolo from
1507–24. The commission to Araldi for St Catherine was one of her first commissions: L. C. Schianchi, *Correggio* (Florence: Scala, 1994), 22–6.

[89] Now scattered across Europe in Dresden, Paris, London, and Naples. For
illustrations, ibid., nos. 6, 16, 55. For the London example, *L'opera completa del
Correggio* (Milan: Rizzoli, 1960), ill. 1. Only those in Paris and Naples are of the
mystical marriage.

[90] K. D. Uitti, 'Women saints in the vernacular, and history' in Blumenfeld-
Kosinki and Szell, *Images*, 247–67, esp. 254–6.

[91] *The Book of the City of Ladies* (London: Pan, 1983), 219. For an analysis of
Pizan that sees her admiration of virgin saints as part of her refusal to accept the

should be added, is such treatment confined to women writers. Partly through the influence of two powerful female patrons it was to be an Augustinian canon, Osbert Bokenham, who wrote the first all-female hagiography in the 1440s, with thirteen lives of women saints, including that of Catherine.[92] Not only does he omit all the misogynist references found in the contemporary Capgrave biography,[93] he even converts one of them into a means of enhancing Catherine's status. The philosophers are made to protest that just one of them would be enough to defeat her, only to discover that even fifty of them cannot trounce her intellect.[94] Again, St Catherine's College Cambridge was founded by a man in 1473 exclusively for male education; nonetheless it was dedicated to the scholar Catherine as its patron.[95]

Many modern feminist theologians continue to seek some direct pattern in the life of Christ that will justify positions of power or education for women. Some of these attempts can be quite sophisticated and impressive, such as Elisabeth Schüssler Fiorenza's treatment of Jesus as 'Sophia's prophet', where the grounds given are his use of the Wisdom tradition (which in Hebrew imagery is of course feminine), and his corresponding

contemporary tendency to equate woman with body, B. Semple, 'The male psyche and the female sacred body in Marie de France and Christine de Pizan', *Yale French Studies* 86 (1994), 164–86.

[92] The two patrons were Elizabeth de Vere, Countess of Oxford, and Lady Elizabeth Bourchier, Countess of Eu.

[93] A recent commentator, though, urges against any simple reading. Her suggestion is that 'the ambiguity and open-endedness of his narrative may well be attributable to the too many uncertainties—political, moral social, dynastic—in 1440s England. Capgrave could only incite readers to think, then leave them to their own devices': K. A. Winstead, *Virgin Martyrs* (Ithaca: Cornell University Press, 1997), 167–80, esp. 177.

[94] Bokenham, *Legend*, xxxi–ii, 12, 130–2. It is just possible, though I think unlikely, that the philosopher's symbol of the heavenly sphere generated the notion of the wheel of torture, and that this in turn produced the marriage ring: L. Réau, *Iconographie de l'art chrétien* (Paris: Presses universitaires de France, 1958), III, 266.

[95] When this happens, it is unclear how far she is thought of as a real person as distinct from a symbol like Wisdom or Philosophy, but men are certainly found commissioning paintings of her in a teaching role linked with real-life saints such as Ambrose: P. Tinagli, *Women in Italian Renaissance Art* (Manchester: Manchester University Press, 1997), 165–7.

practice towards women.[96] But one cannot help wondering whether the medievals were not better advised. We need an analogy for a very different situation, not the pretence that the women in the narrative of Jesus were either powerful or educated. The legend was of course presented as literally true, but that should not distract us from the way in which it actually functioned: as a symbolic indicator of women's entitlement to education and certain other forms of freedom, including the possibility of intimate communion with Christ as Lord and Lover, unmediated by men. Thereby a challenge was given to the existing values of society and new values postulated. The extent of the popularity of Catherine's legend is one indicator of the underlying appeal of these values, but no less important to note is the way in which her legend helped shape subsequent patterns of living sanctity. If Catherine of Siena provides an example from the fourteenth century, the impact of the latter on Josephine Butler demonstrates a continuing indirect influence even as late as the dawn of the twentieth century.[97] I will reserve to Part Three detailed consideration of the sense in which these values might be seen as embodying truths. Suffice it to say for the moment that the very indirectness by which these were expressed granted the legend a certain kind of subversive power which could work as a leavening undercurrent in the society of the time.

Margaret of Antioch How sophisticated the medieval imagination could be is well illustrated by the use to which our other saint was put. For, despite being like Catherine a virgin, Margaret became the patron saint of childbirth, and as such was used to argue for a high dignity and religious significance for that particular feminine role. To see how this could be so one needs first to disabuse oneself of purely negative images of virginity. While undoubtedly praise of virginity did often indicate a deep suspicion of sexuality, it is important to note the way in which it could also be read

---

[96] E. Schüssler Fiorenza, *Jesus: Miriam's Child, Sophia's Prophet* (London: SCM Press, 1994).

[97] Although now best known for her campaign against the mistreatment of women entailed by the Contagious Diseases Acts, Josephine Butler (d. 1906) was also a prolific writer. Her biography of Catherine went through several editions: *Catherine of Siena* (4th edn, 1885).

symbolically as a positive sign of liberation from external oppression: all those forces that conspired to make life so difficult for women would not necessarily have the last word. Moreover, prior to the Black Death there was in Europe a considerable surplus population who were required by economic necessity to remain single; such stories of the triumph of virginity at least claimed for such people some degree of status and worth.[98]

It is only once we take into account such factors as these that we can begin to understand Margaret's significance, but first a brief word about her more general background. Partly depending on whether or not one identifies her with the Greek Marina, some scholars find evidence of Margaret's cult as early as the fifth century, with Pope Gelasius already condemning it as apocryphal at the end of that century in 494.[99] Further confusion was caused by whether or not she was to be identified with the Margaret associated with the Pelagia group of legends. Eventually, all three were to be given three separate feast days, but there is little doubt that in the popular mind they were often confused. The last named Margaret wore male clothing in order to be admitted to the monastic vocation, and thus it was that Margaret of Antioch came to inspire and justify Joan of Arc's similar behaviour.

Margaret of Antioch, however, had also survived being swallowed by a dragon. She was disgorged unharmed. It may not be a very complimentary image of pregnancy, but one needs to recall how dangerous and frequent pregnancies once were until recent times. It did have something of the character of a war for survival, and it was for this reason therefore that Margaret became the pre-eminent symbol for Christian women engaged in this struggle. Though facing a different form of pain, she had gone almost as far as Christ himself to the brink of death and come back. That is no doubt why Raphael in his 1518 painting of the story chose to portray the moment at which Margaret emerges triumphantly

---

[98] Heffernan, 286–8. The notion of the virgin-martyr as privileged intercessor is stressed in E. Duffy, 'Holy maydens, holy wyfes' in W. J. Sheils and D. Wood (eds.), *Women in the Church* (Oxford: Blackwell, 1990), 175–96, esp. 188–91.

[99] E.g. E. A. Petroff, 'Transforming the world: The serpent-dragon and the virgin saint' in idem, *Body and Soul: Essays on Medieval Women and Mysticism* (New York: Oxford University Press, 1994), 97–109, esp. 98.

from the monster.[100] She too had been 'resurrected' beyond the
pain of 'death', the traumatic suffering with which pregnancy so
often concluded. In the previous century her presence (with a
dragon) can even be detected on the bedpost in van Eyck's famous
painting of the *Arnolfini Marriage*: the couple are being given due
warning of what is to come.[101] Bearing children had in effect been
declared a saintly, a Christ-like activity, which art now also
endorsed. That was no doubt one reason why Margaret is declared
in some Lives, like Catherine, Christ's spouse. Particularly marked
is the contrast between the opening of Theotimus' tenth-century
Latin version of her *Life* and Wace's twelfth-century French
version. Whereas the former began by promising to tell how
Margaret 'fought the devil, defeated him and was crowned', the
latter offers a life in which Margaret 'had her love turned upwards
towards God the highest . . . she was God's handmaiden and
spouse'.[102]

That move from martial to marital imagery has been seen as part
of a more general social trend in which there is less stress on the
majesty of God and more on the possibility of an intimate relationship with the Son.[103] Even so, the imagery of battle never
entirely disappears from Margaret's story, if only because of the
effectiveness of the image for childbirth: the child will emerge
from a troubled womb just as Margaret does after being swallowed
by the dragon. It is fascinating to observe the various strategies
employed to underline that victory. Only one of the eleventh-
century English versions retains the Latin's use on Margaret's lips
of Christ's declaration that 'I have conquered the world'; the
others resort to what seem to me less successful ways of making the
same point.[104] Again, whereas in some versions tension is carefully
built up through Margaret not at first knowing the nature of her

---

[100] Now in the Louvre, Paris.

[101] The painting is in the National Gallery, London.

[102] D. L. Mockridge, 'Martial imagery in six late twelfth and early thirteenth
century Vitae of female saints' in L. L. Coon, K. J. Haldane and E. W. Sommer
(eds.), *That Gentle Strength: Historical Perspectives on Women in Christianity*
(Charlottesville: University Press of Virginia, 1990), 60–78, esp. 62 and 74, n. 11.

[103] Ibid., esp. 67–9.

[104] M. Clayton and H. Magennis (eds.), *The Old English Lives of St. Margaret*
(Cambridge: Cambridge University Press, 1994), sec. 22; 137 and 217, but not
171; cf. John 16: 33.

opponent, in others we have Margaret's prayer that she may see her enemy and he is mentioned by name from the start.[105] This varied employment of different kinds of technique to create an atmosphere of fear and suspense indicates that the writers have deliberated carefully over how best to convey the power of the story. The precise character of the symbolism too varies over the centuries. It is, for instance, only with the fourteenth century that the image of virginity assailed also becomes especially prominent in Lives of the saint.[106] We mistake the authors' intentions if we read this as no more than evidence for a growing obsession with sexuality.[107] Martyrdom had become a remote possibility in medieval Europe, whereas virginity assailed could easily be read both literally and as a powerful symbol of external oppression generally. As an image it may not be to modern taste, but it is also to that same century and to Bokenham that we owe a ringing declaration from Margaret that has no analogue in any of the eleventh century Lives. When asked whether she is from a slave family, she declares that 'servitude has nothing to do with me, for I am a Christian'.[108]

For us, dragons speak only of medieval gullibility,[109] and we ignore their symbolic power, a power which we shall examine in more detail in the next chapter. Suffice it to say here that they are one of the great biblical symbols of the power of evil, and the dragon functions similarly here. All the terrors of childbirth, we are being told, could be defeated through identification with Christ, for it was the cross that Margaret wore round her neck that ultimately achieved her release from the dragon's belly. Note, however, that it was identification with Christ not through identical patterning but by innovation into a radically

---

[105] Clayton and Magennis. *English Lives*, sec. 12; 163; contrast 123, 205.

[106] Anonymous fourteenth century *Life* discussed in Petroff, 'Transforming the world', 100–5; Bokenham, *Legend of Holy Women*, 7–27.

[107] For the opposed position on Margaret, E. Robertson, 'The corporeality of female sanctity' in Blumenfeld-Kosinski and Szell, *Images*, 268–87.

[108] One might contrast Lydgate's treatment, where Margaret is made 'discreet in speech and modest in demeanour', perhaps in response to worries about the rhetoric of freedom coming from the Lollards at the time of writing (*c.* 1415): Winstead, *Virgin Martyrs*, 133–41.

[109] Though there are occasional examples to the contrary: E. Stuart, *Spitting at dragons: Towards a Feminist Theology of Sainthood* (London: Mowbray, 1996).

different context, both in the nature of the symbol and in its application. Direct copying was tried. Dame Julian of Norwich spoke of Christ as Mother, and, partly because medieval biology thought of a mother's milk as simply blood in another form, paintings of Christ feeding us from his/her breast are to be found.[110] But that was clearly the wrong track. As with Catherine's claim to education and influence for women, so consideration of Christ-like living under conditions of pregnancy necessitated moving to a new context, without precedent in any of the more traditional saints' lives which merely repeated the pattern of Christ's own.

In response to those who object that there was scriptural precedent enough in the numerous stories of pregnant women within the Bible, not least the experience of the Virgin Mary herself, it is important that two key differences should be noted. First, throughout most of Christian history Mary was unable to provide an adequate parallel since it was assumed that, given the way in which her pregnancy reversed Eden, it must have been exempt from the consequences of original sin and so have involved no pain.[111] Secondly, and more importantly, even if that had not been the view, Mary could still not have functioned adequately in this role. For she necessarily did something that Christ as a man could not do, whereas the way Margaret's legend was interpreted made an explicit connection and thus claimed for women an *imitatio Christi* even in a situation apparently excluded from any such possibility, at least so far as direct patterning was concerned. In short, analogical relationship now became the issue, not simple copying, and that was to have momentous consequences for the future practice of Christianity. To mention but one, celibacy could no longer be seen as necessarily the highest state. No less important, though, was what this allowed for the role of women, in questions of childbirth, influence, and education. No wonder that Joan of Arc saw these two saints as the inspiration of her own unconventional imitation of Christ.

---

[110] C. Walker Bynum, *Holy Feast and Holy Fast* (Berkeley, Cal.: University of California Press, 1987), 270–2 and ill. 25.

[111] In Genesis 3: 16 the pains of childbirth are made one of the consequences of the fall; cf. also 1 Tim. 2: 15.

Fictional writing as the modern medium

As that astonishing linkage of Margaret and the dragon with pregnancy well illustrates, the medieval mind had an extraordinary
capacity to think laterally as well as imaginatively. Our own age,
by contrast, is often more wooden. Instead of sexuality as a symbol
for other values, for instance, often we find everything reduced to
a purely sexual reference. By way of illustration consider one
recent treatment of yet another mythological saint, Veronica, the
woman who preserved Christ's image on a cloth.[112] Sexual
imagery is found everywhere;[113] even the touch of the woman
with the haemorrhage is taken to 'suggest the imperceptible
quickness of sexual arousal'.[114] Rather disarmingly, as justifications
for such flights of fancy we are urged towards 'the adoption of an
open, mixed method that does not fear intuition and speculation'.[115] My point is not that the particular book lacks the weight
of scholarly research; it does not. Rather, my concern is that, if we
are prepared to legitimize such flights in one direction, we ought
also to recognize the capacity for truth to be generated, when
intuition and imagination move in very different directions.

Even where history was wildly distorted, the medieval imagination still sometimes succeeded in retaining some underlying truth.
An illustration to the point is what happened to the seventh-
century St Oswald. Thanks to Bede we know quite a lot about
him, but when his cult spread to the continental mainland his
identity underwent a huge transformation. Instead of being based
in Northumbria, he was made a king of Germany or Norway and
even acquired the raven of the pagan god, Woden. Yet, the
underlying symbolic message was retained, in a mission to convert,
with the raven itself made instrumental to, and symbolic of, that
mission.[116] What I suggest we need in our own day, as we seek to
apply the teaching and narrative of Christ's life for ourselves, is a

[112]   E. Kuryluk, *Veronica and her Cloth* (Oxford: Blackwell, 1991).

[113]   In one of the earliest examples in the book the cloth is identified as the
'womb' and Jesus' face as the 'penis': ibid., 8.

[114]   Ibid., 91–3; cf. Mark 5: 21–42.

[115]   91; for some other examples, 87, 115, 148, 153–4, 177, 186, 195.

[116]   A. Jansen, 'The development of the St. Oswald legends on the continent'
in C. Stancliffe and E. Cambridge (ed.), *Oswald* (Stamford: Paul Watkins, 1995),
230–40, esp. 240.

similar imaginative capacity to maintain continuities, while yet accepting the need to envisage very different worlds and applications.

In the twentieth century we became conscious as never before of the extent of God's kenosis in Christ, of the degree to which God entered into the particularities of the human condition. While such an approach has undoubted benefits, it also brings with it its own distinctive problems. The simple christological test that was once used in determining human sanctity is no longer adequate, if it ever was. What we need is not identity of miracles or even identity of life style, but something much more difficult to assess, the working out of a similar graced life in very different circumstances: not Christ as Sophia or Mother, but women as spiritually wise or trustingly pregnant in their own right. The fictitious lives of Catherine and Margaret began that trend, but the Church as a community has still a long way to go. Those declared saints are still overwhelmingly clerical and male, and not surprisingly this is reflected in the various liturgical calendars employed by the churches.[117] The Church still fights shy of identifying sanctity in industry, business, politics, war, or sexuality; in short, in most of ordinary human life.

That is one reason why, it seems to me, for many people, the exploration of discipleship and sanctity in the modern context has largely passed from the sphere of the Church and its theologians to the nearest modern equivalents that are to be found to those fictitious Lives which we considered earlier. By that I do not mean the attempt to retell the story of Christ himself in modern terms. Seldom is that successful. Perhaps the most powerful portrayal in recent years has been Pasolini's film *The Gospel according to St Matthew*; yet it kept very close indeed to the biblical text. Deviations can sometimes produce greater engagement, as in the more central role given to Mary Magdalene in the musical *Jesus Christ Superstar*, but such modernizations can easily slip over the edge into what only alienates the believer, as in so many responses

---

[117] Even in the twentieth century the proportion of women declared saints by the Vatican has only reached 20 per cent. The Church of England's modern liturgical calendar has sought a better balance, but is inhibited by its failure to raise the feast-day of any women from the history of the Church to the status of a red-letter day.

to Scorcese's *Last Temptation of Christ*.[118] The basic difficulty seems to be how to portray perfection without reducing this to priggishness or arrogance, and innocence without this implying *naïveté*. So Dostoevsky's *The Idiot*, Melville's *Billy Budd*, or Mauriac's *The Lamb* make us reflect, but they do not necessarily make us immediately think of Christ.[119] Judaism, lacking a requirement for such perfection, at least avoids that difficulty, but it too experiences problems with recreating its past. Joseph Heller's *God Knows* is a rare example of a figure from the Hebrew canon being used effectively to raise religious issues for our own day.[120] The better strategy has usually been to explore possible answers through settings nearer to our own time, as in the writings of Singer or Potok. That, I suggest, is also true of Christianity. If we assume something like the traditional understanding of Christ and his significance, then there is a need for imaginative distance to be retained in recognition of the fact that Jesus lived in a very different world. Imaginative closeness only becomes relevant when we consider the impact of his resurrection existence in the here and now of the believer's experience. Even then, that closeness must mean an ability to mediate across time, not the pretence that Christ's earthly life was uniquely without the usual temporal, conditioning restraints.

One reason for the enormous popularity of television soaps is the ability they give the viewer to help negotiate his or her own morality and life style. Instead of abstract reflection, one thinks the issue through by means of story. Difficulties in relationships are constantly being explored, as are attitudes to aspects of life which may be new to the experience of some viewers, such as gay partnerships or drug addiction.[121] Only occasionally is the Church

---

[118] *Jesus Christ Superstar*, unlike so many modern portrayals, avoids the twentieth-century obsession with implying a sexual relationship. José Saramago's *The Gospel according to Jesus Christ* (London: Harper-Collins, 1993) is the most recent novel of this kind to have met with a favourable literary reception.

[119] Melville and Mauriac are discussed in F. W. Dillistone, *The Novelist and the Passion Story* (London: Collins, 1960), 26–68.

[120] *God Knows* (London: Jonathan Cape, 1984). It is instructive to contrast this treatment of King David with that by Allan Massie where the story is well told but without any deep religious dimension and a predictable modernization in making David bisexual: *King David* (London: Hodder & Stoughton, 1996).

[121] Gay relationships have been explored in the TV soap *Eastenders*, and lesbian in *Emmerdale*, where the possibility of a priest blessing the relationship also featured.

depicted as playing some role in these explorations, presumably largely because to those outside Christianity it is seen as essentially a system of rules, whereas it is precisely the exception that is to the fore in such dramas.[122] Yet for most of its imaginative history Christianity has also been concerned to handle the exception, as the prominence given to Mary Magdalene itself indicates. It was a religion for where things had gone wrong, rather than one of self-justification. That is why it seems to me that it is not the retelling of the story of Christ that is required, but the discovery of what a Christ-like life might be like in flawed situations, and this is in fact what many a modern novelist has attempted to explore.

Not of course that the attempt is by any means confined to the novel, soap, or film. One way of reading the extraordinary outbreak of grief at the death of Princess Diana in 1997 is to view her as a figure who could help great numbers of the population negotiate their own flawed lives and those of their family and friends. Whatever in fact motivated her, Diana could be seen as a flawed individual like themselves (a single mother betrayed by the various men in her life) nonetheless trying to do good in the world under difficult circumstances.[123] But the novel perhaps offers the most opportunity for sustained reflection. The rise of the novel as a substitute means of reflection to Scripture has not gone unremarked,[124] but no less important is the way in which it has sometimes functioned as a supplement to what the Bible offers. Indeed, I suspect that many a Christian may already be using novel reading as just such a medium without being at all conscious that this

---

[122] In Britain only the long running radio serial, *The Archers*, gives any significant place to religion, and that seems in large part because of its setting in a village. A sympathetic portrayal of a priest, though, has recently occurred in *Eastenders*, but one must immediately add that his life has been 'spiced' by adultery. In American soaps, particularly those about younger age groups, such as *Friends* or *Party of Five*, religion is conspicuous by its absence.

[123] The language of 'saint' has appeared frequently in discussion of Diana's life. For example, the period 1985 to 1992 is described by one author as that of mother, saint, and sex idol: J. Burchill, *Diana* (London: Weidenfeld & Nicholson, 1998), 152. But insufficient attention has in my view been paid to the fact that part of her attractiveness seemed precisely to lie in the flaws.

[124] One aspect of this issue is discussed in Ch. 5. For defence of the view that 'saints' Lives are in some way the origin of Western narrative, G. G. Harpham, *The Ascetic Imperative in Culture and Criticism* (Chicago: University of Chicago Press, 1987), 67–88, esp. 85.

is in fact what is happening. At least one great novelist makes the connection quite explicit, for in her Prelude to *Middlemarch* George Eliot prepares the reader for what follows by suggesting that the central female figure, Dorothea Brooke, should be seen as a version of St Teresa of Avila operating under different social and historical circumstances.[125]

Certainly, in our own day, a period of religious decline, it is astonishing how resilient Christian reflection through literature has proved to be. Some have explored the darker side of Christianity in its doctrines of fall and sin;[126] others issues of faith as struggle or loss;[127] yet others the whole question of psychological growth in self-perception and religious perceptivity.[128] All these are important, but in terms of a link with our earlier discussion most important are those who consider the question of sanctity. One shared element, well illustrated by the story of Mary Magdalene, is the willingness to engage with flawed perfection. There is, however, one major contrast. Whereas in that earlier tradition the flaw was seen almost invariably as placed in the past prior to conversion, many a contemporary novelist encourages us to detect saintliness *despite* the presence of continuing faults. Thereby we are challenged to think anew the relation between sanctity and conventional goodness. This is too large an issue to do little more than raise here, but as examples of this kind of approach one might mention Graham Greene, R. C. Hutchinson, Ken Kesey, Iris Murdoch, and Patrick White.[129] Though only two of these writ-

[125] The reference back to Scripture is done more indirectly through other characters such as Casaubon and Bulstrode. Eliot writes as an agnostic, and that is perhaps why, despite her sympathy, her conclusions are quite pessimistic: cf. the views of Leslie Stephen in B. G. Hornback (ed.), *Middlemarch* (New York: Norton, 1977), 657–63.

[126] Most obviously perhaps, William Golding (d. 1993) in such novels as *Lord of the Flies* or *The Spire*.

[127] John Updike even used the novel to offer a powerful critique of Barthian theology as an undermining, rather than enhancement, of faith: *Roger's Version* (Harmondsworth: Penguin, 1987).

[128] Susan Howatch's much underestimated six novels about the history of the Church of England in the twentieth century are a case in point.

[129] Significantly, Patrick White called his own autobiography *Flaws in the Glass* (Harmondsworth: Penguin, 1981). R. C. Hutchinson provides a rare example of a novelist willing to pursue the issue of sanctity under conditions of war.

ers had anything like a commitment to traditional Christianity, as with artists generally, we should not deny their ability to help inform Christian self-reflection.[130]

The novels of Graham Greene or Ken Kesey's *One Flew Over the Cuckoo's Nest* are good illustrations of the way in which in so much modern literature a type of sanctity is depicted that challenges conventional categories. Thus despite, or perhaps because of, his conversion to Roman Catholicism, Greene allows himself to detect holiness in attitudes and actions that would normally merit the Church's condemnation. Rose in *Brighton Rock* and Scobie in *The Heart of the Matter* both contemplate suicide as a legitimate furtherance of the demands of love, while in *The Power and the Glory* we are invited to view the whiskey priest as a better witness to Christianity than many of the more conventionally pious. Most of Kesey's readers miss the christological allusions, but such subtlety adds in my view to the success of *One Flew Over the Cuckoo's Nest*. The rough diamond McMurphy (appropriately played by Jack Nicholson in the film version) helps to give dignity to the inmates of a mental hospital where he is a fellow patient, and leads twelve of them out for a brief bout of freedom in the world outside, only to be subject to a lobotomy on his return.[131] In this case we have none of the explicit allusions to religion that characterize the work of Greene, but McMurphy's battle with Big Nurse does invite us to question how adequate our distinctions between ultimate goodness and badness really are.

The life of Jesus has in effect moved from being a set of specific examples for close copying to the status of being an analogous case, that requires imaginative re-identification under very different circumstances, and for that our greater debt is now to the imaginative work of novelists or their equivalent on stage or in film. Assessing the full implications of this for Christian spirituality

---

[130] Greene and Hutchinson. Murdoch has on occasion described herself as a fellow-traveller, but how complicated these issues can be is well illustrated by Patrick White's self-description. He speaks of himself as 'a lapsed Anglican egotist agnostic pantheist occulist existentialist would be failed Christian Australian': *Flaws*, 102.

[131] The allusive character of the religious references is seen in the way in which the headphones for the electric shock treatment are described as a 'crown of silver thorns over the graphite of his temples': (London: Picador edn., 1973), 222.

and morality seem to me as yet in their infancy. All I can hope to have done here is offer some pointers as to where further reflection might be required. To those who may object that my argument has in effect made the lives of the saints and even Scripture itself redundant, I would protest that this is very far from being the case. We will still need to test the adequacy of modern explorations of sanctity against the pattern set by Christ. My basic contention is that this cannot anymore be seen to be a simple or straightforward matter; it will require real imaginative effort on our parts to think through the implications of living under different circumstances and in different contexts. Even novelists can experience difficulties. Whether by design or not, one notes that Michèle Roberts' depiction in *Impossible Saints* in effect makes them creatures of our own day rather than theirs, while even where greater imaginative effort is made to reconstruct the different reality of a past world, this can sometimes be spoilt by conspicuous historical howlers.[132] So we must not underestimate the problems involved. But equally we should not resist because it requires us to expand our horizons well beyond Scripture. Not only does the history of the Church offer us a rich resource which, if properly understood, could be reappropriated in the pursuit of Christian self-understanding, but precisely because the novelist is required to exercise imagination he or she can open up possible scenarios for us that might not even have occurred to the more prosaic minds among us. Henri de Lubac warns us that 'the saint of tomorrow will scarcely conform to our ideas'.[133] In trying to comprehend what discipleship might mean, we need to be prepared to hear the voice of God mediated not only through the pre-eminent example given by Christ but equally in the varied

[132] M. Roberts, *Impossible Saints* (London: Virago, 1998). Although the novel interweaves the life of someone made contemporary with Teresa of Avila and the reworking of stories connected with various legendary saints, the focus is almost wholly modern, without any attempt to engage with values different from the author's own. By contrast, Melvyn Bragg's *Credo* (London: Hodder & Stoughton, 1996) makes a serious attempt to re-create the savagery and poverty of seventh-century Northumbria, but is spoilt by occasional reference to such things as a second baptism or the possibility of women celebrating mass: 226–7; 340.

[133] H. de Lubac, *The Church: Paradox and Mystery* (Shannon: Ecclesia, 1969), 122–7, esp. 124.

attempts that have been made both within the Church and on its fringes to work through that example under new conditions.

My argument has given such a major role to fictional explorations that it may seem as though I have jettisoned any value for real life-saints, perhaps any value for the risen Christ himself. That was very far from being my intention. To see why the role of both nonetheless continues to be essential, I turn now to the final chapter of this Part of the book, and so to consideration of heaven and the tradition of 'the last things'.

3
Heaven and the defeat of the Beast:
Social aspects of discipleship

IN the two previous chapters I considered two rather different ways of appropriating Christ for the present. First, consideration was given to how effective a device an expanded version of the figure of Mary Magdalene might be in enabling us to participate in the story of Jesus: her growth in discipleship and in communion with Christ could also be our own. Then we observed how the stories of saints have functioned in the past, and in particular the major role they acquired in bridging space and time, together with what I labelled 'metaphysical distance', but I ended by observing that different strategies might need to be employed in our own day, as we seek to apply Christ's example and teaching under quite different historical circumstances. Some of the most important issues raised by the two chapters revolved round questions of narrative: in the case of Mary Magdalene the desire to place ourselves in that original narrative of Christ's life; with regard to the saints the need to tell a different narrative as new questions and challenges arise. Customarily, however, we expect of narrative that it should have some appropriate ending, and so it is to that question of the end or conclusion of discipleship that I now wish to turn.

For most of Christian history there has been a tension between two different sorts of ending, one that speaks of heaven as a present reality to which some go immediately after death; the other of the final resolution for all occurring at the end of history. Much contemporary theology rejects the former view as irrelevant or even perverse; instead, it insists, all our emphasis should be on an eschatological hope to be fulfilled in this world. While in no way wishing to deny the imaginative power of a this-world hope and its appropriateness in giving fresh confidence to the oppressed and marginalized, in the first half of the chapter I shall seek to challenge what has become almost a consensus within contemporary Protestant theology, that with such a future hope there remains no further need for the image of heaven as already populated. On the contrary, I shall argue, it is only belief in the post-mortem survival of the 'saints' that allows the social character of Christian discipleship to be taken seriously,[1] and indeed without it even to speak of Christ as risen itself becomes problematic. Thereafter, I shall turn to consider what role might remain for the alternative ending in history, if heaven as present reality has been restored to a central role. Because so much that is excellent is currently being written on its positive side, I shall have little to say on such hopes. Instead, my focus will be on what are usually regarded as the more negative aspects of the traditional imagery. Here too, I shall challenge the prevailing consensus, and suggest that there is much to commend in the way in which notions such as hell, judgement, Satan, and Leviathan have in fact functioned within the Christian tradition. 'The defeat of the Beast' thus remains pertinent to how Christian discipleship should be conceived. What was eventually seen to be a misguided emphasis on eternal punishment nonetheless helped generate strong notions of social interdependence within the Body of Christ, as well as more nuanced understandings of the nature of evil. The story is a complex one, but it does seem to me to indicate discipleship rightly adapting to a framework in effect no longer given by Scripture alone.

A heaven of saints as present reality

As with the example given in Chapter 1 of the status of women, here too there is an insidious temptation for modern theology to present itself as a recovery of biblical insights, lost through the distortions of tradition. Thus the recovery of a psychosomatic

---

[1] Whether 'saints' is interpreted widely as in the biblical sense or more narrowly is not directly pertinent to my argument here. So, although I shall omit inverted commas in what follows, the reader should be alert to the possibility of both meanings.

understanding of ourselves as unitary beings rather than combinations of two distinct entities, body and soul (dualism), it may be said, unites with our fresh appreciation of the importance of the natural environment to make the biblical image of the eschatological renewal of all things in Christ at the end of time the most plausible version of the Christian hope.[2] Among contemporary theologians Jürgen Moltmann has been particularly conspicuous in trying to reclaim such an image for contemporary Christianity; indeed he has written that 'the eschatological is not one element of Christianity, but it is the medium of the Christian faith as such'.[3] The result is that we find him asking, rhetorically, 'is there any way of talking about the heaven of glory except in terms of a visionary future of a new earth?' only to find his answer neatly encapsulated in the formula 'we call the determined side of this system "earth", the undetermined side "heaven",' in effect thus making heaven exclusively the future destiny of this world rather than an alternative to it.[4] The recovery of the biblical view is thus taken to imply a 'sleep' of consciousness or perhaps only survival in the memory of God until Christ restores us to life once more at the end of history. A similar stress is also for many reflected at the very heart of modern eucharistic prayers, with their declaration: 'Christ has died; Christ has risen; Christ will come again', and as such contrasts markedly with what became the most common way of reading the preface to the Sanctus in the 1662 Book of Common Prayer. For, whatever Cranmer's original intentions may have been, the phrase 'with angels, and archangels, and the whole company of heaven' was soon taken to imply the presence of the redeemed already in heaven alongside the angels.[5]

Yet, despite the weight of contemporary opinion now ranged on the other side, it would be unwise in my view to proceed to any simple, automatic endorsement of the biblical picture, as

---

[2] It is no doubt for this reason that Romans 8: 18–25 has become the most quoted, some would say the most overworked, passage in contemporary discussions of the future Christian hope.

[3] *The Theology of Hope* (London: SCM Press, 1967), 16.

[4] J. Moltmann, *God in Creation* (London: SCM Press, 1985), 170 and 163.

[5] Almost certainly not Cranmer's intention. Medieval liturgies such as Sarum had mentioned each type of angel by name; so Cranmer was presumably simplifying at this point, using 'company' in its military sense, to imply the various other ranks of angelic beings.

though nothing could be said in favour of the rather different direction taken by later tradition. That the contemporary emphasis more accurately reflects the dominant biblical view I would not wish to deny. Modern biblical scholarship has exploded once and for all attempts such as those of Harnack to exclude eschatology as a significant element in early Christianity.[6] Even so, closer scrutiny of the New Testament, as of the later Church, suggests a more complicated pattern, with the two models running in tandem throughout. If one was dominant in Scripture, and another for most of the Church's history, we need to explore the reasons why this was so, before pronouncing on the validity of either or both. My discussion therefore opens with a brief survey of how the two competing concepts fared over the course of Christian history, and why. Thereafter, four arguments will be offered, to justify the more authoritative position given to heaven as a present reality in later Christian tradition. Perhaps, though, the most difficult issue of all, and the one which most stands in the way of serious engagement with any notion of a present heaven in contemporary belief, is its adequate conceptualization, and so this section will end with something being said on how current non-dualist understandings of human beings might still allow for the possibility of immediate post-mortem survival. Both the arguments and the subsequent attempt at conceptualization will be concerned to discover how heaven can be made, as it were, 'to come alive'. This is a tricky issue since the imagination can both enliven and destroy the plausibility of belief, as treatments of the last days also amply illustrate. Nonetheless, the attempt must be made, since without it the doctrine will remain without any direct impact on the life of Christian discipleship. First, however, a brief word on the history of attitudes to the two rival views, and in particular why, though the Bible must have the first word, it need not have the last.

Rival accounts contested through history

As already noted, to my mind it seems altogether too simplistic to represent the New Testament as exclusively eschatological and the later Church as focused equally strongly on the alternative

---

[6] As in his classic, *What is Christianity?* (1900; reissued by Fortress Press, Philadelphia, 1986).

perspective. It is more a matter of the two notions running side by side, with now one dominant and now the other. This becomes especially clear, once we introduce the related issue of the competing themes of immortality of soul and resurrection of body. Whereas an earlier generation of biblical scholars detected an overwhelming dominance of belief in a future resurrection of the body, more recent studies suggest a more varied scriptural pattern.[7] Indeed, it has even been suggested that belief in immortality may have come first, as a way of declaring that, despite the tortures imposed on the bodies of Jewish martyrs, their souls would survive.[8] The way in which the ascent imagery of apocalyptic literature was used to suggest major post-mortem transformations, including exaltation to the life of angels, also seems to suggest a more fluid picture.[9] Even so, while the corrective is welcome, that a future resurrection is the principal biblical perspective must still be conceded.[10]

Equally, account must be taken of a more complex picture in the history of the later Church. Certainly, already in the apostolic fathers, in passages contemporary or almost contemporary with the canon, we apparently find the post-biblical Church moving in a rather different direction, with the focus now upon the immediate post-mortem state. Take, for instance, this early instance from Clement of Rome: 'Peter . . . having given his witness went to the place of glory that was his due . . . Paul went out of this world and was taken up to the holy place.'[11] Yet the views of Irenaeus only a century later demonstrate the absence of any uniform pattern. His adoption of millenarianism may have been in part motivated by his desire to combat Gnostic undervaluing of the material world, but, whatever the reason, he ensured a continuing place for

---

[7] One might contrast O. Cullman, *Christ and Time* (London: SCM Press, 1962) and K. Stendahl, *Immortality and Resurrection* (New York: Macmillan 1965) with the much more varied pattern argued by G. W. E. Nickelsburg, *Resurrection, Immortality and Eternal Life in Intertestamental Judaism* (New York: Oxford University Press, 1972) and J. Barr, *The Garden of Eden and the Hope of Immortality* (London: SCM Press, 1992).   [8] Barr, *Eden*, 53–6.

[9] M. Himmelfarb, *Ascent to Heaven in Jewish and Christian Apocalypses* (New York: Oxford University Press, 1993), esp. ch. 3.

[10] Though by no means with as strong a margin as was once thought. Even in the New Testament other perspectives are found, while in the Old Testament resurrection is seldom mentioned.

[11] First letter of Clement to the Corinthians, sec. 5 (my trans.).

the alternative end-of-history perspective in Christian thinking.[12] However, rather than speaking of only two competing positions, it is perhaps more accurate to speak of 'many facets . . . many hopes—and many fears', as experiment was made with quite a number of different possible scenarios.[13]

During the patristic period renewed interest in an impending final judgement seems more often than not to have gone with pessimism about the present, whether because of persecution or because of the disintegration of society that followed the gradual collapse of the Roman empire.[14] Later church history reflects, as we shall see, a similar pattern, with added impetus from certain significant dates such as the turn of the millennium or AD 1500. Such significant dates, fuelled by pessimism about the world, combined periodically to restore an earthly eschatology to the central place in Christian thinking, but, even with this qualification, it remains possible to speak, as in the biblical case, of one viewpoint predominating, though in this case it is reverse of the biblical. Mainly through combining ideas of immortality of the soul and resurrection of the body, a very active intermediate existence could be (and was) postulated, and it is in fact quite rare to find patristic writers rejecting any significant, active role for the soul on death.[15] Even so it took until 1336 before there was any official Church teaching to the effect that the fate of the individual is determined immediately upon death; in Pope Benedict XII's decree *Benedictus Deus* he speaks of the righteous enjoying upon death 'an intuitive, face-to-face vision of the divine essence'.[16]

---

[12] C. E. Hill in *Regnum Caelorum* (Oxford: Clarendon Press, 1992) uses the contrast between Irenaeus and earlier patristic views to argue, somewhat implausibly in my view, that the latter was in fact the biblical position, and that therefore even the book of Revelation needs to be interpreted in this light.

[13] The view of B. Daly in *The Hope of the Early Church* (Cambridge: Cambridge University Press, 1991), 216.

[14] Ibid., e.g. 65, 124, 205.

[15] The Syrian writers, Aphrahat and Ephrem, are among the very few to take the notion of 'sleep' literally: ibid., 72–6.

[16] For an account of his conflict with his predecessor, John XXII, see C. W. Bynum, *The Resurrection of the Body* (New York: Columbia University Press, 1995), 283–91. My translation of *Benedictus Deus*, cf. Denzinger and A. Schönmetzer (eds.), *Enchiridion Symbolorum* (Freiburg: Herder, 36th edn, 1976), 297.

A number of factors account for that delay. One was undoubtedly the complexity of possible post-mortem schemes. Were all
Christians to go to heaven, or only some? Was a period of preparation necessary? If so, what form might this take? Secondly, the
dominant biblical picture never totally disappeared. Throughout
Christian history, there have been periodic resurgences of eschatological conviction, particularly at significant dates, and with such
resurgences concern for the present state of the dead has once
more receded into the background. Then, finally, note must be
taken of the assumption that in any case no official pronouncement was necessary, since even within the New Testament itself
due acknowledgement had already been made of the presence of
the dead with Christ in heaven.[17] Much of this 'evidence' was
premised upon contentious readings of particular verses;[18] even so,
the influence of such readings should not be discounted.

Though some of the details of this picture were subject to
severe challenge at the Reformation (most notably the notion of
purgatory) its essentials remained largely unchanged, with many
theologians continuing to speak of an active life immediately after
death, while also holding to a more distant final consummation.
Far more significant than the Reformation in undermining
consensus in fact has been the widespread collapse in modern
times of belief in the possibility of an existence for the soul independent of the body. What implications that might have for
conceiving of life surviving continuously beyond death we shall
consider in due course. But, to many, such reflection will seem
pointless, if the dominant biblical picture points in a different
direction, and that I have already conceded, even if the weight is
not quite so decisive as is sometimes claimed. Taking revelation
seriously, it will be said, must involve interpreting its minor key in
relation to the dominant melody, the sense of Scripture as a whole.

But must this necessarily be so? What if there are conditioning
factors which explain the dominant stress of the New Testament
but which are no longer applicable to us? That might justify us in
endorsing the approach of the later Church and reversing the

---

[17] Undoubtedly the most used verse in this context are Christ's words to the
penitent thief: Luke 23: 43.
[18] Perhaps the most notorious was the use of 1 Cor. 3: 13 to argue for the
doctrine of purgatory.

balance between the two perspectives, even though this in effect means demoting or 'correcting' the dominant biblical perspective. God would then still have revealed our ultimate destiny to be with him, but the details of how this is to be conceived awaited further adjustments and corrections in the process of his continuing dialogue with his Church. The specific cultural factor I have in mind is the widespread New Testament belief in the imminence of the end of the world, or at least that world as presently constituted. Such a belief would inevitably preclude much interest in the interim state of the dead, since all believers would soon be reunited anyway. If that were so, it becomes scarcely surprising that we find Paul telling us little, except that the dead 'sleep' or are 'unconscious' until then.[19] After all, he expected that the period of unconsciousness would not last long. He saw himself among those who would be 'left alive until the Lord comes' and 'it is far on in the night; day is near' (I Thess. 4: 15; Rom. 13: 12 NEB. cf. also Phil. 4: 6; 1 Cor. 7: 29).[20] Again, in Mark chapter 13 the end appears to be linked with the impending fall of Jerusalem, while in the book of Revelation it is also associated with the author's own times—probably, the reign of Domitian. Though the shock of the resurrection of Jesus could have of itself generated such a belief among his followers, it seems quite likely that Jesus held similar views himself. That way, an urgency would have been given to his mission which it might not otherwise have had.[21] To posit that the revelation of an ultimate destiny for humanity with God should be mediated through such a distorted understanding may well be for some too much to stomach, but to cavil thus is surely to pull the

[19] O. Cullman, *Immortality of the Soul or Resurrection of the Dead?* (London: Epworth 1958), 50. D. E. H. Whiteley, *The Theology of St. Paul* (Oxford: Blackwell, 1964), 268–9, attempts to argue instead, from passages such as Phil. 1: 23 and 2 Cor. 5: 8, for an immediate post-mortem resurrection of the body, but the probabilities seem to me to be in favour of Cullman being right, and that these other passages should therefore be interpreted in terms of Paul's expectation of the imminence of the end.

[20] For the view that apocalyptic is central to the interpretation of Paul's thinking, and not merely an 'ornamental husk' easily removed, J. C. Beker, *Paul the Apostle* (Edinburgh: T & T Clark, 1980), 135–81, esp. 140.

[21] Cf. Balthasar's argument in e.g. 'Glaube und Näherwartung' in *Zuerst Gottes Reich* (Einsiedeln: Benzinger, 1966), 9–24; translated in part in M. Kehl and W. Löser (eds.), *The von Balthasar Reader* (Edinburgh: T & T Clark, 1982), 135–40.

biblical community out of its specific historical context and postulate a quite unhistorical pattern of divine action. God communicated his desire to share his life eternally with us; what precisely
that entailed, however, had still be to be wrestled with, as indeed
the Church continues to do to this day, as it faces the new challenge of a non-dualist understanding of ourselves.

That in doing this the modern Church is attempting nothing
new is well illustrated by the fact that even within the canon we
can detect moves in a different direction, as some writers try to
extricate the Christian message from any firm connection with
belief in the imminence of the end. Luke's Gospel is an obvious
case in point. Some of the words attributed to Christ in this Gospel
are most easily taken to speak of a present life for the dead, as in
the parable of Dives and Lazarus or in Jesus' promise to the penitent thief, both unique to Luke (Luke 16: 31; 22: 43).[22] In addition, one observes how Luke's alterations to Mark downplay the
latter's stress on the imminence of the end, as, for instance, in
Luke's dissociating the destruction of Jerusalem from the end of
the world, or his alteration of Jesus' words before the High Priest
from future expectation to present reality.[23] This suggests attempts
already taking place within the canon to extricate an appropriate
ending for the individual's narrative from that more suited to a
corporate conclusion and now relegated to a more distant
prospect. Why it was so important for that trajectory to be pursued
further is what I now wish to explain.

Heavenly saints and their significance

Purely negative arguments seldom, if ever, engage the imagination. So, were worries about the conditioned character of New
Testament stress on a resolution at the end of time the only factor
to be placed on the other side, this would hardly be sufficient of
itself to carry the day. But in fact there is much at stake, including
even the coherence of Christ's own survival of death. What those

[22] Though Christopher Evans notes various attempts at reconciliation with
the New Testament elsewhere, he postulates a confused situation, in which 'non-
Jewish' influences have played their part: *Saint Luke* (London: SCM Press, 1990),
613–14; 873–4.
[23] Contrast Mark 13: 14 ff. and Luke 21: 20 and 24; Mark 14: 62 and Luke
22: 69.

who object to heaven as present reality fail to consider is the social
dimension of human existence in general and the way in which
not only its reality is threatened without a living community of
saints, but even any meaningful notion of the continuing existence
of Christ's own humanity. To see why this is so, I offer below four
arguments of differing kinds. Though seldom explicitly formulated
in the past, each argument does seem to me to have had an impact
on the imaginative consciousness of the Church, and so helped to
bring about the change of focus. All are premised on the assumption that the Church as the body of Christ entails mutual interdependence. As we shall observe, this is to be found not only among
its ordinary members, but even between the head and its limbs.
We begin, though, with a more obvious form of dependence.

Christ's impact on the dead   Perhaps the most obvious consideration to note is the way in which delay seemed to reduce the social
impact of Christ's own resurrection to apparent ineffectualness.
Proclaimed Lord over all death and all history, on the alternative
scenario it now looked as though these 'first fruits' were without
any significant effect until the long-distant future. All we are left
with is Christ's resurrection as an isolated exception without any
immediate relevance to our lives in the here and now. It was
precisely to counter such a claim that various, now largely forgotten images were developed, such as Christ's descent into hell or
Jesus as the new Samson. But I want to begin with a more familiar context, that of martyrdom, and the roots of these later notions
within the New Testament itself.

Precisely because martyrs seemed most closely to pattern their
death after Christ's own, it is perhaps scarcely surprising that they
were the first to be thought to follow him immediately into glory,
and not be halted until some indefinite future. In all probability
Luke is already making such an assumption in his description of
the martyrdom of Stephen,[24] and in this he is followed by our
earliest post-biblical record of a Christian martyrdom, where the
martyr's immediate access to heaven is assumed; 'may I be received
this day into your presence', declares Polycarp,[25] and this quickly

[24] In my view, the most natural interpretation of Acts 7: 54–60, with
Stephen's death seen as the natural continuation of his vision of the living Christ.
[25] *Martyrdom of Polycarp*, 14.

became the norm for all subsequent martyrdoms. Indeed, the beginnings of such an argument can be detected already within the canon itself, in the notion of Old Testament saints being liberated there and then by Christ's resurrection (Matt. 27: 52. cf. 1 Pet. 3: 18–22). Jerome is one of many writers who makes this thought explicit: 'before Christ Abraham was among the dead below; after Christ the robber is in Paradise.'[26]

Such a belief is reflected in early interpretations of the clause in the Apostles' Creed that speaks of Christ's descent into hell.[27] Indeed, so much was its reference to 'the underworld' taken to imply this sense that the Latin was later modified in the Roman Breviary to make the point clear.[28] In recent years it has become fashionable to reject such an application, and instead interpret the clause as a way of affirming Christ's total identification with the sinful dead. Perhaps the most impressive presentation of this view comes from Balthasar.[29] Rejecting the Reformation equation of Christ's entry into hell with the crucifixion itself, he insists that alienation from the Father became still greater on Holy Saturday. It is not that Christ has no impact upon the dead, he suggests, but that the mythical language of the descent to liberate them describes an event that lies beyond any sequence in our own temporal dimension; so the issue is only confused if celebrated as though it were part of the same process. But while the caution against too literal a reading is wisely given, it is hard not to regard his own suggestion as any less mythological, with its implicit assumption that death is itself a form of punishment.[30]

The great advantage the earlier tradition had is the concrete expression it gives to an immediate impact for Christ's own resurrection. Representative humanity has won through to a new level

---

[26] *Letter*, 60.3 (my trans.). Sections 2–7 constitute an impassioned plea that Christ's resurrection must have an immediate impact. Cf. also J. H. D. Scourfield's commentary in *Consoling Heliodorus* (Oxford: Clarendon Press, 1993), esp. 98–9.

[27] For early interpretations of its significance, J. N. D. Kelly, *Early Christian Creeds* (London: Longman, 3rd edn, 1972), 378–83.

[28] The original Latin seems to have been 'descendit ad inferna,' whereas the Breviary has 'descendit ad inferos.' The Latin has thus moved from a reference to place and things infernal to human beings and the more neutral 'below'.

[29] H. U. von Balthasar, *Mysterium Paschale* (Edinburgh: T & T Clark, 1990), 148–88.

[30] For some problematic examples, 164, 166–7, 173.

of relationship with God, and this is something that can be shared immediately with others. The story is told in a greatly expanded and lively form in the so-called *Gospel of Nicodemus*, which almost achieved canonical status before its demotion at the Council of Trent.[31] Yet its influence continued long after, in part because of its repeated and highly effective use of the refrain from Psalm 24: 'lift up your heads, O gates! . . . that the King of glory may come in,' and can even be detected in one of Charles Wesley's best loved hymns:

> Christi has burst the gates of hell
>
> . . . . .
>
> Christ has opened Paradise.[32]

In Eastern Christendom the image in effect came to be the normal way of representing Christ's *anastasis* or resurrection, and there are some particularly fine artistic examples of this, such as the fresco at Chora in Istanbul, which portrays Christ drawing both Adam and Eve out of hell, with Abel and John the Baptist waiting to join them.[33]

It also led to an unexpected Old Testament type for Christ, in Samson. Initially his story sounds very unpromising material, with talent dissipated in an orgy of self-advancement and self-seeking, but his feat in carrying off the gates of the pagan city of Gaza to the Hebrew shrine of Hebron, forty miles distant, pointed the way to an alternative reading, as an anticipatory image for Christ himself carrying off the gates of hell. More importantly, it also offered the opportunity to re-read Samson's life as a whole in the light of Christ's; it could be used to speak of how the warrior's victory might be won, not by brute force but through the path that led to suffering on the cross. Allusions to Samson thus often

---

[31] A highly composite text, to which Vincent of Beauvais gave this name in the thirteenth century. The descent passage has been dated as early as the second century. For Latin text, H. C. Kim (ed.), *The Gospel of Nicodemus* (Toronto: Pontifical Institute, 1973), 35–47 (XVII–XXVII); for an English translation, W. Schneemelcher (ed.), *New Testament Apocrypha* (Cambridge: James Clarke, 1991), I, 501–36, esp. 521 ff. For an example of its continuing influence, J. De Voragine, *The Golden Legend* (Princeton, N. J.: Princeton University Press, 1993), I, 222–4.

[32] From 'Love's redeeming work is done', verse 2.

[33] This early fourteenth-century fresco is in the apse of Kariye Camii, Istanbul.

functioned as challenges to later historical figures with characters like Samson's to rewrite the narrative of their lives according to this very different pattern.[34] It is a process which continues with Milton's *Samson Agonistes*. In that drama Samson ceases to be the bluff, arrogant warrior (that role is transferred to a freshly invented character, Harapha the Philistine), and instead we discover someone seeking repentance and spiritual renovation. Angrily, he rejects his father's attempt to offer an alternative explanation of his past life:

> Appoint not heavenly disposition, Father,
> Nothing of all these evils hath befallen me
> But justly; I myself have brought them on,
> Sole author, I sole cause.[35]

'Eyeless in Gaza', Samson thus reflects on the follies of his past life. Though it would be tempting to find behind these sentiments the blind poet himself reflecting in a similar way upon the failures of the Commonwealth Revolution through which he had lived, there is little in Milton's writings to suggest that he blamed himself for what had gone wrong.[36] At most, all we can say is that Milton opens up for his readers the possibility for such self-reflection. A rather unedifying tale was thus reappropriated to indicate how Christ's resurrection could transform the social body of which he was the head.

The way in which the story of Samson is thus rewritten retrospectively alerts us to a similar process at work in the imaginative tale of the harrowing of hell, from which it is ultimately derived. Christ's life, we are being told, affects not just the future but also the past. Whether because heaven is in a different temporal stream from our own world or because those already dead are given some

[34] This is one possible explanation for the popularity of the image on Northumbrian crosses, such as that at Masham.

[35] Lines 373–6. Ironically, in Handel's adaptation, the best known aria, 'Honour and arms', is given to Harapha.

[36] Milton seems to have thought that through saintly discipline of life he did all he could do with the folly of others. Though not widely supported, there are also scholars who think that *Samson Agonistes* was in any case written before 1660: e.g. W. R. Parker, *Milton: A Biography* (Oxford: Clarendon Press, 1968). For Parker's reasons for dating the poem to 1647, II, 903–17; for his identification of analogies and disanalogies with Milton's life at the time, I, 313–22.

anticipation of what will happen in Christ, his death and resurrection are seen as already making their impact on past history. The skull at the foot of the cross in so many paintings is often misread as merely a reference to the meaning of Golgotha,[37] whereas rather more is being claimed: the skull was intended as Adam's and, symbolically, the allusion was thus to two representative deaths, that of the old Adam and the new, and their very different results. The image of Christ's descent into hell then carries that contrast to its legitimate conclusion, with Adam represented as the first to be led out from captivity. The new humanity's impact upon all of us is no less immediate than that of the old, and one social identity is replaced by another.

Implications for Christ's own humanity   If Christ's impact on the dead remains deeply problematic unless New Testament hints are carried through to their logical conclusion, even more troubling is what is implied about the nature of Christ's humanity if this is the only human nature presumed to exist in heaven until the consummation. The doctrine of the ascension speaks of the permanent exaltation of his humanity to heaven, but 'God in one man isolated from all others would not even be a God in man, for a man in isolation is not a human possibility'.[38] In other words, would it not be odd to speak of the incarnation as an entering into the essentially social and interdependent character of what constitutes humanity, only for this to be denied once that humanity is exalted to heaven?[39] Admittedly, one could talk of his relation with those still on earth, but it would be an odd sort of human life if that was the only form of contact he had with those of the same nature as himself across several, perhaps countless, millennia. The essentially social character of human beings would effectively have been denied. Certainly, for Augustine heaven is inconceivable unless it be social.[40] Though Aquinas wondered whether human friendships might detract from the perfect vision of God, other medieval writers such as Bonaventure and Giles of Rome took as

[37] 'Skull', as at Luke 23: 32. 'Calvary' is the Latin equivalent. Presumably, the site was near a burial ground.
[38] So A. Farrer, *Saving Belief* (London: Hodder & Stoughton, 1964), 155.
[39] The question of the dependence of Christ's humanity on others both on earth and in heaven will be taken up once more in Chapter 5.
[40] *City of God*, XIX, 5 and 17.

firm a line as Augustine in their view that heaven must necessarily be social in character: a *societas perfecta*.[41] One might also note the strange incongruity in so much contemporary theology of the way in which the same person, including Moltmann himself, can be found advocating a strong social doctrine of the Trinity, yet effectively denying the need for a social identity for Christ's continuing humanity.

Admittedly, that notion of heaven as perfect society had its negative side, in attempts at description conforming all too closely to the society of the writer's own day. So, for instance, in the 1868 best-seller *The Gates Ajar* by E. S. Phelps, heaven has become little more than an extension of the Victorian home and its values. Again, while in the sixteenth century, no doubt in part reflecting changes in church structures and in the aspirations of the rising middle classes, the Reformers moved closer to an egalitarian model, to the Middle Ages with its much less fluid society this seemed almost an impossibility, and so a rigid hierarchy is transposed to heaven. In the twelfth century, for instance, Hildegard of Bingen dresses her saints in silk and white shoes, while in the fourteenth we even find Langland—rather surprisingly in view of his political beliefs—consigning the penitent thief to eat his food off heaven's floor.[42] Yet there was another side. However inadequately, such accounts did sometimes help to provide a critique of existing society and its ways of valuing people. The Bible had already set a precedent in assigning the penitent thief to heaven, rather than to where the nature of his offence might have implied. In similar vein Dante often confounds the expectation of contemporary and modern reader alike. To mention but one example, we find Cunizza da Romano in heaven despite her often tempestuous and complex love-life.[43]

A recent detailed survey of the great variety of such depictions over the centuries concludes by drawing a stark contrast between

---

[41] Aquinas, *Summa Theologiae* 1a 2ae, 4.8; Bonaventure, *Sentences* III.31.3; Giles, *Quodlibeta* 6.25.

[42] *Piers Plowman* XII, 202–5.

[43] *Paradiso* IX, 13–66. Cunizza had had four husbands, two of whom she deserted, and at least two lovers. Dante rightly saw the earthly love as foreshadowing the more heavenly of her later years. Not that Dante's judgement was always as astute. Note his condemnation of the saintly Celestine V to hell for his abdication of the papacy: 'il gran rifiuto' (*Inferno* III, 60).

past and present: 'Scientific, philosophical, and theological scepti-
cism has nullified the modern heaven and replaced it with teachings that are minimalist, meagre and dry.'[44] As I hope my
discussion as a whole will indicate, the reasons for such retreat are
complex, and each requires careful addressing. However, one
cannot help wondering whether one key factor was not a simple
failure of imaginative nerve. Because we are now aware of the
considerable extent to which such descriptions of the society of
heaven mirror the concerns of the writer's own day, it is easy to
jump to the negative conclusion that this is all that they do. But
comparison with a similar phenomenon in respect of the person
without whom that heavenly society would not exist indicates the
inadequacy of this conclusion. For portraits of Christ himself to no
less a degree projected the values of the writer's own times,[45] but
this is by no means all that they have done: they have also reflected
back on that society, and offered to it various aspirations and challenges. For instance, we can be certain that, if heaven is hierarchical, its form of hierarchy will be exercised very differently from
what we encounter in this world. So, it seems to me a mistake that
the Church now retreats so decisively from any description of such
a future. For not only are such portrayals the only way of ensuring that heaven once more engages our imagination and so helps
us towards a longing for closer identification and existence with
Christ; they also enable us, however fallible they may be in detail,
to clarify what Christianity in fact offers as its ideal of society when
wholly directed by Christ. That is a matter of no small moment if
it is indeed true that the humanity Christ has in heaven remains,
like ours, essentially social.

The one body: relating living and dead   Then there is the issue of the
question of 'the communion of saints', whether it really makes
sense to talk of a single body of Christ that bridges the divide of
death unless there is at least some impact of the one on the other.
Apart from any longing to be reunited with one's loved ones,

[44] C. McDannell and B. Lang, *Heaven: A History* (New Haven: Yale
University Press, 1988), 352.
[45] Ably demonstrated in J. Pelikan, *Jesus Through The Centuries* (New York:
Harper & Row, 1987). The same point could also be made synchronically by
looking at the variety of portraits of Christ and heaven in different geographical
areas and cultures.

think of all the ambiguities and tensions in our relations with others which remain unresolved at death. Are we really to say that Christ has no power to effect any transformation in these relationships except in the understanding of those still living? What of the forgiveness longed for from the dead? Can there be no assurance of this being granted in the here and now? What of the help the dead once offered us in our earthly pilgrimage? Is that all now at an end? Are the dead now irrelevant until the end of time? On this scenario Christ surely once more ceases to be Lord of history. Rather, history's dead weight falls upon us, with Jesus' resurrection incapable of providing good news of history's transformation except in the far distant future.

This argument would clearly have appealed to at least one early martyr, Perpetua. As she prepares for her death in AD 203, a vision confirms her in her belief that her younger brother who had died of cancer of the face at the age of seven is now cured, and another on the part of her companion that her parish priest and bishop who had died unreconciled are now at one.[46] Again, Augustine has no doubt that remembering his dead parents at 'God's altar' can have an important effect on their status in the here and now.[47] Of course, some of these concerns can be presented as rather narrowly selfish, with the real focus being peace of mind or reassurance for those still on earth, but this is by no means the whole story. What, for instance, of the desire to extend forgiveness to those who may have done one great wrong while alive, but whom one was psychologically unable to forgive before they met their death? To say that God recognizes the change of mind is scarcely adequate, since the person most directly affected remains unreconciled. Conversely, for the living to know, if that were possible, that they have already been forgiven by the dead is surely quite different from hoping for an eventual reconciliation at some distant, unspecified future date.[48] It thus looks as though issues of forgiveness could cloud almost permanently the lives of the living and of the dead, unless heaven is acknowledged as a present reality. To some, God's forgiveness may seem alone relevant, but that

---

[46] *The Martyrdom of Perpetua* 7 and 13.   [47] *Confessions* 9.13.
[48] Whether such knowledge is possible or not is a complex question, but those who have prayed in this way have certainly often acquired the subjective assurance that this has indeed happened.

is surely to adopt a solipsistic attitude, as though our relations were with God alone and not also with the social reality of which he has made us an inescapable part.

One reason why such an argument has so often been resisted in the past has been that it appears to legitimate not only prayers for the dead, but also prayers addressed to them (most obviously, to the saints) and this, it will be said, detracts from the unique role of Christ in our salvation. Though historically this has no doubt often been so, it is far from obvious that it need carry any such implication. This becomes particularly clear once one asks how such desire for reconciliation could be communicated to the dead. Presumably, all such knowledge would need to be mediated through God, and so the indispensable role of Christ would remain intact. Likewise, in asking prayers of the saints it need not be supposed that they have any privileged access to our minds. That would make them more than human, and so destroy their shared identity with us. Rather, what is being sought is that God allows them to be made aware of what it is for which we pray, and how much of this is communicated and in what form would remain entirely within the divine discretion. Some will recoil from such interaction between the two worlds because of a general resistance to any notion of God acting in our world. That is too large a issue to address here. For others, the worry will stem from a quite different source, from opposed understandings of the nature of heaven, particularly those sympathetic to the Thomist atemporal conception of the beatific vision. My final argument addresses that concern.

The need for a common history The previous three arguments find various degrees of explicit or (more usually) implicit echo in the history of Christian thought and spirituality. In our more historically conscious age we may add one more. For it surely makes no sense to think of us all rising at the same time and immediately being capable of interrelations with one another. The idea that we could immediately relate to an Augustine, Cuthbert, or Hooker is absurd. We ourselves are products of a scientific world, but even were we to confine ourselves to the contents of the Christian faith, major problems would emerge, such as different attitudes to providence or pain, or certain things once regarded as self-evident where most of us now take a different view, such as usury or contraception or the status of women. Thus, to have any hope of understanding one another, these earlier figures would need to live imaginatively through subsequent history, and, if imaginatively, why not in some sense the real thing?

One might of course argue that God would infuse all the necessary knowledge to make such relations possible, but the history of the concept of infused knowledge is not a happy one. It was used by Aquinas to try and explain how Jesus could know certain things that human beings could not know naturally,[49] but modern theology has largely abandoned the idea and accepted that any such notion would detract from his full humanity. Much the same might be said for a timeless beatific vision. Not only are there problems about the notion of timelessness in general,[50] but applying it to human beings raises particularly acute issues, since temporal sequence seems so much bound up with the way we think and acquire understanding of who we are. One thought follows another, and we need to follow through their sequence and interrelation before we are prepared to adopt new ideas and new perspectives. Perhaps the issue can be put at its starkest by observing that, the more marked the difference between our former state and our new existence, the more likely we would be to doubt our continued identity as the same person. As one philosopher has put it, 'what matters in survival is mental continuity and connectedness'.[51] Surprisingly, many of those theologians most keen on the notion of narrative are also those who advocate a future instantaneous state of perfection at the end of history. Could it be that doctrinal considerations are being allowed to subvert the more obvious implications of narrative theory? If narrative is fundamental to who we are, it is hard to see why that importance should cease beyond the grave.

In part, of course, the narrative of our lives is imposed upon us, dictated as it is by circumstances. But there is also an important sense in which we choose our own narratives, through highlighting some incidents and downplaying others. In heaven that narra-

[49] *Summa Theologiae* 3a, 12.2.
[50] N. Pike, *God and Timelessness* (London: Routledge & Kegan Paul, 1970); R. Swinburne, *The Coherence of Theism* (Oxford: Clarendon Press, 1977), 210 ff.; A. Kenny, *The God of the Philosophers* (Oxford: Clarendon Press, 1979), 38–48.
[51] D. Lewis, 'Survival and identity' in A. O. Rorty (ed.), *The Identity of Persons* (Berkeley, Cal.: University of California Press, 1976), 17.

tive will at last conform to God's view of us, but it still makes a difference how this conformity is achieved. For, if it is imposed rather than discovered, there will remain an important sense in which it is not our own. God would have merely dictated a new identity of doubtful continuity with our old, whereas what is surely required is some real and intimate connection with who and what we once believed ourselves to be. That way not only could philosophical issues of identity be eased, but also an approach developed that is more consistent with the non-compulsive type of divine action displayed at the heart of Christian revelation in the incarnation. It is in this connection that there is to be found, I believe, a continued, proper and legitimate role for the notion of purgatory, not in the sense of a place of punishment but as descriptive of the process of painful self-discovery whereby through God's grace we shall learn how he has viewed our lives to date.[52] Re-ordering the narrative of a lifetime can hardly be the matter of a moment, as deep-seated sin is discovered in unexpected places and reasons are found for rejoicing in areas of life to which hitherto little or no value has been assigned.

Time too will be needed to adapt as the world changes and its present inhabitants become more and more distant from the dead in concepts and ideas, unless, that is, the latter are allowed also some conception of such changes, and so can in some sense share in the world's history. It would be easy to parody what I am advocating here. I am certainly not suggesting that every detail of later history should be available to the dead; nor is it my view that history must be shared because of the inevitability of progress. On the contrary, it has been a recurring theme throughout my two volumes that the contemporary Church often needs to recover insights that were once commonplace in earlier generations. So, learning in the next life will inevitably sometimes involve moving closer to the mind-set of a Benedict or Luther rather than necessarily the dead always having to adapt to the living. My point rather is that our identity is so heavily shaped by our specific temporal and geographic circumstances that we cannot simply be changed in a flash into a new identity and so, if the change must occur gradually, why not in parallel with our own world? Even

---

[52] For a more detailed consideration of the issue: D. Brown, 'No heaven without purgatory', *Religious Studies* 21(1985), 447–56.

with the world at an end, there is still no need to think of such temporal developments ceasing, for, developing an insight of the Cappadocian fathers, we may think of heaven as in part constituted by endless exploration of the infinite riches of God:

> This truly is to see God: never to have found the satisfaction of one's desire. But one must always, by looking at what it is possible to see, be fired on towards the desire to see more. Thus no limit should interrupt growth in the ascent to God, since no boundary to the Good can be found nor is the progress of the desire for the Good cut off because it is satisfied.[53]

One English philosopher suggests that heaven would be as boring as Elena Makropoulos finds her life in Janáček's opera, *The Makropoulos Case*. She has taken an elixir of life and for the past three hundred years has been permanently aged forty-two. The result is that her life has now become for her a matter of 'boredom, indifference and coldness'. 'In the end it is the same' she says, 'singing and silence.' So she refuses to take the elixir any more and dies.[54] But if I am right here, the comparison is quite inapposite. God both in himself and in the society he provides can provide an infinitely rich environment whose joys would not wane. Whether we think of God as inside or outside of time, temporal progression and developing social relationships are integral to human identity, and so, however the relation between God and humanity in heaven is conceived, it must still be mediated within such a frame but, so far from that being something to regret, it demonstrates how seriously God takes the kind of creatures he had made us, with progression continuing to be integral to what we are.

Nevertheless, there remains one last objection to be faced, itself perhaps the most problematic, since it involves a question of principle, namely whether such a heaven can ever be given adequate conceptualization given current understanding of the nature of human beings. For, it may be asked, has not decline in belief in

---

[53] My trans. of Gregory of Nyssa's *Life of Moses*, para. 239 in *Sources Chrétiennes* (Paris: Éditions du Cerf, 1955), 1, 109; cf. Gregory Naz., *Or.* 38.7.

[54] B. Williams, 'The Makropoulos case: reflections on the tedium of immortality' in idem, *Problems of the Self* (Cambridge: Cambridge University Press, 1973), 82–100, esp. 82.

the possibility of the independent existence of the soul ruled out such a notion from the start?

Conceiving life after death: soul and body

Hitherto I have been concerned to identify reasons for endorsing the Church's move in a different direction from the predominant biblical witness. Now, however, I must face the objection that, however right in motivation that move may have been, it is fundamentally undermined by the way in which that post-mortem existence was conceived. However, far from accepting that criticism, what I want to suggest is that previous generations were indeed right to endorse immortality of the soul, even though in our own day we need a different approach that antici-pates the language of resurrection of the body at the last day. Theologians have long since accepted that revelation does not disclose scientific truths, but the point seems to me to apply equally to those areas where science overlaps into questions of philosophical coherence. The Church of the past adopted the best available philosophical psychology of its day, and we should not hesitate to do likewise.

It is often argued that to describe ourselves as essentially soul was a Platonic corruption of the original Christian heritage, espe-cially as it necessarily carries with it a world–denying, anti-mater-ial message. But this seems to me not only to confuse Platonism and Gnosticism, but also, even more fundamentally, to ignore why soul was postulated as our essential characteristic in the first place. That the movement should begin with a philosopher who regarded love of physical beauty as a primary means of spiritual advancement illustrates how unfair the accusation is.[55] Equally, the reason why dualism was postulated was not any hostility to the body as such, but rather because of the highly plausible Greek assumption that like can only be known by like, and so if the divine is immaterial, so must also be some crucial aspect of ourselves. The fact that immortality of the soul was made an arti-cle of faith in both the Roman and Presbyterian confessions shows

[55] Plato's positive attitude in the *Symposium* is paralleled in Neoplatonism by Plotinus's extended attack on Gnosticism in *Enneads* 2.9.

how deep such assumptions went.[56] Indeed, there is some evidence to suggest that the reason why resurrection of the body found such easy acceptance among the Jews was that the belief arose at a time when they had still not quite extricated themselves from a semi-material conception of God.[57]

It is in fact much more difficult to comprehend how the gap between material (human) and immaterial (divine) is bridged, once we think of ourselves as essentially non-dualist psychosomatic unities, whose only hope is the resurrection of the body. Indeed that would seem to me one of the major factors favouring the decline of Christian belief in the modern world. Yet both scientific and philosophical considerations do point overwhelmingly towards the rejection of dualism.[58] To use a popular contemporary analogy, in so far as we have a soul, it is more like the program or software that can have no life or activity, unless it is appropriately related to some piece of hardware—in this case, the body. This is not to suggest that human beings are no more than mechanistic computers, but it is to imply that 'the complex information-bearing pattern' that gives us our identity cannot function without being embodied in something at least analogous to the material.[59]

Karl Rahner attempted to solve the problem by suggesting that at death the soul immediately enters into relation with the world as a whole, with the world thus in some sense functioning as the

---

[56] For the declaration at the Fifth Lateran Council in 1513: Denzinger and Schönmetzer, *Enchiridion Symbolorum*, 353–4. The *Westminster Confession*, ch. 32, declares that 'their souls (which neither die nor sleep), having an immortal subsistence, immediately return to God who gave them'.

[57] Everything, of course, depends on how literal some descriptions of God were intended. But it is perhaps not accidental that the patristic writer firmest in defence of the resurrection of the body—Tertullian—also had (under the influence of Stoicism) a materialist conception of God.

[58] For an illustration of the debate, S. Shoemacher and R. Swinburne, *Personal Identity* (Oxford: Blackwell, 1988); for a defence of dualism, R. Swinburne, *The Evolution of the Soul* (Oxford: Clarendon Press, 1986), esp. 145–60; for the range of present positions, D. M. Rosenthal (ed.), *The Nature of Mind* (New York: Oxford University Press, 1991), S. Moravia, *The Enigma of the Mind* (Cambridge: Cambridge University Press, 1995).

[59] The phrase is adopted by the Doctrine Commission of the Church of England in its rejection of dualism in *The Mystery of Salvation* (London: Church House Publishing, 1995), 10–12, esp. 12. For the use of the analogy in a novel, S. Howatch, *The Wonder Worker* (New York: Knopf, 1997), 44.

soul's new body.[60] However, it is hard to make sense of this proposal, since each of us would cease to have our own individuating matter. Difficulties such as this will appear to some to provide ample confirmation of the truth of the original biblical claim, that everything must now await resurrection on the last day. But against that needs to be set the fact that modern scientific developments have not only narrowed the possibilities, in other ways they have also widened them. Thus current talk of 'parallel universes'—more than one space or matter—opens up the option of analogous worlds to our own rather than confining our imagination to fulfilment in this world's terms. Heaven could then be pictured as indeed existing in the present, and as enjoying in some sense an analogous material reality to our own. This is emphatically not to say that heaven is such a parallel universe, as though one day it might be open to scientific investigation, but rather that the notion provides a useful handle for thinking about heaven as alongside our world rather than totally above or beyond it, and so as purely 'spiritual' in a way that precludes humanity from ever entering its domain.[61] Even were we to confine talk of a postmortem body to the eschaton, that body still could not be strictly identical to the one we possess now;[62] so in postulating an interim body that has only an analogous relation to our present existence the difficulties involved are not necessarily any more acute. But to this it may be objected that such an interim body flies in the face of Christian tradition. To see why this is not so, two points need to be made.

The first concerns potential impact on the definitive significance commonly claimed for the resurrection at the end of time.

---

[60] *On the Theology of Death* (New York: Herder & Herder, 1971); for a good introduction to his ideas, M. Murphy, *New Images of Last Things* (New York: Paulist Press, 1988).

[61] The analogy might also be developed to provide a means of conceiving how the humanity of Christ could be present to us in the Eucharist: D. Brown, *Continental Philosophy and Modern Theology* (Oxford: Blackwell, 1987), 169 ff., esp. 176–7.

[62] Even if the biblical injunction for a different kind of body were ignored (1 Cor. 15: 35–50), there still could not be strict physical identity because of the number of bodies over time that have used the same matter, while there is need in any case for a different kind of body if the resurrected body is not, like its predecessor, to be subject to the same inevitability of physical corruption.

It may be said that an earlier 'resurrection body' would radically undermine that pattern, but this is quite untrue. A first resurrection could only undermine a second if the first were in every sense complete. Yet, however far advanced we conceive the saints in heaven to be, even Christ himself, there is still something obvious and important lacking—the presence of those who are destined to join those already there. Christ's will, and thus by implication that of his saints, includes a desire for all creation to be included within his purposes, not only humanity but also the natural order as a whole. So it is quite untrue that on this scenario only trivial things await fulfilment at the consummation of the present world order.

Secondly, it would be a mistake to suppose that such a notion of a first resurrection is a total novelty. For such has been the influence of the perception of ourselves as embodied beings that we find a continuous tradition of willingness to conceive of our initial post-mortem state as already in effect in some sense embodied. In the case of Origen, for example, only God is conceived of as being purely immaterial; matter is the principle of division, and so post-mortem existence consists in acquiring a different body, not in abandoning body altogether.[63] Indeed, Origen's talk of the soul as a 'principle' requiring a body sounds not too dissimilar from the computer analogy used above.[64] Another Christian Platonist, Synesius of Cyrene, is equally clear in his assumption of the necessity of a body,[65] which demonstrates how misleading it is to characterize Platonism as purely concerned with soul. In fact, even as late as the seventeenth century, the astral body of Neoplatonism was still being defended by Christian Platonists such as Ralph Cudworth.[66] Equally, however, there is no shortage of illustrations from more mainstream Christianity. Hilary, for instance, describes the soul as a refined form of corporeal substance, while to cater for visions of the dead Augustine insists that even prior to the general resurrection souls must possess 'some sort of likeness of the body'.[67] Again, in the Middle Ages we find Dante using the

[63] A. Scott, *Origen and the Life of the Stars* (Oxford: Clarendon Press, 1991), ch. 9.   [64] E.g. *Contra Celsum* 5.23; 7.32.

[65] J. Bregman, *Synesius of Cyrene* (Berkeley, Cal.: University of California, 1982), 145–54.

[66] 'The Astral Body of Neo-Platonism' in Proclus, *The Elements of Theology*, ed. E. R. Dodds (Oxford: Clarendon Press, 2nd edn, 1963), 313–21, esp. 321.

[67] Hilary, *in Matt.* 5.8; Augustine, *De Genesi ad litteram* 12.32.60–33.62.

Roman poet Statius to explain his theory of aerial bodies, while Bonaventure's version of hylomorphism meant that all souls automatically have their own matter.[68] Even Aquinas's resistance to any suggestion of matter until the Last Judgement looks decidedly less hostile once placed in its own proper context. For in effect 'the thirteenth century revolutionised eschatology by moving much of what we mean by body into soul,' as, for example, in its insistence that the soul on its own can experience physical pain.[69]

So I conclude that, just as the doctrine of the ascension should be seen as no mere addendum to Christ's resurrection appearances but as indispensable to a proper completion of the personal narrative of the earthly Jesus, so also it is essential that such a completion be affirmed for humanity more generally. The idea that at the ascension Christ in anticipating the eschaton functioned entirely as an individual acting on his own would by implication deny the nature of his humanity as essentially social like our own. By contrast, when envisaged as surrounded by a Church whose members, like him, have been allowed to bring their personal narratives to completion, he can then give expression to the hope for all of us still on earth that through the incarnation culminating in the ascension the permanent significance of our humanity for God was thereby effectively declared. Take away the 'saints' in heaven, however that term is understood, and we end up with the incarnation as only a brief episode in the divine life, with even Christ's own humanity not properly restored to him until the eschaton. Little wonder, therefore, that the Church sought to bridge the intervening period with images of Christ's continuing social existence.

As we shall discover, social questions also play a key role in correctly appropriating imagery associated with the end of history. It is to that issue of the eschaton that I turn next.

The defeat of the Beast

At the beginning of this chapter I observed that in much contemporary theology there has been a significant recovery of the

---

[68] Dante, *Purgatorio* 25.2–109; Bonaventure's version of Aristotle's notion of matter providing the potentiality for form, unlike that of Aquinas, required angels and souls also to consist of matter.

[69] C. W. Bynum, *The Resurrection of the Body* (New York: Columbia University Press, 1955), 155.

imagery of eschatology. To its credit, this has brought with it both a new sense of the Church's identification with the poor and oppressed and renewed emphasis on the value of all aspects of the material order. Unfortunately, though, not only has this recovery, as we have seen, also been combined with short shrift for the image of heaven, it also often goes with curt dismissal of the more negative symbolism that has been associated with the end-times in Christian tradition. Rather than pursue the positive imagery, then, which has been in any case well treated elsewhere, here I want to challenge current neglect of the negative side of the tradition; not, though, by claiming that the imagery was without fault but rather by drawing attention to those developments from which there might still be something to learn. In outline, what I shall contend is that through its imagery of battle and judgement the Christian imagination developed not only a more powerful sense of social interdependence than we find in the New Testament but also a deeper sense of the problematic character of sin. This is not to deny the lead given by Scripture, but it is to claim that we do later tradition a disservice if we do not also acknowledge the acuity of the way in which these notions were further developed.

That the issues are not nearly as simple as they are often presented can be illustrated by the question of how the book of Revelation should be read. It is fashionable to claim it for a this-world eschatology, but in fact it is often hard to work out at any particular moment whether the author is envisaging a this-worldly or other-worldly resolution.[70] Again, it is unfair to claim that hope for this world only becomes truly radical once an other-worldly heaven is denied. There is a long, continuing and rich history of such radical hope throughout Christian history. Equal care then needs to be taken not to prejudge what the more negative imagery that talks of a final defeat of evil was really intended to convey. Mythological language has often been employed to characterize the nature of that defeat, and this is reflected in the title chosen for this second and final section of the chapter: 'The defeat of the

---

[70] He talks of 'a new heaven and a new earth' but also of there being no further need for sun or moon: 21.1 and 23. Again, the new Jerusalem is envisaged as coming down from heaven but also as reaching up to heaven like some huge and more successful Babel (its skyscrapers are approximately fifteen hundred miles high): 21.2 and 16.

Beast'. To refer to the book of Revelation once more, it is here for the first time within the biblical corpus that Satan, serpent, and dragon are all identified, with its story culminating in the chaining of the dragon for the thousand-year reign of the saints and then his final casting into the lake of fire and brimstone for eternal punishment (Rev. 20: 1–10). Evil was thus presented as a Beast that had to be overcome, but what did that mean, and would it retain the same significance in later Christian history?

Apart from scriptural precedent, there is also a deeper reason for my choice of title. In considering the history of such imagery, it is very easy to suppose that all that lurked behind further developments of the imagery in later Christianity was a cruel and rather nasty literalism which contemporary Christianity has rightly jettisoned, whereas what I want to suggest is that the mythological language in fact helped to bring about its own demise. Continuing imaginative explorations were eventually to open up the prospect of 'defeat' for the more nasty or 'beastly' aspects of such imagery. Even the abandonment of belief in hell as a place of eternal punishment was, as we shall see, not unconnected with the kind of applications given to related imagery. Some striking imagery of how dependent we are on others within the community for ultimate salvation helped undermine the notions of absolute responsibility to which hell laid claim, while increasingly, as the imagery was used to challenge rather than reassure believers, the focus of condemnation moved away from others and towards self-reflection. Appearances not withstanding, there was thus, in my view, a real advance in moral and religious perception that forced the eventual demotion of certain elements in the biblical witness and a deepening awareness of the true significance of others.

To explore how this happened, my discussion proceeds by three stages. First, we shall look at the most obvious symbols of the final victory over evil, particularly the last judgement and hell, then more closely at how the enemy is perceived, particularly Satan himself, and finally at the means of defeat, where the imagery of two quite different kinds of battle with beasts will be contrasted, the legends of Leviathan and of the Unicorn. We begin, though, with the imagery that is still most familiar, of a Last Judgement and of some human beings assigned to hell as a place of eternal punishment.

The final victory: communal preparation for judgement

Here I want to begin by considering some of the reasons for hell's demise but less as an issue in its own right and more as preparatory to some comments on the way in which the very awfulness of the doctrine not only helped generate strong social cohesion as one way of warding off its consequences but also eventually allowed that social view to turn back on the doctrine to offer its own critique. In due course three forms of social cohesion will be examined, in the rituals once associated with death, in the invention of purgatory, and in the imagery used to depict the Last Judgement, but I shall begin with the issue of hell as a place of eternal punishment.

Hell and eternal punishment   Here there are some parallels with what has happened to heaven in modern times, as well as also some obvious contrasts. Heaven has receded from Christian consciousness almost by default. There has been no sustained attack on the notion; rather, various difficulties have been left hanging in the air, and so of themselves done their destructive work. The idea of hell by contrast has been subject to repeated assaults over several centuries, with the result that now even those on the more conservative wing of Christianity are often found in effect eliminating the notion. Annihilation is then claimed as the true meaning of the relevant passages,[71] though as exegesis the interpretation seems to me to lack all plausibility. Comparison with other views of the time suggests that eternal punishment would have been the natural reading, while in their specific context the parallel with eternal reward surely implies something equally unqualified (as in Matt. 25: 31 ff. and Rev. 14 and 20). At most what could be argued is that Matthew has made more prominent and definite what was probably only a minor part in Jesus' own teaching.[72] Another tack might be to argue from those

---

[71]   C. Pinnock, 'The fire that consumes' in *Hell: Four Views* (Grand Rapids, Michigan: Zondervan, 1992). It is equally evident in more popular evangelical writing: e.g. J. Stott and D. Edwards, *A Liberal Evangelical Dialogue* (London: Hodder & Stoughton, 1988), 320.

[72]   The phrase 'weeping and gnashing of teeth' occurs six times in Matthew, and only once elsewhere (Luke 13: 28); 'outer darkness' only in Matthew, and that three times. The only relevant Marcan passage seems obviously metaphorical: D. E. Nineham, *Saint Mark* (Harmondsworth: Penguin, 1963), 258.

passages that speak of God's desire for salvation for all,[73] but, if so, it is important to be clear about what we are doing. As integrated a reading of Scripture as possible has ceased to be the aim. Instead, it is a case of allowing one set of passages to cancel out another. If then asked for a justification, it is far from clear that the answer can be generated entirely from within the Bible itself. In effect, what we seem to have is yet another case of revelation continuing beyond Scripture, as the Church's later self-understanding, aided by a different cultural context, finds itself challenged to offer a critique of some of the implications that were once drawn by the biblical writers. Though I begin by examining the nature of that critique and endorse it, I shall go on to suggest that the consequences of the survival of the doctrine for so long were not nearly as uniformly negative as are usually supposed.

Apart from Origen and his disciple in this, Gregory of Nyssa,[74] there is no major figure in the history of Christian doctrine who seriously doubted the appropriateness of the belief in hell as eternal punishment until the seventeenth century, and so it would be more natural to look for an explanation for hell's demise in changing wider cultural assumptions rather than narrowly in inspiration from aspects of the biblical text itself. Quite a number of factors seem to have played their part. Not least is the emergence of a different approach to human self-understanding, and the impact that had on how the human relation to God was perceived, in particular what we might reasonably be entitled to expect of God. Though the consequences were much wider, the change is perhaps most marked in respect of attitudes to punishment. The doctrine of hell was premised on the assumption that we owe everything to God (without him we would not exist), while he owes us nothing. The result is that while on such thinking nothing that we can do can make up for our debt, anything on the other side, precisely because it is an offence against an infinite obligation, is seen as necessarily carrying infinite penalties. The presumption is commonplace throughout the history of Christian

---

[73] 1 Tim. 2: 4; 4: 10; Rom. 11: 32; 1 Cor. 15: 22 and 28. More obscurely, to these are sometimes added 1 Pet. 3: 19–20; 4: 6.

[74] Fire is treated as purgative rather than destructive in response to Celsus' objections: *Contra Celsum* 5. 14 ff. For Gregory of Nyssa's views, *Oratio catechetica* 26.

theology, in otherwise very different thinkers. Anselm, for instance, makes the point integral to his atonement theology, while Calvin's doctrine of double predestination is unintelligible except against such a background.[75]

Yet already by the time of Calvin the roots of hell's demise were present. Rising human expectations were to lead in the following century to formulation of the notion of natural rights and all that this was taken to imply. The quite different way in which the issue of theodicy was presented from now on provides another illustration of how large a change was taking place in human self-understanding; there is a definite move away from arguments based on the nature of God to those focused upon human beings.[76] Natural law had spoken of certain claims that could be made upon us; natural rights now spoke of the claims that we could make on others, including by implication even on God himself. Some Christians continue to find any notion of our having claims against God deeply problematic, as though all notions of grace are thereby undermined. But the parallel with human parents shows that this need not be the case. To assert (in the modern idiom) that parents have duties to their children despite the fact that they have given them life does not mean that children must cease to feel any great debt towards them. Rights are about basic obligations; gratitude and grace arise when something further and beyond duty is offered. So we may see this recognition in the case of God as strengthening, not weakening, Christ's teaching and example, in respect of the value he assigned to each and every individual. We are not God's playthings or chattels, any more than we are one another's.

To recognize that God has obligations and that therefore we have rights against him no less than against our fellow human beings inevitably spelt the death of the argument that infinite debt must generate the legitimacy of infinite punishment, since now there was something to be weighed on the other side. Initially, in the seventeenth century this led not to the rejection of all punishment but

[75] Anselm, *Cur Deus Homo*, esp. 1. 20–1; Calvin, *Institutes of the Christian Religion* 3.21–4.

[76] An obvious example is the decline in use of appeal to *plentitudo boni* (the view that God as Goodness allows his goodness to overflow into lesser levels of goodness which bring with them concomitant evils), and by contrast the increasing importance attached to the free-will defence.

rather to objections only against its alleged infinite extent.[77] In the nineteenth century the pressure was increased still further as the notion of limited liability entered the field of economics and thus of morality as well.[78] Twentieth century pessimism about the extent of human freedom has then carried that process one more stage by questioning whether punishment has any justification at all, unless it is corrective. To some degree the Church itself directly contributed to hell's demise, since there seems little doubt that much of the prominence given to the idea resulted from ecclesiastical attempts at manipulation of human conduct, and that in itself could raise significant doubts about underlying credibility. Was concern for truth really what was at stake, or was it rather a very human attempt to use any convenient idea at hand as a means of exercising control and power over others? Even more liberal churchmen seem to have inclined to the belief that the lower classes would misbehave unless this threat were held over them.[79] Yet, to be fair, that same assumption is to be found even among those inimical to Christianity.[80]

Were this the whole story, it might seem that revelation was at the entire mercy of its cultural context, and hell simply functioned as an unfortunate falsehood until the rise of the question of rights forced an alternative perspective. Certainly it is implausible to claim that rights in general are a biblical notion, far less rights against God. Even so, the value that the New Testament assigns to individual worth did help lay the foundations for such a concept, and so contributed, however indirectly, to the critique that was eventually to be offered of moralities based exclusively on duties and obligations. Significantly, even someone like Locke, who combines natural rights with continued willingness to say something in defence of the doctrine, puts the emphasis very differently

[77] The limited period of punishment was seen either as ultimately redemptive or as purely retributive and followed by annihilation: D. P. Walker, *The Decline of Hell: Seventeenth Century Discussions of Eternal Torment* (London: Routledge & Kegan Paul, 1964), esp. 67–70.

[78] B. Hilton, *The Age of Atonement* (Oxford: Clarendon Press, 1988), 255–97, esp. 277; for nineteenth-century attitudes more generally, G. Rowell, *Hell and the Victorians* (Oxford: Clarendon Press, 1974).

[79] In the seventeenth century, examples include John Tillotson and Thomas Burnet: Walker, *Decline*, 6.

[80] So much so that Voltaire makes the issue central to his discussion: 'L'enfer' in *Dictionnaire philosophique* (Paris: Flammarion, 1964), 173–6.

from the past, less on our obligations and more on the dignity of the free choice given to us by God.[81] Such notions of human dignity, one might observe, came not simply from the general teaching of the New Testament but more specifically from the incarnation. The worth assigned to humanity that is implied by God himself becoming one of us, while not explicitly ruling out the possibility of the doctrine, did mean that severe testing was required to check that there was not after all a fundamental conflict. But if the recognition of natural rights helped identify such a conflict, so also did two other factors, both connected with how moral responsibility is conceived.

The first was increasing recognition of the complexity of our own motives, and so realization of how hard it is sharply to differentiate between those fit for one destiny rather than another. Ironically, the existence of the doctrine in some ways itself contributed to that new perception. For it would be hard to deny that the mythology gave a seriousness to human conduct and decision-making that the modern world often lacks, and so demanded of Christian discipleship more extensive reflection upon one's underlying motives that is the practice with most of us today. Human beings were seen as engaged in creating a type of character that would be fundamentally orientated in one direction or the other: either to heaven or to hell. Even in a period when firm belief in the reality of hell was in decline, the image could be of great dramatic power. A good illustration of this is Don Giovanni, as portrayed in Mozart's opera of the same name; what is at stake is powerfully underlined by him deliberately choosing the flames of hell in full consciousness of God's impending judgement.[82]

If human free choice is taken seriously, such a rejection of the divine purpose would seem to represent a coherent option, and this may be one reason why in more recent years, though still not admitting eternal punishment, the pendulum has swung against dogmatic universalism.[83] Yet in most modern usage, Christian or

[81]   E.g. *An Essay Concerning Human Understanding*, 2.21.72.

[82]   As well as being warned by Donna Elvira and Leporello, he sees the statue of the Commendatore coming to life.

[83]   As in the report of the Doctrine Commission of the Church of England, *The Mystery of Salvation*, 198–9. The pendulum has also swung against interpreting Barth as a universalist: J. Colwell, *Actuality and Provisionality: Eternity and Election in the Theology of Karl Barth* (Edinburgh: Rutherford House, 1989).

otherwise, the image of hell functions as little more than a device for identifying intense unpleasantness.[84] Closer to the original sense are expressions such as 'hell would be too good for him', indicating as it does absolute condemnation of some particular form of behaviour. The worry, though, is whether such sentiments do anything more than pander to human vindictiveness.[85] More salutary, therefore, in my view is one characteristic way in which the image has functioned in the past, as a means not of condemning others but of challenging believers themselves. Heaven is after all not something to which any of us can claim entitlement, but rather crucially dependent on what kind of dispositions we have at death:

> My God, I love thee; not because
> I hope for heaven thereby,
> Nor yet because who love thee not
> Are lost eternally.
>
> .   .   .   .   .
>
> But as thyself has lovèd me,
> O ever loving Lord![86]

That self-addressed seriousness is what seems to me most worth recovering from earlier tradition. There are of course elements in Scripture that already point in that direction. What, though, is seldom adequately acknowledged is the degree to which the images associated with the last things actually intensified and accelerated that process, however much their primary focus appeared, nominally at least, to lie elsewhere in judgement falling on those outside the Christian community.

This is an issue to which I want to return when we look more closely at how the image of Satan and the Antichrist have functioned in the past, but for the moment let me draw attention to another factor contributing to hell's demise, and that is the extent

---

[84] M. Wheeler, 'The limits of hell: Lodge, Murdoch, Burgess, Golding', *Journal of Literature and Theology* 4 (1990), 72–83.

[85] True perhaps even of Peter Berger's 'argument from damnation' as a pointer to the transcendent: *A Rumour of Angels* (Harmondsworth: Penguin, 1971), 70 ff.

[86] *New English Hymnal* (Norwich: Canterbury Press, 1986), no. 73: seventeenth-century Latin hymn formerly attributed to St Francis Xavier.

to which associated imagery stressed social interdependence and so in effect raised the question of whether judgement entirely directed upon individuals was altogether the right category. The rituals and imagery developed prior to the Reformation spoke of us surviving death into a better beyond only as part of the body of Christ, whereas once a more individual stress arose the prospect of hell placed so impossible a burden on the individual soul that it was perhaps inevitable that it would in the end collapse under its own weight. Not all will agree with that verdict. Even so, those social aspects are worth investigating in their own right. Not only will they help indicate the wider context the doctrine once had, as contrasted with the narrow individualism to which it was eventually made subject; they will also allow us to observe the Church imaginatively trying to work through the consequences of speaking of all Christ's disciples as interdependent within the one body. How this worked out in practice I shall consider under three headings: the rituals of death, the invention of purgatory, and the imagery of the Last Judgement.

The rituals of death and interdependency   It is a commonplace to remark that death has replaced sex as the great unmentionable, but even among Christians prepared to discuss the topic, death has lost much of the resonance it once had. In part this is because most of us now die at a relatively advanced age, and often in hospital rather than at home; so it often comes as a relief, and among strangers. Even so, there is no reason in principle why the Church should not attempt to recover the significance death undoubtedly once had, in providing what we might describe as a focused assertion of one's fundamental identity. In essence, what earlier practices sought was concrete expression of the conviction that it was only as a member of the one body of Christ, the Church, that one's death had a meaning, since only thereby could death further one's development and growth into a deeper expression of that identity beyond the grave. The point may seem an obvious one, but in fact that desire led to some marked contrasts from our own day. For instance, modern crematoria are almost always on the edge of towns and not much visited once our bodies are burnt. Cemeteries in the ancient world were likewise far from the town centre, for the dead could bring pollution and disease. But all that changed with Christianity.[87] Taking their cue from Christ's resurrection, first the saints—the holy dead—and then gradually the entire Christian community were brought either within or beside the church for burial. One was buried not as an individual but as part of a community or, if there was not enough room, one's bones were put in a charnel house, also consecrated and in or near a church.[88]

As with medieval wills, historians of the past have often seen in such behaviour little more than insurance policies, but, though undoubtedly such thoughts sometimes played their part, as a complete interpretation it would be grossly unfair. The common practice of leaving something to the Church or the poor, as with burial next to the church, was felt to declare one's identity, to say something about the sort of person one conceived oneself to be, as one prepared to face one's God.[89] But more relevant to our theme, it also spoke of interdependency and vulnerability. One sought burial in church, as also the prayers of the living, because one realized the seriousness of one's condition, and that one's fortunes in the next life were not simply dependent on one's own faith or actions alone but also equally on others: one had lived as a social being, and so that was the only way one could pass beyond death. Bodies were even all made to face east, to emphasize that what was awaited was not individual immortality but a shared resurrection.

Coffins were not invented until the thirteenth century, and even then their role was purely as repeatedly used conveyers to the place of burial; so with the corpse placed directly in the grave a powerful reminder was given of the fragility of human survival, and those reminders continued in the form that memorials took, with flat slabs there to remind the great of the necessity for humility, as also skeletons placed beneath even the most ornate of

[87] For the earlier contrast, P. Brown, *The Cult of the Saints* (London: SCM Press, 1981), esp. 1–22.

[88] For the details of medieval practice, P. Ariès, *The Hour of our Death* (New York, 1981); P. Binski, *Medieval Death* (London: British Museum Press, 1996). The latter, though, is probably exaggerating when he talks of half the population seeking burial in church: 72; contrast 77.

[89] E. Duffy, *The Stripping of the Altars* (New Haven: Yale University Press, 1992), 355.

tombs.[90] There could scarcely have been more forceful declarations that without God's mercy and grace only worms can have any say in our future destiny. No less integral, though, was acknowledgement of human interdependency, the extent of one's debt to others within the community of faith. By the eighteenth century funerary monuments were to become largely a matter of personal glorification,[91] whereas in earlier ages the deceased's social role had been what was most stressed, not primarily, I think, as a means of glorifying the dead (though that no doubt sometimes played its part) but in effect as a form of prayer that the deceased's former importance to others and mutual interdependency should continue to be recognized beyond the grave. If this is doubted, one needs only to recall the extent to which the portrayal of personal characteristics was avoided, and the religious rather than secular role of an office stressed. Edward I, for example, was buried in the vestments used at his coronation, while true-to-life portraiture was commonly avoided in favour of features that appropriately identified social role.[92]

The invention of purgatory   Though claims have been made to date the origin of the doctrine very precisely within the medieval period,[93] and it is true that this is when the doctrine assumes particular prominence, there is no shortage of anticipations which imply an evolving doctrine.[94] Though many factors were involved,[95] one key element was growing self-reflection that

[90]   As in that of Archbishop Chichele (d. 1443) in Canterbury Cathedral.

[91]   The change was a gradual one, and certainly not coterminous with the Reformation. Thus many paintings and monuments in the sixteenth and seventeenth centuries continued to stress the importance of charity and social interdependence as well as the seriousness of death. This is also reflected in some social practices such as 'sin-eaters', poor people provided with food at a funeral. For some examples, N. Llewellyn, *The Art of Death: Visual Culture in the English Death Ritual c.1500–c.1800* (London: Reaktion, 1991), e.g. 13–15, 74.

[92]   For further examples and the argument over whether to provide natural features was to 'counterfeit' true identity, Binski, *Medieval Death*, 102 ff.

[93]   Notoriously, largely because it is conceived of as requiring a specific spatial location, its origin is dated precisely to 1170 in J. Le Goff, *The Birth of Purgatory* (London: Scolar Press, 1984), 135, 154 ff.

[94]   Perhaps as early as the second century if such a dating is accepted for the relevant passage in the *Sibylline Oracles* 2.313 ff.

[95]   Other factors identified by Le Goff include less interest in apocalyptic (230 ff.), the rise of a middle class (7,131) and changing concepts of justice (209 ff.).

forced the realization that even the saved could not pass to the next life unscathed and that to effect this transition it would therefore be necessary to draw upon the resources of the community of faith as a whole. Both aspects of the claim were made subject to rather crude calculations, but these should not be allowed to disguise the importance of the underlying contentions nor their capacity to be expressed in terms more acceptable to our own day.

Consider the individual dimension first. At the time this was worked out in a rather crudely applied retributive theory of punishment that suffers from as many problems as the premises upon which the doctrine of hell was based. Nevertheless, the underlying notion still seems to me to be defensible: that at death we remain incomplete, and completion to enter God's presence must necessarily require purgation of self, in painful self-discovery and transformation, even if we have no particular reason to believe that this will be achieved through punishment. The traditional doctrine was intended to apply only to those whom God at death had already destined for heaven; so the doctrine's demand for self-examination and purgation was already strongly self-referential for the Christian, and one finds this fully reflected in the mystic, Catherine of Genoa's moving *Treatise on Purgatory*.[96] Centuries later, a similar emphasis was to be given in T. S. Eliot's powerful lines:

> We only live, only suspire
> Consumed by either fire or fire.[97]

One modern commentator, having observed that clocks were invented at the same time as purgatory, suggests that insistence upon progress and accomplishments within a finite time span is the modern world's secular equivalent.[98] Whether so or not, like that modern obsession the doctrine, even in its corruptions, added weight to the need to turn reflection inwards. So, even though the

---

[96] Translated as *Purgation and Purgatory* (London: SPCK, 1979). For a helpful exposition and discussion, F. von Hügel, *The Mystical Element of Religion* (Cambridge: James Clarke, 1961), I, 281–94, II; 182–58.

[97] T. S. Eliot, *Four Quartets*, 'Little Gidding', IV, *Collected Poems 1909–62* (London: Faber & Faber, 1963), 221.

[98] R. K. Fenn, *The Persistence of Purgatory* (Cambridge: Cambridge University Press, 1995), esp. 2.

passage in Paul, to which appeal was constantly made, meant no such thing (1 Cor. 3: 11–15),[99] its use did after all have a certain legitimacy, in endorsing the need for such painful self-reflection, both this side of the grave and beyond.[100] Indeed, a plausible case can be made out for suggesting that Protestant thought is as deeply indebted as Catholic to the notion of purgatory in generating demands for critical self-reflection.[101]

But no less important was the social side. Here too it received crude expression, with notions such as a 'treasury of merit' and Masses and other devices employed as a means of reducing the number of days due in purgatory. At one level chantry chapels can of course be seen as attempts to buy salvation, but they did at least force the admission from the wealthy and powerful that their ultimate fate depended on the willingness of others to continue to act as they requested.[102] There was also a more laudable side in the love and care shown by those who made regular petition on behalf of their now dead loved ones. That element could also find an acceptable sense today, if we think of the prayers of the living as offered in solidarity with those now required to undertake a difficult voyage of self-discovery. But there is also another social element worth noting, and that is the way in which much that is wrong with us has a corporate dimension. One might think, for example of attitudes to those of other races or to women. Sometimes it is corporate guilt that has to be explored, and that would seem best tackled socially, just as mutual wrongs might best be faced together rather than separately. So purgatory could itself in part be a social exercise.

Expressed thus, it may now be possible to give some sense to what to the modern mind can often seem as the most perverse of pursuits, namely detailed descriptions of human attempts to explore 'hell' or purgatory. We noted earlier the way in which Christ's descent to the dead functioned as an integral element in

---

[99] The contrast with a purgatorial doctrine of merit is well brought out in C. W. Fishburne, ' I Cor 3.10–15 and *The Testament of Abraham*', *New Testament Studies* 17 (1970), 109–15.

[100] The final verse does seem to imply some kind of post-mortem purgation.

[101] The Puritan Richard Baxter is explicitly compared with Catherine of Genoa in Fenn, *Persistence*, Op. cit., 73 ff.

[102] Often suitably reinforced by benefits to them in turn, many chantry chapels, for instance, also functioning as educational establishments.

the interpretation of the Apostles' Creed. The event was envisaged as taking place after the crucifixion. So Christ was already dead at this point. Nonetheless, almost certainly it was that visit that set the precedent for others, this time involving the living. Examples are to be found in writers such as Gregory and Bede.[103] Perhaps best known are the three Irish versions.[104] Certainly, it was the Patrick legend which led to the most sustained attempts to enter hell, a papal ban eventually proving necessary in order to forbid such adventures and their description.[105] At one level such stories can be read as mere literary creations; at another as a form of didactic and threatening morality.[106] But amidst all the features of an adventure tale, sight should not be lost of the way in which such stories were intended to provide reassurance to the community as a whole that a heavenly destiny was indeed possible. The hero has to face numerous obstacles, but because of his trust in Christ he returns to earth, just as one day, we are being told, by similar trust he will be able to get beyond hell and into heaven; but not that individual alone, since the point of the tale is his role as representative hero, thus assuring all his fellow believers that a similar ascent remains possible for them also.[107] We are thus left in no doubt about the seriousness of the obstacles to be faced, but equally they are declared not to be insuperable.

Thus, despite superficial parallels, giving 'hell' or purgatory a specific location seemed to have functioned differently from interest in where the original Garden of Eden or 'Paradise' was to be found. Although the issue attracted the attention of explorers such as Marco Polo, Henry the Navigator, and Christopher

[103] Gregory the Great, *Dialogues* IV, 31; Bede, *Ecclesiastical History of the English People* V, 12.

[104] *Voyage of Brendan, Vision of Tundal, St Patrick's Purgatory.*

[105] For accounts of those who made the attempt, G. P. Krapp, *The Legend of St Patrick's Purgatory* (Baltimore, 1900), 31 ff. The entrance was closed by papal order on St Patrick's Day, 1497.

[106] These are the two features most stressed by D. D. R. Owen, *The Vision of Hell: Infernal Journeys in Medieval French Literature* (Edinburgh: Scottish Academic Press, 1970), though later French writing is found to be less serious in its purpose than Anglo-Norman: 77, 131–2.

[107] C. M. Loffler, 'The pre-Christian conceptions of time, death and eternity as reflected in Irish mythology', *Analecta Carthusiana* 117 (1987), 5–43, esp. 24–5, 34–5.

Columbus,[108] surprising as it may seem, the search for hell actually offered a more optimistic vision than attempts to locate that perfect garden: the latter told only of an earlier defeat, whereas the former spoke of the possibility of the Body of Christ as a whole obtaining through Christ's grace fresh victories. Indeed, attempts to locate Eden inevitably demoted the rest of the natural world, since it had by comparison inevitably to be seen as inferior; as a result, it took until the Romantic movement before nature was accorded full value on its own, without any supplement required through supposed human improvement.[109] That contrast warns us that decoding imagery is seldom as simple as it might initially seem, but it also affords a more important lesson. Paradise is the notion that apparently remains more faithful to Scripture, but in fact it is the less biblically rooted image of purgatory which, I believe, better secures the Christian conceptual scheme. With its belief in the imminence of a new dispensation, the New Testament had little time to reflect on intermediate states, but that should not, and did not, preclude the subsequent Church from such reflection, nor should it preclude us in our own day.

Images of the Last Judgement   With the rituals of death and the intermediate state of purgatory alike seen in essentially social terms, it can come as no surprise that the final denouement also had a strongly social dimension. Historians often stress the threatening character of medieval depictions of the Last Judgement. That there was this side cannot be denied, but it is not the whole story. A favourite location was in the tympanum above the main entrance to the church, at the west or north door. Such a positioning needs to be taken seriously, for thereby the message was conveyed that those who took the message to heart could now pass safely beneath to enter the Church's fold. Sometimes, even a touch of humour was used to convey the point, as in Gislebertus' magnificent Romanesque tympanum at Autun, where we find the

---

[108] J. Delumeau, *History of Paradise* (New York: Continuum, 1995): for Marco Polo, 79; for Henry the Navigator, 92–3; for Columbus, 54, 156; for the related legend of Prester John, believed to live nearby, 71–96.

[109] K. Bazarov, *Landscape Painting* (London: Octopus, 1981), esp. 9–79. One need only think of the medieval attitude to roses: their thorns are a sign that we live in a fallen world.

archangel Michael tampering with the scales, to secure a favourable verdict, and a family of young children even jumping and dancing as they cling to the angel who leads them on.[110]

In Eastern Christendom one form of iconography was to become dominant, the so-called Deesis, in which we find John the Baptist and Mary as representatives of old and new covenant respectively, interceding on behalf of the faithful. Because in the West a fixed iconography for the scene was never developed,[111] it is hard to generalize, but, as in the East, there are almost always some signs of the key part played by the support of others in securing one's ultimate salvation, even if it is harder to predict who will be given this role. One reason why this more positive side is not always noted is because some of the best-known artistic examples of the genre also tend to be the fiercest, with emphasis on the severity of the judgement clearly taking precedence over any sense of the triumph of a shared social identity. One need only think of what Michelangelo does in the Sistine Chapel, where even Mary seems to recoil from her Son while the artist represents himself with the flayed body of Bartholomew; or again one notes how Verdi treats the *Dies Irae* in his *Requiem* where orchestration and choral writing alike suggest an explosion of terror. If Fauré's version is at the other extreme, with its reduction of this central hymn to a single line and the omission of all else that might seem threatening, there is no shortage of musical and artistic examples that offer something in between. As an artistic example, consider Rubens' large *Last Judgement* of 1615.[112] Whereas the damned descend to hell as distinct and separate individuals, the saved form an interlaced column of intertwined bodies, with saints and angels beckoning them on. If the diaphanous robes and surfeit of flesh is not exactly to modern taste, there remains no doubt about the confidence expressed in communal interdependence. In that painting also, Michelangelo's stern Christ is gone; instead, Christ's kindly face is turned wholly to the saved in a gesture of welcome.

---

[110] D. Grivot, *Twelfth Century Sculpture in the Cathedral at Autun* (Colmar: S.A.E.P., n.d.), 4 and ill. 44.

[111] E. Kirschbaum (ed.), *Lexikon der Christlichen Ikonographie* (Freiburg: Herder, 1972), IV, 516: 'allerdings entsteht kein kanonisher Typus wie in Osten, sondern fast jedes Gerichtsbild verkörpert eine Neuschöpfung.'

[112] In the Alte Pinakothek, Munich: illustrated in F. Baudouin, *Rubens* (London: Bracken Books, 1977), 96.

Nor is that pattern unknown in the medieval world; indeed, there are quite a number of medieval portrayals of Christ as gentle judge.[113]

So, while this is by no means always so, I would contend that even in respect of the Last Judgement some amelioration to the impact of the images was commonly provided through the same social emphasis that we have detected elsewhere in the evolving history of Christian attitudes to death. Once, however, detached from such emphases, hell was rightly seen as too great a burden to bear. That, though, does not entail that such attitudes should now also be abandoned along with hell. The Reformation rightly protested at some versions of interdependence which seemed to usurp the role of Christ, but in its anxiety to correct distortions it produced its own lack of balance in turn: implausibly, Christ was expected to do everything. Yet the whole trend of modern sociology flies in the face of any analysis that would try to limit the only two relevant elements in such a situation to Christ and individual believer. For better or worse, much, perhaps even most of what we are, is conditioned by a cluster of various social influences. In building that admission into its theology and imagery of discipleship, an earlier age not only acted wisely, it also carried significantly further the insights offered by various New Testament images. Both Paul with his talk of the body of Christ and John with his symbol of the vine had already set the pattern, but in their desire to maintain a christocentric emphasis, what was missing was the recognition that not all could be referred back to Christ and so of necessity significant aspects had to be delegated and mediated through others.[114] If I may refer back to the previous chapter, there we witnessed how slowly came the recognition that Christ's example needed to be mediated, if its proper impact in different social circumstances was to be understood; equally then, in my view, the Church is still learning how much any talk of discipleship at all must mean significant mediating roles for others.

[113] As in Carlisle's Cathedral's early fourteenth-century Great East Window.

[114] 1 Cor. 12: 14 ff can of course be read as already making such an admission, but it is one thing to say everyone has a role, quite another to insist that Christ's role is indirect and in some ways now undertaken by others. It is possible that the move in Colossians and Ephesians to distinguish Christ as 'head' of the body rather than himself constituting the whole body (as in the major Pauline epistles) is an attempt to cater for just this point.

Individual discipleship towards the Christian's ultimate destiny can only be given adequate sense if it is described against the wider backdrop that constitutes a corporate pilgrimage of faith.

It is often said that if such a strong emphasis on social interdependence is accepted, this inevitably weakens our ability to talk of individual human responsibility for sin. Certainly it could, and no doubt sometimes did, but what is interesting about post-biblical developments is that, so far from this in general happening, what we witness is a greater readiness to turn the critique inwards on oneself. How and why this happened is our next topic for consideration.

Satan and the enemy as the near-other

Most modern academic theology seems too embarrassed by the nature of the imagery that came to be associated with evil in Christian history to be prepared to give it any sustained attention. That is a pity because such curt dismissal is usually based on a superficial reading of what the imagery was intended to convey. Here I want to draw attention to two key aspects, first the positive role exercised by objectification of evil, and then secondly the way in which, so far from being directed exclusively at condemnation of others, it came to play a central role in self-critique. Hence the appropriateness of the heading of this section which speaks of the enemy as 'the near-other': 'other' as objectified, but 'near' in terms of the object of critique. How that contributed both to a deepening and to a transformation of biblical perceptions will also be indicated as our discussion proceeds.

Objectifying evil: making sense of a supernatural opponent   Some versions of Christianity continue to make extensive use of the imagery of Satan and of the related idea of the Antichrist, Satan's principal henchman at the end of history. Though often dismissed as merely the ranting of fundamentalists, the phenomenon deserves to be taken more seriously, if only because its influence stretches more widely into society as a whole. Novels and films that portray the demonic achieve acceptance and indeed plausibility among many otherwise indifferent to religious belief. In *The Stand* the world's best-selling novelist, Stephen King, even succeeds in getting his readers to accept an apocalyptic scenario, in the course of which, at Las Vegas, the Devil finally discloses his true identity, with horns and all.[115] There would seem no denying that for many in the modern world belief in supernatural evil is more credible than its opposite, and this would seem confirmed by the more indirect way in which modern culture commonly represents supernatural good, as in the film *Star Wars*.[116]

In trying to comprehend why this should be so, no doubt many factors should be taken into account, not least the often saccharine portrayals of goodness among the devout. Of particular relevance, though, in my view is the way in which we commonly experience the pressure towards evil as something larger than ourselves. This has nothing necessarily to do with attempts to evade responsibility; rather, due note needs to be taken of the common human experience of being overwhelmed by evil, its sheer strength to overpower our wills despite us apparently knowing better. From this of course nothing follows about the existence of some mastering external pressure, far less that its character is supernatural, but expressed in this way it does serve a useful, imaginative role in conceptualizing the nature of the struggle that confronts human beings. Evil is much more than some local difficulty that can easily be contained within our own backyard or inner consciousness: 'we are not contending against flesh and blood, but against the principalities, against the powers, against the world rulers of this present darkness (Eph. 6: 12 RSV).' Nor is it the case that the better we become, the less likely we are to feel such a cosmic dimension to our struggle. On the contrary, almost certainly Jesus himself had visions of the Devil,[117] and that pattern was to be repeated in the experience of many a saint.

While thinking in this way could throw us into pessimism as we

---

[115] S. King, *The Stand* (London: Hodder & Stoughton, 1978; uncut version, 1990). The film version makes particularly good use of the horns, in having them emerge only when the Devil's will has been thwarted. Significantly, it is the heroes' refusal of violence that ultimately destroys Satan's power.

[116] The extent of the film's influence is well illustrated by the widespread use among the unchurched of the image of a 'Force' as the best way of describing a sense of divine presence or power. Statistics repeatedly disclose that a majority of those who profess belief in God conceive of him impersonally: J. Astley, 'Non-realism for beginners?' in C. Crowder (ed.), *God and Reality* (London: Mowbray, 1997), 100–112, esp. 100, 111; W. Kay. 'Belief in God in Great Britain 1945–96', *British Journal of Religious Education* 20 (1997), 28–41, esp. 32, 34, 36.

[117] Cf. *Tradition and Imagination*, 308–13, esp. 311.

contemplate the forces ranged against us, for the Christian to think
thus cosmically has some clear advantages. Not only does it remind
us that the gospel call involves a radical call to *metanoia*, a complete
change of mind and direction, it also underlines the fact that any
temptation set before us is essentially 'other': it is not part of our
true selves as God intended them to be. Make temptation purely
internal, and one path might seem as much a reflection of who we
really are as any other. Yet, despite the prevalence and acceptability of such language beyond the circle of the Church, all this may
still sound like special pleading. To see why it is not, we need to
look first at the question of the origin of the concept of a supernatural evil figure.

One recent study postulates that this in fact lay in the desire to
demonize opponents within one's own inner circle, first within
Judaism and then subsequently as applied to heretics within
Christianity.[118] While, as we shall see, such motivations undoubtedly played a role, it cannot be the full story, if only because the
entire effectiveness of such accusations depends on the assumption
that there is some more dreadful external, supernatural evil with
which the opponents have allowed themselves to be identified.
More important therefore, so far as origin is concerned, must be
the way in which it allowed a clearer expression of what is at stake
in both divine and human willing and choosing. Thereby the failure of earlier strands in Scripture to make any distinction between
what God really wants and what he merely permits was overcome,[119] while in the human case a new focus on human choice
could now emerge, with a sharper contrast drawn between what
truly flows with the will of providence and what must be seen as
an aberration from outside that stream. The obvious biblical example to quote is the transfer of ultimate responsibility for a
condemned census away from God and towards Satan,[120] but
there are numerous examples from inter-testamental literature. A
controversial instance is the way in which the author of the book
of *Jubilees* transfers responsibility for the intended sacrifice of Isaac;

[118] E. Pagels, *The Origin of Satan* (London: Penguin, 1995), passim, e.g. xix,
13, 34, 49, 149.
[119] The best-known fusion is God hardening Pharaoh's heart: Exod. 4: 21; 7:
3; 14: 4. In the last case, it is even treated as God's strategy to 'get glory over
Pharaoh and all his host' (RSV).
[120] Contrast 2 Sam: 24: 1 and 1 Chron. 21: 1.

no longer directly part of God's plan, it is left to a satanic figure to take the initiative.[121] Such externalization of evil could of course have led to an excusing of human conduct (and no doubt sometimes did),[122] but overwhelmingly it seems to have operated in a different direction, with a much greater seriousness about the possibilities opened up by choice. Opponents were repeatedly blamed for yielding to Satan. There was no inevitability about the evil becoming part of the individual concerned.

These origins are important in clarifying the ontological status of such language, for it appears that what gave the stimulus to such belief was more the way in which evil was experienced as a pressure from without, less any sense of it being a wholly independent reality. At all events, that would help explain why not only was any ultimate duality resisted but also why confusion persisted for so long about how much should be directly attributed to the hand of God. It also might help make better sense of why precise conceptualization of this alternative world was so slow to emerge. There is no need to repeat here the story of the origin of the various terms, except to note that Satan, Lucifer, and a multitude of other figures were only slowly forged into the concept of the Devil with which we are so familiar today.[123] Surprisingly perhaps, studies of iconography reveal no fixed form until relatively modern times, and in fact throughout most of Christian history the Devil has been given numerous guises, Indeed, initially there was a reluctance to offer any depiction at all.[124] One commentator on

---

[121] *Jubilees* 17: 15–18: 19, esp. 17: 16 and 18: 12. The satanic figure is known as Mastema. Yet, though Abraham is portrayed as seeing all temptation as coming from evil spirits (12: 20), nowhere is his own responsibility denied, or the ability of God to use such temptation.

[122] The main conclusion drawn by L. Link in *The Devil: A Mask without a Face* (London: Reaktion, 1995), 192.

[123] Early demons include Azazel (Lev. 16: 8, 10: 26) and Lilith (Is. 34.14). Satan is used positively in the story of Balaam as the angel who halts his ass's progress (Num. 22: 23–5), and in the story of Job (1: 6 ff.) no hostility to the purposes of God is implied, despite the effect of his proposal on Job. The first clear, purely negative reference only emerges with Zechariah (3: 1–2). The New Testament adds Beelzebub (Mark. 3: 22), and makes the link with the serpent (Rom. 16: 20) while one must wait for Origen and Jerome for the definitive forging of the link between Isaiah 14: 12–15 and Luke 10: 18 to create the figure of Lucifer.

[124] Link argues that one must wait until the ninth century for a definite appearance: *Devil*, 72.

this history has suggested that such shadowy vagueness comes from Satan being seen as the dubious outsider or 'Other', what one does not wish to be.[125] The imagery and language would then be a way of focusing one's concern not to be a certain sort of being, and thereby a way of raising what one's fundamental loyalty and identity is. Hostility to the near outsider would then follow from this characterization as a consequence, not as a cause.

Satan was thus not invented as a way of dealing with near opponents; rather, the temptation to demonize them comes precisely from the fact that objectively they often are the greatest perceived threat to one's identity. The near outsider is where temptation is strongest to move in a different direction, and that is of course precisely what gave the Tempter his particular power in respect of the temptations of Christ himself.[126] Although I have used the language of 'invention', nothing I have said thus far entails the non-existence of supernatural evil. Nonetheless, the nature of the origin of such imagery should at least alert us to the fact that questions of ontology are not the primary rationale for such symbolism, and so we put the emphasis in the wrong place if ontological questions are seen as more fundamental than questions of meaning and truth. Certainly, there is little conceptual difficulty in the notion that a non-material Creator might create non-material, intelligible beings like himself and capable of both good and evil. The real problem with the traditional picture lies not in the existence of such beings as such but rather in the idea that they might have been granted some independent initiative to cause evil in our world, as though God were prepared to stack the cards decisively against us. That objection, though, would not hold against the supposition that some individuals might deliberately court such beings and invite them in as participants in their plans.

The analysis offered here is therefore not intended as a way of definitively determining whether such beings exist or not. Instead, the discussion illustrates how sometimes the truth intended by imagery can exist on a quite different plain from ontology. Even if Satan and his minions do not exist, the language remains a

---

[125] Ibid., 16, 183.
[126] Similarly, Athanasius' *Life of Anthony* is masterful in its portrayal of the Devil using temptations most consonant with the hermit's deepest longings and desires.

useful, perhaps even essential, tool in allowing the otherness of evil to be fully and easily acknowledged: no domestic difficulty is indicated but a force greater than what can easily be countered by one single individual. If that allows a natural opening for talk of the need for divine grace, and appeal to the help of one's fellow Christians, we have already noted that the most insidious form of threat comes when that Other is also near. Although this realization did sometimes open up vindictive tendencies, it also, I believe, enabled the imagination not only to subvert some of the less pleasant aspects of the biblical text but also carry forward its notion of *metanoia* into a continuing demand for transformation. Hell in effect became self-addressed.

From demonizing others to turning judgement inwards   Traditional Christian imagery of the Last Judgement is often portrayed as, on the one hand, providing an unattractive, self-satisfied reassurance for those within the fold while, on the other, directing nasty, spiteful threats to those beyond its pale. That it sometimes functioned in this way cannot be denied, but what I want to suggest here is that one can detect another current that becomes increasingly prominent as imaginative exploration of the issue proceeds. So preoccupied is the New Testament Church with the need for an initial decision for or against Christ that judgement is overwhelmingly directed beyond the community, whereas once the hope of any speedy emergence of the kingdom receded and a more ambiguous Church had emerged, one finds more sustained reflection on the possibility that the real point of the imagery should be moved from the threat posed by a distant 'other' to that proceeding from what is most 'near', namely oneself. I shall begin by briefly noting some of main problems generated by trajectories from the biblical text, then elaborate, at rather more length, the ways in which these came to be modified in the history of artistic representation, before returning once more to Scripture to consider how the history as a whole, biblical and later, should now be appropriated.

It seems hard to deny that some unfortunate precedents were set by the New Testament, not least the readiness to identify specific individuals as the object of God's wrath. For instance, when Paul's talks of a forthcoming 'lawless one', his choice of expression appears to imply that he has some specific individual in mind (2 Thess. 2: 8 RSV),[127] and, though scholars continue to disagree as to precisely which emperor is intended by the book of Revelation, here too there is little doubt that a specific individual is being portrayed as Nero redivivus.[128] So, though Tyconius, Augustine and others tried to keep the emphasis on Jesus' talk of a plurality of false Christs (Mark 13: 5 and 21–2), it was perhaps inevitable that again and again in Christian history fresh identifications for the Antichrist would be attempted, among them Muhammad, Saladin, Pope John XXII, and the emperor Frederick II,[129] not to mention those of our own day. Also unfortunate was the fact that it took until the twelfth century before the belief began to decline which Irenaeus had deduced from Scripture, that the Antichrist would have a Jewish ancestor.[130] The ferocity of much later imagery had also ample precedent not only in the book of Revelation but also in Matthew's presentation of hell,[131] while the 'them and us' contrast in that Gospel and still more so in John could easily appear to legitimate similar presentations in later centuries. Even the parable of the sheep and the goats that now commonly functions as such a powerful and moving injunction upon Christians to act in generous love towards those outside the fold, was almost certainly originally intended by Matthew in the opposite way: as a damning judgement upon non-believers who failed to help Christ's disciples when in need.[132] So, such attempts to identify specific figures as under judgement cannot really be

---

[127] This is more literal than 'that Wicked' (AV) or 'the Rebel' (JB).

[128] The gematria for the Hebrew 666 of Rev. 13: 18 is 'Nero Emperor', while the reference to the deadly wound at 13: 3 implies that Nero is already dead.

[129] The first two because of the military threat of Islam, Frederick II because of his treatment of the papacy, and Pope John XXII because of his opposition to the Franciscan Spirituals.

[130] B. McGinn, *Antichrist* (HarperSanFrancisco, 1994), 199. Irenaeus deduces that he will come from the tribe of Dan from the absence of that tribe in Rev. 7: 4–8 combined with Jer. 8: 16: *Adversus Haereses* 5.30.2.

[131] As in the characteristically Matthean 'wailing and gnashing of teeth': e.g. 13: 42.

[132] A common view among biblical scholars, e.g. J. C. Fenton, *Saint Matthew* (Harmondsworth: Penguin, 1963), 402; H. B. Green, *Gospel According To Matthew* (Oxford: Oxford University Press, 1975), 206; G. N. Stanton, *A Gospel for a New People: Studies in Matthew* (Edinburgh: T & T Clark, 1992), 207–31, esp. 214–18. As Fenton implies, Matthew may have narrowed the focus of one of Jesus' parables for his own purposes.

claimed to be out of character with New Testament attitudes as a whole.

Were this all that could be said, it would be easy to read later history as no more than repeated attempts to reapply the already failed literalism of the New Testament picture, stemming each time from fresh political crises in the author's own day. But a more complicated story needs to be told. Often the end of the world was not at all imminent in the mind of writer or painter, and, even when this was taken to be a real possibility, it often went with the conviction that delay could be achieved through repentance.[133] Indeed, though the demonizing is rightly seen as problematic,[134] what is encouraging about the later history of such imagery is the extent to which it set itself free from a primary condemnation of others and opened up into a new summons towards penitence on the part of the listener, viewer, or reader. Though this is also true of many of the written texts,[135] major examples are not wanting from the history of art. Let me, therefore, offer some representative examples from three different historical periods, the thirteenth, the fifteenth, and the nineteenth centuries.

Among the many examples of illustrated commentaries on the book of Revelation,[136] the earliest surviving English cycle as well as one of the most beautiful is a cluster that probably all derive from a single archetype.[137] Though we lack personal details about the first illustrator, we can deduce from the way in which he handles his material that he was no mere slavish copyist of already existing meanings, whether inherent in the accompanying commentary by Berengaudus or even in the original biblical book

---

[133] Hippolytus (d. 235) thought two centuries still remaining (*Commentary on Daniel* 4.23–4), while Lactantius (d. 325) suggests that prayer and penitence can make a difference (*Divine Institutes* 7.25).

[134] Pagels ends her book on Satan by urging that reconciliation must replace demonizing: *Origin*, 183–4.

[135] Of the examples included in (B. McGinn (ed.), *Apocalyptic Spirituality* (New York: Paulist Press, 1979), Lactantius, Adso, Joachim, and Savonarola all have such appeals: 78, 96, 117, 204–7.

[136] Catalogue and bibliography is provided in 'Census and bibliography of medieval manuscripts containing apocalypse illustrations: 800–1500', *Traditio* 40 (1984), 337–79 and subsequent articles by R. K. Emmerson and S. Lewis.

[137] There is a very fine detailed study by S. Lewis, *Reading Images* (Cambridge: Cambridge University Press, 1995). For earliest, 57; for related manuscripts, 340–4; for debt to *Bible moralisé*, 202–3.

itself.[138] So, for instance, though he shares with the commentator a lack of interest in eschatological imminence, he departs from him in almost eliminating anti–Semitic references.[139] Likewise, he does not hesitate to alter the biblical text in order to provide a more effective linking of incarnation and the ultimate defeat of evil,[140] while at the same time the basic imagery is frequently enriched by subtle visual and word plays.[141] All this is done to ensure increased focus upon his primary message, which is a summons to both personal transformation and participation in reform of the contemporary Church. To effect this purpose the author of Revelation is treated less as author and more as fellow participant in his vision of what change might mean, with his own longing for reform indicated in numerous ways, among them by John sharing in the tonsure of priests of the time. The net result is that the illustrations function best as an invitation to a personal pilgrimage, whereby heavenly realities are employed to sharpen and challenge our perception of earthly ones.[142] The resources of the imagination are thus enriched to ensure that we can see our present world and its faults in a new light.[143] Instead of the canonical work's heavy concentration on the faults of others, and in particular those of imperial Rome, through the illustrations its message has in effect been transformed into a summons to continuing personal conversion and change.

From the end of the fifteenth century comes Signorelli's memorable frescoes in the cathedral at Orvieto. Since the Second

---

[138] Berengaudus' exact date is unknown, but he wrote sometime after the destruction of the Lombard kingdom in the eighth century. Another major artistic tradition that was influential on the continent derives form Beatus' seventh-century commentary. For a brief survey of the situation in thirteenth century England, P. Brieger, *English Art 1216–1307* (Oxford: Clarendon Press, 1957), 159–70.

[139] For question of imminence, Lewis, *Images*, 225; for reduction in anti-Semitic references, ibid., 217–18.

[140] Rev. 12: 6 and 13 are eliminated in order to ensure that Woman and Child can be present for Michael's battle with the dragon; ibid., 267–8.

[141] As in the use of a peacock (*pavo*) to suggest the fear (*pavor*) created by the sound of the trumpet: ibid., 246 ff., esp. 253.

[142] 'Peregrinatio in stabilitate' is Lewis' description: Ibid., 33; cf. 338.

[143] Lewis is prepared to speak of a sacramental participation, and throughout she stresses how the illustrator is no mere passive receiver of the text, but engaged in a complex, interactive, new creation: ibid., xxii, 259–65.

World War interpretation of his portrayal of a preaching Antichrist has been dominated by perception of the work as a sustained attack on the views of the reforming friar, Savonarola,[144] but this ought really never to have carried conviction, for by the time Signorelli signed the contract for the commission Savonarola was already dead and his power and influence largely a thing of the past.[145] What sustained such an interpretation amounted to little more than the fact that Orvieto was a papal city belonging to Alexander VI, one of Savonarola's principal opponents. Much more plausible is the suggestion that here too we have a summons to personal repentance and to a new way of viewing our world, though this time with more heavily political overtones.[146] Roundels of Cicero and Lucan on the zoccolo or surrounding skirting board remind us of the heavy price of civil strife, while the central image makes us members of a crowd listening to the Antichrist, the inflammatory consequences of whose words are clearly indicated both by the rearing horse of pride represented on the podium from which he speaks and by the various murders already take place, close at hand.[147] So far from Alexander VI being given support in his attack on Savonarola, the presence with us, as a fellow member in the crowd, of his bellicose son, Cesare Borgia, alerts us to a more complex position, while the inclusion of Alexander the Great as yet another member of that same crowd may be a covert way of criticizing the pope himself.[148] That may still sound like an externally directed critique, but one needs to recall that Orvieto was in fact a papal city, and so the natural pride the local populace would have had in their identity. Moreover, not only is some more explicit censure directed against the Church

---

[144] So A. Chastel, 'L'Apocalypse de 1500: la fresque de l'antéchrist à la Chapelle de Saint Brice Orvieto', *Bibliothèque de l'Humanisme et Renaissance* 14 (1952), 122–40. He is supported in A. Paolucci, *Luca Signorelli* (Florence: Scala, 1990), 44.

[145] Savonarola was burned at the stake on 23 May 1498; the contract was signed on 5 April 1499.

[146] The argument of J. B. Riess, *The Renaissance Antichrist: Luca Signorelli's Orvieto Frescoes* (Princeton, N. J.: Princeton University Press, 1995).

[147] For Cicero and Lucan, ibid., 31–2; for the artist's strong attempt to involve the viewer, 54; for a literary parallel from the same century for the symbolism of the rearing horse, St Antoninus, *Summa* 3, 725–6.

[148] For the presence of the Borgias, 55, 70. Pope Alexander VI shared with Alexander the Great not only the same name but also some military pretensions.

through the portrayal of a group of quarrelling theologians behind the main crowd, too preoccupied with their disputations to face the destruction all around them, but also we as onlookers are implicitly addressed; the general positioning of the fresco forces us to perceive ourselves as part of the crowd that is being encouraged towards self-seeking ambition and thus to question whether we too are not in the process of succumbing to the Antichrist's will.

With the nineteenth century I want to consider less one specific painting and more the emergence of a new genre, sometimes labelled 'the apocalyptic sublime', in which painters in effect abandoned the traditional biblical imagery of the last times in favour of either non-biblical ways of making their social critique or else redirected alternative biblical symbolism to this purpose. To understand why this occurred we need first to trace the history of the relevant iconography from the fifteenth century onwards. Although Signorelli was one of the most important influences on Michelangelo's *Last Judgement*, in determining the long-term pattern of iconography for apocalyptic themes it was his contemporary Dürer who was to have the more lasting influence.[149] His fifteen Revelation woodcuts of 1498 were to find countless imitators, as well as some who attempted to improve upon their basic pattern; for instance, his *Four Horsemen of the Apocalypse* underwent numerous modifications and variations during the American and French Revolutions and well on into the nineteenth century.[150] Yet, that influence was not without its heavy price, because Dürer's literal adherence to the text of the book of Revelation meant that the ability of the imagery to speak to viewers declined at the same rate as readers' capacity to find the biblical text meaningful in itself. The result was that by the nineteenth century the whole pattern of last-times iconography had become deeply problematic, and a desperate search was initiated for alternative imagery. The apocalyptic theme was now represented by scenes as varied as the Deluge, Belshazzar's Feast, or even Hannibal's crossing of the

---

[149] Though his woodcuts offer a heightened sense of action, Dürer's attempt to substitute one medium for another (visual for text) does in my view result in excessive literalism. But for high artistic praise, cf. E. Panofsky, *The Life and Art of Albrecht Dürer* (Princeton, N. J.: Princeton University Press, 4th edn, 1955), 51–9.

[150] In part mediated by J. H. Mortimer's influential *Death on a Pale Horse* of 1775.

Alps.[151] In part this was occasioned by decline in biblical literalism,[152] but a freer association of imagery also played its part. So, for example, in Deluge paintings a snake frequently appears, while the painter, John Martin, has no hesitation in including a chronologically inappropriate Tower of Babel in his picture of Belshazzar's feast to drive home his apocalyptic theme.[153] One of the most celebrated paintings of the nineteenth century, its scale is such that we are forced to reconstruct what is happening by placing ourselves within its canvas, and thereby of course, as with Signorelli's frescoes, we learn our lesson, of judgement on human pride and arrogance.[154]

The nineteenth century by no means marked the first resort to alternative imagery. Even one of Signorelli's contemporaries, Botticelli, can be found adopting a different strategy, in his desire to express his commitment to Savonarola's reform movement and the apocalyptic fervour that went with it. Not for him explicit depictions of the Antichrist or Last Judgement, but Mary Magdalene at the foot of the cross representing a penitential Florence and snakes and demons lurking in the subtext of his marvellous *Mystical Nativity*, to indicate the definitive battle still to come.[155] From the mid-sixteenth century comes what is for me one of the most powerful attempts to continue use of the traditional imagery, from the penultimate year of Lorenzo Lotto's life. Living in retirement at Loreto, he painted a picture of the archangel Michael defeating the Devil in which the Devil appears as a more beautiful version of Michael himself. The near-other is

[151]   The theme of Turner's first vortex painting of 1812. The landscape of the Alps as 'characters of the great apocalypse' is also a Wordsworthian theme: *Prelude* VI.570.

[152]   Many painters of the time, such as Benjamin West and William Blake, were influenced by Swedenborg. John Martin attacked much of the morality of the Old Testament, including Abraham's sacrifice of Isaac.

[153]   In his famous *Tower of Babel* of 1563, now in Vienna, Bruegel similarly uses the tower to pass judgement on the economic boom then occurring at Antwerp: R-M. and R. Hagen, *Bruegel* (Cologne: Taschen, 1994), 14–21.

[154]   M. D. Paley, *The Apocalyptic Sublime* (New Haven: Yale University Press, 1986), has an illuminating chapter on Martin (122–54), as well as treatments of some other relevant figures, including Benjamin West, de Loutherbourg, Blake, and Turner.

[155]   For illustrations and commentary, B. Deimling, *Botticelli* (Cologne: Taschen, 1994), 78ff.

here clearly identified as alluring and tempting, precisely because his values and projects are so deceptively close to one's own.[156] But unfortunately the strength of Dürer's example and increasing biblical literalism mean that such penetrating use of the traditional imagery was soon to be merely a feature of the past. Whether artists can ever restore to the imagery the power it once had or whether it has now been for ever relegated to the status of the semi-comic, I do not know.[157] I remain convinced, though, that its imaginative element of self-critique is well worth recovering.

The most common strategy in response to the perceived history of Christianity's past is to recommend the avoidance of all judgement on others, but, if I am right about this more complex history, what is required instead is the recognition that any such judgement must always go with readiness to acknowledge the way in which the person making the judgement is also implicated. The consequences for our reading of Scripture I shall consider in a moment, but first let me illustrate some of the difficulties in the modern retreat from judgement on others. One recent analysis of biblical attitudes to future judgement repeatedly recommends the avoidance of judgement in the present.[158] The resultant stress on concern for the victim is refreshing, but unfortunately it can bring with it distortions of its own. Take that author's own example of those suffering from AIDS.[159] In order to avoid judgement, all sufferers equally are described as 'victims', but would it not be a more challenging gospel to say that, even if the sufferer were maximally culpable in leading a life of extreme promiscuity or in complete disregard for the welfare of others, he or she should still

---

[156] J. Bonnet, *Lorenzo Lotto* (Paris: Adam Biro, 1996), 173–5. The picture was painted in 1545, and of course finds part of its rationale in the notion of Lucifer as beautiful ('Light-bearer').

[157] Perhaps the nearest equivalents in twentieth-century art have come from German Expressionism. Under the influence of Nietzsche, Ludwig Meidner used apocalyptic landscapes as a way of urging the necessity for the Apollonian past to be destroyed, in order that a better (Dionysian) future be created. But, whereas before the First World War this message was entirely directed outwards, from 1916 onwards one finds the message made self-referential and an increasing sense of the importance to his artist of his own religion (Judaism): C. S. Eliel, *The Apocalyptic Landscapes of Ludwig Meidner* (Munich: Prestel, 1989), esp. 17–19, 59, illus. 60, 78.

[158] J. Alison, *Living in the End Times* (London: SPCK, 1997), e.g. 98, 125–6, 149, 153, 156, 157.   [159] Ibid., 158.

receive our care and compassion? Even if there were no prior
expression of penitence, the person is in need, and that should be
sufficient summons to action. The danger otherwise is that not
only will we be constantly searching for redescriptions that turn
people into acceptable victims, but also we will refrain from
judgement when judgement is in fact essential to the proper
conduct of any manageable human life. To continue with the
same illustration, it would be one thing to show compassion
towards sufferers in their need, quite another to help people with
promiscuous attitudes to further their designs. A related problem
is the disturbing way in which Christians can so often be found
refusing judgement in one area where they have some sympathy
and yet being ferociously judgemental in another where antipathy
is strong. But the National Front supporter who is permanently
disabled in a riot surely demands our compassion no less than the
promiscuous AIDS 'victim'. What is needed is greater willingness
to see the complexities of human behaviour that make us all a
mixture of good and evil. The National Front supporter is also
sometimes the victim through poor housing or little chance of a
decent job, just as sometimes contemporary Israelis can be the
oppressors, despite the dreadful things that were endured by some
of their ancestors during the Holocaust.

That is why it seems to me particularly important to acknowledge that Scripture itself has this same strange mixture.[160] It has
nasty sentiments against opponents that need to be faced and
purged, not treated as though they were really something quite
different. Nor will it do to pretend that such sentiments are
confined to the Old Testament. Even some of the finest passages
of Isaiah are tinged by the desire to see Israel's enemies reduced to
slavery, and, if not as extreme as the author of Deuteronomy,
there is still little sense of valuing other peoples in their own
right.[161] Yet, when we turn to the New Testament, the book of
Revelation offers few signs of having moved much beyond such
attitudes. Not only is it assumed that the great mass of pagans will

---

[160] Throughout Alison's discussion, he maintains that his consistently compassionate approach constitutes the various texts' actual meaning. E.g. of Matt. 25:
31 ff we are told that 'this is in no way a description of a future gathering beyond
the grave' (157).

[161] Deut. 20: 16–18; Isa. 41: 11–16; 49: 22–6; 60: 10–14; 61: 5–6.

be subject to dreadful punishments, including perhaps the non-Christian Jews who are called 'the synagogue of Satan' (Rev. 2: 9; 3: 9).[162] even Christian opponents willing to compromise on relations with Roman institutions are accorded similar treatment (Rev. 2: 14–16 and 19–23).[163] Were their faults serious, this might be understandable, but, so far as we can deduce, their position on matters in dispute was not that dissimilar from Paul's.[164] None of this is to deny the presence of numerous passages that offer a powerful critique of Roman society, not least in its economic aspects,[165] but once again we must avoid pretending that justice is the only concern even where the obvious reading is a rather narrow vindictiveness.[166] The introductory seven letters disclose an author willing to indulge in some degree of critique of his supporters,[167] but because he fails to make his subsequent visions sufficiently self-addressed, they lack an important dimension that the later Church was to supply: 'The two-edged sword, after all, might fall on us.'[168] That is why I would not hesitate to describe some later adaptations, such as the artistic examples we considered

---

[162] In the latter verse it is promised that they will 'bow down before your feet' (RSV) in much the same way as Isaiah talks of the Gentiles.

[163] The second passage is unqualified in its narrow vitriol. Cf. 1 John 5: 16, probably to be taken in conjunction with 2: 18 ff., and so further evidence of how unforgiving the biblical church could be.

[164] 'The sum total of the Nicolaitans' offence is that they took a laxer attitude than John to pagan society and religion': G. B. Caird, *Revelation* (London: A. & C. Black, 1966), 38–41, 43–5, esp. 39. Cf. E. S. Fiorenza, *Revelation* (Edinburgh: T & T Clark, 1991), 132–6. Contrast 1 Cor. 6: 12 ff. etc.

[165] R. Bauckham, *The Climax of Prophecy* (Edinburgh: T & T Clark, Edinburgh, 1993), 338–83; J. N. Kraybill, *Imperial Cult and Commerce in John's Apocalypse* (Sheffield: Sheffield Academic Press, 1996).

[166] E.g. P. Richard, *Apocalypse* (Maryknoll, N.Y. : Orbis, 1995): 'The violence in Revelation is more literary than real'(4); 'The function of these texts is not to generate violence or hatred, but rather to express the situation of extreme oppression and suffering that the people of God are experiencing' (31).

[167] Most obviously to Laodicea: 3.15–17.

[168] This is the interpretation actually given to the book itself by Patrick Grant, but I fail to see the evidence for it: *Reading the New Testament* (London: Macmillan, 1989), 108–26, esp. 125. Much wiser in my view was his subsequent admission that in their conception of the making of the ideal city Vergil and Revelation were not unnaturally joined by the later literary tradition: *Personalism and the Politics of Culture* (London: Macmillan, 1996), 47–75, esp. 71 ff.

earlier, as both artistically and morally superior.[169] Not only do they frequently get beyond the rather dry literary character of John's 'visions',[170] much more importantly they are premised on the assumption that all judgement of others must include and be conditioned by self-judgement.

Of course, Rome was in numerous ways wicked, but so too was the author of Revelation in what he desired to happen to the wealthy opponent he labelled 'Jezebel'.[171] Indeed, when we recall that almost certainly he would have condemned Paul, we appreciate that the answer must lie not in wholly endorsing the book's contents, but in the recognition that God does not always speak through perfection but also through human weakness, and so his message today could with as much plausibility come through the promiscuous AIDS sufferer or violent National Front supporter as through the Church representative whose sins will be no less real, even if usually more hidden. The New Testament has much to say on the need for conversion, but much less about the continuing presence of evil in the converted. It is the strength of the Christian imaginative tradition that, once that early enthusiasm of attempting to create the perfect community waned, the artists modified the biblical imagery to offer a more realistic presentation of human nature: one in which the focus of judgement must first and foremost always be directed upon ourselves, for it is only by facing that near-other that we will be enabled to deal with the real evil that also confronts us beyond ourselves. It was thus entirely appropriate that Matthew's passage about the sheep and goats eventually came to be seen entirely in terms of a self-addressed critique.

One further consequence followed from such modifications.

---

[169] The artistic issue is best examined by considering a range of artistic examples, such as are offered in N. Grubb, *Revelations: Art of the Apocalypse* (New York: Abbeyville, 1997). On the whole, literal visual equivalents strike one as strange or quaint rather than awe-inspiring. Contrast, for instance, Turner's fine version of *The Angel Standing in the Sun* with the *Morgan Beatus* manuscript on the same theme: 34–5; or the failed literalism of the Angers Tapestry's Beast from the Sea with its more imaginative treatment of the bleeding sea of the second trumpet: 24, 62.

[170] Their literary character is accepted by Fiorenza, *Revelation* 29. Cf. A. Farrer, *The Revelation of St. John the Divine* (Oxford: Clarendon Press, 1964), 24, 28.

[171] She is to be thrown on her sickbed, and her children struck dead: Rev. 2: 22–3.

Making the imagery self-addressed inevitably brought the desire for its condemnation not to be absolute, but rather conditional on the absence of sufficient signs of repentance, and so whether any particular scenario will occur is seen as entirely provisional. By contrast, although the New Testament fully accepts that the destiny of particular individuals can change through repentance, there is little to indicate that the shape and timing of the last days as a whole is open. The idea is of God himself acting to bring about one particular future, with little or nothing that we do able to affect the issue either way. Indeed, so concerned is the author of the book of Revelation to preclude an alternative future that he even repeatedly informs us that no one will repent (e.g. Rev. 9: 20; 16: 9; 16: 11). There he is in marked contrast to attitudes that emerge in later history, where we find the repeated conviction that the end could indeed be delayed by our actions. So, for instance, what interested John Martin with Belshazzar's feast was the potential judgement it offered on British imperialism, but he did not postulate the inevitability of such a judgement. Again, both Signorelli and Botticelli believed that repentance could produce a different kind of world, one in which no necessity attached to the work of the Antichrist or other demons, just as in the Berengaudus Apocalypse we are constantly made aware that we can create a different future, if only we are prepared to join in commitment to reform of ourselves and of the Church.

One modern writer has remarked on the way in which the novel came into being at precisely the time at which apocalyptic thinking was in retreat, and suggests that part of what was happening was a search for alternative endings.[172] There was still the desire that life should have a structure, even if the structure could no longer plausibly be provided by Scripture. With the decline of communism in Eastern Europe grandiose futures are now out of fashion, though piecemeal strategies had in any case long since usurped their place in the West.[173] Yet something is surely lost unless we are allowed to see both our lives as individuals and our

---

[172] F. Kermode, *The Sense of an Ending* (Oxford: Oxford University Press, 1966), 67, 175–6. He also suggests that tragedy substitutes for the terrors of the end: 27, 30, 84, 88–9.

[173] As in the phrase 'piecemeal engineering', used so effectively in his attack on Marxism by K. R. Popper, *The Open Society and its Enemies* (London: Routledge, 5th edn, 1966), I, 157 ff.

corporate existence as having some sense of direction. Not only is hope essential to the human condition, but any sense of fulfilment is dependent on projects tackled and, if not accomplished in our own lifetimes, at least sown for future generations to reap the benefit. Since, however, I am deliberately confining myself here to the less discussed, more negative side of the traditional picture, this is not the place to attempt even a cursory sketch of what that future might be like. It is though the place to insist that, however characterized, that future must include the new emphases developed within later Christianity, of the more open and undetermined character of the world's future destiny, as well as of Bible and Church in no less need of redemption and transformation than what lies beyond their pale. By that remark I certainly do not intend to imply that God's revelatory hand is weak in Bible and Church, but I do wish to claim that its power is immeasurably weakened if Christians do not acknowledge the presence of evil and corruption even in the presence of what they hold most dear, including of course themselves.

The community of faith will thus only defeat the Beast when through God's grace it comes to full recognition of the presence of the Beast in itself and what it most values. That conclusion, though, has been reached without explicitly considering the Christian tradition's use of the imagery of beasts as such. So I want to end this chapter by examining two such contrasting usages. As we will discover, they nicely anticipate some of the issues that will be considered in the next part of this work.

Means of defeat: Leviathan and Unicorn

I want to end with the imagery of these two beasts, partly because the use to which they were put illustrates so well how thinking does not always proceed by logical inference but sometimes develops imaginatively, simply through symbolic images being put to new uses. But there is also a more particular reason, for that very development reflects precisely the patterns observed in the previous two sections, with the changing treatment of Leviathan reflecting the turn inwards I noted in the immediately preceding section, and some versions of the story of the Unicorn exhibiting the same stress on social interdependence that we found to be one incidental consequence of a strong doctrine of hell. In the Bible, although there are some hints of a more nuanced application, in the main Leviathan is an unqualified symbol of evil. In the ancient world as a whole, though, the related figure of the dragon was given a more ambiguous reference, and it is fascinating to observe this also eventually reflected in some later Christian versions of the legend. Thereby, I shall suggest, the seductive character of evil was more clearly identified, and reflection along the lines already indicated in this chapter endorsed. In the case of the Unicorn, although mistranslation secured its place both in the Vulgate and in the Authorized Version of the Bible, the significant development of its legend is firmly post-biblical. Perhaps that is why two quite different versions struggled for mastery. Both could appeal to biblical precedent, but I shall contend that one captures better than the other the most effective means of characterizing the significance of the incarnation as mutual interdependence.

Leviathan and the ambiguity of evil   Leviathan is one of the beasts we regularly find mentioned in eschatological contexts. The book of Revelation in describing the final battle with a dragon and its two assistants, the monster from the sea and the monster from the land,[174] was thus drawing upon a long-standing tradition of symbolizing the ultimate forces of evil in this way. Indeed, it may well be the most ancient of all forms of representing evil. Certainly, a myth of combat with such a monster occurs in many ancient civilizations,[175] and there seems little doubt that Leviathan is itself an adaptation of the Canaanite seven-headed dragon, Lotan. Originally, however, it was employed to indicate how the powers of chaos were restrained and an ordered world brought into existence; only gradually did it move to a future reference, as a way of mopping up, as it were, what remained of opposition to God. In the Old Testament we also find it used as a symbol of threatening forces in the intervening time, such as hostile

---

[174] For the dragon, Rev. 12: 7 ff.; for the sea and land monsters, 13: 1–18. Though not named, the former is usually identified with Leviathan and the latter with Behemoth.

[175] For a variety of different forms in various Middle-East cultures and possible influence on Greek thought, N. Forsyth, *The Old Enemy: Satan and the Combat Myth* (Princeton, N. J.: Princeton University Press, 1987), 21–89.

empires,[176] and it is that notion of the Beast in some sense already defeated, being defeated and still to be defeated that also informs subsequent, post-biblical usage.

So, for instance, death was sometimes seen as itself the monster, and Christ's descent into hell portrayed as his forcing apart of the jaws of the Beast, in order to set the dead free; in this version Adam was quite often shown as himself leading the way.[177] To contemporary Christians paintings of saints battling in a similar way against dragons can appear merely naïve rather than inspirational, whereas a painting like Uccello's *St George and the Dragon* is in fact drawing on this long-standing tradition of the combat myth to suggest that significant, interim victories over evil are also possible, as the community of faith advances towards the Beast's final defeat.[178] However, because in these combats normally only one individual is involved, such images could easily become dangerously individualistic, hinting, as they do, that final victory might depend on only a few great heroes struggling all by themselves to defeat the enemy.[179] It is fortunate, therefore, that a social dimension is to be found in what appears initially to be one of the strangest aspects of the myth, the idea that on Leviathan's defeat his body will provide a feast for the whole community. All who joined in the fight will share in the final triumph over evil:

> when at God's board
> the saints chew pickled Leviathan.[180]

---

[176] E.g. of Assyria, Ezek. 29: 3–5, of Egypt, Isa. 51: 9–11. For a discussion of these and other such passages, J. Day, *God's Conflict with the Dragon and the Sea* (Cambridge: Cambridge University Press, 1985), 88–139. As in most recent scholarship, the source of the imagery is assumed to be Canaanite rather than Babylonian.

[177] As well as various biblical verses (e.g. Isa. 5: 14, Ps. 22: 21, 1 Peter 5: 8), Scandinavian influence has also been proposed: G. D. Schmidt, *The Iconography of the Mouth of Hell* (Cranbury, N. J.: Associated University Presses, 1995), 24–31.

[178] R. Foster and P. Tudor-Craig, *The Secret Life of Paintings* (Woodbridge, Suffolk: Boydell Press, 1986), ch. 3, esp. 28–35.

[179] Care, though, is needed in interpreting symbolism. In Rev. 12: 7 ff. John mentions other angels, but appears to exclude any human help for Michael. By contrast, Epstein's statue of Michael on the front of Coventry Cathedral, though bereft of any other presence human or angelic, nonetheless clearly intends a reference to the corporate struggle to triumph over evils such as Nazism.

[180] W. H. Auden, 'Tonight at Seven-Thirty': *Thanksgiving for a Habitat* X, 19–20, in *Selected Poems*, ed. E. Mandelson (London: Faber & Faber, 1979), 271.

Auden's evocative image, if not exactly canonical, does at least derive from biblical times.[181]

More directly scriptural is the image of Leviathan as God's plaything (Ps. 104: 26). It is possible that no more is intended than an indication of how powerless evil is before God's majesty and might, and that might also be what lies behind the use of Leviathan in Job. But the latter's fascination with the description of the animal could be read as indicating a more nuanced view: that there was also something attractive in the beast.[182] If so, that approach would accord more closely with attitudes in general in the ancient world, where the image of the Beast is used to indicate the seductive attractiveness of evil, and thus what might give the Beast its real power. In its original Greek usage 'dragon' simply meant a large snake, and there is no shortage of evidence from the ancient world to suggest that snakes were seen as ambiguous: capable of delivering deadly bites but also (because of their ability to slough their skin) viewed as symbols of healing and new life. That ambiguity was also transferred to their larger cousins, the dragons. Chinese, Japanese and Mexican thought are all rich in positive imagery.[183] In this context the Roman fascination with monsters is particularly intriguing. It has been argued that it represented the simultaneous attraction and repulsion of a tightly regulated society that desired to escape the limits imposed upon it, but at the same time acknowledged the necessity of having such restraints. The popularity of combat with wild beasts in the arena therefore functioned as a useful safety-value where that dynamic could be played out without any permanent deleterious consequences for imperial order.[184] Even if the analysis is accepted, no strong underlying

---

[181] 2 Baruch 29: 4–5 envisages the two monsters, Leviathan and Behemoth, providing nourishment for all God's chosen at the last days. The slightly earlier 4 Ezra 6: 52 merely records that God has kept them to feed whom he will.

[182] Job 41: 1–34 can be read as expressing fascination with the crocodile as Leviathan's more natural manifestation.

[183] For Chinese, Japanese, and Mexican attitudes, S. R. Canby, 'Dragons' in J. Cherry (ed.), *Mythical Beasts* (London: British Museum Press, 1995), 14–43, esp. 22–31, 42.

[184] Impressively argued in C. A. Barton, *The Sorrows of the Ancient Romans: The Gladiator and the Monster* (Princeton, N. J.: Princeton University Press, 1993), esp. 29, 36–8, 103, 136, 187. Central to the argument is the way in which growth in their popularity corresponds with an increasingly restrictive exercise of imperial power.

moral dimension could be claimed for such attitudes, but they do at least illustrate how the strange, the disordered, and the inexplicable can at once attract and repel.

Though in worship of the Canaanite god of healing the snake was also used as a positive symbol,[185] it is impossible to establish conclusively any comparable ambiguity in biblical representations of snakes and dragons. The incident during the exodus when an image of a snake is used to effect healing almost certainly was simply a case of apotropaic medicine, while John in alluding to the incident in his Gospel may have intended no more by it than to note the power of the cross to ward off evil and so bring salvation.[186] Even so, it might well better accord with John's theology overall, were the re-applied image allowed to suggest the Saviour sloughing his own skin at the resurrection and thereby bringing new life like the snakes of old.[187] Certainly, in later Christian tradition the capacity for the evil power of dragons to be turned into good is to be observed in the legends of quite a number of the saints.[188] Indeed, it is even true of Uccello's painting to which reference was made earlier, inasmuch as the chain which binds the princess to the dragon looks suspiciously like the pet's lead which it will soon become.[189] The fact that in these modifications to combat stories the taming of evil replaces its destruction suggests the ambiguities inherent in the monster now carried one stage further: what good there is in the Beast can be retrieved. In effect, the ambiguity of evil in the other is thereby fully recognized, just as the attractiveness of the dragon acknowledges similar mixed forces in ourselves.

These ancient Christian legends are in the main strongly optimistic. Quite otherwise is the version of the Leviathan tale that has

[185] The symbol of the snake functions in a similar was for the Canaanite god, Eshmun, as it does for the Greek god of healing, Aesculapius.

[186] Num. 21: 6 ff. is normally read as a case of sympathetic magic. What one makes of John 3.14–15 will depend on how far one sees John as fundamentally inspired by the Old Testament or also by his wider cultural context.

[187] Cf. D. Brown, *The Word To Set You Free* (London: SPCK, 1995), 25–8.

[188] As e.g. in the stories of Blessed Ammon and St Simeon Stylites: H. Waddell, *Beasts and Saints* (1934; London: Darton, Longman & Todd, 1995), 8–11, 20–1.

[189] The original is in the National Gallery, London. For illustration, A. Paolieri, *Paolo Uccello* (Florence: Scala, 1991), 37.

become best-known in recent times, Hermann Melville's novel *Moby-Dick*.[190] Melville leaves us in no doubt that he intends an allusion since the whale in his story is referred to on quite a number of occasions as a leviathan. The central figure of the novel, Captain Ahab, is in pursuit of this particular whale to exact justice from it for the harm it has previously done him, but in the process that very pursuit destroys him, as the evil he projects upon the whale become his own self-destruction. The power of the story is well illustrated by the profusion of visual imagery which it has generated, as indeed by the variety of fresh insights and reflections it has been held to justify, not always compatible with one another.[191] What I find particularly fascinating about the novel, though, is the way in which Melville postulates the eventual destruction of good individuals where their opponent is characterized as wholly bad.

That seems to me the inherent danger in the dominant biblical pattern. Its strength lay in the fact that by objectifying evil as a great monster it clearly acknowledged evil's continuing strength and power.[192] But, precisely because in the biblical version the monster remains wholly other, it fails to force a deeper analysis of the ambiguities in what confronts us or recognition of similar well-springs within ourselves. Earlier I noted the possibility that the description of Leviathan in Job might point to a more complex attitude. If so, that is good, but the more common view is to say that Leviathan is there to put a stop to all questions, with God's creativity underlined as indicative of an absolute power which brooks no challenge.[193] The legends attaching to our other beast,

[190] 'Recent times' because, though published in 1851, it was not until the 1920s that it came to be generally recognized as a masterpiece. The delay can be explained by Melville's ambiguous attitude towards nature and God being out of tune with the optimistic spirit of the Transcendentalism of the time.

[191] For a detailed study, including hundreds of illustrations, E. A. Schultz, *Unpainted to the Last: Moby-Dick and Twentieth Century American Art* (Lawrence, Kansas: University Press of Kansas, 1995). Rockwell Kent stresses the triumph of life in the whale (48–9), Boardman Robinson humanity weighed down (65–6), Jackson Pollock unpredictability (131–4), Frank Stella human vitality (152), and Gilbert Wilson pride's destruction (161 ff.).

[192] Here I part company with Forsyth's view that internalization of the myth is pure gain: e.g. *Old Enemy*, 291, 439–40. The advantage of the myth is the way in which it stresses that evil remains a problem very much larger than ourselves.

[193] Perhaps the most natural way of reading Job 38–42, including their reference to Behemoth and Leviathan in chs. 40 and 41.

the Unicorn, indicate a Church imaginatively dissatisfied with that latter view.

The dependent unicorn   Partly because already in Greek thought its existence was presumed,[194] and partly because the authors of the Septuagint were uncertain as to the identity of one particular animal,[195] a one-horned creature passed into the Vulgate and thus into recitation of the Psalms. Even as late as the seventeenth century the creature was still believed to inhabit more distant parts, and so we find the unicorn in the Authorized Version of the Bible, as well as in Coverdale's translation of the Psalms.[196] How the legend arose that it could only be tamed by a virgin need not concern us here.[197] What does matter is the way in which the animal came to function not only as a symbol for purity,[198] but also of the incarnation itself.

Taking its cue from a passage in Job, the tradition came to speak of the power of Christ being enticed to lie gently in the purity of Mary's breast.[199] Yielding to virginity might not be a fashionable notion for our own age, but, if its wider associations with inno-cence and goodness are allowed to stand, there might still be something important that can be salvaged from the tale. To see what that might be, however, we need to think symbolically,[200] and appreciate in their own right the numerous, beautiful images

---

[194] Ctesias claimed to have seen one in the fifth century BC.

[195] 'Wild ass' or 'oryx' are the most common modern translations of passages such as Num. 24: 8 and Deut. 33: 17, where the strength of the animal is very much stressed.

[196] The belief was reinforced by the conviction of many that they were in possession of such horns. For the historical search and the uses to which they were put, O. Shepard, *The Lore of the Unicorn* (London: George Allen & Unwin, 1930), esp. 101–90.

[197] It appears in the *Physiologus* and so could be as early as the third century: J. Duchaussoy, *Le Bestiaire divin* (Paris: Le Courrier du Livre, 1972), 190–2.

[198] As in a rather fine back panel of 1472 for a painting of Battista Sforza, a tertiary Franciscan and wife of Federico dal Montefeltro: M. A. Lavin, *Piero della Francesca* (London: Thames & Hudson, 1992), 112–15.

[199] 'Will the unicorn be willing to serve thee, or abide by thy crib?' (Job 39: 9. AV). Basil of Caesarea set the precedent for the future by giving an incarna-tional thrust to this passage and calling Christ 'the Son of Unicorns'.

[200] S. Baker, *Picturing the Beast* (Manchester: Manchester University Press, 1993) detects a declining ability to read animal symbolism, and contrasts attitudes in the First World War with those in the Second: 44–55.

that were generated of Christ's power resting in apparent weakness rather than allow ourselves to be distracted by the obvious sexual connotations. The horn is of course a sexual image, but it is there not to speak primarily of sexuality, but rather of the implied power yielded in love. One of the finest examples of the once common genre known as the *Hunt of the Unicorn* is now in the Cloisters Museum in New York. Of its seven tapestries perhaps the most memorable is of the unicorn's powerful and energetic body at ease within a fenced enclosure, the *hortus conclusus* of Mary's body. The suggestion of God's power being mastered by the merely human can of course easily raise anti-Marian hackles, but the image is, I think, misread if it is seen as simply intended to compliment Mary. What is really at stake is the capacity of even divinity itself, despite all its power, to be 'possessed', provided the pursuit is undertaken in the right spirit.

It thus speaks of a dignity given to human beings to seek after and find God (cf. Acts 17: 27). Some will object that the image gives too little attention to the priority of grace. For them much more satisfactory will be the variant form of the iconography to be found in a late fifteenth-century group now in the Cluny Museum in Paris and commonly entitled *The Lady and the Unicorn*. Hitherto thought to be a depiction of the five senses, it has recently been plausibly argued that their theme is in fact the soul's progress, with lion and unicorn vying for mastery but the unicorn wining in the end as it carries off the lion's flag and leaves its mistress holding only its standard.[201] Particularly intriguing is the way in which as the story advances the lady herself comes to adopt one key feature of the unicorn, with her own hairstyle reflecting the unicorn's pointed horn. In an analogous way one of the Rosicrucian classics tells of a lion breaking its sword in two in the presence of a unicorn.[202] Such variants restore the initiative to the unicorn, and so perhaps make it easier to understand how the image could ever have come to be associated with monarchy as a symbol of power: even to this day the British royal standard consists of rampant lion and unicorn.[203]

---

[201] For illustrations and detailed analysis, G. Büttner, *Die Dame mit dem Einhorn* (Stuttgart: Verlag Urachhaus, 1990).

[202] J. V. Andreae, *Die chymische Hochzeit Christiani Rosenkreuz* (reprinted Basel, 1978).

[203] One of the two lions of England was replaced by the unicorn as the emblem of Scotland at the Union of the Crowns under James I and VI.

It is to the latter image that W. H. Auden is closer in his poem *New Year Letter*. Both Leviathan and the unicorn in fact appear. So, while on the one hand reminding us that:

> The average of the average man
> Becomes the dread Leviathan

the poem ends with an address to the unicorn:

> O Unicorn among the cedars,
> To whom no magic charm can lead us,
> .   .   .   .   .   .
> Disturb our negligence and chill,
> Convict our pride of its offence
> In all things, even penitence,
> Instruct us in the civil art
> Of making from the muddled heart
> A desert and a city.[204]

His view of the significance of Leviathan hits, in my view, exactly the right note, and well encapsulates what I argued earlier regarding the development of a more ambiguous beast. With his attitude to the unicorn, though, I remain less happy. Human beings are seen as required to be purely receptive, and indeed Auden informs us that 'only the passive listener hears'. But even the Cluny unicorn had to await the lady's response, while the Cloisters version allows real initiative to Mary. On that scenario what in effect we have is divine power seeking its own calming and domestication, but unsuccessful until the Virgin draws the hitherto unrestrained power into her lap. The translation of such a resonant image into prosaic English can easily suggest the denial of the relevance of divine grace, but I doubt if that was ever the intention. The hint is not only of Mary graced by acquiring a new dignity as a result of the creature in her lap but also God himself. She needs him to shine, but so also does he need her.[205] Mutual dependence is thus asserted, and so the recurring theme of this chapter reaffirmed.

---

[204] W. H. Auden, *New Year Letter* in *Collected Longer Poems* (London: Faber & Faber, 1974 ed.), 120 and 129–30.

[205] The extent of Christ's dependence on others and on his social context is repeatedly affirmed in my *Tradition and Imagination*, esp. Chs. 2 and 6, as also in Ch. 5 of this volume.

The story I have attempted to tell in this chapter is a complex one, but I hope that its basic structure is by now clear. It has taken till modern times for Christians to retreat from the trajectory of hell as a place of eternal punishment, as originally set, particularly by Matthew and the author of the book of Revelation. It took significantly less time to retreat from a purely this-world eschatology. The danger for the modern Church is that in a world which has returned to a conception of ourselves as essentially enmattered, later advances in understanding (with an already existent heaven of 'saints') will simply be jettisoned. Equally, the long history of hell will be seen in purely negative terms without reference to the richer view of social interdependence and the ambiguity of evil that also came with it.

Part One of this volume has been concerned with the general structure of discipleship. In Part Two I want now to go on to consider two specific examples of changes in revelatory understanding, to illustrate how important it is to take account of the historical situatedness of all such discipleship. Each of the two issues can be made to relate to the two beasts with which this chapter ended. With Leviathan I noted the way in which its projection as something unqualifiedly evil gradually gave way to a more ambiguous presentation of both it and ourselves. In Chapter 4 we shall observe how changing treatments of human suffering as mediated through reflections on the Book of Job also gradually move away from purely external accounts towards demands for interior transformation. Likewise, in Chapter 5 we shall observe how the tension already observed in the use of the legend of the unicorn between Mary as purely passive figure or as something more runs right through the history of attitudes to what was involved in her commission and its significance.[206] On the surface so different, what the two issues share in common is the way in which the stories of both Job and Mary were profoundly affected by the impact of changing human experience.

---

[206] To talk of 'the hunt of the unicorn' gave an active role to Mary, whereas the story could all too easily be presented in terms of the unicorn as the real hunter, in search of pure pasture. For one further illustration of this tension between active and passive hunt, see Plate 3 of this book.

PART TWO
The impact of changing experience

IN this part of the book I shall examine two quite different biblical figures, whose treatment over subsequent centuries has diverged considerably from their biblical starting points. Inevitably what happened to one of them—the Virgin Mary, the subject of Chapter 5—is much the better known, but no less dramatic changes occurred in treatments of the story of Job (the topic of the earlier Chapter 4). Linking an undoubted historical figure such as Mary with someone who may never have existed may seem odd,[1] but, though in my discussion of Mary consideration will be given to the extent to which the biblical narratives that concern her are historical, this is not where our primary focus will lie. Rather, I want to use the two figures to illustrate the way in which the biblical narrative, far from closing options, has in the past operated as a powerful stimulus towards new insights into the nature of discipleship, Jewish as well as Christian, particularly in response to changing patterns of human experience. Wider cultural changes mean that suffering has not always been experienced in the same way, and neither has the impact on Christians of the image of Mary.

It seems to me implausible to suggest that the resultant insights derived from the inherent meaning of the text alone. Although, as we shall see, it is possible to identify some promising biblical trajectories, not only was the precise course they eventually took heavily dependent on other factors, sometimes the net result was

---

[1] Ezekiel (14: 14 and 20) links Job with two other ancient worthies, Noah and Daniel, but even if the author of the canonical text intended to refer to the same Job (outside the Bible it is a well attested name), it still would not follow that any of the details of the story had a basis in history.

a critique of the some of original emphases of the biblical text. This is not to deny that text considerable insights of its own, but it is to insist upon its limitations. The book of Job was the indispensable launch-pad in the search for appropriate Jewish and Christian responses to suffering, but it was not to be given the last word, nor in my view should it be. Even when insights from the New Testament are added, important though these are, further reflection was, and is, required. The reader should not misunderstand me. I am not making a point about philosophical approaches to the problem of evil, which in any case would be to judge Scripture by the wrong criteria.[2] What concerns me here is an appropriate religious response to innocent suffering, and the way in which that has changed enormously, as developing human experience opened up new issues and various writers through God's grace were given insight into how suffering could be perceived differently in the light of those changed circumstances.

Similarly, I shall argue that it is only by taking seriously the various contexts in which assertions were made about Mary that we can assess fairly their truth or otherwise. My main reason for taking her as my other example is the huge transformations that have occurred over the centuries in her image, both for the good and for the bad. That very ambiguity will enable me to highlight some of the ways in which a developing tradition can go wrong. What I shall contend is that Mary often functioned by means of a kind of displacement, through, for example, taking on some of the functions of Christ or the Holy Spirit because these had failed to receive adequate expression elsewhere. Even the imagination will be found sometimes compounding the problem rather than giving aid. Nonetheless, what is encouraging is how that history also illustrates the capacity of the developing tradition to correct itself. Virginity refused to be confined as a purely negative image, despite the pressures in that direction, while the continuing battle between representations of Mary as passive or as active ensured that a single model for women never became the exclusive norm. Even so, it was an uphill struggle, since right at the beginning the

---

[2] For my own approach to the philosophical problem, D. Brown, 'The Problem of Pain' in R. Morgan (ed.), *The Religion of the Incarnation* (Bristol: Bristol Classical Press, 1989), 46–59; for a range of approaches, M. M. Adams and R. M. Adams (eds.), *The Problem of Evil* (Oxford: Oxford University Press, 1990).

New Testament presentations tend to treat her, in my view, either as passive instrument or at most representative figure rather than specific individual. Nonetheless, lurking just beneath the surface of the biblical text is a more adequate way of relating to Christ through her. That might suggest a simple return to Scripture, but that is not in fact where my argument will end. There is a need to take seriously the range of experience that has been reflected in reactions to her throughout the course of Christian history, from the Byzantine Pulcheria to the Cistercian Bernard, in Luther no less than Bernadette. These suggest a way of deepening our reading of the significance of the incarnation that allows us not only to make sense of the imaginative expansion of her role in the story of Jesus but also to find permanent significance in their mutual interdependence.

What above all these two present chapters share is the conviction that two thousand years of history (or more in Job's case) require greater realism in the way theologians think about revelation. The idea that a small pocket of time could contain all the answers, even seminally, I find little short of absurd. History invariably throws up new ways of viewing our experience, and what has given Christianity its strength over the centuries is not mere repetition of the past but an ability to respond to new circumstances in new ways. New understandings of virtue and particular providence (Job), or of family indebtedness and virginity as empowerment (Mary), are but a few of the issues which the following pages will raise. Yet, while I regard each of my examples as significant, the more general question should not be forgotten: whether, cumulatively, they do not argue for a different way of conceiving revelation and the relation of the Christian faith to its foundational texts.

4

Job and innocent suffering

As already noted, our concern here will not be so much with the so-called problem of evil and its more technical philosophical or theological resolution, as with religious attitudes, with how believers have chosen to face the onslaught of unmerited suffering, and in particular with what the practice of discipleship has meant in such a context. The Book of Job represents one such response, but it is by no means the only possible reaction. Throughout much, if not most, of subsequent Jewish and Christian history Job has in fact functioned less as a text with a specific meaning and more as a handle for investigating alternative responses. More recent Christian writing has tried to reinstate a presumed original intention, but that has in my view brought impoverishment rather than enrichment. To see why, I propose to trace the discussion historically, from the canonical Job through *The Testament of Job*, Gregory the Great, Aquinas, Calvin, and Blake. What I hope to demonstrate is that these later and often much despised interpretations do sometimes constitute significant advances on the canonical text, and that the Christian community today is the poorer if in its response to innocent suffering it is not allowed to build upon these rewritings of Job's story. However, first we need to set the canonical work in its own context of revolt against earlier approaches.

Setting the context: alternative responses

In order to set the canonical book in its proper context we need first to look, more generally, at how the issue of suffering is viewed in the Old Testament. Though there are some references to an alternative perspective such as testing or purgation (e.g. Gen. 22: 1; Deut. 8: 2–3; Isa. 48: 10), overwhelmingly the picture that emerges is one of blessing or reward answering to obedience or righteousness, and punishment to its opposite, sin.[1] Within that frame Paul's reading of Genesis 2–3, particularly as this was filtered later through Augustine, makes Christians immediately think of original sin and its devastating consequences (Rom. 5: 12–21),[2] but in fact nowhere in the Old Testament outside of these opening chapters is appeal made to this explanation, still less to a theory on such a grand scale as Paul and Augustine were to make of it. After all, in itself the passage only tells us that the labour of man and woman will get more difficult (3: 16–19), not that any predisposition to evil on the part of their children would also follow. Almost as little evidence exists to suggest that humanity was generally conceived to have supernatural forces ranged against it. Certainly talk of Satan as an independent, evil power is late,[3] and the identification of the serpent with the Devil even later.[4] However, occasionally we do find the sea-monster Leviathan personified as a supernatural source of evil (Isa. 27: 1; 51: 9–10; Job 7: 12; 26: 12). Yet, that is but a small qualification to the general pattern: explanation is sought within the actions of human beings themselves.

The most common pattern is social rather than individual. This is illustrated by the repeated threats and promises of the prophets, where the fate of the nation as a whole is at stake. It is also to be found in much of the historical writing. Deuteronomy alternates promises and threats upon the community as a whole, while in Kings we have as a repeated refrain, as monarch succeeds

---

[1] Although 'blessing' indicates that the initiative remains with God, the link is so often made that in practice from the human perspective 'reward' was perhaps the normal way in which the relation was seen.

[2] For the differences between Paul's thought and Augustine's, N. P. Williams, *The Ideas of the Fall and Original Sin* (London: Longman, 1927), esp. 123–57, 36–84; D. E. H. Whiteley, *The Theology of St. Paul* (Oxford: Blackwell, 1970), 50–3.

[3] In Job 1: 6–2: 7 and Zech. 3: 1–3, though acting as 'devil's advocate' he is still part of the heavenly court; it is only in 1 Chron. 21: 1 that Satan is made personally responsible for evil, replacing 'the anger of the Lord' of 2 Sam. 24: 1.

[4] Though some argue the other way, that the Genesis tale is an origin story demythologized, with the serpent turned into one of God's creatures; cf. G. von Rad, *Genesis* (London: SCM Press, 1972), 87–8.

monarch, the havoc caused by God's anger at their sins 'by which they made Israel to sin'.[5] Normally, it is the community immediately in view that is seen as the object of punishment or reward, but occasionally this is transferred to a subsequent generation, most conspicuously in the case of the Ten Commandments (Exod. 20: 5); here the effect is negative, but a more positive result is not unknown.[6] Since this is in some ways a natural extension of the concept of social responsibility (that guilt attaches to whatever unit—nation, tribe, or family—acts together), one might have thought that the notion would have occurred more frequently in Scripture than in fact it does. Presumably the reason why it does not is because an explanation is then required as to why the appropriate punishment is delayed, while those most closely involved appear to escape.

The irony is that, had such a general theory been maintained at full force, then it is unlikely that of itself it could ever have come under pressure as an explanation. Whatever disaster happened, this could always have been attributed to the wrongs of a previous generation, and the problem of innocent suffering might thus never have reached consciousness. In a similar way Hinduism has been prevented from ever raising anything analogous to the Western issue by its doctrine of karma, with someone suffering in the present always capable of explanation in terms of the punishment due from a presumed evil earlier life. Yet the apparently unassailable theory did break down, perhaps because loosening of social ties caused by sharper differences in wealth, a divided monarchy, and so forth made strong notions of corporate responsibility increasingly difficult to sustain. At all events, though the notion of punishment applying to families rather than individuals is found in a number of places in the Old Testament (e.g. Num. 16: 25–33; 2 Sam. 21: 6 and 9; Est 9: 13; Dan. 6: 24), it is interesting to observe that in one case where divine approval for such a connection can most easily be deduced from the context (Josh. 7: 25), the Septuagint omits the reference to the perpetrator's

---

5 For Deuteronomy e.g. 28–30; for Kings, e.g. 1 Kings 16: 12–13.
6 For example, Abijam is treated kindly for the sake of his ancestor, David: 1 Kings 15: 1–5. Although I think it unlikely, 'to the third and the fourth generation' of Exod. 20: 5 could possibly refer to several generations under the one roof rather than to punishment exacted at a later time and on subsequent generations.

family also being included in the burning and stoning.[7] That later reading probably represents a rival Hebrew tradition about what it was appropriate to attribute to a hero like Joshua, the administrator of the punishment, far less God himself. If so, the emendation may be read as implicit endorsement of the prophet Ezekiel's critique of more corporatist notions in his ringing declaration of individual responsibility: 'The soul that sinneth, it shall die' (Ezek. 18 and 33: 10 ff.; esp. 18: 20 AV). Yet that runs parallel in his writings with a continuing acceptance of the fact that in God's act of judgement against the land, the righteous will suffer, no less than the guilty (e.g. 21: 3 ff.). In trying to comprehend such tensions in his thought some Old Testament scholars have suggested that the general idea was not so much one of direct divine action as of the working out of the internal consequences of nature or of history,[8] but this seems to me to put the issue too much in modern dress. In a world without a clear conception of natural law or historical process, inevitably everything was seen as directly under the hand of God, however mediated, and so what these contrasting verses in my view represent is Ezekiel being pulled, inconsistently, in two different directions.

It is in any case a simplistic understanding of history to suppose that one account ever totally displaces another; they can often run side by side for centuries. This is something which we shall observe in some detail later, but in the interim one need only reflect on the way in which even today those affected by serious illness often first seek some causal explanation in terms of a fault requiring punishment. So, similarly, we should not think that the greater prominence given to individual punishment ever totally displaced the earlier social view. However, stress on individual responsibility did generate some obvious, immediate difficulties. The confidence, for instance, of some of the psalms in a direct equation between prosperity and merit (e.g. Ps. 37, esp. 1–2 and 25) contrasts sharply with others which express reservations or even doubt. Psalm 73 has sometimes

---

[7] Burning had already been mentioned at verse 15; so this cannot be used as an argument against the originality of the second half of verse 25, where Achan's family are specifically included in his punishment.

[8] E.g. K. Koch, 'Is there a doctrine of retribution in the Old Testament?' in J. L. Crenshaw (ed.), *Theodicy in the Old Testament* (London: SPCK, 1983), 57–87.

been interpreted in the light of Israel's subsequent religious history, with belief in the after-life seen as endorsed, or appeal made to the value of some powerful religious experience,[9] but it is hard to read it naturally in any other way than as written by someone who initially hesitates over such a direct correspondence between sin and punishment, only finally to yield to its endorsement.[10]

But perhaps nowhere is confidence in such correspondence more explicitly asserted than by the author of Chronicles who argues back from general principle to how the story must now be told.[11] The wicked seventh-century king Manasseh had reigned for fifty-four years, while good King Josiah died on the battlefield of Megiddo in 609 BC, aged a mere thirty-nine. Whereas the author of Kings simply records these exceptions to his theology without explanation (2 Kings 21: 1–17; 23: 29–30), the Chronicler argues that Manasseh must in reality have repented in order to have enjoyed such a long reign, and Josiah must really have done something wrong to have suffered such a tragically early death. The result is the provision of a divine command that was disobeyed in the latter case, and a prayer of penitence in the former (2 Chron. 35: 21–2; 33: 12). A further consequence was the composition of the moving and beautifully balanced Prayer of Manasseh that is to be found in the Apocrypha. The fact that it was never uttered is of course irrelevant to its merits as a prayer.

What this brief survey surely indicates is the lack of either consistency or any clear pattern of development in Old Testament attitudes. Though himself not entirely consistent, Ezekiel appears to be rejecting a position that is to be found in a near contemporary, the author of Kings.[12] Yet it is a position to which Chronicles

---

[9] For former, A. Weiser, *The Psalms* (London: SCM Press, 1962), 505–16; for latter, W. Eichrodt and R. J. Williams in Crenshaw, *Theodicy*, 33–4 and 50–1.

[10] Contrast v. 2 and 16–20.

[11] We can certainly infer from this that the author did not find the Kings version edifying or instructive for his readers. Whether he would have drawn a stronger historical inference that therefore the events did not happen this way is harder to say. He might have thought them a rare exception to the pattern of divine action; alternatively, since his own text allows of no exceptions, he may have deduced the stronger claim.

[12] M. Noth proposed a date *c.* 550, F. M. Cross two recensions, the first *c.* 620: F. M. Cross, *Canaanite Myth and Hebrew Epic* (Cambridge, Mass.: Harvard University Press, 1973), 274–89; M. Noth, *The Deuteronomistic History* (Sheffield: University of Sheffield Press, 1981).

returns several centuries later in a more intensified form, with the kings certainly punished for their sins but those sins also bringing retribution on the nation as a whole. Throughout most of subsequent Jewish and Christian history theologians in the two communities have continued to try to apply such answers, and even as late as the twentieth century at least one distinguished historian attempted to interpret the two world wars in categories of divine judgement.[13] Though Job challenges any such close connection between suffering and providence as reward or punishment, as we shall see, it was to take many centuries before the possibility of more plausible, alternative connections came to be acknowledged. The authority of these earlier approaches, I would suggest, therefore lies not in any of their specific answers but in legitimating the search for a deeper understanding of the divine will.

The Book of Job: rival readings

The basic structure of the book is too well known to require more than a brief reminder here. In the opening prose section, at the suggestion of Satan who functions here as an angel in God's court, Job, 'a blameless and upright man' (Job 1: 8 RSV), is made subject to numerous disasters. In the poetry sections which then follow Job, unaware of Satan's machinations, argues with his three friends and a later, younger arrival, Elihu, over the cause of his misfortune. Job continues to protest his innocence, while the others seek for some cause in past misconduct. Finally, God speaks from the whirlwind (38–41), Job repents of challenging God's designs (42: 1–6), and in a final prose section has all his material possessions more than amply restored to him. Yet, while discussion of the issue in this form will be new to the canon, no matter how early or late the book is assigned, it can by no means claim to be the first detailed treatment in the Near East of the religious issues raised by suffering. Already in the second millennium the topic was being raised among Israel's neighbours,[14] and while the Egyptian paral-

---

[13] H. Butterfield, *Christianity and History* (London: Collins, 1957), 67–91.

[14] For examples V. H. Matthews and D. C. Benjamin (eds.), *Old Testament Parallels* (New York: Paulist Press, l99l), 201–24.

lels are not particularly close,[15] one Babylonian document (variously called 'The Babylonian Theodicy' or 'The Sufferer and the Friend') has the same dialogue structure, and another ('Babylonian Job') is seen by some as the inspiration behind the first, prose version in the Hebrew Bible.[16] That is important to acknowledge, as questions do not arise out of thin air, but from specific cultural contexts: for instance, the absence of belief in immortality as a form of compensation in earlier Babylonian thinking exerted a pressure towards further reflection which was absent from Egypt. Scholars continue to dispute if and how the text grew but, fortunately, that is a matter that need not concern us here. Job's complaints would lack the power of specificity without the opening prose section; so we can be sure that, even if from a different author, the poetry was intended to expand upon the basic prose plot.[17]

The fundamental issue that needs to be addressed is how God's answer from the whirlwind was intended to function, and so what kind of attitude it was supposed to evince on the part of the believer. Three types of answer may usefully be distinguished: that it was intended to put an end to further debate; that it spoke of a type of God in respect of whom such questions were inappropriate; and that a specific answer was after all given, in a particular type of reassuring experience. Such answers could of course be complementary rather than mutually exclusive, but for the purposes of analysis it will be easier to consider them separately in turn. As will emerge, I want to challenge the adequacy of all three as answers, as well as in large part, if not entirely, their correctness as accounts of authorial intention. Nonetheless, my objective is not wholly negative since in so doing I hope to indicate why there was a certain naturalness to subsequent developments.

An end to further debate?

In the late twentieth century there was much talk of the impossibility of a post-Auschwitz theodicy, and theologians and continental

---

[15] For possible reasons, R. J. Williams, 'Theodicy in the Ancient Near East' in Crenshaw, *Theodicy*, esp. 47–8.

[16] Cf. N. H. Snaith, *The Book of Job* (London: SCM Press, 1968), 19–33.

[17] For similar views, cf. J. G. Janzen, *Job* (Atlanta: John Knox Press, 1985), 23.

philosophers were quick to reprimand analytic philosophers for the inappropriateness of continuing to raise the problem of evil.[18] In the context of such a debate it is tempting for those opposed to analytic treatments to view the Book of Job as a natural ally, but is this so? To begin with, it would seem odd to postulate that a text that explores issues without restraint should itself have as its primary message the impropriety of any such similar unrestrained investigation. To quote the old proverb, what is sauce for the goose should also be sauce for the gander! Admittedly, even biblical scholars unsympathetic to the text sometimes draw the same conclusion. Crenshaw, for instance, declares that 'Job's silent submission before an awesome display of power amounts to loss of integrity' and 'an argument against humanity'.[19] But the problem with such an interpretation is that, while it does much to explain the four chapters of God's concluding speech from the whirlwind, it leaves unresolved the great mass of the poem. Could someone who thought the questioning and challenging of God's purposes inappropriate really have allowed his pen unlimited license over the previous thirty or so chapters? After all, it is not as though they are polite challenges; in the eyes of many they border on the blasphemous, and, if so, the author of Job in writing them must be subject to the same accusation.[20]

It is fortunate, therefore, that other commentators have suggested a very different approach: that, so far from intending to stem the tide of any further debate, the author's wish was to secure permanent openness to further discussion. A modest version of this thesis is supported by David Clines and Donal O'Connor who speak of 'bipolarity' or 'two different levels of intentionality' in the conclusion.[21] The effective rebuke to both Job and his friends

---

[18] E.g. P. Ricoeur, *The Symbolism of Evil* (Boston, Mass.: Beacon, 1969), 314–15; K. Surin, *Theology and the Problem of Evil* (Oxford: Blackwell, 1986), 26–7.   [19] Crenshaw, *Theodicy*, 6.

[20] Certainly, the author leaves us in no doubt that the objections of the friends have been overruled. What is less clear is whether Job's own complaints have been satisfactorily answered, and, in particular, whether in allowing the complaint and debate once to have been pursued at such length similar discussions and complaints are not thereby implicitly legitimated.

[21] D. J. A. Clines, *Job* (Waco: Word Biblical Commentary, 1989), xxxix; D. O'Connor, *Job, His Wife, His Friends and His God* (Dublin: Columba Press, 1995), 156–7.

(seen in Job's repentance and God's admonition of his friends, 42: 1–7) means that two responses are in fact possible to the text: one which takes silent acceptance as the proper answer to God's words from the whirlwind, and the other which continues to legitimate all that questioning and challenging which Job continuously hurls against God in his frustration and anger.

David Penchansky goes even further. For him 'conflicting voices in the book of Job clamour to be heard. Most readings of Job are deficient because they attempt to harmonise, compelling the book to say only one thing. Job embodies a powerful example of the disparate text, an act of literature that is characteristically unstable, a place of conflict.'[22] That is why, he argues, there is so much dissonance in the book: a pagan setting for a Jewish writing;[23] a Job who is both pious and rebellious, perhaps blasphemous; an answer that is no answer; and so on.[24] Even the prologue is hardly as clear as it is often taken to be, since already in its opening chapter any automatic association of suffering with retribution has been called into question.[25] Indeed, it is possible to carry Penchansky's point about the prologue further, since, despite the frequency with which commentators lambaste the *naïveté* of the God who yields to Satan's challenge,[26] it is hard not to read this element in the story except as a very effective critique of the God who does finally emerge from the whirlwind, who is no less arbitrary. Penchansky, though, in my view goes too far in suggesting that the author intended no answer at all to the problem of evil, and a wholly open concept of God.[27] Yet it is surely not implausible to suggest some shared features with the fashionable deconstructionism of our own day, in the author's implicit questioning of the finality of his own answer, no less than that of others.

This kind of open interpretation is one which has also been elaborated by Gerald Janzen and Walter Reed,[28] the latter in

[22] D. Penchansky, *The Betrayal of God: Ideological Conflict in Job* (Louisville, Kentucky: Westminster, 1990), 9.

[23] As in the opening verse, probably a reference to Edom.

[24] Penchansky, *Betrayal*, 32–4, 31 and 47, 71.

[25] Ibid., 38. Cf. Job 1: 21.

[26] E.g. N. C. Habel, *Job* (London: SCM Press, 1985), 85: 'a deity unwilling to avoid a challenge and driven by a desire to be right at all costs'.

[27] Habel, *Job*, 70–86.

[28] Janzen, *Job*; W. L. Reed, *Dialogues of the Word* (New York: Oxford University Press, 1993), ch. 4.

particular asserting that 'it is not too much to claim that Job offers a critique of the Hebrew Bible as a whole'.[29] The point is that it is possible to detect parodies of all three of Israel's major traditions. Thus, it is not just the aspirations to knowledge of the Wisdom tradition that are mocked in the friends' speeches, there is even a direct parody of Psalm 8.[30] Again, not only does Job make a recurring appeal to some form of legal settlement between him and his Maker, he wants an alternative to the laws inscribed on the tablets at Sinai: 'Oh, that my words were written! Oh, that they were inscribed in a book! Oh, that with an iron pen and lead they were graven in the rock for ever! (Job 19: 23–4 RSV)'[31] Finally, even the prophetic tradition is implicitly assailed, with the last arrival, Elihu, a thinly veiled version of Israel's archetypal prophet, Elijah (they are both variants of the same name), and, as if to confirm this fact, Elihu is the only one of the four friends to claim to speak under divine inspiration (e.g. Job 32: 8 and 18–22).[32] Reed's final judgement on the book is therefore the need for continuing 'dialogic cross-talk'.[33] Readers will vary in their estimate of how convincing they find such an analysis, but the fact that the poetic sections even permit such an interpretation surely argues for a more open-ended approach.

But, if that is a conclusion that may be drawn from the poetry, more surprisingly perhaps, a similar inference is also possible from further reflection on the prose. For, if the poetry is the attempt to translate into more abstract terms what was already a piece of haggadah, why may that haggadic tradition not continue in fresh attempts to tell a plausible story that will help human beings to make sense of their lives?[34] Haggadah of its very nature continues to evolve, and so with the images of this story 'overdetermined,

---

[29] Reed. *Dialogues*, 120.   [30] In Job 7. Note esp. vs. 17–18.

[31] Even with the allusion to Sinai accepted, it might still be argued that he wants his words added to Sinai rather than in competition with them, but against is the absence of explicit reference to Job as obedient to the Law.

[32] Against might seem to be the way in which Elihu opens his speech with verbose preliminaries (32.6–22), but, if a parody is being attempted, then some unfair comparisons might be exactly what one would expect.

[33] Reed, *Dialogues*, 138.

[34] The argument of Leslie Fielder, 'Job' in D. Rosenberg (ed.), *Congregation: Contemporary Writers Read the Jewish Bible* (San Diego: Harcourt Brace Jovanovich, 1987), 331–45, esp. 340 ff.

polysemous, finally inexhaustible'[35] it was perhaps inevitable that the story would continue to be rewritten, even if at one level it does look as though the poetry intended to call curtains (in the divine speech). In short, although an answer of sorts was attempted, the final shape of the book as a whole argues for a quite different conclusion: the legitimacy of continuing exploration.

A God beyond questioning?

A second major strand in interpreting God's answer from the whirlwind comes in the supposition that what is presented within the speech is a type of God in respect of whom the questions raised earlier should now be seen as inappropriate. On this view God's character is beyond the good and evil in terms of which the dialogue has hitherto been structured. One recent advocate of this approach comments:

The book represents a critique of the human, all-too-human effort to see the world in purely 'moral' terms, or to imagine that the world and its God are under obligations analogous to the obligations human beings bear towards each other in this vale of beauty and calamity . . . The obligations of morality are obligations *we* are under; if God himself is under obligations we cannot know what they are. But we can see the goodness in the world he creates and rules.[36]

These remarks come from a philosopher, but similar sentiments are to be found in many a biblical scholar. Norman Habel, for instance, writes:

God freely chose to bless Job with good, just as he chose to afflict him with evil. Job experienced the freedom of God by being afflicted even though innocent and by being blessed even after defying God and accusing him of being demonic. The integrity of Job and God is confirmed, but integrity has taken on a new meaning that transcends conformity to a mechanistic moral or natural law of reward and retribution . . . God creates the space in his order for the freedom of humans and the freedom

---

[35] Ibid., 342.
[36] J. T. Wilcox, *The Bitterness of Job* (Ann Arbor: University of Michigan Press, 1989), 223–4. Author's italics.

of God, for the integrity of mortals and the integrity of God . . . Job, like God, comes to transcend the moral order by his innocent suffering.[37]

As a final example, consider Dermot Cox. Arguing that the real focus of the book is not suffering but the nature of God,[38] he comes to the conclusion that the God who is revealed

is a poet, an artist for whom suffering is a necessary catalyst for creativity . . . A world in which no lion killed to survive, in which no eagle soared in dispute of the laws of logic, would not be a world of wonder. Only one who believes that a 'perfect' and 'reasonable' world existed, a world in which everything could be explained and fitted together like a jigsaw, could formulate the principle that a just God could not be responsible for suffering. But there is a different kind of God: the one Job meets in the theophany—the divine poet.[39]

In one sense these commentators are of course right. Those key chapters evince no concern with morality; instead they speak of a God of mysterious and at times puzzling creativity, as in their depiction of the ostrich (39: 13–18). The references to God's control over the two monsters Behemoth and Leviathan might possibly be read as moral control, given the way that Leviathan in particular functioned in Israel's history as a symbol of evil (Job 40: 15–41: 10),[40] but the difficulty with such a contention is that, if so, this is nowhere implied, far less explicitly stated. In short, though the analogy of God as the unsympathetic ringmaster responding to the uncomprehending clown is too harsh,[41] at the very least it must be conceded that morality has been demoted onto quite another level.

Yet, even if valuable insights into the character of divine creativity can be salvaged from the speech, the question still needs to be asked whether the price paid has not been too high. In brief, the problem is that the presentation seems to demean both God

---

[37] N. Habel, *Job*, 60–9, esp. 67–9.

[38] D. Cox, *Man's Anger & God's Silence* (Slough: St. Paul's, 1990), 21–31, esp. 25–9. [39] Ibid., 126–7.

[40] For a discussion of the role of Leviathan more generally, the final section of chapter 3 of this work.

[41] The analogy is E. Swados' in 'Job: He's a clown' in C. Bushmann and C. Spiegel (ed.), *Out of the Garden: Women Writers on the Bible* (London: HarperCollins, 1994, 204–20).

and humanity. God is demeaned because it ceases to be clear why we should call him 'good', and that affects not just his moral status but also his worship, since worship means 'worth-ship'. Likewise, humanity is demeaned because by definition the range of possible relations with God is reduced. For human freedom, creativity and love are all subject to moral assessment; yet none of these find mention in the divine speech. Biblical scholars in their commentary on the text frequently expand the passage in some such way, but the truth must be admitted that in the defining speech of the book they find no such place, and as such it remains woefully inadequate. The passage cries out for some expression of concern for humanity if worthiness for worship is to be sustained, and this is in fact what we find later versions of the tale attempting to provide.[42] So, while I tend to agree that the author's main response lay in terms of an acceptance of the ultimate mysteriousness of God, it was his failure to integrate that sense of mystery with any notion of how this relates to the goodness of God that ensured continuing exploration of the issue. The tension had to achieve a more satisfactory resolution.

Ironically, whether intentionally or otherwise, the author is better at exploring a deeper sense of human morality than he is of divine. In theory, the plot requires that Job be of unimpeachable innocence, but in practice what we find are quite a number of hints to the contrary, and it is the tension between the two which helps generate a debate that will run for centuries, thereby deepening Jewish and Christian moral reflection. It seems, therefore, a particular pity to me that René Girard should have chosen to extend his influential theory of the scapegoat to this book, thereby reinforcing the modern tendency to read the plot in black and white terms.[43] While there are some superficial similarities to the classical notion of the scapegoat, as in Job's once universal popularity succeeded by

---

[42] It might be argued that these objections are mitigated by Job 1–2 and 28.12 ff. Yet neither passage seems to me to exhibit deep concern, while both are widely regarded as being from other hands. For the latter, G. von Rad, *Wisdom in Israel* (London: SCM Press, 1972), 148 ff.

[43] Girard's two key works are *The Scapegoat* (London: Athlone Press, 1986) and *Things Hidden since the Foundation of the World* (London: Athlone Press, 1987); an excellent survey is provided by J. G. Williams, *The Bible, Violence and the Sacred* (San Francisco: Harper, 1991).

universal loathing (Job 29: 2–25 and 19: 13–19),[44] its application in this specific case founders on lack of evidence. There is nothing, for instance, to suggest that his friends needed someone to blame for something or that they were envious of his previous status. Girard praises the text for giving us a 'privileged tool of demystification',[45] in allowing us to see the process at work, but significantly to establish this he has to deny that the divine speech is any proper part of the original text;[46] yet, linguistically, there is nothing to indicate that this might be so. Much wiser is one of his expositors who draws a rather different message, 'whether or not they are additions': that they warn against any 'transcendent amorality or new "higher morality" ' as just as insidiously destructive of the value of the individual as the older threats of social conformity.[47]

Although they are only hints, there is some evidence to suggest that the author viewed Job in a more ambiguous light than most modern readings tend to suppose. Very occasionally, even Job himself appears to doubt his own innocence. Most translations indicate only a slight wavering at 9: 20–2, but the Jerusalem Bible may be right in indicating something more substantial: 'Though I think myself right, his mouth may condemn me; though I count myself innocent, it may declare me a hypocrite. But am I innocent after all? Not even I know that.' Also to be noted is the fact that if we carefully distinguish poetry and prose as from different hands, then further ambiguity arises. For in the poetry God fails to endorse Job from the whirlwind, while in the concluding prose section the reprimand to the friends[48] could be read as a reference back to the opening prose section alone where Job accepts his misfortune from the hand of God unlike the friends who had failed to say anything (Job 1: 21 and 2: 13; cf. 'not spoken').

But in many ways more interesting are the ambiguities inherent in the portrayal of Job himself. Take his attitude to his wife. From 19: 17–22 we learn that his physical maladies make him repulsive to his wife. Yet, while he laments that fact as part of the catalogue of his own misfortunes, nowhere does he speak with sympathy of

---

[44] R. Girard, *Job the Victim of his People* (Stanford, Cal.: Stanford University Press, 1987), 3–13.   [45] Ibid., 38; cf. 100, 108.
[46] Ibid., 101–3.   [47] Williams, *Bible*, 175–8.
[48] 'You have not spoken to me what is right, as my servant Job has': Job 42: 7 RSV.

her lot, now presumably enduring comparable poverty; nor indeed does he enter into her sense of loss over her children. Instead, in his defence against the charge of adultery, he wishes humiliation on her, not himself: 'If my heart has been enticed by a woman or I have lain in wait at my neighbour's door, may my wife be another's slave, and may other men enjoy her' (Job 31: 9–10 NEB).[49] Some commentators try to mitigate the evil by speaking of 'a conception of solidarity strange to us',[50] but, though there was certainly a difference of attitudes,[51] it is hard to believe that any society would endorse the integrity of someone who exonerated himself so totally from any punishment falling directly upon himself.[52] Indeed, the passage opens with such an emphatic declaration of sexual purity that one cannot help wondering whether something rather different is being said between the lines, whether deliberately or not: 'I have come to terms with my eyes, never to take notice of a girl' (Job 31: 1 NEB). Though elements of Judaism did fall into the prudery that so damaged the history of Christianity, it would be odd if it were being endorsed here, when the text as a whole shows such little interest in the observance of law. That later tradition felt it necessary to reflect more deeply on Job's wife should therefore occasion us no surprise.

Another puzzling element in his conduct is his attitude to the poor. There is much in Job's speeches that speak of apparent concern for the poor and marginalized, among whom Job now numbers himself. This has even led the doyen of Liberation theologians, Gustavo Gutiérrez, to interpret the book with that concern as its primary focus.[53] But, while Job is quick to blame God for his neglect of the poor (e.g. 24: 4–12), he fails to acknowledge his own

---

[49] It could be argued that the following two verses allow some impact on himself, with his adultery seen as calling into question his posterity (cf. RSV). But, not only is it unclear whether this is the meaning, some commentators, including the NEB editors, also doubt whether the verses are original.

[50] J. H. Eaton, *Job* (Sheffield: Sheffield Academic Press, 1985), 21.

[51] For another example, cf. Judges 19: 1–30 and P. Trible's comments in *Texts of Terror* (London: SCM Press, 1984), 65–91.

[52] At most one might claim that he saw dishonour to his wife as punishment on himself. But it is hard to fill this out in an acceptable way without appealing to modern romantic notions of love which are not even hinted at in the text. The loss seems to be more one of personal honour or self-esteem.

[53] G. Gutiérrez, *On Job: God-Talk and the Suffering of the Innocent* (Maryknoll, N. Y.: Orbis, 1987).

faults. His pride in his own generosity to the poor is described at length (e.g. 31: 16–40). Yet, significantly, in one isolated verse (which Gutiérrez fails to discuss) a rather different picture emerges. Talking perhaps of the ancient equivalent of travellers or gypsies he remarks: 'But now they make sport of me, men who are younger than I, whose fathers I would have disdained to set with the dogs of my flock' (Job 30: 1 RSV). It is hardly enough to make us side with Eliphaz's accusations against him (22: 6–9), still less to speak of an authorial intent to undermine Job's pretensions; the mention is after all so casual, and may well reflect the author's own limitations on charity. But it is one of a number of indications of smugness or self-satisfaction that was to set later tradition on a more profound course of moral reflection than the book itself offers.[54] However much justified, the overweening pride that we find Job displaying in his erstwhile achievements thus secured a very different analysis of morality. Chapter 29, for instance, would be an acceptable eulogy for a saint, but scarcely from the person's own mouth.[55] Turning away from the book's wholly externalist account (in terms of deeds), later tradition looked more deeply into the heart. An altogether higher plane was thus secured, and while a great contemporary spiritual writer like Cardinal Martini can pretend that it is from the Book of Job that his own reflections derive (that lack of self-knowledge lies at the root of all sin),[56] we must pronounce otherwise. The text made the trajectory necessary, but the real achievement was still to come.

An answer in human experience?

It remains now to deal with the last of the three common interpretations of God's words from the whirlwind, that the intention was after all to give some kind of answer in terms of human

[54] Even if such attitudes would have been regarded as morally acceptable at the time of the book's composition, and so in some sense my critique could be said to be anachronistic, it still indicates well why further developments were virtually inevitable.

[55] The chapter begins with the consequences of his friendship with God, but ends in a rather revolting self-satisfaction at being the constant object of others' admiration. E.g. 'they waited for me as for the rain' (v. 23 RSV).

[56] C. M. Martini, *Perseverance in Trials: Reflections on Job* (Collegeville, Minnesota: Liturgical Press, 1992), e.g. 36–8, 67–80, 84–6.

experience of the divine. This has been a repeated pattern of explanation both in earlier times, and throughout the twentieth century, something that is well illustrated by one collection of articles where the theme recurs in contributions from Arthur Peake in 1904, Oesterley and Robinson in 1934, and H. H. Rowley in 1963.[57] Here, for instance, is Peake's comment:

It is the vision of God that has released him from his problem. His suffering is as mysterious as ever, but, plain or mysterious, why should it vex him any longer? He has seen God, and has entered into rest . . . The soul's certainty is the soul's secret . . . If we know God, no other knowledge matters.[58]

Nor is this a peculiarly English approach. Walther Eichrodt comments in similar terms

The freedom of the creator, which is strongly emphasised, is no cruel caprice . . . It includes a mysterious inner bond between the creator and the creation, on account of which people feel themselves addressed and seized in the depths of their being . . . This inner transport wrought by the power of the creator, which, since it is absolutely miraculous, is able to convince one of its higher right and to still all doubts, is the actual content of God's speeches and the final refutation of all rational theodicies.[59]

But despite the undoubted distinction of the scholars who support such a line, this just will not do. For the insuperable objection remains that nowhere are we told that the experience of the speech, as distinct from its content, is integral to the argument. Rather, it seems to function, like Satan, as no more than a literary device, a mere vehicle for conveying a point. Were it otherwise, one would have expected the author to dwell on Job's participation in the experience, or at the very least to allude to it, but in the six verses allotted to his response this finds no mention. To see how far this is from being the author's intention, one need only contrast the passage with the degree of personal interaction that

[57] N. N. Glatzer (ed.), *The Dimensions of Job* (New York: Schoken, 1969), 197–205, 205–14, 123–8. [58] Ibid., 203–4.
[59] W. Eichrodt, 'Faith in providence and theodicy in the Old Testament' in Crenshaw, *Theodicy*, 17–41, esp. 34–5.

one finds in more obviously experiential accounts, such as Moses at the burning bush or Isaiah in the Temple (Exod. 3: 1–4, 17; Isa. 6: 1–13).

Yet, unsatisfactory though these answers are, they do point to an important dimension of the issue which is too often ignored. It is too often assumed that what is at stake is a purely philosophical or theological issue, and the result is that no account is taken of what is really central in leading a religious life, the more spiritual or pastoral questions that make possible the practice of discipleship. One of the few scholars to acknowledge this is Ernest Nicholson, who observes that therein lay the motivations even for the 'solutions' which the author is concerned to attack:

Theodicy is not primarily an intellectual exercise but has a strong pastoral function. For an ancient Israelite it was a comfort to know, when misfortune struck, that the fault lay in oneself and that repentance would bring forgiveness and restoration of well-being from a merciful God, or that such misfortune was divine 'testing' which would be followed by renewed blessing for one whose heart was proved to be true to God.[60]

While his own proposed answer also, I think, founders as an interpretation of Job through lack of evidence from within the text itself[61] his remarks do underline the necessity for the search for such a pastoral solution, and thus legitimate the later rereadings of the book, to which I now turn.

Trajectories developed within Judaism

The history of Christian interpretation will be considered shortly, but it will be helpful to consider first what happened within Judaism. Here each of the three elements I distinguished in the previous section were to be subject to significant further developments. Their starting points were, however, the conclusions we reached rather than the proposed reading of Job with which in each case we began. So to reflect this fact, different sub-headings will be used below. How far these developments are interpreted as

---

[60] E. Nicholson, 'The Limits of theodicy' in J. Day, R. P. Gordon, and G. M. Williamson (eds.), *Wisdom in Ancient Israel* (Cambridge: Cambridge University Press, 1995), 71–82, esp. 73.   [61] Ibid., 80–2.

trajectories from authorial intention and how much as hidden potentialities of the text will of course depend on the reader's response to the previous section. Although either scenario would be compatible with the notion of continuing divine revelation, clearly the easier stimulus to further reflection would have been for an earlier version to have appeared explicitly in the text. Otherwise, it will be more a case of God using the wider cultural context to stimulate fresh ways of approaching the text.

An open searching

The first conclusion we reached, it will be recalled, concerned the open character of the text, the way in which it implicitly invited further exploration of the issue of theodicy. The most obvious development here was in the introduction of post-mortem existence, but also to be observed are some subtle, and other not so subtle, modifications of the scheme which the book had apparently already rejected. An example of the former comes from the first-century BC rewriting of the story, *The Testament of Job*.[62] Instead of the capricious deity of the original responding to Satan's challenge without Job's knowledge, Job himself is made to provoke Satan's attack by his refusal to compromise with him.[63] Psychologically, we therefore have the very different scenario of Job joining in the battle against evil rather than being merely the subject of divine whim. But there are also many more pedestrian attempts to fit him into the traditional punishment scheme. For instance, we find it suggested that Job's suffering was in fact deserved because he had acted as one of Pharaoh's counsellers.[64] How far such thoughts could go is well illustrated by a fifteenth-century Spanish sermon,

---

[62] For a strong defence of the unity of the work, with the author seen as using various devices to integrate and develop existing traditions, particularly the Septuagint, B. Schaller, 'Zur Komposition und Konzeption des Testaments Hiobs' in M. A. Knibb and P. W. Van den Horst, *Studies on the Testament of Job* (Cambridge: Cambridge University Press, 1989), 46–92.

[63] Ch. 6–8; T. H. Charlesworth (ed.), *Old Testament Pseudepigrapha*, (London: Darton, Longman & Todd, l983), I, 841–2.

[64] *Exodus Rabbah* 21.7; for further references and analysis, J. R. Baskin, *Pharaoh's Counsellors* (Chico, Cal.: Scholars Press, 1983), 14–16; the theme is also taken up by E. Wiesel, *Messengers of God* (New York: Summit Books, 1976), 212–15.

in which the preacher insists upon Job's guilt, arguing that the case was comparable to Joseph's brothers who received a delayed punishment for their crimes; so when we suffer, we must look more deeply into our own hearts.[65] It is a solution which we must beware of dismissing too patronizingly. For the canonical text itself had provided some ammunition for preceding in this way. In its canonical shape, at the end Job is finally rewarded; so it looks as though, while severing the necessity for any such connection, the book did not exclude the possibility altogether of some connection continuing to exist. This, as we shall see, is an important point to be borne in mind later when corresponding Christian attitudes are noted.

However, this was by no means the norm. Instead, over-whelmingly resort was had to the notion of resurrection, a notion which scholars would now generally agree formed no part of the original discussion. Sometimes the tradition itself recognizes this, as in the *Zohar*'s criticism of Job's denial of an after-life.[66] More typical is the pattern set by the Septuagint. The canonical book ends, 'And Job died, an old man and full of days', whereas the Septuagint significantly adds 'and it is written that he will rise again with those whom the Lord raises up'.[67] A similar pattern emerges in the *Testament*. Job is made to utter a great psalm of affirmation, while the burial of his children is declared unnecessary because of his certainty that they are already with God in heaven.[68] How deeply such a different version of Job's story became entrenched within the tradition is well illustrated by the Book of Tobit. Since it is normally dated at least a century earlier than the *Testament*, presumably this influence has been mediated from the Septuagint, but the parallel in attitudes between the two works is striking.[69]

[65] M. Saperstein (ed.), *Jewish Preaching 1200–1800* (New Haven: Yale University Press, 1989), 169–79.
[66] *Zohar* (SPCK, 1983), 93–4 and 235, n., with further references.
[67] Here, and elsewhere, I have used the Lancelot Brenton translation which also provides Greek original in parallel columns: (Grand Rapids, Michigan: Zondervan, 1851). The restoration of Job's fortunes in the canonical work could be seen as a kind of resurrection, and so as providing a trajectory towards the approach adopted in the Septuagint.
[68] Ch. 33 (Charlesworth, *Pseudepigrapha* I, 855–6); ch. 39. 11–12 (ibid., 859).
[69] The most striking parallel, though, is only preserved in the Vulgate (and in Hebrew and Aramaic fragments from Qumran): 'The Lord allowed this testing to happen to him (Tobit), so that the example of his patience might be given

Targums are notoriously difficult to date, but likewise the *Targum of Job* leaves us in no doubt of the necessity of introducing a life beyond the grave, even if the author is not always entirely consistent.[70] He seems uncertain whether the wicked will rise again,[71] but is in no doubt about the future of those who trust in God.[72] Somewhat surprisingly, seventeenth-century Judaism was even willing to consider the possibility of reincarnation.[73]

Most commentators reflecting on this history view what happened as no more than the artificial imposition of alien ideas upon a text that should rightly bear a very different meaning. But more needs to be heard on the other side. If, as I have argued, the author of the canonical text may well have seen himself as initiating a debate, not closing it, then each of these later versions could be viewed as making their own legitimate contribution. Indeed, the contribution could be described as essential. Today it is fashionable to deride the relevance of the after-life, but this is done from the comfort of the affluent West without regard to that large mass of humanity for whom life remains essentially nasty, brutish, and short. To those who object that nothing can compensate for certain forms of pain, the reply may be made that the point is not compensation, but completion, that how the suffering is endured can be given a meaning as transitional to a deeper relation with God. Thus, while not discounting the search for reasons, the focus moves almost imperceptibly from a 'why' question to a 'how', or perhaps simply to a different form of 'how'. For, as the remark quoted earlier from Nicholson indicates, even those who supported a punishment explanation, also wanted a 'how' that could make the suffering pastorally endurable. Yet even so, there remains this difference, that the placing of the believer's suffering in a wider context ensured that instead of looking externally for some fault, a more internalist approach could develop and flourish. What really mattered was how the suffering was experienced.

---

to later generations, just like that of the saintly Job' (2: 12 Vulgate; my trans). The passage as a whole (2: 10–23) is instructive in this respect, with mention of a future life at v. 18.

[70] For possible dating, *The Targums of Job, Proverbs & Qohelet* (Edinburgh: *The Aramaic Bible*, T & T Clark, 1991), 5–8.

[71] Contrast 14.12 and 15.21.   [72] E.g. 5.4; 11.17; 36.7.

[73] Saperstein, *Preaching*, 303–26.

Morality deepened

That more internalist approach is also what we find reflected in the moral changes made to Job's story, our second major area of interest. Although the following three questions overlap, one way of viewing subsequent developments is to see the canonical book stimulating deeper reflection in response to such questions as these: What is it to be good? What are the proper limits of anger? and, What resources are required for one to be good?

One of the striking contrasts between the canonical book and The *Testament of Job* is the specificity of the latter compared with the former. Instead of vague generalities, the later author insists upon specifying particular acts.[74] Not only that, these acts indicate a real engagement with valuing particular individuals and their problems, in a way in which the canonical book's general allusions to help for the widow and orphan singularly fail to provide.[75] It is almost as though in the earlier case standard categories for relief are being mentioned, rather than real sympathetic concern for their problems. At all events, note how the *Testament* expands Job's boast that his doors stand open into a sympathetic concern that the poor may always be able to obtain relief without being made to feel any embarrassment in their necessity, or how Job's claim that he made widows 'sing for joy' is turned into practical measures for their enjoyment and entertainment.[76] Here is real human warmth and compassion.

A similar pattern emerges if we consider later treatments of Job's wife. As we saw above, within the canon she is given short shrift. In the Hebrew there is only one brief exchange between husband and wife, when she urges him to 'curse God and die', and he rebukes her for speaking 'as one of the foolish women', declaring: 'shall we receive good at the hand of God, and shall we not receive evil?' (Job 2: 9–10 RSV). The Septuagint, however, considerably expands the text to make Job's wife a full participant in his lot. Not only does she lament the loss of her children, but in her attempt to support Job who is 'upon a dung heap outside the city',[77] she has become 'a wanderer and a servant from place to place and

---

[74] Chs. 9–15; 842–5.   [75] E.g. 29.12–13; 31.16–17.
[76] Job 31: 32 and *Testament* 9.8; Job 29: 13 RSV and *Testament* 14.1–5.
[77] V. 8. The Hebrew merely has 'among the ashes'.

house to house, waiting for the setting of the sun, that I may rest from my labours and my pangs which now beset me'. It is into this context that advice to Job is set, and it is now couched in a significantly different way. Instead of the strong 'curse' of the Hebrew we have 'say some word *eis* the Lord and die'. Whether merely a weaker version of the curse formula (*eis* as 'against'), or urging a prayer for death (*eis* as 'towards'), the intention clearly is to make her appear in a less hostile light, even though the Hebrew's 'as one of the foolish women' is retained. As if in confirmation of the fact, in the Greek, unlike the Hebrew, Job looks her full in the face (*emblepo*), and instead of making a generalized statement about 'receiving' good and evil, particularizes it to the two of them: 'If we have received good things at the hands of the Lord, shall we not endure evil things?' The changes in tense and verb are surely not without significance. Putting the conditional clause in the past underlines already shared benefits from the hand of God, while the different verb in the main clause indicates the need to join one another in patient endurance.[78]

In *The Testament of Job* the exchange is greatly expanded (chs. 21–6). His wife's plight is heightened, with her begging for bread and even being forced to sell her hair. Though on this version we are left in no doubt that 'some word against the Lord' is how the author read the Septuagint passage (cf. 26: 3), the other expansions have still further softened the significance of this lapse, as does the later incident that records her death (chs. 39–40). Mourning her children's death, she is granted a vision of her dead children now crowned in heaven, and 'died in good spirits'.[79] It is perhaps under such Jewish influence that Islam developed its own distinctive story to illustrate Job's good relations with his wife. Of the Qur'an's three references to Job, only one makes a very brief allusion to Job's wife, with Job instructed to 'take in thy hand a little grass, and strike therewith: and break not thy oath'.[80] However,

---

[78] For some further useful remarks on these verses, O'Connor, *Job*, 21–42.

[79] For an example of how *not* to read the text, cf. J. Lamb, *The Rhetoric of Suffering* (Oxford: Clarendon Press, 1995), 17–23. So convinced is he that it must reflect prejudice against the 'marginal female' that he asserts that 'the *Testament* buries Sitis in the mud of the byre'; 21.3. In fact, though she dies there with 'the living animals standing weeping over her', she is given an honourable burial by 'the poor of the city'.

[80] Sura 38. 44. The three passages in question are 6.84; 21.83–4; 38.41–4.

this was expanded in later Islam to suggest that what had really happened was that Job had temporarily lost his temper with his wife when she urged him to 'curse God and die'; so God urges him to keep the letter of his oath but not the spirit, since, now understanding his wife's frustration, he will beat her only with a 'wisp of grass'.[81]

So, whether we consider individual acts of charity or Job's relations with his wife, it does look as though, far from limiting the range of morality, the later tradition sought, quite correctly in my view, to deepen its application. Instead of vague generalities, on the human level it has become a matter of valuing individuals in their own unique particularity. In a moment we shall consider one specific change in Job's relation to God, but these moral reflections about human morality also had their general effect on how the relation between God and Job was conceived. Within the canon Abraham is called a 'friend of God',[82] and that image of intimacy was taken up as one possible explanation of why either Job himself could speak so freely with God, or else why Moses had to be the work's author, as already in intimate communion with God.[83] Very much later the Jewish philosopher, Moses Maimonides (d. 1204), was to argue that the book should be read as indicating how one might grow towards a disinterested love of God. 'Satan' becomes an internal evil impulse, which it is the intention of the speech of Elihu in particular to correct.[84] Though as an account of intended meaning the interpretation is utterly implausible, its very existence illustrates how further questioning could indeed enrich rather than undermine understanding of the divine-human relation.

Hitherto my sympathies have been very much with later developments rather than with the canonical writing. However, there is at least one area where there seems almost universal modern

---

[81] Cf. A. Y. Ali edition of *The Holy Qur'an* (Leicester: Islamic Foundation, 1975), 1227, n. 4202.

[82] 2 Chron. 20: 7; adopted in the New Testament, James 2: 23.

[83] For friendship and bold speech, Philo, *Quis Haeres Sit?*, 4.19 ff; for the connection between Moses and Job, I. Jacobs, *The Midrashic Process* (Cambridge: Cambridge University Press, 1995), 21–78, esp. 72–5.

[84] M. Maimonides, *The Guide for the Perplexed* (New York: Dover, 1956), 3.22–4; 296–307; for a helpful discussion, O. Leaman, *Moses Maimonides* (London: Routledge, 1990), 168–76.

consensus that the canonical version has the edge over the developing tradition, and that is on the question of anger. Later accounts, it is maintained, emasculate Job by depriving him of his right to rail against the human condition. Certainly the contrast is marked. The canonical Job asks, 'What end have I to expect, that I should be patient?', whereas in *The Testament of Job* he draws patience as the main lesson of his life: 'Now then, my children, you also must be patient in everything that happens to you. For patience is better than anything.'[85] The Septuagint stands somewhere in between. Job's complaints are at times softened, particularly where God is directly mentioned. For instance, instead of saying 'I desire to argue my case with God' (Job 13: 3 RSV), in the Septuagint we find this put as follows: 'I will reason before him, if he will.' But even so the general feel of the text remains much closer to the canonical writing than it is to the *Testament*.

That the canonical text underscores a point of great importance, I would not wish to deny. As any hospital chaplain or bereavement counsellor would amply testify, anger is an almost indispensable part of coming to terms with pain. Those who attempt to suppress their resentment against God, against themselves, or against their immediate family (or a combination of all three), either take longer to heal or find themselves venting their displaced anger elsewhere. Yet, though this is the first and essential word that needs to be said on the subject, it is hardly the last. The pain can become unendurable if the individual is unable ever to get beyond his or her anger; it then functions like a frustration that has no release or a festering wound that has no cure. At first sight, it might seem as though the canonical work does indeed allow one to get beyond that initial stage. But this is far from clear. No sooner are Job's complaints answered from the whirlwind than his fortunes are restored, whereas with the typical sufferer the pain continues even after the anger is suppressed or subsides. What we therefore need is some account of how to behave beyond the working through of one's anger, and this the canonical book singularly fails to provide. Thus, while it is entirely proper to criticize later accounts insofar as they fail to legitimate anger, they may also be read as attempting to answer that further issue of how one is to behave at the point beyond anger. Patience may not be a fashionable virtue, but it does

---

[85] Job 6: 11 NEB; *Testament* 27: 6–7.

play an integral part in ensuring that the sufferer can turn his or her mind to other things besides the pain, and so give life fresh meaning. Perhaps, therefore, progression from Hebrew through Septuagint to *Testament* should be read not as the story of continuing decline, but as each indicating essential stages in the soul's advancement towards dealing adequately with the presence of pain: from anger through confusion to patience. This is not necessarily to suggest that any of them exhibit their roles to perfection (for instance, the patience of Job in the *Testament* is too self-assured), but it is to insist that they were each in their own way raising indispensable questions.

Job's status as a righteous pagan also stimulated further moral reflection, in particular over the question of the sources of morality. Could a non-Jew lead the good life or not, and, if so, how?[86] The issue, though, focused not on Job alone. Also represented in the discussion were the prophet Balaam as an example of the wicked pagan and Jethro, Moses' father-in-law, as the archetypical proselyte.[87] The blackening of Balaam seems to have intensified as a result of the positive Christian use of some of his words,[88] but even Job did not always fair particularly well. Though the majority view from the Tosefta onwards[89] was that Gentiles could be saved, it was sometimes suggested that Job had had enough compensation in this life, while, if great praise were heaped upon him, this is sometimes because he has been turned into a Jew, as in the Targum which even has him lament that he is not 'like infants which never saw the light of the Law' (3: 16). Both the Septuagint and the *Testament* make him an Edomite descended from Esau, and so, apart from one lapse in the *Testament* (45: 3), the intention does seem to have been to make him, at the very least, a *separated* brother. Implicit recognition was thereby given to the possibility not only of goodness outside of Israel but of God acting beyond Israel's confines to comfort those in distress. Moral

---

[86] For a detailed study of the application of the question to the three figures mentioned below, J. R. Baskin, *Pharaoh's Counsellors* (Chico, Cal.: Scholars Press, 1983). For Job, 7–32 and 116–17.

[87] For Balaam, Num. 22–24; Deut. 23: 5–6; Josh. 24: 9–10; that Jethro was a proselyte was inferred from Exod. 18: 12.

[88] In particular Num. 24: 17, which was interpreted as a prophecy of Jesus' acknowledgement by the magi.

[89] Tosefta refers to 'Additions' to the late third-century Mishnah.

horizons were thus, however slowly, being widened, though it needs to be noted that the canonical text through its opening verse also presumably intended such widening (though it is done so discreetly that today most readers fail to notice).

An experiential resolution

The last area of development which I would like to mention concerns the question of religious experience. Here a huge change is observable with the *Testament*, in that an extensive role is now given to intimate experience of God. In a confident psalm Job asserts that his destiny lies with God. The language employed implies some kind of connection with Merkavah mysticism, the major mystical tradition that had its source in Ezekiel's vision of the divine chariot: 'My kingdom is forever and ever, and its splendour and majesty are in the chariots of the Father.'[90] That declaration is made while Job still endures, but the connection is taken up once more at the end of the book. In the last few chapters (46–53), Job hands over 'magical' sashes to his three daughters. Not only have these helped to cure their father (47: 5–11), he promises them that 'these cords will lead you into the better world, to live in the heavens' (47: 2).[91] All three daughters are then temporarily transported, speaking the language of angels (48–50), while, as their father dies, they see 'the gleaming chariots' coming for his soul (52: 6). Though to the modern mind any mention of magic is seen inevitably to detract from the value of any claim to mystical experience, it is as well to note that major Merkavah texts make similar kinds of connections without any apparent feeling of incongruity.[92] It is also now thought that the imagery of Merkavah mysticism may have had some influence on Paul.[93] Whether so or not, the important

[90] *Testament* 33.9; Ezek. 1: 4–28.

[91] Although I have used the language of 'magic', it is as well to recall that the ark of the covenant, the hem of Jesus' garment and Paul's handkerchief are all accorded not dissimilar powers in Scripture: 2 Sam. 6: 7; Matt. 9: 20; Acts 19: 12. 'Holy' or 'quasi-sacramental' might be less pejorative terminology, but would not immediately indicate the presence of extraordinary powers.

[92] J. Dan, 'The religious experience of the Merkavah' in A. Green (ed.), *Jewish Spirituality* (London: SCM Press, 1985), 289–307, esp. 305–6.

[93] A. E. Segal, *Paul the Convert* (New Haven: Yale University Press, 1990), 40–52.

point to note is the search for a deeper relationship, a more sustained experience of the divine, than the canonical work appears to allow. The magical sashes are thus symbols of the power of divine grace to carry one through the worst of ills, through transforming and intimate experience of God.

In the search for a more adequate resolution of the dilemmas raised by innocent suffering, each of the three types of development which we have discussed seem to me to make a distinctive, though not unconnected, contribution. In effect, each tries to place the sufferer on a new level of relationship with God. That is most obvious with the mystical experience with which our discussion ended, but the prospect of life after death implies a continuing relationship, while increasing the specificity of morality speaks of its demands as more than mere conformity to external rules and commands; its essence has become the valuing of relationships, both human and divine. What we might call 'personalizing the answer' is also what we shall find happens in respect of Christianity. An increasing internalization is to be noted, though this is combined with what from one particular perspective might be described as a retreat, namely increasing reassertion of there after all being some connection between suffering and punishment.

Christian internalization and retreat: Gregory to Calvin

Before identifying what I consider the defining characteristics of Christian developments, I want first to give a brief indication of what happened in the liturgy and in art. I begin, though, by noting the various ways in which Jewish and Christian reflection interconnected. Though the last important reference in the West to the *Testament* was in the sixth-century Gelasian Decree,[94] and thereafter it was virtually unknown until modern times (the two principal Greek versions were rediscovered in the nineteenth century), it had already left its permanent imprint upon Christianity. The Epistle of James' reference to 'the patience of Job' (5: 11 AV) is most naturally taken as either a direct allusion or deriving from

---

[94] Where the work is described as 'apocryphus': 5.6.4. Although ascribed to Pope Gelasius (d. 496), the standard critical edition adopts the later date: E. von Dobschütz, *Das Decretum Gelasium* (Leipzig: Heinrichs, 1912), esp. 306.

similar exegetical assumptions. Clement, writing *c.* AD 96, unqualifiedly adopts the Septuagint's account of Job as a firm believer in
the resurrection.[95] His willingness to use other pseudepigraphical
texts such as 1 Enoch and the *Assumption of Moses* may possibly
imply that the *Testament* also played its part in forming his thinking. With greater confidence it can be asserted that some of the
Testament's most characteristic strains survived throughout the
Middle Ages, however mediated. Painted on the eve of the
Reformation, Dürer's famous picture of Job and his wife with two
musicians indicates two distinctive, recurring elements: Job being
helped by his wife and by music.[96] The widely disseminated
Apocalypse of Paul (available in a fourth-century Latin translation)
had suggested that it was Satan and not his wife who had tempted
Job to curse God, while at Chartres we find the feet of husband
and wife charmingly intertwined. As noted above, music played a
major role in the *Testament*; for reasons which are unclear, in the
medieval tradition this is sometimes transformed into a tale in
which the musicians are rewarded by scabs or worms which eventually turn into gold.[97] One must not, however, create a misleading impression of mindless conformity to one particular pattern.
The story continued to be used as a vehicle for further reflection,
now in one direction, now in another as, for instance, with the
English *Life* showing maximum sympathy for his wife[98] and the
illustrated *Biblia Pauperum*, by contrast, identifying her as suitable
for matching Christ's tormentors.[99]

[95] First Epistle to the Corinthians 17.3; 26.3.
[96] Jabach Altarpiece, Wallraf-Richartz Musuem, Cologne; e.g. M. Bailey,
Dürer (London: Phaidon, 1995), no. 26. Bailey does not take sides on how Job's
wife should be interpreted. Panofksy sees her as a tormentor, but I have adopted
the view of Wölfflin in the text: E. Panofsky, *The Life and Art of Albrecht Dürer*
(Princeton, N. J.: Princeton University Press, 4th edn, 1955), 93–4; H. Wölfflin,
The Art of Albrecht Dürer (Oxford: Phaidon, 1971), 137. For further dicussion, see
Plate 4 of this book.
[97] As in the Middle English *Life of Job* and the Middle French play *La Patience
de Job*; for further discussion of the medieval literature, L. L. Besserman, *The
Legend of Job in the Middle Ages* (Cambridge, Mass.: Harvard University Press,
1979), esp. 66–113.
[98] Cf. esp. lines 113–119, where this has become Job's only fault deserving
reprimand.
[99] A good later example comes from the seventeenth century: C. Wright,
Georges de La Tour (Oxford: Phaidon, 1977), no. 24.

One recent major study of the history of the iconography of Job detects a continuing pattern of artistic representation of Job as rebel against conformity: 'Artists convey the conviction that Job is not simply a model of submissiveness, but that his image punctures the dishonesty or self-deception of conventional religionists.'[100] While some of the author's innovating proposals strike me as plausible, others strain credibility to the limits.[101] Part of the problem is that he seems to envisage the artists directly meditating on the biblical text rather than development in their images being mediated through an existing theological and artistic tradition.[102] The result is that the influence of Pope Gregory is consistently underplayed,[103] and even the kind of impact the *Testament* had, in my view, misconceived.[104] Yet the study is an exciting one because it does indicate the openness of the developing artistic tradition, not least in its capacity to develop through Job a response to the new scourge of syphilis in the sixteenth century.[105] But that would seem to me a rare instance of where the artistic imagination was in

[100] S. Terrien, *The Iconography of Job Through the Centuries: Artists as Biblical Interpreters* (University Park, Pa.: Pennsylvania State University Press, 1996), 266. This is the summary of his view that he offers in the 'Postscript', but it is repeated many times, beginning as early as xxxiv.

[101] As an example of the former, his impressive arguments for reading Job's wife positively in the painting by George de La Tour commonly called *Job Mocked By His Wife* (166–9); as an example of the latter, his priestly reading of her role on an eighth-century sarcophagus (28–9), or his view that Giordano's *Job and His Comforters* is intended as an attack on the council of Trent (185–7).

[102] 'As far as the Jobian theme is concerned, the sculptors of Gothic cathedrals give evidence of having studied Scripture thoroughly rather than the theological treatises of scholars and clerics' (Ibid., 80). Why should either be true?

[103] For instance, in his treatment of the Chartres carvings the key role of Gregory in treating Job as a type of Christ is ignored and instead the absence of his influence noted in the positive treatment of Job's wife: 73 ff. Yet the same sentence which he quotes to justify talk of Gregory's misogyny is immediately preceded by the christological typology: *Moralia* Preface 6.14.

[104] He envisages artists reading the work (e.g. 45), for which there is no evidence, whereas its images appear to have been mediated through oral tradition.

[105] Job became a patron of sufferers in much the same way as Sebastian was of those afflicted by the plague. Terrien argues plausibly for the influence of such ideas on major artists such as Bellini and Dürer, while he even succeeds in finding an impressive twentieth-century example in a work by the Canadian artist, Raymond Bishop: 127–45, 224–5.

advance of the literary.[106] Indeed, even if what is sought is precedent for revolt against 'patient Job', one might note that this could have as easily come from what might initially seem the most conformist and orthodox setting possible: the liturgy.

Admittedly, the Breviary's daily readings followed a predictable pattern. Although Job was set in its entirety for the daily Matins readings during September, their force was considerably muted by the required daily antiphon: 'The Lord gave and the Lord has taken away; blessed be the name of the Lord' (1: 21). But quite otherwise was the version for the Office for the Dead which was authorized from the seventeenth century onwards.[107] Here in the Matins order all nine readings were drawn from the Book of Job, and, although the penultimate expressed resounding confidence in the resurrection (19: 25–27), all the rest, drawn from Job's own words, exhibit anger and resentment. Even the last (10: 18–22) declares that it would have been better, had he never been born. Pastorally, this seems to hit exactly the right mood, in marked contrast to many modern funeral liturgies which fail to catch any sense of ambiguity, far less anger. A similar criticism might be made of modern set-readings for Sunday worship. Over a three-year cycle the Roman Catholic Mass introduces the congregation to only two passages, while there is only one in a two-year cycle of eucharist readings in the Alternative Service Book of the Church of England. None of them could do much to further the understanding of such an important pastoral dimension.[108]

However, our attention needs to be focused elsewhere if we are to identify the most significant contributions which the Christian tradition came to make in the continuing task of interpreting the agenda set by the Book of Job. The eighteenth century represents something of a watershed; so we shall treat the modern period separately. Prior to that point, two main contributions may be identified, one positive and the other negative. The positive

---

[106] For another, note my discussion of Blake later in this chapter.

[107] For further details, P. Rouillard, 'The figure of Job in the liturgy' in C. Duquoc and C. Floristan (eds.), *Job and the Silence of God: Concilium*, 169 (1983), 8–12.

[108] The Roman Catholic lectionary has Job 7: 1–7 and 38: 1–11, the Anglican 42: 1–6.

concerns internalization, the negative too narrow an understanding of particular providence.

To describe the work of Pope Gregory (d. 604) as a positive contribution will strike some as sounding the depths of human perversity. That great historian of Christian thought, Harnack, has not a good word to say about this man who 'reduced the spiritual to the level of a coarsely material intelligence'.[109] More than anyone else he was responsible for securing 'patient Job' as the norm of interpretation for most of Christian history. Whether in its full thirty-five books or in the various short compendia that were available,[110] his *Magna Moralia* became the standard point of access in applying the canonical work to a life of Christian discipleship. Homes Dudden observes that as a commentary it is 'well-nigh worthless';[111] Beryl Smalley, while not dissenting, notes 'how suitable it was for educational purposes'.[112] That is no doubt true (his audience were quickly initiated into a wide range of Christian doctrine and practice); yet that should not make us retreat altogether from the notion of commentary.

Certainly it bears no comparison to a modern commentary, and frequently the text becomes a mere handle upon which Gregory can fix quite independent thought. This is particularly true of the allegorical reading which he offers in addition to the literal and the moral. With the latter he finds allusions to the contemporary Christian, whether individual or Church as a whole, while with the allegorical Job is taken to be a prophet who always also speaks of Christ. The opening section in which Job's seven sons and three daughters are interpreted as a covert indicator of the twelve apostles (both perfect numbers) and the three orders within the Church (clergy, celibate, and married) does not inspire confidence;[113] still

[109] A. Harnack, *History of Dogma* (1898), V, 262–73, esp. 262.

[110] G. R. Evans, *The Thought of Gregory the Great* (Cambridge: Cambridge University Press, 1986), 145.

[111] F. Homes Dudden, *Gregory the Great* (London: Longmans, 1905), I, 194.

[112] B. Smalley, *The Study of the Bible in the Middle Ages* (Notre Dame, Indiana: University of Notre Dame Press, 1964), 34.

[113] *Moralia* 1.19–20. Yet such an approach is not altogether without its advantages. One might note, for instance the way in which the presentation of Job's friends as heretics, speaking a mixture of truth and falsehood and awaiting reconciliation, does create a more engaged sense of debate: Pref. 6.15; 8.17. (*PL* 75.525–6).

less, when Job's suffering 'without cause' is turned into its opposite,[114] or what the canonical work clearly refers to God is ascribed
to Satan.[115] Nonetheless, lurking behind all of this is a profound
insight that does, I believe, represent a significant advance. If the
Septuagint and the *Testament* succeeded in personalizing Job's
ethics, Gregory succeeded in internalizing them. That was no small
achievement because it ensured that facing suffering could now be
viewed not as something purely external that had to be confronted
alone (the Hebrew version) nor even as something that could be
faced with others (the *Testament*), but something whose final resolution was a matter of internal attitude.

Gregory was himself particularly well equipped to effect this
transformation. Living through troubled times he was convinced
the world was soon to end. Added to that were personal pains,
bowel problems, and fevers. In his introductory, dedicatory letter
he leaves us in no doubt that he feels a strong personal identification with Job's sufferings, and wonders whether it may even have
been 'the plan of divine providence' to throw two afflicted souls
together, 'ut percussum Iob percussus exponerem, et flagellati
mentem melius per flagella sentirem'.[116] A major factor in
Gregory's turn inwards was of course the fact that he saw in sin
one of the principal sources of human unhappiness, but, as his
introductory references to his own physical ailments make clear, it
would be a mistake to read the *Moralia* as though he had simply
changed the question. Conversion of mind was required, whether
the pain was physical or moral. Human beings are conceived of as
ships going against the current; they inevitably fall back unless they
have the right ballast or stability.[117] Virtue and knowledge therefore remain superficial until they are reinforced by the constancy

---

[114] Gregory wrestles with the Vulgate's 'frustra' (2.3) to indicate why the
claim is not true in its most fundamental sense: *Moralia* 3.2.3; cf. 3.14.26 (for
application to Christ).

[115] *Moralia* 13.18–25; cf. Job 16: 7–18. Perhaps, however the most startling
contrast of all is his interpretation of the whirlwind speech, as providing reassurance to Job that Satan and the Antichrist (identified with Behemoth and
Leviathan) can in fact be defeated: *Moralia* 32.12.16 ff. (*PL* 76.645C ff.).

[116] 'That one so shaken might expound the shaken Job, and through his own
batterings feel better the mind of another so battered' (my trans.); Letter to
Leander, 5 (*PL* 75.515C).

[117] *Regula Pastoralis* 3.34; cf. *Mor.* 11.68.

and deeper understanding that can only be generated through suffering. 'The gift which was first taken up in peaceful circumstances is made manifest in tribulation,' and so 'while the darkness of pain is created through blows from outside, internally the light of the mind is fired by the instruction it receives.'[118] Indeed, not only is there never any absolute guarantee, and so constant vigilance is required,[119] but the devout will also be worried by unrelieved external prosperity because this may well prevent the more solid grounding which can come only once a humble dependence upon God has been learnt,[120] and which can only then pass from fear into love.[121] Grace has now become the heart of the story. No wonder, then, that almost every verse of the canonical work had to be reinterpreted since God is no more merely the voice at the end of the tale but integral to its every stage.[122]

Although Aquinas offers what he himself calls a literal reading, in seeing the issue primarily in terms of mental attitude his approach in fact stands nearer to Gregory than it does to most contemporary approaches to the problem of evil. This emerges clearly from his long commentary on Job, where Satan is demythologized into an eternal divine decree and the whirlwind into a metaphor for divine inspiration.[123] More significantly, the dialogue is conceived on the model of a medieval *disputatio* or debate, with a progressive argument that culminates in God's final speech. Job's 'light sin' (*levitas*) is the purely intellectual and somewhat arrogant way in which he has presented the truth to his friends: 'careless speech which seemed to smack of pride'.[124] The friends' more serious fault lies in their complete misunderstanding of providence. The final resolution of good and evil lies beyond

---

[118] My trans.: Pref. 2.6 (*PL* 75.519C); *Mor.* 3.9.15 (*PL* 75.607A).

[119] E.g. *Mor.* 5.11–12.

[120] 'The devout, when they see the prosperity of this world fall to themselves, are shaken by a dreadful thought . . . they fear, lest divine justice detects a wound in them, and while heaping on them external gifts, drives them from interior benefits.' (my trans.): *Mor.* 5.1.1 (*PL* 75.679C).

[121] *Mor.* 24.28–9; cf. *Letters* 7.23.

[122] For further elucidation, A. Bocognano's 'Introduction' in *Grégoire Le Grand, Morales sur Job* (Paris: *Sources Chrétiennes*, Les éditions du Cerf, 1974), 212, 7–32; C. Straw, *Gregory the Great* (Berkeley, Cal.: University of California Press, 1988), 236–60.

[123] *Literal Exposition of Job* (Atlanta, Georgia: Scholars Press, 1989) on 2: 1–6; 92; on 38: 1–5; 416.   [124] Ibid., on 42: 1–10; 469.

the grave; in the meantime suffering is there to be used. For, though Thomas toys with the idea that the point of the suffering is merely to make Job's virtue more public,[125] the heart of his answer seems to be that, while we can never know for certain why some particular hardship occurs,[126] we do know that particular providence exists,[127] and that, provided our reason remains in control, with God's grace this can then be turned to good effect.[128] The bottom line for Thomas, as for Gregory, is thus a question of mental attitude, the imposition of a different value system on the world rather than any external assessment of goods.[129] The canonical work had as its answer insisted upon a different value system for God; the Christian tradition has now come to assert instead a different value system for humanity.

In trying to comprehend why that change occurred, it would be pleasant if all could be ascribed to reading the Book of Job in the light of Christ, but matters are seldom that simple. Certainly, as the Gospels amply illustrate, Jesus offered a less ambiguous God than Job's, one essentially characterized by love of all, and he also preached an internalization of the law. But even Jesus had little to say on the question of suffering itself. Moreover, the contention is not implausible that in some ways the theology of the New Testament set back the severing of the connection between sin and suffering, inasmuch as so much of its atonement theology insisted that the rationale of Jesus' death lay in him bearing the penalty for our sin. This is not to deny that what Jesus taught had the potential for eliciting a new focus, but my suspicion is that it needed some further spur, and that, I suggest, was provided by monasticism, for it developed such demands for sustained internal reflection that extending the internalization of morality to the reception of suffering could happen almost imperceptibly. At all events, it seems no accident that the person most responsible for communicating this change to Western Christianity, Gregory, was himself a monk.

---

[125] Ibid., on 23: 8–13; 302–3.   [126] Ibid., on 23: 8–13; 303–4.

[127] Ibid., on 7: 14–18; 153–4; on 27: 1–8; 325–6. Here, like Maimonides, he stands in opposition to Aristotle's rejection of particular providence.

[128] Ibid., on 6: 1–10; 137–40; on 9: 15–21; 174. He takes more seriously than Gregory, though, the negative impact of pain: cf. e.g. his comments on 17: 11.

[129] Cf. E. Stump, 'Biblical commentary and philosophy' in N. Kretzmann and E. Stump (eds.), *The Cambridge Companion to Aquinas* (Cambridge: Cambridge University Press, 1993), 252–68.

But, if there was in this what seems to me a positive advance, one negative feature also needs to be faced. Not all will agree that it should be regarded as such, but that at any rate is how I intend to argue. Earlier we noted the way in which the canonical work did not altogether exclude the possibility of there being some connection between virtue and reward, sin and punishment. Indeed, its canonical shaping with its prose conclusion seemed to imply merely delay in implementing the connection. That element of delay was taken up within the Christian tradition in the notion of resurrection, but it was also combined with the supposition that, though the Book of Job had excluded any necessary connection between sin and punishment in this life, it had not eliminated the possibility altogether. In other words, punishment remained open as a reading, though no longer required. How this came about we shall consider in a moment, but a few brief remarks first on resurrection will be appropriate.

As with the Jewish tradition, so also with the Christian, resurrection did come to dominate the interpretation of Job. Perhaps mainly now because of Handel,[130] the book's best-known verses (Job 19: 25–6) continue among the general public to be taken to speak about resurrection, though no such meaning was intended.[131] The Vulgate, following the Septuagint, had given the passage that meaning, as with many another verse, but in the Fathers the process was carried much further. Indeed, for Ambrose even Job's 'Let the day perish wherein I was born' (3: 3 AV) came to acquire that sense! He 'wished that the day of his birth might perish in order that he might be granted the day of resurrection'.[132] The more positive side of the belief, in showing God's concern for those who have been harmed in this life, I have already attempted to delineate above. Unfortunately, that aim also went with a very crude form of calculation, which is well illustrated by Gregory's approach. Every fault, he tells us, necessitates

---

[130] *Messiah*, part III, no. 45.

[131] E.g. denied in Jerusalem Bible footnote; contrast Jerome, *Liber contra Joannem Hierosolymitana* 30 (*PL* 23. 381–2); but for a modern scholar prepared to say something on the other side, cf. Habel, *Job*, 302–9.

[132] *De excessu fratris* II, 32: optavit perire diem generationis suae, ut diem resurrectionis acciperet. Cf. Gregory, *Moralia* I, 186.

its corresponding punishment[133] and so, if not rectified in this life, it will be in the next. Though it is often said that this view generated a form of works righteousness (and to some degree it of course did), what such a critique often ignores is the wider context of a general pessimism about how difficult it was in any case to get to heaven; so it brought little self-assurance, as indeed Gregory's own case illustrates.

Much more damaging in my view was the continuing assumption that the way in which suffering befell a particular individual was deliberately planned by God, whether as a form of test, purgation, or punishment. It is often said that the New Testament severed any possible connection with punishment,[134] but we need to ask ourselves whether this really was so. Luke 13: 1–4 and John 9: 2–3 (both unique to each evangelist) may initially seem quite clear. But the immediately following verse in the Luke passage reinstates the possibility of a connection with its threat that 'except ye repent, ye shall all likewise perish' (13: 5 AV), while of the John passage C. K. Barrett wisely remarks that its implication at most is that 'not all sickness could be ascribed to sin'.[135] In other words, the universal application of the theory is being denied, not its legitimacy *tout court*. As a matter of fact the contrary assumption is made quite a few times in the New Testament, as, for example, at Mark 2: 1–12, 1 Corinthians 11: 30 and James 5: 14–16. Also the already noted tendency to interpret Christ's death in terms of punishment strengthened the possibilities of connections elsewhere, as did the viewing of the consequences of original sin in similar categories.[136] Then to this must be added the contentious issue of how the teaching of the Bible should be viewed as a whole. Nowhere, for instance, does the New Testament condemn the general account of history in terms of rewards and punishment which permeates so much of the Old Testament. So it does seem

[133] 'Deliquenti Dominus nequaquam parcit, quia delictum sine ultione non deserit', *Moralia* 9.54.

[134] Cf. e.g., D. Nineham's contrast between later Church and Bible, *Christianity Medieval and Modern* (London: SCM Press, 1993), 20.

[135] C. K. Barrett, *The Gospel according to St. John* (London: SPCK, 2nd edn, 1978), 356; contrast John Marsh's lack of caution in *Saint John* (Harmondsworth: Penguin, 1968), 376–7.

[136] Augustine laid much stress on Job 14: 4–5 as helping to establish the doctrine; e.g. *Comm. Rom.* 5. 1, 5, 9; 7.18.

to me not implausible to claim that the continued assertion of some connection that has dominated the Church's view of the world until modern times was in fact the direction towards which tradition in the form of Scripture was itself pointing. If so, it becomes all the more imperative to be clear about what might legitimate a challenge to such a position.

That such a perspective governed Protestant as much as Catholic readings of Scripture seems confirmed if we take the case of Calvin. He preached a series of sermons on the Book of Job amounting to over seven hundred pages of a closely printed folio.[137] Calvin has no doubt that the text speaks of the resurrection, though occasionally Job 'speaketh like an unbeliever'.[138] More pertinent to our purpose here, he is convinced not only that nothing happens except by divine providence,[139] but also that, while we are not always punished according to our sins,[140] punishment can come even for the sins of our fathers.[141] He is not very sympathetic to the plight of Job, whom he sees as being disciplined because he has succumbed to being 'sleepy in the time of our prosperity'.[142] The result was that when troubles came he forgot to give thanks for benefits past and so, though like David called a 'mirror of patience', it is David in Psalm 22 who sets the better example.[143] Calvin, as one might expect, is insistent that no one has any right to expect anything of God.[144] Nonetheless, because his doctrine of particular providence requires him to believe that prosperity and adversity are alike sent directly from God, reasons are in fact offered as to why one might befall an individual rather than another. In the case of the wicked he contends that any prosperity they may enjoy is for their own confounding while in the case of the faithful he urges that it should be treated with caution, lest, as with Job, the discipline of affliction should lie just over the horizon.[145] But perhaps the most distinctive feature of Calvin's

[137] A facsimile of the 1574 English translation was reprinted in 1993 by the Banner of Truth Trust, Edinburgh; all reference are to this edition.

[138] Serm. 28; 128.   [139] Serm. 5; 23.   [140] Serm. 33; 151.

[141] Serm. 74; 349.

[142] Serm. 110; 519. Sermon 154 is particularly severe on Job: 722–6.

[143] Serm. 12; 52. Elsewhere, Psalm 73 is used to illustrate the way in which David had been similarly subject to doubts about divine providence: 9; 40.

[144] Institutes, 3.14.5, quoting Job 41.11.

[145] Serm. 32; 150; Serm. 107; 502.

analysis is the way in which he insists on the extent to which, though we should trust divine providence, its ways remain largely inscrutable to us in this world. Indeed, it is this underlying notion that generates the particular angle Calvin gives to the divine speech from the whirlwind. In effect, its argument has become that providence is clearer in nature than in history, but precisely because of that clarity in nature we can trust to God to ensure that history also in due course receives a similar just ordering.[146]

Some worrying examples of Calvin's willingness to identify God's punishment taking effect on his contemporaries are on record.[147] But neither such attitudes as these nor what some call his excessive moralism should blind us to the extent to which, so deeply immersed in Scripture as he was, Calvin accurately reflects the Bible's teaching as a whole, even if he fails to observe some of the complexities of the Book of Job in particular. Yet, however, qualified, it would not be fair to end these remarks on Calvin on a purely negative note. His sermons on Job are in fact full of deep psychological insight, and do much to accelerate the internalization approach to the problem of evil which we have already witnessed in both Gregory and Aquinas. The difficulty remains though, as we turn to the modern period, whether internalization and particular providence could continue to be maintained together in such close harmony.

Modernity: the revolt against particular providence

Though at the beginning of the modern period belief in particular providence still remained strongly entrenched, cracks in its armour would soon emerge. The increasingly frequent appearance of robust defences was one small indicator that all was not well. Pierre Bayle's *Dictionnaire historique et critique* of 1697 had thrown down the gauntlet.[148] Though some have sought to defend his

---

[146] For a helpful exposition of that aspect of his argument, S. E. Schreiner, *Where Shall Wisdom Be Found? Calvin's Exegesis of Job from Medieval and Modern Perspectives* (Chicago: University of Chicago Press, 1994), 91–155, esp. 135 ff.

[147] E.g. Letter to Viret, 14 November 1546; quoted in W. J. Bouwsma, *John Calvin* (New York: Oxford University Press, 1988), 95–6; Bouwsma is one of those who complain of his 'moralism'.

[148] An enlarged second edition appeared in 1702.

avowed loyalty to Calvinism,[149] a sceptical reading seems the more natural. Certainly, he does not hesitate to ridicule orthodox explanations of suffering, comparing them to the notion of 'a father who allows his children to break their legs so that he can show everyone his great skill in mending their broken bones, or to a king who allows sedition and disorders to develop through his kingdom so that he can gain glory by overcoming them'.[150] Leibniz's *Theodicy* of 1710 was in part intended as a response. Leibniz's claim that this is the best of all possible worlds is too well known to need further elucidation here. Each and every detail of the world has been so ordered that it generates a harmonious, rational whole: 'God, by a wonderful art, turns all the faults of these little worlds to the greater adornment of his great world. It is like the findings of perspective where certain good designs appear only confused until one relates them to their true point of view as seen by means of a glass or mirror.'[151]

It is often forgotten that there was a similar debate in England. Thomas Hobbes' *Leviathan* of 1651 was of course primarily a work of political philosophy, but his title, as he himself admits,[152] was derived from the Book of Job. It is a book which he interprets as removing particular providence from the world and substituting in its place absolute divine right,[153] and it is into this context that Leviathan as an image for the power of the human sovereign fits naturally. Although some have sought to interpret his remarks at face value and see him, like Bayle, as someone unjustly parodied for what was a sincere attempt to defend the sole authority of revelation,[154] once again this seems to me implausible. Certainly he is one of the targets behind Alexander Pope's 1733 poem *An Essay on Man*. Although Pope urges:

> Know then thyself, presume not God to scan;
> The proper study of Mankind is Man,[155]

---

[149] E.g. J. Kilcullen, *Sincerity and Truth: Essays on Arnauld, Bayle and Toleration* (Oxford: Clarendon Press, 1988), e.g. 58–60.

[150] P. Bayle, *Historical and Critical Dictionary*, ed. R. H. Popkin, (Indianapolis: Hackett, 1991), 166–79, esp. 176; entry under 'Paulicians'.

[151] *Essais de théodicée*, 2.147 (my trans.)

[152] *Leviathan* (London: Collins, 1962), 2.28; 284.

[153] Ibid., 2.31; 312–13.

[154] E.g. F. C. Hood, *The Divine Politics of Thomas Hobbes* (Oxford: Clarendon Press, 1964).   [155] *Essay on Man* 2.1–2

the poem is in fact a sustained attempt to show the interdependence of all things for the good, with even our self-serving instincts ensuring the promotion of family and the cultivation of others' esteem. It is all summed up in the poem's most famous lines:

> All nature is but art unknown to thee;
> All chance, direction which thou canst not see;
> All discord, harmony not understood;
> All partial evil, universal good;
> And, spite of pride, in erring reason's spite,
> One truth is clear, Whatever is, is RIGHT.

In making the reference to pride's failures so prominent, it is possible that an allusion to Hobbes is intended, since the latter's favourite description of Leviathan was as 'king of all the children of pride'.[156]

Yet, despite such public declarations, Pope did feel something of the force of the argument on the other side. Within the poem itself when the argument gets rough, he sometimes repeats the language of the canonical work,[157] while in another poem, *The Epistle to Lord Bathurst,* he tells of 'a plain good man' like Job who is successfully corrupted by riches and 'curses God and dies' (339–402). Nonetheless, *An Essay on Man* enjoyed enormous popularity throughout Europe, even Voltaire describing it as 'the most beautiful, the most useful, and the most sublime poem ever written in any language'.[158] But it was also attacked, partly because of a rather free French translation.[159] Samuel Johnson provided English versions of some of the critical comments, and even wrote a burlesque of the poem's theology in his 1759 work *Rasselas.* Pope was, however, defended at a very early stage by the controversialist and theologian, William Warburton, who in the 1740s had argued that Job should be interpreted allegorically and not literally; it was written, he suggested, during the Babylonian captivity, with the 'friends' symbolizing the foes of the Jewish people. That contention helped to keep the Book of Job prominent in the public

---

[156] *Essay* 1. 289–94; Hobbes, *Leviathan,* 284; Job 41: 34.
[157] *Essay* 1.157; cf. Job 28: 26 and 37: 3; *Essay* 1.257–8; cf. Job 25: 4–6.
[158] M. Mack, *Alexander Pope: A Life* (New Haven: Yale University Press, 1985), 541 and n. 899. [159] Ibid., 736–41.

debate, as did the shock of the Lisbon earthquake on All Saints'
Day, 1755 when about 40,000 people were killed, many of them at
church. Though Voltaire's parody of particular providence in his
Candide of 1758 was to have more lasting influence, the fact that
one theologian (William Sherlock) sold a hundred thousand copies
of his providential version of the Lisbon events demonstrates how
strong the rival position continued to be.

But a change was afoot, perhaps best typified by the change of
mind of the philosopher Immanuel Kant. In his earlier writings he
had subscribed to the Leibnizian view; at one point he even
recommends that we should 'accustom our eye to these terrible
catastrophes as being the common ways of providence, and regard
them even with a sort of complacency'.[160] However, his 1791
essay, 'On the Failure of All Philosophical Attempts at Theodicy',
represents a major change of view. He employs as his key one
particular verse from the book: 'God forbid that I should justify
you; till I die I will not remove mine integrity from me' (Job 27:
5 RSV). While its use in other hands might have been a declaration of non-belief, in Kant's it was not. As his more developed
position two years later in *Religion within the Limits of Reason Alone*
makes clear, what he sought was to make human freedom central
to a practical 'solution'. We are not the passive instruments of
providence; it is up to us to respond in our freedom to the situation, and in that response we discover what is meant by grace.

Kant did not immediately win the day, but it does seem as
though this is the position towards which the Church has been
moving over the succeeding two centuries. Thus inconceivable
today would be the once common interpretation of the Irish
Potato Famine as a judgement of God, or the words of a memor-
ial tablet in a Dumfries cemetery from 1832. Commenting on the
four hundred and twenty citizens who had died of Asiatic cholera
that year, the slab informs us: 'That the benefit of this solemn
warning might not be lost to posterity this monument was erected
from collections in several churches in the town.' An elucidatory
reference to Psalm 90 is offered below: 'Their torment was to
destruction, and saying, Return, ye children of men.'[161] In other

---

[160] Quoted in A. Loades, *Kant and Job's Comforters* (Newcastle: Avero, 1985),
105; for the contrast between the earlier and later Kant, ibid., 101–58.
[161] Monument in St Michael's churchyard, Dumfries, south-west Scotland.
Which translation of Ps. 90: 3 was used is not clear; it is not the AV.

words, the epidemic is seen as a judgement on those who died, and a summons to those still alive to repent.

In trying to understand what has led to the abandonment of such attitudes, it would be absurd to suppose only one factor responsible. As we have seen, continuing reflection on the book of Job played its part, but that can hardly be the whole answer, if only because the text only ruled out any automatic connection in all cases, not one that was delayed or that applied in some instances and not others. Clearly the impact upon the European consciousness of such a major disaster as the Lisbon earthquake and the arguments surrounding it must also have played their part. But arguments are seldom successful of themselves, and in any case Europe had been subject to even greater disasters in the past, such as the Black Death, and at that time the notion of particular providence had emerged, if anything, strengthened.[162]

Christopher Lamb in his wide-ranging study of attitudes to the Book of Job in the eighteenth century observes how it functioned as a focus for the move towards particularity and self-reflection in English literature.[163] If we may develop his argument a little, it was not that such attitudes had not existed before, but that now there was the desire to see each situation (and the individual in it) as unique; so there arose a conflict with the explanations of particular providence because, though in theory particular, such explanations tended to reduce to a few standard types. Individuality was being asserted, of which the replacement of the language of natural law by that of natural rights was another sign. That too helped to undermine any strong adherence to particular providence. Government was now seen as up to us, and not part of a given divine dispensation as in Romans 13. It is a process which has continued into the twentieth century. Almost no adherent of any of the three main monotheistic religions would have thought contraception compatible with their faith prior to about 1900. Who came into the world and who left it was seen as very much part of the providence of God. When considering Rome's current dilemmas it is salutary, therefore, to recall that the Anglican

---

[162] The Black Death was most commonly interpreted in terms of divine judgement.

[163] J. Lamb, *The Rhetoric of Suffering* (Oxford: Clarendon Press, 1995), especially chapters on Richardson and Fielding, 226–73.

communion only abandoned its opposition as late as 1930 (the Lambeth Conference of 1908 had given an unconditional condemnation). One way of viewing such changes is of course to see them as no more than adaptation to secular values. But there is another option, and that is to recognize that the full implications of the infinite value attaching to the individual already enshrined in Jesus' teaching and practice could only come to full consciousness once certain possibilities and perceptions of freedom were present within the society itself. Particular providence can so easily sound manipulative, rather than giving choice to the individual how to respond.

But a new sense of freedom and personal integrity is only half of what has emerged from this continuing engagement with the issues raised by Job. It set new parameters for any practical theodicy, but it did not itself actually provide such a theodicy. I want therefore finally to consider William Blake's illustrations for the Book of Job as indicative of perhaps the most important way of coming to terms with suffering in this new understanding of experience as no longer directly engineered by God. Blake's illustrations have often been interpreted in purely psychological terms, with God simply as an aspect of Job's personality,[164] but closer attention to his writings and practice demonstrate conclusively that this cannot be so. Prayer and vision played an integral part in Blake's life and he held with absolute conviction a belief in personal survival after death.[165] He also seems to have consciously sought some sort of identification with Christ, even though at the same time he remained deeply suspicious of all forms of institutionalized Christianity where he saw Christ usurped as a tool of conservatism.[166] Thus for Kathleen Raine he is England's 'greatest Christian artist', and the significance of his Job engravings, which

---

[164] Here J. H. Wicksteed's 1910 work *Blake's Vision of the Book of Job* (revised edition, 1924; reprinted New York: Haskell House, 1971) has been particularly influential; for a more recent example influenced by Jung, A. Solomon, *Blake's Job* (London: Palamabron Press, 1993).

[165] B. Lindberg, *William Blake's Illustrations to the Book of Job* (Turku, Finland: Abo Akademi, 1973), 74, 152–66; J. King, *William Blake: His Life* (London: Weidenfeld & Nicholson, 1991), 214–15, 222, 229.

[166] King, *Blake*, e.g. 201, 210; D. Fuller, *Blake's Heroic Argument* (London: Crook Helm, 1988), e.g. 16–17.

he did late in life,[167] is for her to be compared to that of Bach's B-Minor Mass and Shakespeare's *King Lear*.[168] Certainly the two painters for whom Blake most consistently expressed admiration,[169] Michelangelo and Fra Angelico, also both had a profound religious motivation underlying their art.

Though the engravings are replete with biblical quotations (occasionally subtly modified),[170] what in fact we are offered in this account is a version which departs in numerous ways from the biblical version, presumably with the intention of offering a significantly different message. But it is by no means idiosyncratic, since it reflects fully the stream of tradition which had preceded it. We may begin by observing some parallels with the *Testament of Job*. Job's wife again plays a major role (she is to be found in no less than eighteen out of the twenty-one sketches); it is Satan rather than the biblical 'great wind' which brings down the house on top of Job's children; the presence of his ten children in heaven is recorded;[171] and Job's interest in music is represented in the last two engravings. Since the *Testament of Job* did not become generally available in the west again until 1833, elements such as these must have been indirectly mediated, but convincing evidence is available to explain how this might easily have occurred; there was a wealth of art and poetry which had kept such ingredients alive.[172] Even when an image is apparently wholly derived from the Hebrew Bible, as with the potsherd in contrast to the Vulgate's dunghill, to account for its prominence one needs once more to turn to the tradition where it had been assigned a specific symbolic role: as a sign of Job himself being broken and then recovering through being worked upon by God.[173]

[167] Probably in 1821, though earlier versions of some of them do exist. The Butts water-colour set (now in the Pierpont Morgan Library, New York) probably date from 1805–6.
[168] K. Raine, *William Blake* (London: Thames & Hudson, 1970), 26, 186.
[169] King, *Blake*, 223.
[170] Cf. Lindberg *Illustrations*, 107–9. For example, 'tho consumed be my wrought image' is the variant used to conclude the famous AV rendering of Job 19: 25–7.
[171] For the action of Satan, Illustration III; for Job's children in heaven, margins of Ill. XIX. [172] Lindberg *Illustrations*, 139–48.
[173] Job 2: 8; Plate VI and XII; Lindberg *Illustrations*, 133–4.

But perhaps the influence of a developing, imaginative tradition is seen at its deepest when we consider how Blake intended
his art to be interpreted as a whole. For the significance of the
story he takes to lie in how suffering can deepen our discipleship
and patterning after Christ (and Blake himself was at various times
of his life in poverty not far short of destitution).[174] The sending
of Satan is made to correspond with Job giving bread (Illus. V),
to indicate the underlying problem with his character: his apparent generosity is inadequately motivated. The God after whom he
patterns himself is a self-satisfied God, a hint of which has already
been given in the margins of Illustration II with its 'peacock of
pride and parrot of vain repetitions'.[175] Job's physical affliction
with boils is in the biblical account almost an anticlimax, whereas
here it becomes the undoubted culmination of his sufferings
(Illus. VI). Satan's genitals are scaled over, perhaps to remind us
of the way in which Job had become patron saint of those affected
with syphilis,[176] but also to hint at Blake's own conviction of how
a general shame spreads once a conviction of sin has arisen.[177]
Yet, as at Chartres, his wife is joined to him by his feet, while in
the following illustration we see her caring for her husband in a
way that echoes Michelangelo's most famous Pietà at St Peter's in
Rome (Illus. VI and VII). Job's recovery begins when he starts to
rebel (Illus. VIII), and can then see the God he worshipped for
what he is: with cloven hoof (Illus. XI). But even before that, in
the previous illustration the possibility of patterning himself after
Christ had been raised, with his friends mocking him as others
had once mocked Christ. Certainly, there seems little doubt that
the God of the whirlwind (Illus. XIII) is Christ, given his obviously cruciform shape and the way in which he reaches out to Job
with his right hand. Before God himself finally appears on earth
to bless husband and wife (Illus. XVII), Job is given some instruc-
tions on the defeat of evil: that it is a battle with evil on a
monstrous scale, as the presence of the two monsters, Leviathan
and Behemoth indicate (Illus. XV). But the gift of new life finally

[174] Though probably not when the engravings were done, as from *c.* 1821
(possibly 1818) Blake had the support of John Linnell who bought and adequately
paid for whatever Blake wanted to do.
[175] S. F. Damon, *Blake's Job* (Providence, R.I.: Brown University Press,
1966), 14.   [176] L. L. Besserman, *Legend*, 65.
[177] Boils and shame are connected in Blake's *Jerusalem* 21. 3–5.

comes when Job prays for his misguided friends. The text 'Also the Lord accepted Job' is deliberately juxtaposed with that act (Illus. XVIII). He can now happily receive love in the form of gifts, whereas in his erstwhile state he knew only how to dispense justice. In short, a new creature has been born through suffering, with a deeper morality and a better sense of life's significance. Particular providence is thus no longer seen as something imposed, but a freely chosen decision to interpret suffering, however caused, in a particular way and so, correspondingly, shape one's life of discipleship.

Throughout the course of our investigation I have repeatedly drawn attention to an increasing internalization of Job's dilemma. With the Septuagint and *Testament of Job* the story had refocused on relations with specific people, replacing the purely formal ethics with which the canonical book had attempted to demonstrate Job's piety. Then, most obviously with Gregory the Great, but beginning much earlier and increasing as the centuries rolled, there was added emphasis on the solution itself as also having something to do with internal attitudes rather than some formal restoration of prosperity. With that also went the paralleling of Job's misfortunes to those of Christ. Blake, however, has carried that process yet one stage further. Now we have a much more complete integration of ethics and internalization in that the 'solution' to suffering is seen to lie not just in attitudes (patience, faith, and so forth) but also in our capacity to change those attitudes in the light of such experiences. Our freedom now plays an integral part. Related to that perception is also Blake's implicit claim that Christ is actually discovered in the suffering rather than already being there as its exemplar. Job's formal worship and apparent generosity to the poor (Illus. I, IV, V) had first to be undermined before they could be reinstated in a truer form.[178] The righteous Job had finally perished to become any one of us. But he had become one of us not by being made guilty, but through the arbitrariness of his suffering opening up possibilities

[178] The significance of the presence of a Gothic church and of its later substitution by a Druid temple is disputed. Damon (*Blake's Job*, 20) thinks that it may speak of a move away from more formal worship, but elsewhere Blake uses Gothic as an image of the imaginative because of its exuberant and not narrowly geometric style. Perhaps therefore both are simply intended to speak of unrealized spiritual possibilities.

for deeper perceptions of us as we really are and of what we might become.[179]

None of this is to suggest that Blake was unique in having such insights, but he does well illustrate the huge change that has happened in the way human beings view their experience, and so with it how the question of suffering is best handled under these new circumstances. Even though the canonical work's purely externalist account was soon abandoned, for most of the history of the Church Christians still thought of suffering as 'sent', as specifically engineered by particular providence for some definite purpose, whether punishment or otherwise. The revolution that has happened in modern times is that most Christians no longer think in such terms. As with issues as diverse as parenthood or wealth, overwhelmingly what befalls us is seen as a mixture of the accidents of life and our own choices. Yet, far from such a perception forcing God to vacate the scene, it means that he can now achieve an even more central role, as we seek his grace to use those situations creatively. This is the point that Blake saw.

It is a viewpoint which the historical Jesus is unlikely to have shared. The visions of the Devil which so tormented him in his temptations were no doubt for him unqualifiedly real, and in no sense experienced as simply a product of his own imagination. Likewise, in the case of his death his cry of dereliction suggests puzzlement about why it is taking this form, but no doubt that it is from the hand of God: that was something given. We cannot now say for certain whether that puzzlement found its resolution this side of the grave, as Luke and John imply (Luke 23: 46; John 19: 30; contrast Mark 15: 34), or whether he had to await his resurrection. But what, I think, we can declare of that contrast is that it is indicative of the power of God to help us make sense of our experience and give meaning to our suffering, by, like Jesus, calling on his aid. So, great though the distance is between our imaginative world and that of Jesus, it is still one in which the risen

---

[179] Inevitably with so much symbolism and ambiguous textual commentary, a variety of different interpretations are possible. In the body of the text, I have followed what remains the most common reading, but for one which reduces the moral content and instead sees the primary emphasis on spiritual development through a 'dark night of the soul', P. Minney, 'Job's Gethsemane: Tradition and Imagination in William Blake's Illustrations for the Book of Job': M Litt. thesis, University of Durham, 1997, esp. 99–133.

Christ can continue to make a vital contribution. The living Christ comes alongside us in our suffering and can help us make effective use of it, not by offering a response identical to the way in which he faced the issue when incarnate, but rather one in which his own transformed resurrection perception and our own present circumstances will interact to produce a new vision.

The contentions of the previous paragraph have been put so baldly that some readers may find the contrast between Jesus' experience and that of the Christian in the modern world too stark to allow any meaningful discourse about continuities, as well as developments, in the Christian tradition. If so, they need to be alerted at this point to the two chapters of my companion volume *Tradition and Imagination* devoted to detailed discussion of the continuities which exist on the question of Jesus and suffering despite the huge transformations which have also occurred across the centuries.[180] A not unrelated example was offered in the first chapter of this volume with the transformation to which Mary Magdalene was subject after her death. What she and Jesus shared was the subsequent adaptation of the story of their lives to say different things about their significance from how either of them would have understood those lives and their meaning at the time. Though in Mary's case this involved more of what could be categorized as the literally false, nonetheless in both cases I argued that what emerged was after all true in the deepest sense of that term. The final part of this work attempts to give substance to that claim, but first I want to turn to another instance of a woman transformed over the course of the centuries through changing patterns of experience: the mother of Jesus. In this case I shall argue that the Church was not always so successful, though, as the reader will discover, such a concession does not makes my conclusions nearly as predictable as might have been expected.

---

[180] Chapters 6 and 7.

5
Mary and virgin promise

IN the previous chapter we observed how the treatment of Job's story over more than two and a half thousand years reflected among Jews and Christians changing attitudes to, and experience of, suffering, with corresponding resultant changes in the practice of discipleship. Later attitudes could not be characterized as mere decline from the central biblical perspective. On the contrary, while some insights from the Bible need to be retained, others— of equal importance—were to emerge in the later development of the tradition of the book's interpretation. Revelation—what God is saying to us through that particular story—cannot therefore be narrowly confined either to what the book originally meant or to what it is believed to be saying to us today. Instead, we need to take with full seriousness the continuing dialogue in which the community of faith has engaged throughout history with the book's topic by means of imaginative transformations of its content.[1] In the case of Job I was concerned to argue that greater weight should be given to later tradition than is normally allowed. However, I did not intend thereby a uniform pattern of positive, advancing developments. Religious perceptivity can decline as well as progress. What, therefore, I would like to do now is examine a much more ambiguous development where regression is perhaps more prominent, and that is the highly controversial case of the treatment of Jesus' mother. Identifying such regression is

---

[1] Why it is appropriate to speak of a single 'community of faith' rather than of a number of quite distinct such communities is an issue that will be faced when the question of authority is discussed in Part Three. For the moment, though, one might note the way in which even the *Testament of Job* was incorporated into the Christian consciousness.

commonplace. Where my treatment is distinctive is in the claim that things are already going wrong in the New Testament itself, and that this trend is exacerbated in the later history of the Church for similar reasons, through a distorted Christology. Experiential demands were eventually to force Mary into an exalted role, precisely because Jesus was no longer available to fulfil the relevant functions in his own right. Even the imagination, as we shall see, contributed to some notable deformations. Nonetheless, amid all the distortions, some more positive aspects were to emerge, and these deserve due appreciation. As we shall observe, her life and present significance become much more directly relevant to questions of discipleship.

From the Bible: instrument of promise or struggling disciple?

As in my discussion of the figure of Job, so here also I shall proceed historically, and so begin with Scripture. What I shall contend is that in order to highlight the graciousness of God in Christ all four evangelists to varying degrees distort the contribution of Mary, turning her into either passive instrument or ideal, representative disciple, thereby ignoring a more complicated dynamic which, I shall suggest, lies just beneath the text: Mary as struggling disciple. It is a dynamic which many would find incompatible with any literal reading of the virgin birth. While not denying the greater importance of its symbolic meaning, I shall give reasons why it seems to me that there need be no inconsistency.

In assessing how the evangelists view Mary, the infancy narratives would seem an appropriate starting point, and in particular Luke's Gospel since, unlike with Matthew where the story revolves round the actions of Joseph, its primary focus seems to be on Mary herself. She is the one to whom the angel appears, as also the one whose joy at the news of the forthcoming birth is celebrated in the Magnificat. Yet care is needed in our handling of the material. As I argued at length in *Tradition and Imagination*, our modern celebrations of Christmas deviate in numerous ways from the likely intentions of the two evangelists, not least in supposing the child to be the true focus of the narrative rather

than his significance as an adult.[2] If that is so, even less likely is
that Mary is its real or even secondary core, and that is what I shall
argue shortly.

But first the reader needs to be reminded why such a conclusion need not be the final judgement that the Church should make
on the matter. In that previous volume I maintained that, once a
full doctrine of incarnation had developed, it became legitimate to
celebrate the birth in its own right rather than merely as anticipatory of Christ's adult significance. So at least in principle a similar
corrective might be necessary for a proper treatment of Mary, and
that, I suggest, emerges as the Church has become more conscious
of the gradual character of the appropriation of Christ's significance, not least by the biblical community itself. Because it was
only with the resurrection that Christ's full significance began to
become known, the evangelists were faced with no other
recourse—at least if they kept to the narrative form—than to tell
Christ's life rather differently from what had actually happened.
The conclusion of the story needed to be anticipated, so that the
significance now attaching to the past could be grasped immediately. But, unfortunately, while that meant greater clarity about
the ultimate meaning of Jesus' life, it also produced distortions in
its turn, particularly in respect of the Church's later understanding
of Mary. Thus, for example, whether compositions of Luke
himself or of the early Church, the Magnificat and Nunc Dimittis
clearly represent the clarity of conviction and confidence which
the post-Resurrection church had now attained, and which it
could now express through suitable borrowings from the Old
Testament.[3] Not that the sentiments were wrong in themselves,[4]
but they assigned a confidence and certainty to the beginning of
Jesus' life, and thus to Mary, that almost certainly was not there.

Once such a general pattern of reflection is conceded, the question immediately arises as to how far the process may have gone.
For some theologians almost every detail of the infancy narratives

[2] Cf. *Tradition and Imagination*, 75–85.
[3] Magnificat: Luke 1: 46–55; Nunc Dimittis: Luke 2: 29–32; with the former
based on 1 Samuel 2 and the latter on Isa. 49.
[4] Here I deliberately adopt an eccesiastical way of referring to the relevant
passages, to underline my endorsement of their sentiments and significance,
though at the same time challenging their historicity.

is mythological. Certainly, the flight into Egypt and the massacre of the innocents in Matthew's account are used to reinforce Matthew's general thesis that a greater than Moses is now here, as is his presentation of the Sermon on the Mount. But it would be precipitate to infer immediately from such desired parallels the presence of pure invention. Jesus' teaching is unlikely to have been delivered like this on a single occasion, but most scholars would agree that its general content is not too far distant from what Jesus is likely to have said over a number of different occasions. Similarly, the parallel with Moses in respect of the massacre of the innocents should not of itself be sufficient to rouse our doubts about the historicity of the incident. Indeed, what we know of Herod's character from elsewhere would seem to add verisimilitude. Rather, for me the real doubts only begin to arise when the incident has to be set in the context of the already noted gradual growth in Jesus' own self-understanding and that of his followers. A family and community remembering such an incident would surely have implied a different reception for his initial ministry. Even so, for the Christian an important symbolic truth remains firmly embedded in the story: that, though a greater than Moses is here, like Moses he comes as a challenge to the powers that be.

The incident is a good one to consider, because it presents on a smaller scale the larger issue raised by the question of what is commonly called the virgin birth but which should more accurately be labelled the virginal conception.[5] For some theologians such as Pannenberg it is so obviously transitional between an adoptionist Christology that dates Christ's sonship from his baptism and the full pre-existent view of John that he sees no other possible option than rejection, if the full force of the latter is to be maintained.[6] Barth by contrast maintains not only that the notion is fully compatible with a pre-existent Christology but also that it is the best way of preserving the absolute priority of grace in what happened.[7] Neither is a New Testament scholar, but in the most

---

[5] Strictly speaking, 'virgin birth' should be reserved for the claim that Mary's hymen remained intact even after giving birth—a claim sometimes made in versions of the birth which insist that she experienced no pain.

[6] W. Pannenberg, *Jesus God and Man* (London: SCM Press, 1968), 141–50, esp. 143.

[7] K. Barth, *Church Dogmatics* (Edinburgh: T & T Clark, 1958), I/2, 172–202; *Dogmatics in Outline* (London: SCM Press, 1949), 95–100.

thorough investigation of the birth narratives by such a scholar, Raymond Brown also leaves the final decision to doctrine rather than history. For him 'the *scientifically controllable* biblical evidence leaves the question of the historicity of the virginal conception unresolved'.[8] Some would argue that, rather than engage in what turn out to be acrimonious discussions about historicity, concern for the unity of the Church requires us to focus upon the theological significance of the doctrine.[9] At one level that would seem right: its symbolic significance is, as we shall see, what mattered most to the evangelists. Yet, more difficult issues should not be avoided. However indecisively the historical question is answered, it will contribute to our picture of the Mary with whom we are engaged, and whose principal title in the history of the Church has always been that of Virgin. Moreover, even at the symbolic level difficult choices must be made, between competing accounts of what significance was intended to be assigned to that 'virginity', or else ought to be. So it will be profitable to consider each—history and symbol—in turn.

Narrow evidential issues are unlikely of themselves to resolve matters. Even the classic defence of Gresham Machen had to conclude that his four hundred pages of defence only really became plausible when 'the virgin birth is removed from its isolation and taken in connection with the whole glorious picture of the One who is said to be virgin-born'.[10] Unless, for instance, one is inclined on other grounds to believe in miracles, one is unlikely to be persuaded in this case. However, it is important to note that many of the common objections raised against its historicity do not survive scrutiny. There is no evidence, for instance, to suggest that Isaiah 7: 14 helped to shape the belief. On the contrary, its natural meaning is that someone who is currently a virgin will in due course conceive in the normal way. It thus appears that it is belief in the virginal conception which led to the verse being interpreted as a prophecy rather than the influence running the

---

[8] R. E. Brown, *The Birth of the Messiah* (London: Chapman, 2nd edn., 1993), 517–33 and 697–712, esp. 527 (his italics).

[9] E.g. P. W. Thomas, 'The Virginal Conception', *Expository Times* 107 (1995), 11–14.

[10] J. G. Machen, *The Virgin Birth of Christ* (Cambridge: James Clarke, 1930), 381.

other way.[11] Again, most alleged parallels turn out on inspection to be spurious. This is clearly so with most classical and Egyptian parallels where something analogous to sexual relations is maintained. But, even where this is not obviously so, examples favoured by distinguished biblical scholars can still turn out to be quite weak, whether their aim is to establish possibility of influence,[12] or greater historical credibility elsewhere.[13] This is not to contest the existence of belief in virgin births in other religions,[14] only to challenge whether any of the parallels adduced are all that close.[15] Also pertinent is the incongruity of the claim in a context where Jesus being of 'the seed of David' is repeatedly affirmed.[16]

The relevance of anthropological studies is somewhat more complex to assess. In 1966 Edmund Leach initiated an extensive debate as a result of an article in which he denied the legitimacy of inferring any literal claims from this or similar accounts; instead the virgin birth, he argued, was part of a general pattern that had

[11] Cf. C. E. B. Cranfield, 'Some reflections on the subject of the Virgin Birth', *Scottish Journal of Theology* 41 (1988), 177–89, esp. 181.

[12] In *Ancient Christian Gospels: Their History and Development* (London: SCM Press, 1990), 306–7, H. Koester posits a Hellenistic background on the basis of Philo's treatment of four Old Testament wives, but in context (*De Cherubim* 43–7) it is clear that the commitment never goes beyond the allegorical, with Philo primarily concerned to attribute the implanting of virtue to God.

[13] Commenting on the legend that Apollo was Plato's father, we are told that 'the source situation here is better than with Jesus': U. Luz, *Matthew 1–7* (Edinburgh: T & T Clark, 1990), 118, n. 25. The reason adduced is because its first recorded mention was in an encomium given in the year of Plato's death by his nephew, Speusippus. But what this ignores is the fact that the pagan source (Diogenes Laertius, *Lives* 3.2) to which we are referred for this information does not treat it as true (Diogenes opens by referring to Plato as the son of two human parents), and indeed implies by the way in which the legend is introduced ('there was a saying at Athens') that neither did Speusippus.

[14] At least as early as Hesiod's *Theogony* we have gods giving birth without intercourse: 924 ff. for Athena from Zeus and Hephaestus from Hera. The closest parallel may in fact be Mexican, when Quetzalcoatl is conceived by a god breathing on his mother Chilmalman: so R. Laurentin, 'Sens et historicité de la conception virginale' in P. C. Balic (ed.), *Studia mediaevalia et mariologica* (Rome: Antonianum, 1971), 515–42, esp. 517.

[15] R. E. Brown comes to a similar conclusion: *Birth*, 522–4

[16] J. McHugh, *The Mother of Jesus in the New Testament* (New York: Doubleday, 1975), 269 ff.

purely social and relational meanings.[17] The details of the debate need not concern us here. What, however, it did highlight was the extent to which earlier generations or 'primitive' peoples of more recent times were open to alternative accounts of conception, including parthenogenesis, as with the Trobriand islanders or Australian aborigines. One might add to this the widespread belief in medieval Europe that an evil spirit or *incubus* might descend upon a woman unawares and thus generate pregnancy. In none of these cases is the parallel with Mary's conception particularly close, but it does emphasize how very much more open to alternative explanations earlier generations were before the discovery of the ovum by von Baer in 1826.[18]

These anthropological observations are important because they make less credible what for many (perhaps most) is the decisive argument against, namely the difficulty of envisaging how Mary could have possessed such knowledge and it not have profoundly transformed the course of Jesus' ministry.[19] Raymond Brown, for example, observes that not only did neither Mary nor Jesus' brothers show any deep conviction of his status during his earthly ministry 'she communicated no profound christological understanding to his followers who came to understand only after the resurrection and, indeed, at first seem to have proclaimed that Jesus had *become* Messiah . . . never mentioning the virginal conception'.[20] But is such a presentation not to assume that the only two alternatives are either the biblical narrative as it stands or not at all?[21] But, if the presentation of Christ's nature and consciousness was changed in the light of the resurrection by building upon factors already present within the oral memory,

[17] E. Leach, 'Virgin Birth', in *Proceedings of the Royal Anthropological Institute* (1966) 39–49; for a good, overall survey of the debate, J. A. Saliba, 'The Virgin-Birth debate in anthropological literature: a critical assessment', *Theological Studies* 36 (1975), 428–54.

[18] Cf. J. Delaney, 'The meaning of paternity and the virgin birth debate', *Man* 21 (1986), 494–513, esp. 508.

[19] The general ignorance in the ancient world of underlying processes is well illustrated by Eccles. 11.5.   [20] R. E. Brown, *Birth*, 526.

[21] It is a point which can equally be made against Brown's critics, where the tendency is to assume that the only possible response is a defence of complete historicity rather than history and imagination both working creatively together. For an example of the fault, Miguens, M., 'The infancy narratives and critical biblical method', *Communio* 7 (1980), 24–54.

why might this not also be true in respect of Jesus' birth? Even if Mary had experienced a virginal conception, while it would have spoken of God's action, without the certainties with which the text is now endowed it would hardly have spoken of Christ's divinity, and Mary might well have kept quiet until she discovered what the future would bring, especially as to speak out would have invited obvious ripostes about illegitimacy. Although there is no wide acceptance for Jane Schaberg's claim that embedded in the narrative is the implicit admission that Mary had been the victim of rape,[22] it does provide a powerful reminder of what counter-claims might have been made, had Mary made the unusual circumstances of the birth generally known.

None of this is to prove historicity, but it is to claim that from acceptance of the infancy narratives as essentially post-resurrection creations one is not necessarily required to infer that the virginal conception is itself also an imaginative invention, with purely doctrinal content in view. Yet, though the historical objections are in my view weaker than is commonly contended, just as today one is unlikely to be persuaded of the truth of a virginal conception without some appeal beyond history to conceptual considerations,[23] so even then there is no doubt that for the evangelists doctrinal content was their primary concern. It was one key, opening way of indicating Jesus' fundamental significance. That the focus was upon Jesus and not Mary needs first to be acknowledged, before we go on to consider why a larger imaginative role for her was nonetheless appropriate.

As Luke tells the story, Elizabeth's conception in old age anticipates the still more remarkable case of Mary, and as such provides a useful, salutary warning that the point can thus have nothing to do with hostility to sexuality: it is 'a miracle in which the birth by

---

[22] J. Schaberg, *The Illegitimacy of Jesus* (San Francisco; Harper & Row, 1987), e.g. 90.

[23] *Some* concepts of incarnation require it; D. Brown, *The Divine Trinity* (London: Duckworth, 1985), 122–6. There is also the modern problem of how much Jesus might be allowed to inherit from Mary. When earlier generations spoke of Jesus taking flesh from Mary (e.g. Irenaeus, *Adversus Haereses* 3. 21–2) they had in mind a largely passive inheritance, not the possibility of genetic determinations of character. To exclude the latter would seem to require the creation of an embryo *de novo*, with Mary having more the role of surrogate mother, together with all the consequences that might imply.

an infertile woman is escalated to the birth by a virgin'.[24] Both births tell of the inauguration of a new order, and this we find reflected in Mary's song, the Magnificat. But both birth and song are there to stress what God is doing, not Mary. Admittedly, Mary is given a larger role than in Matthew's Gospel, but we should not confuse the original focus of the text with the one which we might now wish to give to it. In this sense at least Barth's stress on the absolute priority of divine grace is right. As the most important recent ecumenical investigation of the text conceded, not only is the Latin version (*gratia plena*) of the angel's greeting quite wrong (the Greek speaks of present favours, not of already existing endowments), even 'Blessed are you among women' merely reflects a common Old Testament form of address, and so prevents us 'from taking it too absolutely, as if it meant that Mary was the most blessed woman who had ever lived'.[25] In short, the intention is not to highlight what Mary has done, but what God has done through her.

That is why it would seem to me a mistake to argue that the text as it stands gives an adequate response to those who object to the Marian tradition as a whole on the grounds that it has encouraged a purely passive attitude on the part of women. The approach is found in a number of feminist theologians, who stress the need for Mary's answer and reflection.[26] But in fact there is surprisingly little within the infancy narrative itself which would justify this conclusion. Mary's fiat is really incidental to the main focus of the text, God's involvement in acting upon her. Her role is not properly as an individual but rather as a foil, so that through her various objections and difficulties the marvellous character of what God is doing may be

---

[24] L. Schottroff, *Let the Oppressed Go Free* (Louisville, Kentucky: Westminster, 1993), 158–67, esp.160.

[25] R. E. Brown et al., *Mary in the New Testament* (London: Geoffrey Chapman, 1978), 127–8 and 136. Austin Farrer even suggested that Luke may have intended by the angel's address no more than a 'charming play on words . . . "Good day to you, since God's so good to you" '; *Interpretation and Belief* (London: SPCK, 1976), 121–2.

[26] E.g. R. R. Ruether, *Mary—the Feminine Face of the Church* (London: SCM Press, 1979), 28; D. F. Middleton, 'The story of Mary: Luke's version', *New Blackfriars* 70 (1989), 555–64.

more effectively highlighted.[27] Even the allusion to a sword piercing her heart (Luke 2: 35) could be a reference merely to the incident in the Temple which follows, since Luke makes no mention of Mary's presence at the crucifixion, and so no indicator of any active or deep involvement in the future mission of her son.[28] Others have found in Barth's claim that the virginal conception reveals 'the limitation of male pre-eminence' a message of liberation for women that Mary can symbolize, but unfortunately, while Barth finds in the event an attack upon the assertiveness of male institutions, what he praises in its place is the passivity of a virginity which 'can merely receive'.[29] As the ecumenical team observe in an unguarded moment, 'this marvellous conception . . . tells us no more about Mary than that she is God's instrument'.[30] So, even if an intended parallel with the ark of the covenant had been proved (different Greek words are in fact used), this would merely have established Luke's high view of Jesus, not something definite about Mary.[31]

A more promising avenue of investigation might be to observe the way in which, though any personal contribution of Mary is downplayed, she does at least seem to have a clear representative or symbolic role. For as many writers, Protestant as well as Catholic, have noted, she is portrayed as one of the *anawim* or devout poor of Israel to whom the gospel has come. It can plausibly be argued that it is in this symbolic function rather than as an individual that Mary is of particular interest to Luke,[32] and,

[27] Expression of her anxieties at 1: 29 and 34 allow the angel to highlight the remarkable character of what God is doing, and so in effect it is the logic of the story as told that requires her assent, rather than any concern on Luke's part to praise Mary. This is not to deny that even so Luke's text leaves open the possibility of an alternative trajectory that could legitimate a different way of approaching the story.

[28] J. A. Fitzmyer, *Luke the Theologian* (London: Geoffrey Chapman, 1989), 72–3.

[29] Barth, *Church Dogmatics*, 1/2, 191–3; endorsed by F. Kerr, 'Questioning the Virgin Birth', *New Blackfriars* 75 (1994), 132–140, esp., 139–40.

[30] Brown et al., *Mary*, 125.

[31] R. Laurentin, *Structure et Theologie de Luc I–II* (Paris: J. Gabalda, 1964), e.g. 73, 79, 151. Similar views are advocated by D. M. Stanley in *Worship* 34 (1959–60), 330–2 and N. M. Flanagan in *Worship* 35 (1960–1), 370–5.

[32] E.g. M. E. Isaac, 'Mary in the Lucan infancy narrative', *The Way* Supp. 25 (1975), 80–95, esp. 84; K. Sullivan, 'His lowly maid', *Worship* 36 (1961–2), 374–9; R. S. Hanson, 'Mary, according to Luke', *Worship* 43 (1969), 425–9.

although this is contested by some scholars such as John Robinson, in all probability such an attribution of poverty may well reflect the historical facts. Even so, it is important to note that only a representative function has been established, not any particular interest in Mary for her own sake, and so we must exercise caution when we consider her role in John, where still more obviously symbolic writing is involved.

Consideration first of a related case will make the issues clearer. It has been argued that despite the promising start at the beginning of his Gospel, Luke soon regressed to a more patriarchal attitude, and that this is what we find reflected in his ascribing the beginnings of the Christian mission in Samaria to a man (Philip in Acts 8), whereas John 4 offers us the truth with the unnamed woman at the well converting many (John 4: 39).[33] But in accounting for the divergence between the two evangelists, there is readily available a more plausible explanation than merely male bias in Luke. The historicity of John's version is not only called into question by the relative ease with which the woman can be used to symbolize the people of Samaria,[34] on the practical level one also needs to note how far the inevitable prejudice against such a sinner, even if she were historical, would naturally inhibit any truly effective mission. Here, as elsewhere in John, resort to symbolism provides a more satisfying explanation. Similar issues, then, arise with respect to the presence in John of Jesus' mother at the foot of the cross. If the incident is historical, it is surprising that she is not mentioned along with the other women whose names are given in Mark and Matthew, and who in any case (in all three Gospels) are described as viewing the crucifixion 'from afar' (RSV). Is it not more reasonable in any case to suppose that friends would guard a mother from watching the death of her son in such hideous circumstances, however much she may have felt that her duty called her to be there? That is of course pure speculation, but we

---

[33] B. Kahl, 'Towards a materialist feminist reading' in E S. Fiorenza, *Searching the Scriptures: A Feminist Introduction* (London: SCM Press, 1993), I, 225 ff.

[34] A parallel is sometimes drawn with the way in which Mary represents Israel in Luke, with the Samaritan woman's five husbands symbolizing the gods of the five nations of 2 Kings 17: 24 ff.; A. R. C. Leaney, 'The Virgin Birth in Lucan theology and the classical creeds' in R. Bauckham and B. Drewery (ed.), *Scripture, Tradition and Reason* (Edinburgh: T & T Clark, 1988), 65–100, esp.78–80.

need to resist the conviction that piety required her to be there, in body as well as spirit. At all events, the general structure of the narrative, particularly the way Mary is addressed impersonally as 'Woman' suggests that John's aim is 'to give her a *representative* status, just like the anonymous "disciple whom Jesus loved".' and not to present 'Mary as an individual in her own right'.[35] That a new family or community is established at the foot of the cross seems generally agreed. Some contend that more must be meant by 'mother', with Mary as Israel now symbolically committed to the care of the Church or, less commonly, as herself the Church now entrusted to its leaders.[36] A further variant suggests that Mary 'symbolises the one who faithfully awaits the messianic times' who can now be admitted into the family of the Church.[37] Whichever version of such symbolism was part of John's intention, the highly impersonal way in which Mary is identified makes it most unlikely that any of them were supposed to apply specifically to her as an individual.

Nevertheless, that move from passive 'instrument' in Luke to explicitly representative disciple in John may perhaps be of more significance for her individuality than might initially appear. For elsewhere John hints (only just) at a model of discipleship in Mary that may actually reflect something highly significant about her actual life. For it has been observed that in the only other place where Mary is called 'Woman' she displays a mixture of incomprehension and compliance and so functions as 'a representative of those . . . for whom misunderstanding is not a permanent obstacle to discipleship'.[38] This, I suggest, is precisely the pattern which emerges from considering the evidence of the Gospels as a whole. For, though Mary is recorded as present with the disciples on the

---

[35] S. Barton, *People of the Passion* (SPCK, 1994), 54–68, esp. 65, 66.

[36] Brown et al. *Mary,* 214–18; V. Eller, 'Mary: Protestantism's Forgotten Woman', *Anglican Theological Review* 62 (1980), 146–51. Mary as Israel would reflect both her age (part of the old dispensation) and her only other major role in John in the miracle at Cana, which likewise speaks of the ending of the old dispensation, with the Jewish water jugs turned into wine.

[37] R. F. Collins, 'The representative figures of the Fourth Gospel, II', *Downside Review* 94 (1976), 118–32.

[38] J. Ashton, *Understanding the Fourth Gospel* (Oxford: Clarendon Press, 1991) 268–9.

eve of Pentecost (Acts 1: 14),[39] for much of Jesus' ministry she seems to have shown incomprehension at his behaviour. Certainly Mark leaves us in no doubt about Jesus' negative response to his mother and brothers (Mark 3: 31–35), and while this could be merely Mark's attempt to emphasize the priority of the eschatological or church family over the earthly, it is more likely that it reflects historical reality. For Mark records elsewhere hostility from family and friends, to which John gives additional support by his observation that 'even his brothers did not believe in him' (Mark 3: 21; 6: 4; John 7: 5).[40] Though in general we are not provided with a motive, one of the passages is most naturally read as indicative, not of envy, but rather of real concern lest Jesus do himself harm. Degrees of disbelief among his family might thus have varied, but all, including his mother, would have been united in seeking to avert the dangers which they saw in his behaviour. Mary's life would thus have been a struggle towards full faith in her son and his mission. Yet, though frequently missing the mark, her faith still culminated in her presence in the incipient Pentecost church.

That is one version of her life-story as a whole that could be told. Luke's Gospel, however, suggests quite another, and herein it seems to me lies the tension which was to dog the subsequent history of the Church. For, though Luke offers a further two passages which could be read to indicate hostility (Luke 8: 19–21; 11: 27–28), such an interpretation becomes implausible as soon as we observe what he has done with Mark's two references. One is omitted entirely, while the other is modified to imply a local hostility that does not include the family.[41] So, in all probability those commentators are right who suggest that 'Luke has eliminated all criticism of Jesus' family and casts Mary, his mother, as the ideal hearer of the Word of God'.[42] While I argued earlier that

---

[39] Some have seen the allusion as purely theological, the intention being to indicate that 'the earthly family of Jesus is now taken up into his spiritual family': C. K. Barrett, *The Acts of the Apostles* (Edinburgh: T & T Clark, 1994), I, 89–90. But given the extreme brevity of the reference, this is hard to credit.

[40] The first verse suggests positive concern, and though it refers this to 'friends', the location is 'home' (v. 19).

[41] Luke 4: 24 speak of a prophet not being accepted in his own country, but omits Mark's reference to family and house evincing a similar attitude: cf. Mark 6: 4.   [42] E.g. Fitzmyer, *Luke*, 76.

the New Testament cannot be blamed for any negative attitudes towards sexuality that were later to be drawn out of the image of Mary as Virgin, it does then look as though the trajectory is already present that will produce the purely passive notions of perfect discipleship that have been so deleterious to women through the ages. The New Testament, no less than later tradition, must therefore share the blame for some of the negative features which were to follow. For overall it does appear as though Luke, having begun his narrative with Mary as passive instrument, then continued in similar vein, with Mary praised for what amounts to unrelieved passivity, in unqualified subservience to the divine will.[43] John at least gave her a representative role beyond merely being one of the *anawim*, but that in no way suggests that he valued her in her own right. So it is only really by burrowing beneath the surface of the evangelists' texts that we find hints of an alternative Mary, one struggling towards full faith in her Son.

If this is anything like a correct account, it suggests two very different trajectories for her future treatment. Inevitably because of the way in which the texts have been read for most of their history, the struggling Mary had to await until modern times the possibility of complete appropriation, and it was the notion of Mary as instrument that the biblical writers passed on to their successors in the faith. That is a point worth stressing since so often it is the later Church that is blamed for such a portrayal, when there it is already in the New Testament. Those negative aspects have been so frequently adumbrated elsewhere, that I shall devote little attention to them in what follows. Instead, my focus will be upon how, almost despite the odds, the imagination retrieved Mary as an ally in the better flourishing of the Christian life. In the case of the New Testament, Mary's individuality was downplayed for the best of reasons: the attempt to clarify her son's significance. In a later section, though, we shall observe how a thoroughly bad Christology could also produce the opposite effect, and lead to the even greater exaltation of Mary.

---

[43] The modern tendency in preaching is to counter such a portrayal by taking her fiat (Luke 1: 38) as indicative of active endorsement of the divine will. But the story has only the conventional Old Testament 'fear' in the divine presence (1: 29–30), and so should not be taken to indicate real mental debate, while ancient theories of pregnancy would naturally suggest an emphasis on 'receiving' rather than a 'giving'.

Fresh insights: Virgin freedom and family indebtedness

In this section I want to draw attention to two key ways in which the imagination retrieved Mary for a more positive role than mere passive instrument or passive hearer of the word. Despite its dominance, the primary New Testament trajectory was effectively undermined through interaction between the wider culture and the hints we have already noted that Scripture gave of an alternative trajectory.

But, first, despite the surfeit of literature that already exists on the inadequacies of later tradition, some brief comments on its more negative side would seem apposite. Certainly, due acknowledgement needs to be made of how badly things went wrong, but we must firmly resist over-simplistic accounts of what happened, too narrowly expressed in terms of the obsessions of our own age. In particular, the sexual card can very easily be overplayed. Certainly, Mary has often been used both consciously and otherwise as a means of controlling women; certainly too, she has in effect at times functioned as a goddess.[44] But to say this still leaves very little explained, since it engages neither with the factors underlying such practice nor with the many other areas where neither explanation holds. That is why one of the best-researched accounts of her cult in recent years nonetheless seems to me deeply flawed, since for all her reference to the beauty at times of what was produced, one senses a lack of imaginative engagement in Marina Warner's account, as her concluding concentration on Ishtar and misogyny well illustrates.[45] Significantly, for instance, there is no attempt to wrestle with the way in which it was deficiencies in presentation of the Christian doctrine of God that lead to the necessity for Mary's divine role, with Christ as representative of judgement rather than mercy or the Holy Spirit treated as

---

[44] For an interesting variant on the argument, whereby a repressive Virgin replaces a liberating pre-Christian goddess, M. Condren, *The Serpent and the Goddess: Women, Religion and Power in Celtic Ireland* (San Francisco: Harper, 1989). The Norman invasion of Ireland is seen as particularly significant in this respect.

[45] M. Warner, *Alone Of All Her Sex: The Myth and Cult of the Virgin Mary* (London: Quartet, 1976), esp. 333–9. On the basis of a brief reference by Epiphanius to a heretical sect known as the Collyridians, Geoffrey Ashe invents a major alternative goddess religion offering freedom to women and waiting to reassert itself: G. Ashe, *The Virgin* (London: Routledge, 1976), esp. 149–71.

a commodity rather conveyor of a personal relationship;[46] no attempt to take seriously the long history of alternative, very different ways of reading her life and role.[47]

Warner's conviction is that the cult's moral treatment of women is now seen to be such that 'like Ishtar, the Virgin will recede into legend'.[48] Other critics are less sanguine. The sociologist, Michael Carroll, has offered an entirely Freudian analysis of Mary's power, but concludes 'there will be a cult devoted to Mary (or Cybele or whatever She comes to be called) as long as there are economic conditions that produce the father-ineffective family.'[49] But what that conclusion belies is his own much wider search for explanations in the body of his text, which make his book much better than it might otherwise have been. So, for instance, Marian apparitions turn out not to be oedipal but hallucinations modelled on some key person in the visionary's family context. My point is not whether or not any of Carroll's particular conclusions are true, but the need to be open to a wide range of explanation, as hugely different cultural factors across two thousand years helped to shape her cult. Two illustrations of more positive and perhaps surprising developments now follow.

The first of which we need to take cognisance is the way in which very different symbolic meanings could be attached to virginity from those pertaining in the infancy narratives. As we have seen, for the New Testament Mary's virginity was merely a sign of something else, the new beginnings that God was initiating through Jesus. All too familiar is its later use to assert a form of purity that was in effect a denial of sexuality. Yet there was also a clear, positive conception which should be noted. The New

---

[46] It is no accident that Mary's role as intercessor for mercy is at its strongest when theories of atonement demanded the last farthing from Christ; no accident that she takes over the role of the Holy Spirit when consideration of the role of the Spirit is at its weakest between Trent and Vatican II. To speak of Mary forming Christ in us or as 'source of grace' is to blur the distinction: cf. A. J. Tambasco, *What Are They Saying about Mary?* (New York: Paulist Press, 1984), 74.

[47] Many instances of views running counter to the dominant trend are given by Hilda Graef in her *Mary: A History of Doctrine and Devotion* (London: Sheed & Ward, 1965); e.g. I, 40, 43, 45, 53, 75, 126, 131.

[48] Warner, *Alone Of All Her Sex*, 339.

[49] M. P. Carroll, *The Cult of the Virgin Mary* (Princeton, N. J.: Princeton University Press, 1986), 224.

Testament image of virginity that promised something other than itself was transformed into a promise for the bearer of virginity herself. The promise of the coming Saviour was, as it were, turned back on the Virgin to give her in her own right through his presence a new freedom and dignity. Once that was seen, it was a promise that could be appropriated by all who called themselves virgins, though as the patristic period well illustrates, the tension with the more negative image continued.

An earlier chapter has already alluded to Peter Brown's positive interpretation of virginity in the patristic period, in allowing women no longer to be defined by their family context.[50] Ambrose, though, may be used to illustrate how ambiguous at times the evidence can be. In his treatise *On Virginity* one finds positive and negative sentiments alternating with no obvious consistency. Women are told to keep the door of their lips closed if they are to hear the word of God and avoid the offence of Eve, only to be told a page or so later that the soul is feminine because it softens the assaults of the body by its gentleness and rationality.[51] Tensions between the two competing approaches seems to emerge early. Oscar Cullmann has described the *Protoevangelium of James*, written perhaps about AD 150 and probably the ultimate source of legends that describe Mary's life prior to her meeting with Joseph, as a work of 'great merit', whose 'whole presentation is impressive and extremely graphic, and is evidence of a sober, sincere and poetic mind'.[52] The most natural way to read the story, in my view, is to take Mary's early commitment to virginity as dedicatory rather than as a means of avoiding pollution, though menstruation is certainly treated in those terms.[53] Jane Schaberg is someone who fails to share any of Cullmann's enthusiasm, finding in the earliest versions of the work a strongly despotic account of

[50] For a strong expression of the contrary view, J. Raitt, 'The vagina dentata and the immaculatus uterus divini fontis', *Journal of the American Academy of Religion* 48 (1980), 415–31.
[51] Ambrose, *De Virginitate* XIII, 81 and XV, 93.
[52] In his introduction to the text in W. Schneemelcher, *New Testament Apocrypha* (Cambridge: James Clarke, 1991), I, 424.
[53] Dedicated herself at the age of three, 'she danced for joy', but at twelve the priests of the Temple decide to remove her from its precincts because of worries about pollution: 7.2–3 and 8.2 (Ibid., 429).

God's action with Mary wholly passive, and the entire focus of the story geared to ward off accusations of Jesus' illegitimacy.[54] With that aim in view, she insists, Mary's parents are even made upper class, to render abuse of their daughter less likely. However, even she concedes that virginity did eventually become the primary focus, particularly in the form we know as Pseudo-Matthew; yet not in a negative way, but rather as an example of Mary exercising free choice in her vocation.[55]

There is of course no reason to believe Mary's youthful commitment to virginity true nor that her birth was a blessing to parents in old age, Anna and Joachim, though the mention of Jesus' birth in a cave may possibly indicate an early alternative tradition to that recorded in the Gospels since it has early attestation also elsewhere.[56] Despite the fact that the entrance of the infant Mary into the life of the Temple was to become one of the twelve great feasts of Orthodoxy[57] and was also to play a major role in Western art, it is one of the clearest indicators of why the apocryphal tradition cannot be true, for the Old Testament shows no tendency whatsoever to value any permanent religious commitment to virginity, male or female, and indeed regards it as a great curse for a human being to be without issue.[58] Admittedly, though, attitudes were beginning to change, as the practice of celibacy at Qumran indicates. Even so, the New Testament offers only an occasional supportive remark that is indicative more of eschatological concerns than of any real commitment to a new value (Matt. 19: 12; 1 Cor. 7: 7). By contrast, whatever faults the new stress on Mary's virginity had, it did at least now allow equal dignity to the woman or man who chose not to define themselves

---

[54] Not all female commentators take such a negative view. For some the purity of Mary has most in common with Roman Vestal Virgins, with the intention being to give Mary an exceptional role but one in no way characterized by hostility to normal patterns of sexuality: B. R. Gaventa, *Mary: Glimpses of the Mother of Jesus* (Columbia: University of South Carolina Press, 1995), 100–25, 133–45, esp. 120–2.

[55] J. Schaberg, 'The Infancy of Mary of Nazareth' in E. S. Fiorenza (ed.), *Searching the Scriptures* (London: SCM Press, 1995) II, 708–27, esp. 720, 725.

[56] Justin Martyr, *Dialogue with Trypho*, ch. 78.

[57] Held on 21 November.

[58] For some examples, Gen. 20: 18; Ps. 113: 9; 127: 3; 128: 5–6.

by their progeny. That was a major innovation in religious under-standing that deserves due credit.[59]

One illustration of its positive benefit to women comes from Constantinople and the key ideological role Mary played in secur-ing a high status for women at the imperial court. Cyril of Alexandria leaves us in no doubt that for him the key issue over the question of defining Mary as *Theotokos* or Mother of God at the Council of Ephesus in 431 was christological rather than Marian.[60] Nonetheless, it is doubtful whether he would have succeeded in his objective, had he not had such fervid support from Pulcheria, sister of the Emperor Theodosius II. As herself a dedicated virgin, not only did she see her own life in Marian terms as seeking metaphorically to bring the Saviour to birth within herself, she also viewed any honour or slight assigned to Mary as implicitly applying to her as well.[61] Her virginity gave her consid-erable freedom both in spending her wealth as she saw fit and in acting as she deemed most appropriate. The result was tactical use of her wealth and power, as well as ostentatious demonstrations of feminine dignity, among which should be noted her entry into the sanctuary on the grounds of the mystical birth of Christ in her own person, her robe being used as an altar covering during the divine liturgy, and her key role in the reception of relics.[62] That this meant that in the process Mary acquired some of the trappings of

[59] Some modern theologians insist that the logic of the metaphor requires that virginity 'symbolises closedness, if anything at all, certainly not openness': J. P. Mackey, 'The use and abuse of Mary' in R. Holloway (ed.), *Who Needs Feminism?* (London: SPCK, 1991), 99–116, esp. 108. But not only does what happened in practice indicate alternative possibilities, if this is 'blatant misuse of the natural range of image and symbol', on the same criteria to use the cross to speak of life would also merit condemnation.

[60] Well illustrated by Cyril's third letter to Nestorius (Ep. 17), where it is only in the penultimate paragraph that he turns to consider Mary: L, R. Wickham (ed.), *Cyril of Alexandria: Select Letters* (Oxford: Clarendon Press, 1983), 12–33 esp. 26–9 (par. 11).

[61] K. G. Holum, *Theodosian Empresses: Women and Imperial Dominion in Late Antiquity* (Berkeley, Cal. : University of California Press, 1982), 130–74, esp. 141–2.

[62] For entry of sanctuary, Holum, *Empresses*, 145; for other two items, V. Limberis, *Divine Heiress: The Virgin Mary and the Creation of Christian Constantinople* (London: Routledge, 1994), 49–50; 52–3; cf. 57.

an imperial cult cannot be denied,[63] but it would be foolish to deny on this basis the considerable impact that the notion of Mary as virgin exercised in a very different direction, in generating not yet another sovereign, but someone with whose independence of life-style the unmarried could identify.[64] Regret should lie not in the strength of this notion of virginity as such, but in the way in which it tried, among other things, to abrogate to itself superiority over the married state. In this respect Jovinian, the opponent of Jerome and Augustine, deserves a better press, as too do the other celibates who insisted upon equality.[65] Much has been made in recent years of the presence of women priests among the Gnostics. Seldom has it been noted that stress on Mary's virginity also resulted in comparable liberties.[66]

Inevitably because of their positions of power, it was male celibates who were to prove most manipulative in their use of the concept. But even here there is a positive side. One illustration may be given from Anglo-Saxon England, where growth of the cult of the Virgin seems closely tied to the tenth-century monastic reform movement as its inspiration.[67] As one historian observes,

[63] 'Empress' in the modern world immediately conjures up negative overtones, but for an impressive argument to the effect that an empress beyond manipulation gives greater freedom to women than the pornographic attempt to control women that so characterizes contemporary society, see the introductory chapter of S. Boss, *Empress and Handmaid* (London: Geoffrey Chapman, 1999).

[64] Limberis seems to me too reductionist in her approach. It is hard to believe that civic religion, particularly in the form of Tyche or Fortuna, could have exercised quite so decisive a role as she envisages, even to the extent of determining Constantine's choice of his new capital (7–21). Where the strength of her book lies is in observing the way in which the extravagance of imperial encomia affect the style of praise of Mary, as in the famous Akathistos hymn (62–97; 149–58).

[65] For an excellent defence of Jovinian, D. G. Hunter, 'Resistance to the virginal ideal in late-fourth-century Rome: the case of Jovinian', *Theological Studies* 48 (1987), 45–64. The support of other celibates for such a view is noted by Jerome in *Epistles* 49.2.

[66] For Gnosticism, e. g. E. Pagels, *The Gnostic Gospels* (London: Weidenfeld & Nicholson, 1979), 60–1, 69; for the Collyridian sect honouring Mary with a female priesthood, Epiphanius, *Panarion* 78.23.

[67] In Ireland there was a parallel development, but much later. Apparently, no churches or monasteries were dedicated to Mary before 1100, only a few between 1100 and 1150, and then a great explosion thereafter. So the two books by P. O'Dwyer, *Devotion to Mary in Ireland 700–1110* (Dublin: Carmelite Publications, 1976), 46; *Devotion to Mary in Ireland 1100–1600* (1979), 10, 42, 76.

'it is difficult to explain why it captured the imagination of the reformers to such a marked degree, unless it be that they wished to adopt as patron saint of the new celibate monasticism a saint who was known above all for her virginity'.[68] Certainly, the reforming zeal of Dunstan went with numerous churches dedicated to Mary, while in an office that may come from Aethelwold's hand it is interesting to observe clergy, monks and the female sex identified as Mary's three principal objects of concern.[69] The notion of virginity as freedom, power, and dedication was also reinforced by the way in which it eventually came in itself to symbolize incarnation. For in the image of the burning bush Mary's virginity was in effect taken to imply a dignity which not even the fire of the divine presence could quench or annihilate.[70] Chaucer is someone who stresses the freedom and status thus implied:

> O moder mayde! O mayde moder free!
> O bush unbrennt, brenninge in Moyses sighte,
> That ravisedest doun fro the deitee.[71]

But if the new understanding of Mary's virginity had a positive function as well as the negative so commonly noted, so too did Jesus' acquiring of a grandmother. It is at this point that I come to consideration of the second of the two innovations which I promised to note, a new sense of family interdependence. For simply to describe the invention of Anne as just a pure flight of imaginative fancy fails as an analysis to reckon with deeper, underlying motivations. Admittedly, the marked growth in her cult in the later Middle Ages was in part due to the accidents of royal patronage, in particular the key role played by Anne of Bohemia (wife of Richard II of England) and Anne of Brittany (wife of Charles VIII and then Louis XII of France), but some real and

---

[68] M. Clayton, *The Cult of the Virgin Mary in Anglo-Saxon England* (Cambridge: Cambridge University Press, 1990), 273.

[69] Ibid., 122 ff., esp. 135; cf. 69.

[70] Based on Exod. 3: 2. First popularized in the east, the image received a considerable boost from the devotional writings of Birgitta of Sweden and Adam of St Victor.

[71] The opening lines of the third stanza of the Prioress' Prologue, *Canterbury Tales*: W. W. Skeat (ed.), *The Works of Geoffrey Chaucer* (Oxford: Clarendon Press, 1894), 181.

definite needs were also met. Most obviously, her invention allowed the incarnation to reflect the normal pattern of medieval life, in its extended family, and so allowed a greater realism to its message. But it also ensured a greater dignity for women, both through balancing the virginity of her daughter and by offering an alternative account of where the greatest debt for the origins of one's Christian faith often really lay, within the family itself and particularly its female members. Medieval Christianity effectively made the point by imaginatively exploring Jesus' origins, as also to some degree that of his immediate followers.

The presence of similar female names in the biblical text was taken as a cue not for potential confusion but instead as an incentive to produce a more integrated family story. It thus became common to suppose that Anne had married three times, giving birth to three different Marys (all mentioned in the Gospels—the Virgin Mary, Mary Cleopas and Mary Salome), who in turn bear Jesus, James the Less and Joseph the Just, and the brothers James and John. The result was not only the acceptance of multiple marriage, but the claim that the most powerful figure behind the apostles was in fact a woman.[72] If this claim is thought far-fetched, in riposte one need only note the way in which the notion worked itself out in art. For example, tree of Jesse versions of Jesus' family tree begin to appear in the eleventh century, but by the beginning of the fourteenth their patriarchal character is being countered by kinship diagrams which make Anne central.[73] Not only that, nativity scenes also become popular in which Mary is entirely surrounded by women, her mother and reputed sisters in particular, with all the men relegated to a back row.[74] That pattern

[72] K. Ashley and P. Sheingorn (eds.), *Interpreting Cultural Symbols: Saint Anne in Late Medieval Society* (Athens, Georgia: University of Georgia Press, 1990), Introduction, 1–68, esp. 3, 11–12, 53.

[73] P. Sheingorn, 'Appropriating the Holy Kinship: Gender and Family History' in ibid., 169–98, esp,170–1.

[74] There are several fine examples in the Wallraf-Richartz Museum in Cologne, particularly from the so-called Older and Younger Masters of the Holy Kindred (*die heilige Sippe*); for a discussion of one of these, Plate 5 of this book. In the Counter-Reformation such portrayals were discouraged, but male protest is already evident in an early sixteenth-century example from an anonymous Swabian artist, now in the Philadelphia Museum of Art. Behind Mary and Anne Joseph and Joachim are placed on a raised dais, to ensure that the viewer does not misconceive the true nature of structures of authority and influence.

is still more powerfully represented by the common form of statuary which in German is known as *Selbdritt*. In this case men are dispensed with altogether, with the infant Christ accompanied only by his mother and grandmother.[75] The sex which exercised the primary influence upon him is thus left in no doubt.[76]

The value of both marriage and womanhood were thus powerfully asserted through the way in which the story of Anne was explicated. It also seems likely that the task of preparing Mary for her role led to greater stress on women's education. In art Mary is frequently portrayed reading the prophecies of her role, but for that reading to be possible she needed a teacher and so, despite the fact that in the original version of the legend Mary was dedicated to the Temple at the age of three, Anne comes to usurp that role and is so represented in art from the fourteenth century onwards. As learning to read prayers was almost certainly how the process of learning began at this time, moral value and religious image could scarcely more closely coincide.[77] None of this is to claim historical truth for the details of Anne's story, but it is to claim another kind of truth: that its images embodied worthwhile ideals which not only acted as a valuable counterpoise to her daughter's virginity but helped carry the Christian revelation beyond its biblical roots which particularly in its Marcan form had denied any indebtedness of Jesus to his family roots.

To be real the incarnation must have meant that Jesus like any other child was heavily dependent upon those who brought him up. Whether we encapsulate that truth in Mary alone or in Mary together with Joseph or in Mary along with her mother remains a secondary issue to that fundamental assertion. But to retain the

---

[75] *Heilige Anna selbdritt*—Saint Anne as herself the third.

[76] A more worrying example of this trend is the type of statuary known as *Vierges ouvrantes*, where statues of the Virgin open up to reveal depictions of all three persons of the Trinity. Though defensible on the grounds that it is only through the incarnation that we know of the Trinity or perhaps as a healthy refusal to countenance tritheism, the way things could go badly wrong is well illustrated by some medieval plays paralleling that image by mechanical actions representing all three persons arriving in the womb at the time of the annunciation: cf. G. M. Gibson, *The Theatre of Devotion: East Anglian Drama and Society in the Late Middle Ages* (Chicago: University of Chicago Press, 1989), 137–74, esp. 144–52.

[77] Cf. W. Scase, 'St Anne and the education of the Virgin' in N. Rogers (ed.), *England in the Fourteenth Century* (Stamford: Paul Watkins, 1993), 81–96.

image of Anne has at least two advantages: it reminds us of a similar need in Mary, and it also frees us from assuming that the only possible norm for upbringing is our own society's nuclear family. Herein lies one of the drawbacks in the gradual replacement of Anne by Joseph which occurs from the sixteenth century onwards. A number of factors seem to have brought about the change: challenges to the historicity of Anne, the Counter-Reformation desire, particularly among the Jesuits, to give greater stress to male responsibility in religion, St Teresa of Avila's strong focus on Joseph and the rising urban middle class's new conception of itself.[78] That Joseph deserves appropriate commemoration is no doubt correct, but we must guard against supposing that because he is more historical he is therefore less liable to distortion. If already in the sixth century we find Joseph wrongly only tolerated in the house as evidence for Mary's continuing loyalty to her vow of virginity,[79] in the twentieth we find a writer willing to speak of 'progressive revelation' in respect of the growth of Joseph's cult, yet insisting that what it reveals is 'the adorable perfection of God the Father in a tangible way', with Mary's obedience to Joseph now paralleled in the obedience of the faithful in the life of priests.[80] What this would suggest is that issues of historicity are less important than the images which narratives, historical or otherwise, are used ultimately to convey.

Of the two issues we have discussed it is, ironically, the one that was subject to greater imaginative elaboration which is likely at root, nonetheless, to contain the greater historicity in respect of its impact on the life of Jesus. For if anything like a kenotic account of the incarnation is accepted, it would seem likely that Jesus' family must have played a major role in helping to shape his consciousness, whereas we can be certain that, even if there was a virginal conception, Mary is unlikely during Jesus' lifetime to have derived from it any of the power and freedom from which her later imitators, both women and men, benefited. Though neither

[78] The last is the view of T. Brandenbarg, 'St Anne and her Family' in *Saints and She-Devils: Images of Women in the Fifteenth and Sixteenth Centuries* (London: Rubicon Press, 1987), 101–27, esp. 124.

[79] St Romanos the Melodist, *Kontakia: On the Life of Christ* (London: trans. E. Lash, HarperCollins, 1996), 7.

[80] A. Doze, *Discovering Saint Joseph* (Slough: St Paul Publications, 1991), e. g. 66–71, 135, 187.

has proved easy, of the two it is also family indebtedness which twentieth-century Christians have found easier to appropriate, even in its least factual form. So, if we take Canada as our example, not only was the vast St Joseph's Oratory in Montreal built in the inter-war period, but also the largest pilgrimage centre in North America (at Beaupré) is dedicated to St Anne.[81] Care must therefore be taken to avoid over-simple generalizations about imaginative truth, as though once deprived of its most obvious relation to historical fact it thereby becomes bereft of any significant connection with historical reality except perhaps its own immediate context.

Experience triumphs over bad Christology

In the previous section, due note was taken of the way in which the New Testament image of Mary as passive instrument was combined with the new element of suspicion of female sexuality to produce a powerful cocktail with potentially very deleterious consequences for women. But because the picture is already a familiar one—at least as an account of what happened in the history of the Church—most space was devoted to two other, less well-known developments: the way in which virginity was almost, despite its inheritance, turned round and used as an instrument of liberation and, secondly, the claim for family interdependence, to which we shall return later at the end of the chapter. Both developments could be interpreted as reactions against already imposed categories for human experience: virginity as passivity; exclusively male trees of Jesse. Here, though, I want to draw attention to a more fundamental, experientially inspired revolt, this time against Christology itself. What we shall observe is Mary being used to counter a thoroughly bad Christology and in the process usurping some roles that might legitimately be seen as Christ's alone. Even so, precisely because she had gained such a status, it enabled Mary to draw the figure of Christ back into a more adequate represen-

---

[81] St Joseph's Oratory was begun in 1924 under the inspiration of an illiterate caretaker, Brother André; the present Basilica of Sainte-Anne-de-Beaupré dates from 1923 (its predecessor having been destroyed by fire), and receives annually nearly two million pilgrims.

tation, only for Reformation and Counter-Reformation to generate fresh problems in their turn.

There is no doubt that over the course of the first millennium
in the popular mind, and indeed in much academic theology,
Mary came to function in the place of Christ as the sinner's friend
and intercessor. It is a transition that is often linked to her growth
into a semi-divine or goddess figure, but two caveats need to be
given against any too simplistic version of this claim. In the first
place, this status is only definitively reached more than a thousand
years after the rise of Christianity and so cannot be explained as
stemming directly from Mediterranean goddess cults; secondly and
relatedly, what seems to have made the decisive difference is not
Mary herself but the Christology of the time. The most famous
theologian of the eleventh century may be used to illustrate the
problem.[82] Anselm offers a severe doctrine of atonement, according to which there is a requirement for infinite satisfaction for the
offence of human sin against God's honour, and Christ is therefore
presented as the divine being alone able to fulfil that demand.
Inevitably this accentuated the sense of distance between Christ
and the rest of humanity, and that is exactly what we find reflected
in Anselm's prayers. Christ through what he suffered because of
our sins stands primarily as our judge, whereas Mary can plead on
our behalf: 'Whose intercession is accustomed more easily to gain
pardon for the accused than she who gave milk to him who is at
once just avenger and merciful pardoner of each and all of us?' As
Anselm himself so eloquently puts it in another of his prayers:
'You have given birth to him through whom the dead come back
to life . . . through your Son you have saved unhappy humanity
from sin . . . Therefore, Lady, you are mother of justifier and the
justified, bearer of reconciliation and reconciled, parent of salvation and the saved.'[83]

Admittedly, there were other trends at this time that could have
generated a quite different result. Not long after Anselm wrote, we

[82] Anselm (1033–1109) completed his work on the atonement *Cur Deus
Homo?* in 1098.

[83] My trans. of *Oratio* 6, 16–18 and 7, 118–26 in F. S. Schmitt (ed.), *Anselmi
Omnia Opera* (Edinburgh: Nelson & Sons, 1946), III, 15 and 23. For more on
Anselm, E. A. Johnson, 'Marian devotion in the Western Church' in J. Raitt
(ed.), *Christian Spirituality: High Middle Ages and Reformation* (London: SCM Press,
1988), 392–414.

find in Rome Mary portrayed as sharing the throne of Christ and equally august and distant.[84] At the other extreme is the hymn *Salve Regina* which, if anything, makes Christ more human and accessible than Mary.[85] But neither were in the end to represent the dominant trend. The stress on Christ's judgement kept him remote or, if combined with tender images, ambiguous, whereas the increasing popularity of the coronation of Mary, however exalted it made her, at least reminded the believer that it was as mother that she had Christ's ear.[86] Although intense devotion to Mary appears initially to have been mainly the preserve of monks and secular clergy, we soon find it spreading widely among the laity through psalters and books of hours, with again her role of intercessor predominating.[87] It was to lead to many stories of Mary's intercession succeeding where all else had failed, as in the story of Theophilus found at Chartres and many other medieval cathedrals and antecedent of the Faust legend,[88] or the tale of her descent into purgatory which influenced the art of both Pisano

---

[84] In the basilica of St Maria in Trastevere *c*. 1140. The image may have arisen partly through use of sculptures and icons in place of actors in liturgical drama, and partly through the reapplication of the imagery of the Songs of Songs to Mary. For example, 4.8. was paraphrased as 'ponam in te meum thronum'. For further details, I. H. Forsyth, 'Magi and majesty: a study of romanesque sculpture and liturgical drama', *Art Bulletin* 50 (1968), 215–23; E. Kitzinger, 'A virgin's face: antiquarianism in twelfth century art', *Art Bulletin* 62 (1980), 6–19, esp. 11.

[85] The hymn is commonly attributed to Hermannus Contractus in the eleventh century. Although Mary is addressed as queen, she is asked to give access to the fruit of her womb rather than explicitly Christ in glory. Ironically, in Calvin's rewriting Christ is addressed as King and instead of vision of his humanity being sought, what is requested is sight of 'the God of gods most high': L. Pearson, 'Salve Regina and Salve Redemptor: Hermann the handicapped and the Calvin connection', *Hymn* 45 (1994), 23–6.

[86] Originally, the theme of coronation was by no means confined to Mary and simply represented a human being now granted eternal life: M. J. Coloni, 'Le couronnement de Marie a Notre-Dame de Paris', *Études mariales: bulletin de la société francaise d'études mariales* (1985), 107–20, esp. 110.

[87] N. Morgan, 'Texts and images of Marian devotion in thirteenth century England' in W. M. Ormrod (ed.), *England in the Thirteenth Century* (Stamford: Paul Watkins, 1991), 69–103, esp. 95–7.

[88] Though in Goethe's version Gretchen takes over the primary intercessory role, the play still ends with a vision of the Virgin Mary: *Faust* Part II, Act V, l. 11989 ff. E. Trunz (ed.), *Goethe Faust* (Munich: Verlag C. H. Beck, 1986), 360–64.

and Giotto.[89] The latter was eventually to be given an unexpected twist in Dostoyevsky's decision to use the Russian version to introduce the famous 'Legend of the Grand Inquisitor' in *The Brothers Karamazov*.[90]

Yet, ironically, precisely because Mary was usurped to perform Christ's intercessory role, a new way of approaching him was in fact eventually opened up. For constant appeal to what seemed to legitimate for Mary the gentler role, namely her motherhood, finally forced upon the Church not only a more human portrait of her but also of Christ himself, as she interacted with him. This trend can clearly be seen in Bernard of Clairvaux, despite the fact that he is sometimes represented as simply endorsing continued growth in an exalted role for Mary. The Bernard with whom we are most familiar is in any case at times more the creation of later history than the reality itself. One example is the famous story of him being fed on the Virgin's milk, which seems to have been first attributed to Fulbert of Chartres and was only attached to Bernard in the fourteenth century.[91] Admittedly, he does urge his readers, 'with every fibre of our hearts, with every desire of our breast, with all our prayers, let us venerate Mary, since such is the will of him who wished that we have everything through her'.[92] But on

---

[89] D. S. Shorr, 'The role of the Virgin in Giotto's Last Judgement' in J. Stubblebine (ed.), *Giotto: The Arena Frescoes* (New York: Norton, 1969), 169–82. Judaism offers a similar story of Rachel succeeding where the patriarchs had failed: cf. J. Neusner, *Jews and Christians: The Myth of a Common Tradition* (London: SCM Press, 1991), 117–29. For different responses to Mary and Rachel in the Bethlehem of today, S. S. Sered, 'Rachel's tomb and the milk grotto of the Virgin Mary', *Journal of Feminist Studies in Religion* 2 (1986), 7–22.

[90] *Brothers Karamazov* (Harmondsworth: Penguin, 1958), 289. For a translation and commentary on the Russian version, only rediscovered in 1857 and probably dating from a ninth century original, P. Pascal, *The Religion of the Russian People* (London: Mowbray, 1976), 57–87. Mary's intercession secures remission of punishment for 'Christian folk' tormented in hell 'from Holy Thursday until Pentecost' each year (75–7).

[91] B. O. McGuire, *The Difficult Saint: Bernard of Clairvaux and his Tradition* (Kalamazoo: Cistercian Publications, 1991), 189–225; C. Dupreux, 'La lactation de saint Bernard de Clairvaux: genèse et evolution d'une image' in F. Dunand et al. (eds.), *L'image et la production du sacré* (Paris: Méridiens Klincksieck, 1991), 165–93.

[92] Sermo in nativitate Beatae Mariae (the Aqueduct sermon), 7 in J. Leclercq and H. Rochais (eds.), *Sancti Bernardi Opera* (Rome: Editiones Cistercienses, 1968), V, 279 (my trans.).

the other side needs to be set his opposition to the immaculate conception, his sparing allusions to her bodily assumption, and his acceptance that the primary reference in Revelation 12 was to the Church and not to Mary. Indeed, apart from his use of the image of the aqueduct Bernard's originality seems to have lain entirely in the strength of the foundation which he gave to a particular form of spirituality. Bernard opens one of his sermons on the Song of Songs by declaring that 'today the text we are studying comes from the book of experience',[93] and it is his identification with Mary as his experiential pattern for love of Christ that was to become so significant for later developments, though Mary is as a matter of fact seldom mentioned in those specific sermons. Whereas Victorine spirituality saw the bride under the image of mystical prophet or seer, Bernard embraces wholeheartedly the potential in the sexual imagery.[94] Some earlier commentators insisted that a sharp differentiation from courtly love was nonetheless retained, but more recent writers have tended to the view that courtly love was also seen as a vehicle towards love of God, and so any absolute contrast between secular and sacred love cannot be maintained.[95] Equally, in both there was a key element of the unfulfilled. In one sermon Bernard speaks of Mary bringing forth splendour, but 'in a shadow'. This has led one commentator to describe Mary's role for Bernard as being 'to catch the light from outside and reorganise it . . . in the endless stream of images' and 'as such she is at the source of the human imagination'.[96]

What such imaginative identification with Mary effected was not fresh doctrinal claims but rather a new way of viewing Christ.

---

[93] Bernard of Clairvaux, *Sermones super Cantica Canticorum* 3.1: 'Hodie legimus in libro experientiae.'

[94] For a general survey of the book's use, A. W. Astell, *The Song of Songs in the Middle Ages* (Ithaca: Cornell University Press, 1990).

[95] The contrast is insisted upon by Etienne Gilson but rejected by Peter Dronke. E. Gilson, *The Mystical Theology of St. Bernard* (Kalamazoo: Cistercian Publications, 1990), App. IV, 170–97; P. Dronke, *Medieval Latin and the Rise of the European Love Lyric* (Oxford: Clarendon Press, 1968) I, 69, 75, 87–97.

[96] M. B. Pranger, *Bernard of Clairvaux and the Shape of Monastic Thought: Broken Dreams* (Leiden: E. L. Brill, 1994), 134–62, esp. 162. The shadow image occurs at the beginning of Bernard's sermon on Mary's nativity, sec. 2: 'She produced the same splendour (as the saints in heaven), but in a shadow, and only because the Most High overshadowed her' (my trans.). The reference is to the Vulgate of Song of Songs 2: 3.

As the Middle Ages advance, though the stern judge never entirely disappears, the intimacy of the believer with Mary and her own intimacy with her Son is in effect used to legitimate the bridging of the middle term and thus a sense of the believer's own intimacy with Christ. The best method of judging the development, therefore, is not doctrinal but experiential: its effectiveness in aiding the imagination's appropriation of the gospel. A good example of continuing tension between the two approaches comes from Dante. Although he continues to speak of Mary as the one who 'breaks the hard judgement there above',[97] he assigns to Bernard the task of inducting us into the divine vision with which the *Divine Comedy* ends, and he is made repeatedly to insist that intimacy with Mary will also bring intimacy with her Son: 'Her brightness alone can dispose you to see Christ.'[98]

It is particularly in connection with presentation of the birth narratives that such developments are first most clearly to be observed, with at times here also a somewhat surprising use of erotic imagery.[99] Eroticism, though, necessarily implies involvement, and this is precisely the way in which the new artistic representations functioned. The tender interaction of Mary with her young son was held not only to legitimate but also in some ways to require a similar involvement on the part of the believer.[100] Although such developments might have yielded a purely passive model, in particular from the annunciation, there were pulls the other way, as for instance in the popular image of Mary herself weaving the robe of Christ's flesh,[101] or in the use of the Magnificat to suggest the possibility of dramatic change, very

---

[97] *Inferno* II, 96 (my trans.).

[98] *Paradiso* XXXII, 86–7. The two last cantos are both relevant. That it is important that Mary remain completely human in this context is stressed by J. Pelikan, *Eternal Feminines* (New Brunswick: Rutgers University Press, 1990), 101–19, esp. 105.

[99] For the role of the annunciation in such mysticism, S. E. Hayes, 'Of Three Workings in Man's Soul' in A. C. Bartlett (ed.), *Vox Mystica: Essays on Medieval Mysticism* (Cambridge: D. S. Brewer, 1995), 177–99.

[100] For a more detailed discussion of the contribution of art in this context, *Tradition and Imagination*, ch. 2; for its role in respect of Christ's death, ibid., ch. 7.

[101] As in the early eighth-century Iona hymn, 'Cantemus in omni die'. Text and commentary' in T. O. Clancy and G. Markus, *Iona: The Earliest Poetry of a Celtic Monastery* (Edinburgh: Edinburgh University Press, 1995), 177–92, esp. 184.

effectively used by Abbot Suger to justify his own major building campaign that was to lead to the invention of Gothic.[102] Mary's percipience was also sometimes used to counter the common image of woman as flesh and man as spirit,[103] while we find women writers themselves proposing that the infancy narratives are misread if female passivity is taken to be their message. So, for instance, Catherine of Siena in one of her prayers declares of Mary that 'in you today our human strength and freedom are revealed', and in particular praises her because Christ 'would never have entered unless you had opened to him'.[104] Again, Birgitta of Sweden even has the shepherds require clarification whether the saviour that is born is as a matter of fact male or female.[105]

None of this is to deny continuing tensions. Although Birgitta was the mother of eight children, she accepted and indeed elaborated upon the way in which Mary's painless giving birth was quite different from her own, while Bernard used their mother's dedication of them as children to justify quite appalling behaviour towards his married sister.[106] Yet, however frequent the regressions, change was certainly on the way. During the lifetimes of Birgitta (1303–73) and Catherine (1347–80) the Black Death ravaged Europe and this gave a powerful impetus towards focusing as much on Mary's presence at Christ's death as at his birth. That too, though, brought dangers. In the case of Birgitta, it even leads her to allow Christ to say: 'As if with one heart, my mother

---

[102] He talks of 'insignificant me' called to 'the enlargement of the aforesaid place'; E. Panofsky (ed.), *Abbot Suger on the Abbey Church of St Denis* (Princeton, N.J.: Princeton University Press, 2nd edn, 1979), 89. For a helpful discussion of the use of the Magnificat in the Middle Ages, J. S. Neaman, 'Magnification as Metaphor' in W. M. Ormrod (ed.), *England in the Thirteenth Century* (Stamford: Paul Watkins, 1991), 105–22.

[103] C. W. Bynum, *Holy Feast and Holy Fast* (Berkeley, Cal: University of California Press, 1987), 262–3.

[104] M. O'Driscoll (ed.), *Catherine of Siena: Selected Spiritual Writings* (New Rochelle, N.Y.: New City Press, 1993), 80–1.

[105] M. J. J. Harris (ed.), *Birgitta of Sweden: Life and Selected Revelations* (New York: *Classics of Western Spirituality*, Paulist Press, 1990), 205; *Revelations* VII, 23. For a useful discussion of Birgitta's mariology, K. E. Borresen and K. Vogt, *Women's Studies of the Christian and Islamic Traditions* (Dordrecht: Kluwer, 1993), 72–5.

[106] For these and a number of related examples, C. W. Atkinson, *The Oldest Vocation: Christian Motherhood in the Middle Ages* (Ithaca: Cornell University Press, 1991), 101–43, esp. 112–13, 120–1.

and I have saved humanity.'[107] But, on the whole, the greater impact was a healthy one, in a more active participation in Christ's narrative for the reader and viewer, no less than for Mary.

As noted earlier, John may well have invented the incident at the foot of the cross to say something about relations within the community or about discipleship. If so, that imaginative element is carried considerably further in the later Middle Ages. Already at the beginning of the fourteenth century Pseudo-Bonaventure had prefaced the crucifixion with a incident that was to find its way into art: the emotionally charged scene of Christ saying farewell to his mother. Another more famous imaginative expansion of the story is the Pietà whose artistic form scholars once thought originated among male mystics in Germany but which more recently has been attributed to female Beguines.[108] Either way, there can be no doubt that this and related images helped secure a strong sense of God's identification with human suffering, as Jesus' agony came to be seen not simply as something done on our behalf but as God the Son coming alongside us in events in which we could become emotionally involved like a mother. This is also the way in which nativity scenes need to be read. Whereas for us today Renaissance paintings in particular often appear merely as pretty pictures, as a matter of fact they are seldom without signs that invite deeper participation, for example, through a symbol in Christ's hand such as grapes, apple or goldfinch or the presence of later saints who had made the requisite appropriation such as Catherine of Alexandria or Francis.[109]

Sadly, however, both Reformation and Counter-Reformation did much to halt the process, though with very different motivations. Luther may be taken as illustrative of the former, not least because his thought does at least display more of a wrestling with questions of imaginative appropriation than is the case with any of

[107] My trans: *Revelations* I, 35. This was to become quite a popular theme.

[108] J. E. Ziegler, 'Some questions regarding the Beguines and devotional art', *Vox Benedictina* 3 (1986), 338–57; J. E. Ziegler, 'The *curtis* beguinages in the southern Low Countries and art patronage', *Bull. Inst. Hist. Belg.* 57 (1987), 31–71.

[109] The following two books offer more than three hundred paintings of Mary with commentary: B. Bernard and C. Lloyd, *The Queen of Heaven* (London: Macdonald Orbis, 1987); C. Kovachevski, *The Madonna in Western Painting* (London: Cromwell, 1991).

the other Reformers.[110] His identification of the problem is clear, that with the negative developments Christ has in effect become a tyrant for anguished consciences, with the result that it is to Mary that people most naturally turn for comfort and reassurance. Yet he does appear to have believed—at any rate off and on—that rather too much would be lost if involvement with Christ through Mary were to be given up. This perhaps explains his recurring inconsistencies not only on doctrinal issues but also on what kind of practical response one should make to her. So, for instance, while his 1521 commentary on the Magnificat places great emphasis on Mary's passive acceptance of divine grace without any merit on her part, one can find within a few lines of one another the acceptance of the legitimacy of asking for her intercessions and the assertion that 'everyone should make an effort to regard himself and God as though God and he were the only persons in heaven and on earth'.[111] Yet his 1522 Christmas sermon asks us to envisage ourselves sitting on Mary's lap and becoming 'her dear child'. Inculcation of example is by no means the sole aim of such an imaginative exercise, for Luther exhorts us to 'see to it that you make his birth your own'.[112] Eight years later in another Christmas sermon his attitude changes once more, and Mary is told: 'I have a greater honour than your honour as his mother. For your honour pertains to your motherhood of the body of the child, but my honour is this, that you have my treasure.' So exclusively christocentric does the emphasis become that we are even told that 'he is more mine than Mary's'.[113] But a 1535 hymn continues to use the language of Revelation 12 to speak of her.[114] One way of

---

[110]   Calvin seldom refers to Mary. He does, however, urge us to 'confess with her that we are nothing'. More surprisingly, there are some grounds for supposing that he held to belief in Mary's perpetual virginity. For a general survey, B. Dupuy, 'The mariology of Calvin', *Sewanee Theological Review* 38 (1995), 114–25, esp. 117, 120.

[111]   *Luther's Works* (Saint Louis, Missouri: Concordia, 1956), Vol. 21, 297–355, esp. 323, 327 for Mary's lack of any particular merit, and 319 for the intercession passage (cf. 355).

[112]   *Luther's Works* (Philadelphia: Fortress, 1974), Vol. 52, 7–31, esp. 16. The congregation are also compared to the animals gathering round the manger (22), while of Mary's labour he declares it to have been without pain (11).

[113]   *Luther's Works* (Philadelphia: Fortress, 1959), Vol. 51, 211–18, esp. 214, 215.

[114]   *Luther's Works* (Philadelphia: Fortress, 1965), Vol. 53, 292–4.

reading such oscillations in attitude is to acknowledge that Luther may well have realized that rather more was at stake than his doctrine of justification. For the Reformation, in depriving the believer of identification with the person who had become the principal other agent in Jesus' story, effectively required him or her to take the seat of a spectator rather than an involved participant. One can of course observe a drama and believe the issue matters, but it will surely matter considerably more if individuals can feel themselves in some sense participants. *Ex hypothesi* one cannot be Christ; so if he is made the only actor in the drama who matters, any such sense of participation must inevitably be lost. It is often claimed that there was a corresponding gain in the sanctification of the home, but, if that is so, commentators have not been slow to point out the obverse side; thereby Luther 'also placed religion clearly within the male sphere'.[115] Mary ceased to mediate a relation with Christ for both men and women, and so the net result was a sharper differentiation of their respective spheres.

Not that the Counter-Reformation fared much better. For the success of Mary in such a role depended on her humanity, and it is precisely Mary's humanity that was being progressively undermined until the reforms of Vatican II. No doubt partly in reaction to her demotion by the Reformation, the most extravagant language of all comes subsequent to it, and indeed is already to be seen in the sixteenth century, as in the Jesuit Peter Canisius playing the card of the incomparable virgin for all he is worth.[116] Some of the Church's official interventions also inhibited her more human role and thus her capacity to mediate the appropriation of her son in the relevant way. Examples would include Counter-Reformation attempts to forbid as indecorous the

[115] With the male now firmly in charge of religion, both in church and in the home: cf. M . Wieser, 'Luther and women: the death of two Marys' in J. Obelkevich, L. Roper and R. Samuel (ed.), *Disciplines of Faith* (London: Routledge, 1987), 295–308, esp. 305. Wieser's stress, though, is somewhat different from mine. She sees the diminution of the female role, in the feminine side of the divine nature as represented by the Virgin Mary, and in the intellectual and contemplative side of human nature as this is expressed in Martha.

[116] Peter Canisius, *De Maria Virgine Incomparabili* (Ingolstadt, 1577), e.g. II, I, 106. Particularly repellent are the views of the École Française of the seventeenth century. Olier describes the Eucharist as instituted out of regard for Mary and her 'like a queen reigning on the throne of God'; cf. H. Graef, *History*, II, 31–43.

baring of Mary's breast or her swooning at the foot of the cross.[117] Certain forms of emotion that had helped the medieval believer were thereby effectively precluded. The development of the rosary as a form of popular piety might constitute another example. First widely disseminated in the form advocated by Dominic of Prussia (d. 1460), some versions offered a much more christological focus than others.[118] Luther found only Marian hyperbole, which was not true of all variants in his day.[119] Nonetheless, the Counter-Reformation trend was towards contemplation of Mary in her own right, as is witnessed by the substitution of her Coronation for the Last Judgement as the fifteenth mystery at the end of the sixteenth century, or the universal adoption in the seventeenth of a coda to the Ave Maria, requesting her prayers.[120]

Reformation and Counter-Reformation, therefore, in my view alike erred. Both in effect failed to notice that the primary problem was christological, and that a powerful experiential corrective had been given which the reforms of both by implication radically undermined. Of the two it might be argued that the more serious flaw lay with the Counter-Reformation, with its tendencies being seen to culminate in two problematic doctrinal definitions of the immaculate conception (1854) and assumption (1950). The issue to my mind, though, is not that simple. While the next section will concede that the dogma of the immaculate conception does represent the culmination of the major negative tendency which has run through the tradition, the next and final section will contend that, when rightly interpreted, the assumption powerfully encapsulates all that is best in these developments.

---

[117] More successful in the latter case than in the former, as, though the depictions are more restrained, Mary nursing the infant continues as a theme in seventeenth-century painting.

[118] In one fifteenth-century set of pictures to accompany use of a rosary Mary is found in only a minority of the medallions (7 out of 15): A. Winston-Allen, *Stories of the Rose: The Making of the Rosary in the Middle Ages* (University Park, Pa.: Pennsylvania State University Press, 1997), 47–52, esp. 49; cf. also 27.

[119] Ibid., 140–1.

[120] Ibid., 60, 145. The latter, though, was already quite common in the sixteenth century

Immaculate Mary: distortion and displacement

That suspicion of sexuality played its part in identifying Mary as immaculate is sufficiently often remarked to need no further consideration here. Indeed, it is hard not to resist the conclusion that one factor in the presentation of Mary at the Council of Ephesus in 431 was already the desire to outdo Artemis' claims to chastity at her famous local shrine.[121] Though such an admission does not affect Ephesus' central affirmation of Mary as *Theotokos* or Mother of God (where the focus is incarnational as a more literal translation clearly reveals—'God-bearer'), it cannot be denied that the orthodox side was aided by a rather dubious Marian piety. This is well illustrated by the sermon of Proclus at Constantinople which initiated the debate, in which he makes several extravagant allusions to 'the stainless jewel of virginity'.[122] Unfortunately, that kind of focus was seriously to distort much of the rest of Christian history. The result is that the promulgation of the dogma of the immaculate conception in 1854 cannot be dismissed as a mere nineteenth-century aberration, but instead must be seen as a deep-seated fault running through much of the Church's tradition. This emphatically does not mean that nothing can be said on the other side, but it does mean that we are forced to come to terms with two kinds of corrupting influence, one deriving from the imagination and the other from theological reflection. We shall now examine each in turn: first, the way in which the imagination can sometimes seriously distort perspective; secondly, how, once Mary is viewed in a certain light, theology is then found displacing concepts in her favour that should rightly belong elsewhere.

Imaginative distortions

Here, while tracing the growth of the doctrine and noting that it was by no means inevitable, my main aim is to draw attention to two key features of that story: on the one hand, the extent to which it was dependent on the imagination being in the grip of a

---

[121] Though Cyril is more strictly christological than Proclus, the second of his two hymns to Mary (*PG* 77.1032–6; cf. 77.992) is embedded in an address to the city of Ephesus where comparisons with Artemis are drawn.
[122] Oratio 1, 'De laudibus sanctae Mariae'.

more fundamental image, that of original sin; on the other, the way in which, though Mary as immaculate was by the nineteenth century to become a standard part of Christian imaginative experience, ironically it was an experience heavily motivated from the top.

Original sin is, at its most basic, the doctrine that all humanity suffers from the consequences of the fall, the sin of Adam and Eve. On one way of reading such a claim, it would seem uncontentious even when applied to Jesus, since even he could not escape— without ceasing to be human—the frailty of our nature and the socially ambiguous context in which it is set, and it is no doubt in this way that we should read Julian of Norwich's endorsement of such a view.[123] Suffering and death might seem similar, but are in fact somewhat more complex. For, though Christ experienced both, this was traditionally seen in terms of voluntary subjection, rather than as part of what it means to be human. Adam through his rebellion became subject to death; Christ chose death to release us from the consequences of Adam's sin. Nowadays, we might wish to express matters differently: that death is an inevitable part of being human. But one element could not be changed without radical alteration to the normal pattern of atonement theology, and that is the consequence Augustine drew from the fall (technically known as original guilt): that all humanity stands under condemnation in virtue of participation in that fall, and so only Christ, as exempt from all sinful tendency, could save us.

The difficulty of reconciling that last assertion with any claim that Mary also shared in such exemption helps explain the long delay until 1854 before the official promulgation of Mary's exemption from original sin. But the potential of the imaginative contrast with Eve (already in Justin and Irenaeus in the second century)[124] assured a long process of anticipation. According to Genesis part of Eve's punishment was pain in childbirth. So, not surprisingly, the inference was quickly drawn that Mary in her absolute obedience could have experienced no pain in giving birth to Jesus, and

---

[123] Julian of Norwich, *Revelations of Divine Love*, ch. 51: 'God's Son fell, with Adam, but into the depths of the Virgin's womb' (Harmondsworth: Penguin, 1966, 148).

[124] Justin Martyr, *Dialogue with Trypho*, ch. 100; Irenaeus, *Adversus Haereses* 3.21.10; 3.22.4.

one finds this notion reflected in writings as different as the second-century *Odes of Solomon* and fourteenth-century *Revelations* of Birgitta of Sweden.[125] Belief in Mary's sinlessness, though, arose more slowly than is often supposed. So, for instance, Irenaeus interprets Cana as a rebuke and Origen speaks of her doubting under the cross,[126] while Athanasius, though full of praise for her, does say that 'she strove to make progress each day, and did'.[127] Chrysostom envisages her despairing at the annunciation, while Gregory the Great at one point takes her as representative of those who like the synagogue 'stand outside'.[128] Yet there is no doubt that by the early Middle Ages the belief in her perfection had become universal, and so she was now the new Eve in the most obvious sense of all.

It was left to Duns Scotus to draw as a further implication of the contrast the conclusion that fittingness required Mary also to be exempt from original sin, and so born without even the disposition to sin which all have shared since Eve's fall.[129] Though a further stage of development, its significance should

---

[125] *Odes of Solomon* 19.8–9 (cf. *Ascension of Isaiah* 11.2–15); ed. J. M. Charlesworth, *The Old Testament Pseudepigrapha* (New York: Doubleday, 1985), Vol. II, 752–3; Birgitta of Sweden, *Revelations* 7.21.6–13 (New York: *Classics of Western Spirituality*, Paulist Press, 1990, 203). Birgitta helped to popularize the notion in England, as in the mid-fifteenth-century wall painting in the Deanery at Durham whose birth scene depicts a radiant Mary standing up with the inscription below: ''Gaude quia deo plena peperit sine pena cum pudoris lilio.' The Latin *pena* (*poena*) nicely captures the connection with original sin, meaning both 'penalty' and 'pain'.

[126] Irenaeus, *Adversus Haereses* 3.16.7 (*Sources Chrétiennes* 211.314); Origen, Homily 17 on Luke (*SC*, 87. 256–8).

[127] My version of the French translation of Athanasius' *Epistola ad virgines*, the original only surviving in Coptic: *Le Muséon* 42 (1929), 197–274, esp. 244–6. Although I agree that perfection is not intended, Hilda Graef puts matters too strongly when she speaks of flaws 'because "bad thoughts" come into her mind': *History* I, 53. The French actually reads: 'ne pas laisser une mauvaise pensée s'arrêter en son coeur' (245).

[128] John Chrysostom, *Homily on Matthew* 4.4.5 (*PG* 57.45); Gregory the Great, *In Evang.* 1.3 (*PL* 76.1086C). Gregory is commenting on Matt. 12: 46 ff., and is quite explicit: 'videlicet Synagoga'.

[129] Though anticipated by others such as Eadmer (who reversed a contrary trend, Lanfranc having suppressed the feast), his defence was the most significant; for an exposition, G. Tavard, 'John Duns Scotus and the Immaculate Conception' in H. G. Anderson et al. (eds.), *The One Mediator, the Saints and Mary* (Minneapolis: Augsburg, 1992), 209–17.

not be exaggerated, for at least two factors made the transition easier than might initially have appeared. The first is that the language of Mary as immaculate was already in use to describe her more limited sinlessness, in large part through her identification with the bride in the Song of Songs and with Wisdom in the book of the same name. The former was taken to declare of her that *tota pulchra es . . . et macula non est in te* (you are wholly beautiful and there is no blemish in you), while the latter uses the expression *speculum sine macula* (mirror without stain) (S. of S. 4: 7; Wisd. 7: 26). Both images could appeal powerfully to the imagination. Secondly, though the rejection of the doctrine by Bernard and Thomas Aquinas is well known, often forgotten is the very limited character of their objections. Both accept that Mary was sanctified as sinless before birth. The potential effects of original sin in her had thus already almost disappeared to vanishing point, although both Bernard and Thomas would have maintained that an important principle was still at stake: that Mary was in a situation of need like other human beings, which Christ was not.[130]

The slowness of theology to adapt to scientific advance is well illustrated by the fact that the most recent doctrinal consequence of the contrast with Eve dates from as recently as 1950, almost a century later than Darwin's *Origin of Species* of 1859. For the way in which the dogma of the assumption was formulated seems to have deliberately left open the possibility that Mary never died.[131] That is indeed what logic requires if one maintains the traditional theology, with Mary totally exempt from all the assumed conse-

---

[130] Aquinas, for instance, declares: 'Beata Virgo contraxit quidem originale peccatum, sed ab eo fuit mundata antequam ex utero nasceretur' (*Summa Theologiae* III, 27.2.); for a very helpful discussion of his reasons, M. Hodges, 'Why did St Thomas reject the doctrine of the immaculate conception of Mary?' (ESBVM—Ecumenical Society of the Blessed Virgin Mary—pamphlet, 1970). Orthodoxy sees a similar principle at stake in its rejection of Mary's exemption: K. Ware, 'The Sanctity and Glory of the Mother of God', *The Way* (1984) Supp. 51, 79–96, esp. 85–92.

[131] Pius XII's encyclical nowhere states that Mary died. In more recent writing the implications for relations with Orthodoxy are either ignored or distorted. For an example, J. Saward, 'The Assumption' in A. Stacpoole (ed.), *Mary's Place in Christian Dialogue* (Slough: St Paul Publications, 1982), 108–24, esp. 118–21, whereas John McHugh honestly wrestles with this problem: 'The doctrine of the Immaculate Conception: reflections on a problem in ecumenical dialogue', *The Month* NS 22 (1989), 330–6.

quences of original sin. Yet we have no reason to believe that human beings with the potential for immortality ever existed in the way the opening chapters of Genesis suggest. Instead, the story needs to be read imaginatively as a story about ourselves: how human self-assertiveness distorts not only our relations with God but also with one another and our environment (with suffering and death as symbols of those consequences). But, if that is so, then Mary could be no more exempt from pain in childbirth or from death than any other human being.

In terms of the general structure of the argument of this book, it would be nice if at this point one could blame such developments upon too much literal-mindedness and insufficient attention to the imagination, but matters are seldom that simple. The Eve–Mary contrast that helped generate such attitudes was, as we have noted, itself an exercise of the imagination and as such part of a more general aesthetics that stressed the symmetry of the balance between the tree of temptation and the cross as tree of life. Not only that, the visual was twice to play a decisive role in securing a firm place for the doctrine, first in the post-Reformation artistic representations which helped prepare the ground for 1854, and then in the visions which both before and after its promulgation helped root it more deeply in popular piety. As we shall discover, the two phenomena were not unconnected.

Consider first the paintings on the subject by El Greco, Velasquez, Rubens, Zurburán, and Murillo (who is responsible for more than two dozen on this theme). Their imagery played a crucial role in advancing popular involvement with the doctrine, and in particular how Mary's relation with the rest of humanity was perceived. For the earlier image of her conception, with Joachim and Anne embracing at the Golden Gate, gave way to portrayals of her on her own, with the stress now on her role being predetermined by God and her purity and innocence reflecting that role. As Francisco Pacheco, Velasquez's teacher and father-in-law, put it in an influential work: 'In this most lovely mystery the Lady should be painted in the flower of her youth, twelve or thirteen years old, as a most beautiful young girl, with fine and serious eyes.'[132] Those 'serious eyes' could reflect her preordained

---

[132] E. G. Holt (ed.), *A Documentary History of Art* (Princeton, N. J.: Princeton University Press, 1982), II, 221–4, esp. 222.

role, which theologians now found anticipated in Old Testament imagery of pre-existent Wisdom, in part aided by an unintended mistranslation by Jerome.[133] Yet we must not suppose that the increasing prominence given to the doctrine was purely the work of theologians or artists, still less merely the result of pressure from below.

The artists in question all worked either in Spain itself or in the Spanish dominions (in Rubens' case in the Spanish Netherlands), and this dominance of Spanish iconography appears to be no accident. In fact, the Spanish monarchy saw its own fortunes as closely bound up with those of Mary, and over several centuries engaged in extensive propaganda on the doctrine's behalf, which the papacy, with varying degrees of success, tried to resist. If Charles V (I of Spain) and Philip II showed some reticence on the matter in their desire to keep their varied dominions united, the same cannot be said for the kings who ruled Spain in the seventeenth century, Philip III and IV and Charles II. Philip III, for instance, had special medals struck in 1619, equating the significance of the doctrine with that of the Eucharist, though the thousands on sale in Rome were confiscated almost immediately.[134] Nor did attitudes change when the Bourbon dynasty succeeded the Hapsburgs. To give only one example, in 1800 Charles III imposed on all universities in Spain a requirement on those teaching there that they swear an oath to defend the position,[135] though of course it was not made a dogma until fifty-four years later. Such advocacy has been plausibly interpreted as a sustained attempt to bolster a flagging monarchy, not through courting popular appeal, as might initially be thought, since the initiatives came from above and not below, but by trying to enlist a yet more powerful monarch (Mary) in support of the Spanish crown.[136]

For whatever reason, the image of the 'beautiful lady' did eventually succeed in firing the popular imagination, and so it was that most of the famous visions of Mary in the nineteenth and twenti-

---

[133] The Vulgate for Proverbs 8.24 is as follows: 'Nondum erant abyssi, et ego iam concepta eram.' Instead of conception, all modern translations refer instead to birth e.g. 'was brought forth' (RSV).

[134] S. L. Stratton, *The Immaculate Conception in Spanish Art* (Cambridge: Cambridge University Press, 1994), 86.

[135] Ibid., 140.

[136] The general implication of Stratton's argument; e.g. 100–1, 138–9.

eth centuries came to take this form, partly under the influence of the famous artists mentioned above; not, of course, through direct contact with their work but rather thanks to the existence of numerous copies and the popularization of their content. Catherine Labouré's vision of the miraculous medal at Paris in 1830 included the address: 'Mary, conceived without sin'.[137] For Bernadette Soubirous at Lourdes in 1858 the beautiful woman remained anonymous until the last vision when she declared herself to be the Immaculate Conception.[138] At Fatima in 1917 the children were instructed to encourage devotion to 'the immaculate heart' of Mary.[139] Given the close resemblance of such visions to existing iconography, it would be very easy at this point to be completely dismissive, and follow those who explain the phenomena as a response to one form or other of crisis in religious belief.[140] But that would be to suppose that the only options are all or nothing, whereas if, as we have already observed, even biblical experience of God is a mixture of truth and falsehood and heavily conditioned by its context, then we ought to expect the

---

[137] R. Laurentin, *The Life of Catherine Labouré* (London: Collins, 1983), 79.

[138] A. Ravier, *Bernadette* (London: Collins, 1979), 22–3.

[139] D. Wayne and J. Flory, *Oh, What a Beautiful Lady!* (Chulmleigh, Devon: Augustine, 1976), 133–4. Not the best book on the subject, but its title (drawn from one of the children's comments) indicates the continuing influence of Song of Songs 4: 7. A complete, brief survey of all such visions without interpretative judgements is offered by M. S. Durham, *Miracles of Mary* (London: HarperCollins, 1995), a more academic survey by S. L. Zimdars-Swartz, *Encountering Mary: From Las Salette to Medjugorje* (Princeton, N. J.: Princeton University Press, 1991).

[140] E.g. Warner speaks of 'the desperate thirst believers have for assurances that the faith is still credit-worthy' (*Alone of All her Sex* 311–2). Victor and Edith Turner see in the Church's support for the visions a response to the undermining of the historicity of the first Eve: 'Post-industrial Marian pilgrimage', J. J. Preston (ed.), *Mother Worship* (Chapel Hill; North Carolina Press, 1982), 152–3. That there was such an element of defensiveness is proved by Pius IX's own words on the day following the 1854 declaration when he talked of the dogma's role to 'destroy this dangerous error of Rationalism, which in our unhappy times not only afflicts and torments civil society, but more deeply afflicts the Church': quoted by B. C. Pope, 'Immaculate and powerful: the Marian revival in the nineteenth century' in C. W. Atkinson et al. (eds.), *Immaculate and Powerful* (Boston, Mass.: Beacon Press, 1985), 181–2. One should also note the element of aggressive self-assertion among Anglican converts in England: J. Singleton, 'The Virgin Mary and religious conflict in Victorian Britain', *Journal of Ecclesiastical History* 43 (1992), 16–34.

same to apply elsewhere. Dogmatism is a danger for the enlight-
ened liberal as much as for religious conservative, as the extraordinary response to the visions at Marpingen in 1873 well illustrate.
Although the violent intervention of troops and the numerous
arrests could be put down to the excesses of Prussian officials, what
is surprising is the extent to which liberal German opinion
supported such repressive measures in the Saarland.[141]

For a start, we should note that on occasion even the participants themselves have expressed caution and reserve. Catherine
Labouré acknowledged that she was sometimes mistaken, while
Bernadette Soubirous consistently resisted identification of her
visions until the last moment and then it was given with hesitation
and without understanding of its significance.[142] Again, if some of
the visions had a strongly vindictive, apocalyptic strain and sometimes produced material which the Church tried to suppress, as
with La Salette and Fatima,[143] that can be balanced by Bernadette's
refusal even at her death to disclose the 'secret' revealed to her,[144]
perhaps because she now dismissed its importance. One should
note that the Old Testament is also replete with unfulfilled apocalyptic announcements of doom, while, as with these modern
visionaries, so also for Isaiah and Ezekiel their visions closely corres-
ponded to what they already knew of God through Temple
worship. God, I suggest, chooses to build upon what individuals
can already comprehend, and so what one really needs is careful
detailed consideration of each instance.

In this respect the research of the American scholar, William
Christian, is impressive. Focusing on what has happened in Spain,
two of his books investigate apparitions of the fifteenth and early

---

[141] D. Blackbourn, *Marpingen: Apparitions of the Virgin Mary in Bismarckian
Germany* (Oxford: Clarendon Press, 1994), esp. chs. 7, 9 and 10.

[142] R. Laurentin, *Catherine Labouré*, 262; Laurentin in his book on Bernadette
repeatedly stresses her earlier resistance to an immediate identification of *Aquero*
with the Virgin and then her incomprehension and resistance to a more personal
formula as substitute for her strange, impersonal way of describing the Virgin: R.
Laurentin, *Bernadette of Lourdes* (London: Darton, Logman & Todd, 1972), e.g.
82–3, 50–1.

[143] In 1879 Melanie, one of the La Salette children, published a book of her
experiences which the Church banned, while the third secret of Fatima was
opened by John XXIII in 1960 but never disclosed.

[144] Account given in V. and E. Turner, 'Marian Pilgrimage', 169–70.

sixteenth century and a controversial grouping from the twentieth. While noting the heavy degree of cultural conditioning, he insists that the most natural reading is that the recipients were sincere in what they claimed, and that some element of positive assessment is possible even for the non-believer. If the earlier period is marked by the way in which 'visions served to strengthen the relations between communities and the forces of nature',[145] the apparitions nearer to our own day were in part 'rejecting the city and the world of commerce that devalued rural sharing and mutual help', and that is why sacred geography is so important to them.[146] Some will see their tendency to occur in backwaters as a sign of the primitive character of the people involved, but equally it might speak of God's concern for the poor and deprived, and that might even apply where there is good reason to doubt the veridical character of the vision.[147] The point is that there is surely no need to go down an all or nothing route.

To me it seems that Bernadette's experience was veridical and did contribute decisively to the great saint she undoubtedly became. What makes me resist her final description of the woman to whom she liked to allude (somewhat impersonally) as *Aquero*[148] is not because such a doctrine could not in principle be given by a vision, but partly because of Bernadette's own hesitations, and, more importantly perhaps, because of the distortions which it produces, through Mary coming to function imaginatively in place of Christ himself.[149] This is not necessarily to blame the visionaries

[145] W. A. Christian, *Apparitions in Late Medieval and Renaissance Spain* (Princeton, N. J.: Princeton University Press, 1981), 206. The last officially accepted apparition was in 1513. Thereafter, there followed ruthless suppression by the Inquisition, presumably because of the independence of judgement implied: 150 ff.

[146] W. A. Christian, *Visionaries: The Spanish Republic and the Reign of Christ* (Berkeley, Cal.: University of California Press, Berkeley, 1996), 396; cf. 302 ff. The visions took place at Exkioga.

[147] While in no way discounting the positive effects of Guadalupe, it is disappointing to discover academics endorsing those effects without also facing the considerable historical problems involved, as in I. Gebara and M. C. Bingemer, *Mary, Mother of God, Mother of the Poor* (London: Burns & Oates, 1989), 144–54.

[148] Bernadette's own preferred description: 'that' or 'it' in the local dialect.

[149] I do not think this true of Bernadette, but think of La Salette, where the children are told by the Virgin that her Son's arm was 'so heavy and pressing' that she could no longer restrain it: Zimdars-Swartz, *Encountering Mary*, 248.

themselves; sometimes more pedantic minds forced them to read their experience in particular ways. But it is to note that, if much of the argument of this book has been that doctrine has given too little attention to imagination, there also remains an essential caveat to be heard on the other side: that imagination itself must also be tested against doctrine. That is not to make one or other redundant, but it is to insist that any adequate approach to the enrichment of the human understanding will need both.

Theological displacement

If the imagination can err, so too can theological reflection. That is to state the obvious. What is unusual in this particular context is the extent to which such error takes the form of displacement: Mary usurped to say things that are more naturally applied elsewhere. I shall begin by noting how this happens in respect of both Christ and the Holy Spirit, but want to end by suggesting that the same phenomenon continues to occur in more recent presentations of Mary's significance. I find it hard to regard modern interpretations of her as the embodiment of 'the feminine' as anything other than claims which, if true, should find their primary justification elsewhere. I begin, though, by noting some of the ways in which functions normally reserved for Christ or the Spirit are transferred to her instead.

The most fundamental objection to the doctrine can be expressed in two related, but different ways: that on this doctrine Mary either ends up with a humanity too remote from our own or else is assigned a status perilously close to divinity. How quickly the former can turn itself into the latter can easily be observed if we list in ascending order of difficulty the kind of objections that have been raised against the various transformations to which Mary has been subject. First, as early Origen theologians are to be found observing, unless there was some sin in her, Christ could not have died for her.[150] Secondly, there was the question of how complete sinlessness could meaningfully be defended without paralleling Jesus' own miraculous birth, and so usurping reflection

---

[150] Origen, *Homily on Luke* 17.6: *Sources Chrétiennes* (Paris: Éditions du Cerf, 1942) 87, 256–8.

more appropriately made in respect of him.[151] Having crossed that divide, it then became all too easy for her to usurp a specifically divine role and take on the work of the Holy Spirit as principal agent in relating us to Christ. Finally, as we noted earlier, whenever an inadequate Christology is present, advocates have not been so slow in requisitioning for her one of the main roles of the Son, and so in effect she became principal mediator of divine compassion and mercy.

There would seem little doubt that this gradual progression is in fact what happened in the history of the tradition, and that its problematic content is still clearly observable today. Here, for instance, is the twentieth-century Polish saint, Maximilian Kolbe: 'The Holy Spirit is the uncreated Immaculate Conception; Mary is the created Immaculate Conception; she is the quasi-incarnation of the Holy Spirit and his Spouse: this gives the basis for an exchange of names and titles between them.'[152] It is a notion made still more explicit by the Liberation theologian, Leonardo Boff, who unqualifiedly speaks of Mary as 'hypostatically united to the Third Person of the Blessed Trinity', in the same way as the human Jesus is to the divine Logos.[153] Though these are extreme expressions and have not found favour in the Roman Catholic community as whole, it would distort the history of the tradition to describe them as isolated aberrations.

At La Salette the children assumed that Mary identified herself with God, since her words were reported as follows: 'I gave you six days' work. I have reserved the seventh for myself.'[154] Such a remark could be put down to *naïveté*, but one detects similar crossing of the boundaries even in outstanding adult saints. Thus, in St Ignatius Loyola's *Spiritual Exercises* Mary is to be found usurping the role of the Holy Spirit in what would otherwise have been a

[151] As in the popular identification of the embrace of her parents at the Golden Gate as itself the point of conception—conception by a kiss, as it were. The Counter-Reformation condemned such a view, and we find this reflected in Pacheco's influential treatise *Arte de la pintura* (Madrid, 1649 reprinted 1956), 2.208.
[152] Quoted by J. Van Den Hengel 'Mary: Miriam of Nazareth or the symbol of the eternal feminine', *Science et Esprit* 37 (1985), 313–33, esp. 325.
[153] L. Boff, *The Maternal Face of God* (London: Collins, 1989), 93.
[154] Quoted by A. Carr, 'Mary model of faith' in D. Donnelly (ed.), *Mary Woman of Nazareth* (New York: Paulist Press, 1989), 7–24, esp. 9.

very obviously trinitarian passage.[155] Again, the way the imagery of
air and breath is applied in Gerard Manley Hopkins' poem 'The
Blessed Virgin compared to the air we breathe' should leave us in
little doubt that its proper object should have been, instead, the
Holy Spirit, however beautiful and moving its current form is.
Prior to the Second Vatican Council even theologians of the stature
of Karl Rahner and Edward Schillebeeckx were contributing to
this general atmosphere. Take the case of Schillebeeckx. Though
he rejected the notion of Mary as co-redemptrix, he did insist that
it is nonetheless legitimate to claim for her that she 'is the mediatrix between Christ and us', as well as unique revealer of the maternal side of God which Jesus as a man could not embody.[156]

Someone who took a very different line was Yves Congar. On
his view Mariology would remain distorted for so long as
Christology was also askew. Two major faults were detected in the
latter: a dominant monophysitism which deprived Christ of any
real humanity with which we could identify, and a stress on judgement which inevitably meant that one had to look elsewhere for
mercy and intercession.[157] Mary as symbol was thus forced into
certain roles precisely because Christ as symbol failed to deliver
them. It was not that imagination had run riot, but that doctrine,
no less than imagination, was forced into new patterns in order to
preserve certain underlying truths, in particular due recognition of
divine compassion and of God's working upon us to bring us into
a deeper relationship with himself.

But if that was one form of displacement, more recent conservative Catholic theology displays, to my mind, another, in its
treatment of Mary as the embodiment of the feminine. To treat
the issues involved fairly, though, it is important that the contrast
should be drawn with more secular versions of the thesis. Since at

---

[155] First Week, Third Exercise, para. 63. In similar vein in a trinitarian passage
of an eighth-century Coptic hymn, we find the petition: O Mary, Mother of
God, / Dwell in us at all times: *Sing the Joys of Mary* (Slough: St Paul Publications,
1982), 110.
[156] E. Schillebeeckx, *Mary Mother of the Redemption* (London: Sheed & Ward,
1964; in Dutch, 1954), 126 and 141–2. For a critique of the early Rahner as well
as the early Schillebeeckx, E. Johnson, 'Mary and contemporary christology',
Église et Theologie 15 (1984), 155–82.
[157] Y. Congar, *Christ, our Lady and the Church* (London: Longmans, 1956),
68–77.

least the time of Feuerbach arguments have been offered to the effect that the divinization of the feminine in Mary played an important and positive role in giving due status to the feminine dimensions of life. For Feuerbach himself, though, such exaltation of the maternal principle helped to conceal God as human projection, which only Protestantism could bring to full consciousness with its obvious felt want.[158] As is well known, the psychologist Jung also welcomed the declaration of the dogma of the assumption in 1950 on the grounds that a proper quaternity had at last been recognized, with the maternal archetype given its due place in the godhead.[159] Such claims strike me as rather patronizing towards women, as though a minority element in the godhead was better than nothing, whereas its introduction would seem merely to reinforce marginalization, unless feminine imagery is legitimated wholesale or else the relevance of gender at all to the divine nature denied. What distinguishes the modern Catholic approach is the use of the feminine to say something primarily about human nature and its relation to the divine. The issue remains, though, whether in this form it is any less of a displacement.

Although Vatican II only narrowly decided for the inclusion of Mary under its treatment of Church and again only narrowly for relativizing 'Mediatrix' and for rejecting 'Mediatrix of all graces',[160] it might have been thought that the Council's more christological approach had finally put an end to Mary as a serious source of contention. But what in fact has happened is that she has been used by conservative Catholics to focus one of the most contentious issues of our time, that of gender and its significance. For, if few would now explicitly endorse Aquinas's view that the feminine must be excluded from God since he is pure act,[161] a more subtle version of his underlying assumptions continues to

---

[158] L. Feuerbach, *The Essence of Christianity* (New York: Harper & Row, 1957) Part I, ch. 6, 65–73.

[159] For a good exposition of Jung with references, T. A. O'Meara, 'Marian theology and the contemporary problem of myth', *Marian Theology* 15 (1964), 127–56, esp. 132–40; for a critique, particularly of his influence on Boff, S. Coakley, 'Mariology and "Romantic feminism": a critique' in T. Elwes (ed.), *Women's Voices* (London: Marshall Pickering, 1992), 97–110, esp. 106 ff.

[160] For further details, see articles by C. J. Peter and E. A. Johnson in Anderson et al. *One Mediator*, 295–304 and 311–26.

[161] Aquinas, *Summa Contra Gentiles* 4.11.19.

plague the understanding of both male and female discipleship, and this is often premised on Mary as model.

The most influential version of such an approach is to be found in the theology of Hans Urs von Balthasar, Pope John Paul II's favourite theologian. Argued sometimes at length, it is his contention that 'because of her unique structure the Catholic Church is perhaps humanity's last bulwark of genuine appreciation of the difference between the sexes'.[162] In essence, the idea is that the feminine is to be equated with receptivity, and as such provides the most adequate model of the proper relationship of humanity in general towards God. Mary can then emerge as the perfect exemplar of our discipleship, particularly where the immaculate conception is affirmed, since hers will then be a life of 'a pure "Yes" to God, one in which the innate propensity to autarchy is totally lacking'.[163]

In assessing such a view, it is important to be fair, and so acknowledge a greater degree of subtlety than this initial presentation may suggest. When, for instance, Balthasar declares that 'over and against Christ—man and bridegroom—the Church is decidedly and primarily feminine,'[164] it might sound as though he is merely concerned with a point about imagery, but in fact his claim strikes at the roots of our understanding of both divine and human nature. God the Father as source and origin of the Trinity is seen as wholly masculine, while the Son in both receiving and giving is a mixture of both differentiations. Humanity as created, however, remains 'essentially feminine when compared to the Creator God'. Balthasar even finds this reflected in the facts of human biology, with 'basic embryonic structure . . . primarily feminine' and male characteristics only forming later.[165] The more active 'male' role is

---

[162] For general presentation, *Theodrama* (San Francisco: Ignatius Press, 1992), II/2: 'Woman's Answer'; for the quotation, *New Elucidations* (San Francisco: Ignatius Press, 1986), 195.

[163] J. Ratzinger, *Daughter Zion* (San Francisco: Ignatius Press, 1983), 78–9. Earlier he had spoken of how Mary 'emerges as the personal epitome of the feminine principle' (28).

[164] Balthasar, 'Epilogue' in L. Bouyer, *Woman in the Church* (San Francisco: Ignatius Press, 1985), 113.

[165] Balthasar, 'A word on "Humanae Vitae" ' in *New Elucidations*, esp. 213–4. For a good exposition of these aspects of Balthasar's thought, D. L. Schindler, 'Catholic theology, gender, and the future of western civilisation', *Communio* 20 (1993), 200–39.

then explicated in terms of a contrast with the symbol of 'Peter', whose sole purpose is to 'lead the bride to her womanly function and fortify her in it'.[166] One surprise is the number of women willing to commit themselves to such a view. So completely did Balthasar's spiritual companion, Adrienne von Speyr, succumb that not only did she sometimes portray herself as the Church to Balthasar's Christ, she even speaks of assuming his physical indispositions in order to leave him room for his work.[167] Nor is she by any means alone among women ready to endorse such views, despite its apparent implications for women's ordination and the status of women generally.[168]

In response the answer is given that such a theology in fact enhances the status of women rather than denigrates it, since women become the culmination of creation as God intended it to be. But this answer is inadequate for at least three reasons. First and perhaps most importantly, it is based upon a poor theology of grace that supposes that because God is always first, always there taking the initiative, therefore we must attribute all we do to him. It is a profound error which Balthasar shares with the Protestant theologian he most admired, Karl Barth, who also speaks of the virgin birth in terms of 'non-willing, non-achieving, non-creative, non-sovereign man' and in the light of such a judgement declares that the more active a male is, the more he must fall under judgement.[169] One might contextualize Barth as an extreme reaction to the overweening confidence in human initiative that then permeated the world about him.[170] But that can only be part of the

---

[166] Balthasar, *Church and World* (New York, 1967), 129. For expositions, J. Saward, 'Mary and Peter in the christological constellation' in J. Riches (ed.), *The Analogy of Beauty: The Theology of Hans Urs von Balthasar* (Edinburgh: T & T Clark, 1986), 105–33; J. Heft, 'Marian themes in the writings of Hans Urs von Balthasar' *Communio* 7 (1980), 127–39.

[167] J. Roten, 'Two halves of the moon' in D. L. Schindler (ed.), *Hans Urs von Balthasar—His Life and Work* (San Francisco: Ignatius Press, 1991), 65–86, esp. 73. For a female critique, T. Beattie, 'A man and three women—Hans, Adrienne, Mary and Luce', *New Blackfriars* 79 (1998), 97–105.

[168] E. g. J. A. Little, 'Sexual equality in the Church', *Heythrop Journal* 28 (1987), 165–78; M. M. Miller, *Sexuality and Authority in the Catholic Church* (Scranton, Penn.: University of Scranton Press, 1995).

[169] K. Barth, *Church Dogmatics* (Edinburgh: T & T Clark, 1958), I/2, 191, 194.

[170] For a good critique along these lines, P. Fiddes, 'Mary in the theology of Karl Barth', *The Month* N.S. 22 (1989), 300–09.

answer. Macquarrie has tried to turn the notion of the immaculate conception from something purely negative, the absence of original sin, to something positive, 'the flowering of the co-working that has been present from the moment at which redemption has begun'.[171] But, while this notion of co-working is welcome with its stress on divine respect for human dignity, it is not clear what sense it has if Mary has been predestined never to sin. The same objection might also be thought to apply in the case of Christ but does not, because in the latter case there is this essential difference that it is part of the definition of who Christ was that his divine nature remain fundamentally in control.

More plausible, therefore, to me is Lindbeck's ecumenical proposal for the doctrine's interpretation: that if the consequences of original sin are as destructive for human freedom as the tradition has sometimes thought, then the doctrine may stand as guarantor of 'God's humility and condescension in waiting for a creaturely "yes" '. It gave Mary the necessary 'space' for a truly free assent.[172] That is to turn the passivity argument on its head: the absence of the restraints of original sin is now postulated, not as removing obstacles to the divine action, but rather as securing a free human response. Even so, the approach would only seem necessary if we assume what seems to me an outmoded doctrine. Because of the way in which human beings have evolved and the social conditioning to which they are all subject, not even Christ could escape the effects of 'original sin' in disposing him in certain directions rather than others. So it is not clear what is gained in speaking of either Christ or Mary as exceptions. Indeed, it would seem to rob them of what makes their example of most value to us, in them facing the same conditions of temptation as we face. But, even if this more radical critique is not accepted, my basic point would stand, that to present male or female discipleship as passive receptivity is to distort what is of most worth in the divine creation. A 'yes' that exhibits no real imaginative engagement with alternatives can hardly be called active decision-making.[173]

---

[171] J. Macquarrie, *Mary for all Christians* (London: Collins, 1990), 51–77,98–115, esp. 113.
[172] G. A. Lindbeck, *The Nature of Doctrine* (London: SPCK, 1984), 96–8, esp. 97.
[173] One might contrast Jesus' own wrestling in the story of the temptation.

A second objection is that such stress on receptivity is especially pernicious in its application to women. Even where a more active image of Mary is maintained,[174] the rhetoric of immaculate conception can draw women back to this more passive, receptive presentation: 'this pure and receptive site where God can enter and remain in all glory and majesty without encountering any opposition or resistance'.[175] These words come from authors very much concerned that we all (women included) should actively engage ourselves on behalf of the poor. But even if we turn back to pregnancy itself, we surely have no more reason to associate receptivity with the woman than the man. The ovum is no less active in the process of the foetus coming to birth, while pregnancy is very much more than a mere bearing: as modern science reveals, the mother contributes both internally and externally by her attitudes and conduct. Given the culture of her day, Mary may well, of course, have been more receptive and passive than her modern equivalent. Paul VI spoke wisely when he urged that the Virgin Mary is 'proposed as an example to be imitated not precisely in the type of life she led, and much less for the socio-cultural background in which she lived'.[176] Balthasar may himself be used to illustrate how misguided the more conventional approach really is. In one extended essay he uses the image of harlot to criticize the Church.[177] Certainly, the image is a frequent one in the Old Testament, but, even if scriptural, one cannot have it both ways. Either the feminine is as capable of the active role as the male, or else the model of faithful obedience

---

[174] The use of the image of Mary as 'mulier fortis' (Prov. 31: 10 Vulg.) was one way in which the medieval tradition attempted a counterbalance: J. Pelikan, *Mary Through the Centuries* (New Haven: Yale University Press, 1996), 88–94, esp. 91.

[175] Gebara and Bingemer, *Mother of God*, 111. Though ascribed to 'patristic reading of the Old Testament' no critique is offered in this section (108–13) which is dealing with the immaculate conception.

[176] Paul VI, *Marialis Cultus* (London: Catholic Truth Society, 1974), 60–1, para. 35. John Paul II is much less forward looking in *Redemptoris Mater* (London: Catholic Truth Society, CTS, 1987), where passive, sacrificial roles are praised for women (para. 46). The result has been quite different responses from women; e.g. A. Loades, 'On Mary: Constructive ambivalence?', *The Way* 34 (1994), 138–46, esp. 138–9.

[177] Balthasar, *Spouse of the Word: Explorations in Theology II* (San Francisco: Ignatius Press, 1991), 'Casta meretrix'.

belongs essentially to the feminine and it is male imagery which we must use whenever we speak of rebellion against God.

If my first objection focused upon humanity in general and my second on women in particular, a third concerns Mary herself, and will help form a natural transition to a more positive treatment. Certainly many of the principal elements in her imagery can be used purely passively. So, for instance, the Latin version of Isaiah 45: 8 was used to suggest Mary as mother earth waiting to give birth to the Saviour,[178] while Mary as enclosed garden can all too readily conjure a negative image of virginity.[179] But neither mother nor virgin need bear such a connotation. Not only can 'mother' imply Mary helping to make Christ who he was, it can also suggest a similar active role in helping our transformation. Likewise, instead of virginity as enclosed garden we can think of it in terms of another image favoured in the tradition, that of the burning bush. For what that image surely entails is not only that Mary was *finitum capax infiniti*, someone who could bear God's presence and survive, but also someone who remained as bush, a human being with all her dignity and freedom retained in their own right.

Assumption: interdependence and promise realized

Though wrongly focused in my view when used as a means of attempting to salvage the doctrine of the immaculate conception, a more active understanding of Mary's discipleship is in fact already easily locatable within treatments of the other main doctrine to which we now turn, the assumption. Though Michelangelo portrayed even Mary flinching before Christ's stern judgement,[180] the predominant image in art, poetry and sermon is quite different: that Mary was always active and never hesitant in her intercession and care for those who sought her aid, whether

---

[178] 'Aperiatur terra, et germinet Salvatorem'; J. F. A. Sawyer, *The Fifth Gospel: Isaiah in the History of Christianity* (Cambridge: Cambridge University Press, 1996), 69–71.

[179] The *hortus conclusus* of the Song of Songs (4.12) need not necessarily imply something 'close-locked' and shut in on itself. Many artists were careful to keep the wall as low as possible, stressing instead the beauty of the garden within.

[180] In his Last Judgement on the east wall of the Sistine Chapel.

we think of her directly pleading in a Last Judgement or using her cloak or veil as a form of protection for supplicants.[181] In fact, belief in the assumption may well have first arisen in the late fifth century in monophysite circles as a way of securing a more obviously purely human figure than Christ who could actively plead our case.[182] It is a role that despite common modern assumptions was actually reinforced by the description of her as Queen of Heaven, since old rules of male succession meant that the title spoke not so much of power in her own right as influence behind the throne.[183] So, however much such talk implied an improper displacement of Christ's true function, at least its stress on an active role for Mary ensured that the different conception of her which I suggested at the beginning of the chapter lay just beneath the biblical text never entirely disappeared.

Not that the form of activity in the later tradition bears much relation to the New Testament's struggling disciple, but even there some continuities can be identified. As we noted earlier, this is particularly true of the patristic pattern of questioning Mary's constant perfection, and its insistence instead upon development in her character. That in itself might seem to tell against the assumption, since one common argument is that 'Mary's body-person was uniquely open to assumption-transformation in light of freedom from sin'.[184] But to say that an achieved freedom is less worthy would surely be to fall into very similar limitations upon forgiveness as characterized the earlier Marian tradition, where she has to substitute for Christ because he cannot forgive.

Integrating this alternative picture of Mary into how we conceive her final destiny might be thought to require the complete jettisoning of past treatments of the assumption.

---

[181] The cloak of the *Madonna della Misericordia* became very popular in Western medieval art; the protecting veil is also found in icons and in the Russian feast of Protection or *Pokrov*; for an attempt by an Orthodox theologian to purge it and other elements of the Eastern Marian cult of christological distortions, E. Behr-Sigel, *The Ministry of Women in the Church* (Redondo Beach, Cal.: Oakwood, 1991), 181–216, esp. 202–4.

[182] So H. Chadwick, 'Eucharist and christology in the Nestorian controversy', *Journal of Theological Studies* N.S. 2 (1951), 163 ff.

[183] The argument of J. McHugh, 'On true devotion to the Blessed Virgin Mary', *The Way* Supp. 25 (1975), 69–79, esp. 75.

[184] M. T. Prokes, 'The nuptial meaning of body in the light of Mary's assumption', *Communio* 11 (1989), 157–76, esp. 171.

Certainly, we have no historical grounds for believing that there was anything particularly remarkable about her death. But from that admission nothing follows about discounting the entire content of the imaginative use to which the image has been put over the centuries. To see why, we need first to make some connections with Chapter 3, and take note of my discussion there of how heaven might best be conceptualized. In brief, I argued that, in view of the indispensability of bodiliness to human identity, humans beings, if they are to survive death, must have something analogous to a body in heaven. So, if Mary is alive at all, she must now possess some such analogue. This is by no means to reintroduce a bodily assumption, by the back door as it were, any more than being committed to the doctrine of the ascension requires us to think of Jesus proceeding like a rocket through the clouds into a different world. Both doctrines alike speak of the presence in heaven of the entire humanity of the two individuals concerned, however conceptualized. In a more pessimistic age Dante had declared that Mary was alone with Christ in wearing 'the double garment' of body and soul.[185] That need not be our own view. The point of the assumption, I suggest, is simply this: that, if anyone is now there with Christ, Mary must be. As Rahner puts it when declaring that she is 'the ideal representation of exhaustive redemption', what this means is that her destiny is 'normal' for all Christians, even if it is not as yet 'general'. For Rahner, what gives Mary this 'special "right" ' is her 'divine Motherhood', but he offers little expansion or explanation of what such a claim might mean.[186] It will be the purpose, therefore, of the rest of this section to develop what grounds there might be for thinking Mary especially privileged in this respect. Two arguments will be adduced: first, her growth into sinlessness; secondly, the way in which to talk of her assumption underlines the incarnation as grounded in human interdependency, with ascension and assumption thus made mutually interdependent.

[185] Con le due stole nel beato chiostro / son le due luce sole che saliro (with the two robes in the happy cloister are the two lights that have ascended); Dante, *Paradiso* 25.127–8.

[186] K. Rahner, 'Interpretation of the dogma of Assumption', *Theological Investigations* (Darton, Longman & Todd, 1961), I, 215–27, esp. 225–6. Cf. also Idem, 'Le principe fondamentale de la théologie mariale', in *Recherches de science religieuse* 42 (1954), 491.

Let us take sinlessness first. In *Marialis Cultus* Paul VI offered a brave admission of the extent to which 'socio-cultural contexts' have adversely affected our understanding of how Mary should be perceived.[187] My worries run deeper than his. At the same time we must resist supposing the tradition an irrelevance. Elisabeth Moltmann Wendel declares that 'women will put more trust in their own imaginations than in the tradition'.[188] The trouble with that proposal is that our imaginations are seldom wider than our own immediate cultures, as, for instance, Fiorenza's focus on the teenage single mother illustrates.[189] It is not that there is anything wrong with such reflections in themselves, but it is only by reminding ourselves of the positive ways in which Mary has functioned in very different circumstances from our own that our vision can be enlarged.

There can be no proof that Mary became sinless, any more than we can fill in the gaps in Christ's life and offer irrefutable evidence in his case.[190] But Acts 1: 14 does present her as a faithful disciple, and by implication therefore present at Pentecost in the following chapter. 'James the Lord's brother' (Gal. 1: 19) is presumably one of her children, and, if so, she would have been part of a wider conversion to full commitment to Jesus' message on the part of her family as a whole. It is presumably the same James who had an experience of the resurrected Lord (1 Cor. 15: 7). Whether Mary was also granted a similar privilege, we are not told. Ambrose deduced that such an event must have taken place, and Pseudo-Bonaventure popularized it for medieval art.[191] John, I have already argued, invented, less plausibly, such an encounter at the foot of the cross. An even earlier anticipation was offered in another common artistic theme, set as Jesus prepares to go to his death, that of 'Christ taking leave of his

---

[187] Paul VI, *Marialis Cultus*, esp. 61–2, para. 36.

[188] E. Moltmann-Wendel and J. Moltmann, 'Becoming human in new community' in C. F. Power (ed.), *The Community of Women and Men in the Church* (Geneva: WCC, 1983), 29–42, esp. 37.

[189] E. S. Fiorenza, *Jesus: Mariam's Child, Sophia's Prophet* (London: SCM Press, 1995), 186–7.

[190] For a discussion of how sinlessness might be defended in Christ's case, *Tradition and Imagination*, 316–21.

[191] Ambrose in *De Virginitate* speaks of the Virgin Mary as the first witness to the resurrection, while Pseudo-Bonaventure in his *Meditations on Life of Christ* offers a detailed account.

Mother', as in the Huber painting recently acquired for the National Gallery in London.[192] Then, as if by way of compensation for the marginalization of the great majority of women throughout Christian history, her role at Pentecost came with the passage of time to be intensified, with her now assigned central place.[193]

Were the biblical incidents by contrast all incontestably historical, it might be possible to dismiss such elaborations as mere invention, but in fact they serve much the same purpose as the infancy narratives or John's account of Mary at the foot of the cross. Using Mary's discipleship as a medium they are there to help build our own. Where they are at fault is not in the use of the imagination, but in failing to allow for development in that discipleship, for that way they might not only have kept closer to history but also have allowed even greater imaginative engagement. Some may object that we ought not to engage with what is not factually true, but, if so, they will soon find themselves distorting Christology no less than Mariology. For, as I argued at length in *Tradition and Imagination*, Christ's true significance is very much larger than the mere 'facts' of his life, either how they were experienced by others at the time or even how he himself experienced them. Similarly, then, with Mary. In retrospect, given the understanding she now possesses, it is as engaged in these events that she would now wish us to put her, and thus also ourselves as fellow disciples.

Liberation theology in particular has made us sensitive to the social dimension of historical and doctrinal 'facts'. But we need equal sensitivity to their imaginative dimension. Doctrine has seldom functioned in isolation, and we distort the truth if we suppose expressions of the assumption to be concerned solely with asserting Mary's new status. Nearly always, whether in poetry or art, our involvement is also at stake. So, for example, even as florid a poem from the seventeenth century as Richard Crashaw's 'On the Glorious Assumption' includes the lines:

> And, while thou goest, our song and we
> Will, as we may, reach after thee.

[192] The acquisition of the Huber (d. 1553) had already been anticipated by a fine Altdorfer (d. 1538) on the same theme.
[193] The seventeenth-century female Portuguese painter, Josefa d'Obidos, makes women even more central by adding the figure of Mary Magdalene and pushing the male disciples to the side; Museu Nacional de Machado de Castro, Coimbra.

Again, paintings of the assumption consistently strive to invite us to share in the disciples' vision. It is a heavenly gaze mediated by our own willingness for an identifying, visionary experience.[194] Even an apparently mundane depiction of the Virgin's death such as Caravaggio's speaks of our need to live like Mary a Christ-like life, for her arms stretched out like a cross and her feet bare in humility speak volumes. Only when we possess a similar attitude, the painting is urging us, can we too pass, like her, through the curtain that forms its background: no mere ornament, but indicative of God's very presence beyond (the Holy of Holies).[195]

Deep-seated Protestant suspicions of Mary may make some readers still resist any such attribution of sinlessness to her. It may therefore be of help if I stress that, though I intend the claim to be significant, it is not a covert way of reintroducing old understandings of what that meant. Thus I am not claiming that she was so from birth, but rather that her life was one of gradual growth into full commitment to her son's mission. She even resisted that mission when it was fully launched, though perhaps for the best of motives.[196] Even Pentecost probably did not mark the end of her growth in understanding. But with the early death of Joseph she alone was able from personal experience to reflect on the significance of her son's life from cradle to grave and beyond, and both Luke and John thought it appropriate to project the ideal of discipleship back upon her earlier life. It seems therefore that of all the disciples she was best placed to represent the struggle of every Christian believer towards the perfection of relationship that is the destiny intended for each one of us, and which in this world is mediated through reflection upon the course of a life with which Mary's alone was fully coextensive.[197]

---

[194] For such an argument pursued in detail, V. I. Stoichita, *Visionary Experience in the Golden Age of Spanish Art* (London: Reaktion, 1995),

[195] P. Askew, *Caravaggio's Death of the Virgin* (Princeton, N. J.: Princeton University Press, 1990), esp. 69–83, 108–32.

[196] With Mark 3: 31 ff. interpreted in the light of v. 21, one could argue that interventions of family and friends were motivated by the attempt to save Jesus from himself, 'mad' actions that would lead to his own destruction.

[197] I have sought to expand on this notion of Mary as model disciple in 'Mary's discipleship and the artistic imagination' in M. Warner (ed.), *Yes to God* (London: Tufton, 1999), 69–82.

But if Mary's growth into sinlessness is one reason for endorsing the assumption, of still greater importance, it seems to me, is
what it says about Christ's dependency upon us. However revolting those images are of Mary trying to assuage her Son's wrath,
they did at least acknowledge that Christ owed Mary something.
It is that thought which we need to take very much further in our
own day. Whether there was a virginal conception or not, we
now know that children in the womb are profoundly affected by
the attitudes and behaviour of their mothers. But Jesus' dependency by no means ceased at the moment of birth. One
Evangelical scholar has suggested that it was Mary who taught
Jesus that he was Son of God and partly for that reason he declares
that he 'can very nearly' accept the truth of the assumption.[198] To
my mind, understanding came more gradually to both. The well-
known hymn of the seventeenth-century Anglican divine,
Thomas Ken, envisages only 'raptures' for Mary at Jesus' birth,
whereas another Anglican, W. H. Auden, more realistically has
her say:

> Sleep. What have you learned from the womb that bore you
> But an anxiety your Father cannot feel?
> Sleep. What will the flesh that I gave do for you,
> Or my mother love, but tempt you from his will?[199]

Parent-child relations are never entirely smooth, precisely because
human identity is formed not only in response to parental example but also in reaction to it. One contemporary female theologian
has suggested that if women 'attribute any place at all to Mary,

---

[198] J. W. Wenham, 'The Blessed Virgin Mary—an evangelical point of view',
The Churchman 86 (1972), 27–38, esp. 34–5, 37.

[199] T. Ken, 'Her Virgin eyes saw God incarnate born' : *New English Hymnal*
182. W. H. Auden, from *For the Time Being (A Christmas Oratorio)* in *Collected
Longer Poems* (London: Faber & Faber, 1968), 171. T. S. Eliot offers a similar
approach; cf. K. Watson, 'Doors in the Rose-Garden' (ESBVM pamphlet, 1988).
For Anglican approaches generally, R. H. Fuller, 'The role of Mary in
Anglicanism', *Worship* 51 (1977), 214–24; R. Greenacre, 'Mother out of sight'
(ESBVM pamphlet, 1989); A. M. Allchin, *The Joy of All Creation: An Anglican
Meditation on the Place of Mary* (London: Darton, Longman & Todd, 1984). The
last is a helpful survey of more positive attitudes within the history of
Anglicanism.

they see her above all as "that woman with the difficult son" '.[200] Whether so or not, that would seem to me exactly right. In the fourteenth-century Simone Martini offered a powerful depiction of Jesus as a petulant twelve-year-old, clearly 'in the huff' at his parent's rebuke.[201] Whether the incident is historical or not, it is hard not to believe that Jesus' identity was forged partly in hostile reaction to his parents' will. Nor should we think of Jesus as always in the right, as though the perfection of adulthood must also be expected of the child. When Max Ernst's surrealist painting of Mary spanking Jesus was first exhibited in 1923, the public outcry was such that it had to be kept in storage for several years.[202] Yet, given the very different attitudes to corporal punishment between then and now, is it not likely that Jesus like any other child would have tested the boundaries, and the limits have been set according to the customs of the time?

In one of his sermons Gerard Manley Hopkins speaks of his longing to see 'the matchless beauty of Christ's body in the heavenly light'. His expectation is to find beauty of mind and of body, yet of a highly individualistic kind. The category of mind will be that of 'genius', while the body will bear the marks of 'neither disease nor the seeds of any' since, even on earth, it was 'framed directly from heaven'.[203] In this description everything is being done to exclude Christ from dependence; he needs the help of no other minds; his body retains its beauty whatever it is fed. It is a position that has frequently been maintained in the history of Christianity, but it surely represents a complete perversion of any

---

[200] E. Maeckelberghe, 'Mary: maternal friend or virgin mother?', *Concilium* 1989, 120–7, esp. 125.

[201] Simone Martini (d. 1344), *Christ discovered in the Temple*, Walker Art Gallery, Liverpool. One might contrast this painting with another in the same gallery and on the same theme, that of Holman Hunt painted in 1862, where Jesus is at most embarrassed by his mother's attentions. For a discussion of Martini's painting, Plate 6 at the end of this book.

[202] M. Ernst, 'Die Jungfrau zuchtigt das Jesuskind vor drei Zeugen', Wallraf–Richartz Museum, Cologne. Ernst's strict Catholic upbringing reveals itself in quite a number of his paintings.

[203] Sermon for 23 November 1879; e.g. in *Gerard Manley Hopkins: A Selection of his Poetry and Prose* (Harmondsworth: Penguin, 1953), 137–9. This critique is pursued in more detail in D. Brown and A. Loades, 'The Divine Poet' in D. Brown and A. Loades (eds.), *Christ: the Sacramental Word* (London: SPCK, 1996), 1–25, esp. 7–9.

adequate understanding of incarnation. As human beings we cannot escape dependence upon one another. We are by the way we are made social beings. The Gospels tell us that Jesus longed for support in Gethsemane, and that such was the hostility in his own home town he was *unable* to perform a miracle (Mark 6: 5).[204] These incidents may not tell us about continuing dependence on his mother, but, if his life followed the normal pattern of human development, then she may have played a crucial role in shaping the sort of character he was. Joseph, by contrast, appears to have died by the time of the decisive moment in Jesus' destiny, the inauguration of his public ministry.

The assumption then speaks of that dependence acknowledged, a dependency that is by no means confined to Mary as those who are his Church today continue to act on Christ's behalf in the world. Christian doctrine has always declared the permanence of Christ's humanity. As I argued in Chapter 3, it makes no clear sense to speak of such a humanity as though either in life or in heaven it were bereft of all the social dimensions that make human beings what they are. The assumption thus completes and guarantees intelligibility to the doctrine of Christ's ascension. So far from undermining Christology, Mariology can thus actually deepen it, both in its imaginative model of discipleship and in its declaration of the presence of Christ's extended body in heaven.

Earlier we noted the problems that arise when Mary is associated with what is seen as the distinctively feminine, with some like Balthasar and Barth finding in it the right model for human response both male and female, and others only a rationale for the further exploitation of women. My own suspicion is that the debate about what is merely cultural and what a true function of gender still remains in its infancy, and that we should therefore be much more free in our application of imagery to either sex, irrespective of its apparent origins. Admittedly, the early precedent set by Syriac Christianity can at times sound exotic rather than convincing, but at least interdependence was thereby acknowledged.[205] The inherent capacity of a developing tradition to

---

[204] Significantly, this was changed by Matthew in the parallel passage, Matt. 13: 58.
[205] In the *Odes of Solomon*, 19 the Father is treated as feminine, Mary as masculine. For a positive evaluation, S. A. Harvey, 'Feminine imagery for the divine:

correct itself is for me powerfully illustrated by the eventual emergence, despite Christianity's strong patriarchal inheritance, of the
notion of Mary as priest.[206] Moves were made to suppress the
notion, but what it offers is a vision of how in fact even Christ's
own sacrifice on the cross was critically dependent on the way in
which he had been nurtured by others. Mary through her care and
education of Jesus sought to offer her offspring to God, and in so
doing made an indispensable contribution to what form that final
offering eventually took.

Even in our own cynical age in which virginity is so often parodied,[207] the notion can sometimes bear positive connotations as
when we speak of 'virgin earth' or 'virgin forests'. But this is no
less true of much of the history of the Christian tradition. A virgin
promise that had once only spoken of fulfilment in the life of
another not only came to speak of fulfilment in its own right in
virginity as freedom, but also, more importantly, of a discipleship
imaginatively relived, the imitation of which can help our own.
For these purposes real life and imaginative reconstruction may be
allowed to blend, for both point in one and the same direction, a
life of increasing faith in her Son. A virginity not of pure receptivity or passivity, but rather of potential awaiting its realization, it
found its promised fruit in due course at Christ's side in heaven,
where it speaks of the continued dependence of his humanity on
ours, no less, of course, than of ours upon his.

the Holy Spirit, the Odes of Solomon and the early Syriac tradition', *St Vladimir's
Theological Quarterly* 37 (1993), 111–39; for a negative, G. P. Corrington, 'The
milk of salvation: redemption by the mother in late antiquity and early
Christianity', *Harvard Theological Review* 82 (1989), 393–420, esp. 407 ff.

[206] Although from 1916 onwards more negative attitudes prevailed, the
notion was endorsed by Pius IX in 1873. For a sympathetic treatment, T. Beattie,
' Mary, the Virgin priest?', *The Month* NS 29 (1996), 485–93.

[207] Most obviously perhaps with the pop star Madonna, and her various
albums such as *The Immaculate Collection* (1990), 'dedicated to "The Pope", my
divine inspiration' (CD notes).

PART THREE
Truth and authority

In the final part of this volume I want to draw together some of the main issues raised both here and in my earlier volume *Tradition and Imagination*. The very possibility of discipleship depends crucially on the plausibility of the wider framework within which its practice is set. In particular two recurring questions need to be faced: first, where authority lies in the process of the developing tradition in which both belief and practice has been moulded by changing narratives; secondly, how the truth content of that tradition is to be understood when placed in a context within which historical 'fact' and imaginative 'fiction' are inextricably combined.

The second question is the one which I shall deal with last in the final chapter, as it seems to me the more fundamental. Across the two books I have offered a series of examples of cases where in my view advance in religious understanding has been achieved through in effect biblical stories being retold. Sometimes there may have been no historical content in the first place, as with Job or possibly even the patriarchs, but even where incontestably there was, as with Jesus, his mother or Mary Magdalene, it has been my contention that the subsequent 'fictional' elaboration has not necessarily led to a reduction of the truth content of the narratives concerned. Of course, inevitably this was sometimes so. One instance offered in the previous chapter was the way in which a doctrine of immaculate conception came to be attached to the Virgin Mary. Sometimes the relevant faith community has seen for itself the inappropriateness of a particular line of development, as in the eventual rejection within both Judaism and Christianity of the suggestion that the command to sacrifice Isaac came from the Devil, or the modern abandonment of reading the life of Joseph as the story of Christ. But we need clearer criteria than the mere test

of time. Some have been indicated in earlier chapters. Their varied
character, however, means that it is important that they be
brought together and some form of overall assessment offered.

That is where my discussion in the final chapter will end. Its
first half, though, will consider what types of claim can be
sustained respecting imaginative writing and art as a vehicle of
truth. Because of the doctrinal character of Christianity, even
those sympathetic to my argument as a whole might be tempted
to conclude that what really matters are the inferences drawn from
the rewritten stories rather than the form of the stories themselves.
So, for instance, my point might be thought to be the truth of
particular doctrines that have been implicitly defended, such as the
divinity of Christ or the present existence of saints in heaven, or
the truth of particular moral positions such as the equality of the
sexes or the illegitimacy of interpreting an individual's suffering as
part of the particular providence of God. But that would be to
engage in a form of reductionism which I would want to challenge. Even if correct in its analysis of the content of the New
Testament, Bultmann's programme of demythologization could
still rightly be criticized for failing to take with sufficient seriousness how indispensable the myths as stories are to the power and
persuasiveness of the gospel. However correct in theory, existen-
tial truths cannot of themselves adequately engage the heart and
the imagination. The point has been well taken by more recent
supporters of what has come to be known as narrative theology.[1]
However, as I have repeatedly sought to make clear in preceding
pages, that approach has in my view two major defects. First,
because often the net effect has been the canonization of a particular narrative—the biblical—with historical questions in consequence either side-stepped or jettisoned altogether, the power of
'fiction', when fully acknowledged as such, to communicate truth
is given very inadequate treatment. Second, because a particular
version is made normative, little or no attention is given to the
factors that have led in subsequent centuries to radical transformations of the narrative or even to the search for substitute or
compensatory narratives, as I argued happened in the case of the

---

[1] For focusing the issues, particularly useful are: G. W. Stroup, *The Promise
of Narrative Theology* (London: SCM Press, 1984); R. F. Thiemann, *Revelation and
Theology* (Notre Dame, Indiana: University of Notre Dame Press, 1985).

Lives of the saints. It is that more complicated picture which will be addressed in the final chapter.

But before that discussion there comes the immediately following chapter, on authority. In the earlier book *Tradition and Imagination* I underlined my concern to maintain a strong emphasis on revelation but noted the need to combine it with a account where tradition becomes revelation's natural medium, both within Scripture and beyond, rather than something to be set in contrast over against it. Although I have spoken of 'trajectories' from the biblical text and of the deposit of faith turning back on itself to 'correct' earlier misunderstandings, the fact that I suggested that such changes arise through interaction with specific social and cultural contexts might easily be taken by a hostile critic to imply the recognition of no authority beyond my own reflections. Nothing could be further from the truth. Ultimately, behind that process I would wish to see the hand of God continuing to involve himself intimately with humanity and our desire to understand the divine purpose. More immediately, however, there seems to me an indispensable role for the community of faith in helping the individual believer determine where that process of revelation has now reached. One intention, therefore, behind the chapter that follows will be to clarify how I conceive the relation between the individual theologian and the Church as a whole. But there is also a more fundamental purpose, and that is to urge a reassessment of the status of conflict within the community of faith. In outline, my argument will be that both within the Bible and beyond more often than not truth has emerged through lively disagreement, and not simply by formal acceptance of an existing deposit or simple deductions from it. The ability to envisage alternative scenarios has thus always been integral to the healthy development of the tradition. Unilinear theories of development must therefore be abandoned, and the search for consensus within conflict be taken with much more seriousness, whether we are thinking of later Church history or even the Bible itself.

Sadly, it is often only a later generation that comes to see the legitimate strengths of both opposing positions. Biblical and later Church history are replete with examples of failures to listen appropriately to different branches of the tradition, still more of failures to listen to the wider society. Of course, that refusal to listen is sometimes exactly what the situation requires. Herein lies one of the great strengths of an existing deposit of faith. But the deposit can sometimes also function as a prison, effectively preventing the appropriation of fresh insights. It is that admission which points to the need for the presence, in some of the faithful at least, of an open imagination that insists upon the exploration of alternative possibilities. Personal subordination to a community of faith is justified because inevitably the totality of corporate insights will be immensely more rich than what can be achieved on one's own. Even so, it is only by some individuals opening up alternative possibilities that the community is itself allowed the chance of moving as a whole in fresh directions. That being so, extremely important though the notion is to any community of faith, its authority cannot safely be conceded the last word, and that is why one further chapter on truth must follow the forthcoming discussion of authority.

6

Apostolicity and conflict: Peter and Paul

THE most famous theological discussion of development was offered by its author as his justification for his move from the authority of Canterbury to that of Rome.[1] Few today would regard the tests Newman offers as persuasive, far less decisive. The continuing significance of the *Essay* is the impetus it gave to less wooden approaches to how development occurs, with entailments from an earlier deposit now accepted as altogether too simplistic.[2] To his credit, that is one of the reasons why to begin with Newman expressed reservations over the subsequent promulgation of papal infallibility in 1870;[3] why too he acknowledged tensions between the prophetic, priestly, and regal aspects of the Church in the 1877 Preface to his *Via Media*.[4] Yet as an Anglican Newman is found expressing a desire for a very simple authority structure. Christ is presented as investing in his apostles the main powers that he himself possesses, and indeed the image of prophet, priest, and king is used to make that point, but without any of the

[1] J. H. Newman, *An Essay on the Development of Doctrine* (1845). For his seven tests, ch. 1, sec. 3.
[2] Well indicated by O. Chadwick, *From Bossuet to Newman* (Cambridge: Cambridge University Press, 1957), esp. chs. 2 and 5.
[3] For some context to his famous remark 'to Conscience first, and to the Pope afterwards', S. Gilley, *Newman and his Age* (London: Darton, Longman & Todd, 1990), 363–81 esp. 375–6.
[4] Section 7 ff. argues that the theological ('prophet'), devotional ('priest') and ruling ('king') aspects of the Church have each a tendency to overstep their proper limits but that this can sometimes serve a useful purpose in securing the legitimate objectives of the Church.

tensions noted that he would later make explicit in his 1877 *Preface*.[5] Did the realities of his new communion perhaps force upon him the beginnings of the recognition of a more complex picture?

However that may be, modern biblical scholarship and the development of non-partisan research into the history of the Church certainly now compel such a recognition.[6] We can no longer think as Newman did of the apostles after the death of Christ acting in unanimity as a college with power to act as 'sole channels of grace' and 'sole governors',[7] and this authority then being transmitted to their successors. Conflict runs deep both in Scripture and in the subsequent history of the Church, and it is impossible to substantiate any claim that truth has always unqualifiedly flowed in one stream and one stream alone. Increasingly, attention is being drawn to a range of positions within the New Testament, with, for instance the views of James, Peter, and Paul no longer easily reconcilable. Similarly, in treatments of the early Church more positive assessments are being offered of heretical movements that were until recently seen in largely negative terms, just as Reformation and Counter-Reformation are being contextualized, not only through greater acknowledgement of their common medieval inheritance, but also in the way in which the decrees of both distort except when read in relation to the alleged faults of the other side: in other words, neither can claim to offer self-contained truths. These are some examples of the historical issues to which attention will be drawn shortly. The reader should note, though, that it is impossible to offer here more than cursory comment on any particular example, and that the examples are intended in any case to be subordinate to consideration of the theological implications of such a changed understanding of the community of faith's past. With that end in view, I shall consider first the pattern that emerges within Scripture itself before turning to a consideration of what happens in the subsequent history of the Church.

---

[5] *Parochial and Plain Sermons* (San Francisco: Ignatius Press, 1987), II, 25, esp. 417. Cf. also VII, 17, esp. 1541–2.

[6] Continuing problems with partisan approaches to Church history are illustrated in J. Kent, *The Unacceptable Face: the Modern Church in the Eyes of the Historian* (London: SCM Press, 1987).

[7] *Parochial and Plain Sermons*, VI, 14, 1299.

Contesting a biblical consensus

My subheading here is deliberately ambiguous, for not only do I
wish to challenge the notion of any simple idea of an Old or New
Testament biblical consensus, I also want to argue that it is in fact
commonly through the process of contest and conflict that a
consensus eventually emerged, to which some authority could
then legitimately be attached. Even that limited claim, though,
may be altogether too much for some scholars. They might rightly
observe that all such forms of consensus came at a price, with the
exclusion of some group or other, as for example in the New
Testament with the Church's eventual rejection of those Ebionite
or Jewish Christians (probably to be especially associated with the
apostle James) who strongly supported continued observation of
the Law. This must be conceded, but equally we need to guard
against the supposition that any proper search for the truth can
ever avoid some losing out. In much modern interfaith and
ecumenical dialogue there is an insidious temptation to identify
tolerance with indifference. This can appear, most obviously
perhaps, in the supposition that the only way to respect those with
whom one disagrees is to declare their opinion as good as one's
own, and thus the conviction can easily emerge that it is only in
issues that do not ultimately matter that one may legitimately
disagree. One unfortunate expression of this idea in ecumenical
dialogue is in the notion that what are labelled *adiaphora* should be
read as implying that doctrines thus characterized are of no intrinsic, or at most only minor, importance.[8] A recent instance of the
same kind of problem in interfaith discussion comes in the work
of a German scholar who equates anti-Judaism in the New
Testament with any suggestion from the Christian side that
continued adhesion to Judaism cannot of itself lead to salvation.[9]
Certainly, it must be conceded that the New Testament does

[8] What is 'indifferent' in terms of structural unity might still play a vital role
in the practice of a Christian's faith. Accepting difference is thus not to be
equated with declaring unimportant.

[9] G. Lüdemann, *The Unholy in Holy Scripture* (London: SCM Press, 1997),
76 ff. For him 'anti-Judaism is the other side of "Christ alone" ' (118), and it looks
as though Christianity could only avoid the accusation if it treated Jesus' teaching and significance as equivalent to that of 'a Reform Jew' (130).

contain some of the seeds for later anti-Semitism and that despite almost all its authors being themselves Jews, but we must surely resist the view that any declaration of disagreement necessarily of itself constitutes an act of hostility. Indeed, it is worth noting that in the original arguments for religious toleration in England, the philosopher John Locke opposed forced conformity not because he held all views on such matters to be of equal worth but because he argued that God valued something more: the free assent of the individuals concerned.[10] In other words, what matters is the degree of respect one accords those with whom one disagrees, not the strength of one's disagreement. It is of course not always easy to keep the two issues separate, but that does not alter the importance of the principle. Christianity and Judaism *may* both lead to salvation, but it is important in the search for truth that all options be kept open, including of course the possibility that neither religion is true.

Because moral, political, and religious views can profoundly affect the way in which we live, inevitably the search for truth in these areas often tends to have an acerbic edge. But there is also another, more positive way of viewing the matter. Because positions are deeply held, it can sometimes take powerful expressions of a contrary view to shock us into taking opponents seriously. Conflict can thus at times be creative in widening horizons, and in compelling either the adoption of one's opponent's perspective or at the very least its incorporation into a wider frame. That, I suggest, is the way in which we should read the conflicts lying just beneath the scriptural text. In a moment we shall consider how such an observation might apply in respect of disagreements among the apostles, but it will be helpful first to set such conflict against the wider background of the way in which the Judaism they had inherited was itself created through contested opinions. In a sense, God's apostles or 'accredited agents' have always been in dispute with one another,[11] and that is how growth in the tradition has occurred.

---

[10] Force can never produce that 'faith and inward sincerity' which alone can 'procure acceptance with God': *Works of John Locke* (1727), II, 243.

[11] For the sense of apostle as Christ's *shaliah* or accredited agent, C. K. Barrett, *The Signs of an Apostle* (Exeter: Paternoster, 2nd edn, 1996), esp. 71–4. The different senses assigned to the term by Luke and Paul is only indirectly relevant to the discussion which follows.

Hearing plural voices: Jewish no less than Christian

Given its probable thousand-year span it is perhaps not all that surprising that a great diversity of opinion is to be found within the Old Testament canon. Attention has already been drawn to some of its features in the earlier volume. Here, while offering additional examples, I want my primary focus to be rather different, not so much on the question of how revelation works as on the issue of what authority might legitimately be attached either to the final result or to the various conflicts themselves. Over the past twenty years or so Brevard Childs has been prominent in arguing that decisive weight should be given both to the final redactional shaping of particular books and to how that final shaping fits into the structure of the canon as a whole. In arguing thus he has offered valuable lessons in how later material can sometimes significantly modify earlier, which can then in retrospect be seen as offering a distorted picture of God's nature or purposes unless read with the complementary later material. An example would be the way in which Amos's message of unrelieved condemnation is given a wider frame by the later redactor's offer of eschatological hope in chapter 9.[12] More recently, Childs's position has become more firmly ecclesiastical, with the Church's understanding of Christ apparently held to be what should finally determine our understanding of the shape of Christian Scripture, both Old and New.[13]

In developing such theories of 'canonical criticism', he has been subjected to some severe adverse comment, partly because of the way in which his method seems to allow later perspectives to determine legitimate interpretation and partly because of the inevitable downgrading of earlier strands in the tradition even though these may well bear in their own right a readily accessible meaning.[14] Although he takes care to make some reference to

[12] B. S. Childs, *Introduction to the Old Testament as Scripture* (London: SCM Press, 1979), 395–410, esp. 405 ff.

[13] In *Biblical Theology of the Old and New Testaments* (London: SCM Press, 1992) he talks of 'the complete canon of the Christian church as the rule-of-faith' (67) with the Old Testament seen as having 'functioned as Christian scripture because it bore witness to Christ' (64).

[14] For some pertinent criticisms, J. Barr, *Holy Scripture: Canon, Authority, Criticism* (Oxford: Clarendon Press, 1983), esp. 75–104, 130–71.

post-biblical exegetical history, there is no wrestling with the possibility that this history might also open up legitimate alternative options as radical as the New Testament had done with respect to the Old.[15] More recently, however, another distinguished Old Testament scholar, Walter Brueggemann, has argued that 'testimony' and 'countertestimony' are integral to the way in which the Hebrew Scriptures developed, and so something irretrievable is lost unless due note is taken of such conflict. His use of this interpretative category is plausibly applied across a great range of cases. Encouraging too is the key role he gives to the imagination in generating alternative narratives and images.[16]

Where, however, he can be faulted is for his postmodernist insistence that God is only available to us through such conflict and that it is somehow destructive of the significance of the text to attempt to dissolve or lessen it.[17] If communities are to make progress and develop, it would seem inevitable that they will try to attempt some resolution of conflict, and, in reflecting on its past, at one level it must be seen as not only natural but also right that any community discussion in the present will need to begin with its existing assumptions about consensus.[18] Therein lies one great strength of Childs' approach. Yet, the danger is that in the process of achieving consensus valid insights will be lost, and that is why there is always a need periodically to revisit sites of conflict, not least to recall the creative role it once exercised. Although it is a huge oversimplification, much of the history of Protestant interpretation of Scripture has been dominated by the assumption that the real core of the Old Testament lies in the prophets and that

[15] Illustrated by his commentary on Exodus where a commendable concern for the history of exegesis is somewhat vitiated by rather predicable praise for Augustine, Calvin and Luther: B. S. Childs, *The Book of Exodus* (Louisville, Kentucky: Westminster Press, 1974).

[16] W. Brueggemann, *Theology of the Old Testament* (Minneapolis: Fortress Press, 1997). Significantly, the book is subtitled 'Testimony, Dispute, Advocacy'. For the role of the imagination: e.g. 67–71.

[17] For his refusal to allow God beyond the text, e.g. ibid., 66, 70, 722, 725. His acceptance of postmodernism is indicated by the title of an earlier book: *Texts under Negotiation: The Bible and Postmodern Imagination* (Minneapolis: Fortress Press, 1993).

[18] For a work that accepts diversity but shows greater concern to place it on the way towards consensus, J. Goldingay, *Theological Diversity and the Authority of the Old Testament* (Grand Rapids, Michigan: Eerdmans, 1987).

this core was then taken up by Paul, while conventional Catholic thinking can be characterized in terms of 'Peter' anticipated in the priestly tradition and presented with particular effectiveness in Matthew's Gospel and in the Epistle to the Hebrews, the one seen as offering a new priesthood and new Law, and the other as reflecting the sacrifice of the Mass. If modern biblical scholarship has required a different interpretation for Matthew and Hebrews, equally Protestants have been forced to acknowledge a more positive role for the priestly tradition, not least because of the Psalms now being seen as central to Temple worship.[19] Even so, there remain conflicts that have not yet in my view been fully integrated. As an example I want to consider first Christianity's perception of its relation to Judaism, and then secondly the related issue of Judaism's own perception of its history.

It is all too easy for Christianity to present itself as a natural, inevitable, and self-contained development from Judaism. But even at its very beginning the issue may not have been quite that simple. For it is not impossible that even the notion of Yahweh itself was fostered through creative dialogue with the surrounding culture. For there is some evidence to suggest that 'Yahweh' began as a local Midianite god, adopted by the Hebrews to symbolize the freedom they now sought.[20] There we are in the mists of early history, where certainty is impossible. What we can say, though, is that increasing recognition is now being given to the role that dialogue with the surrounding culture played within the canon itself. Partly under the influence of Barth, earlier this century many biblical scholars offered accounts of the Old Testament that dismissed the presence within Scripture of any debts to natural reason. But the whole Wisdom tradition tells a different story, and it is to his great credit that this was eventually fully acknowledged by Gerhard von Rad in a book published in the last year of his life, a trend that has been continued in the

---

[19] So long as most of them remained attributed to David, any hint of a connection with the priestly tradition could be quietly suppressed.

[20] R. Albertz, *A History of Israelite Religion* (London: SCM Press, 1994), I, 49 ff. For a more radical view of 'evolution . . . through conflict'. with the exodus seen as an ideology to express the desire for internal reform at the time of the exile, G. Garbini, *History and Ideology in Ancient Israel* (London: SCM Press, 1988), 52–65.

Gifford Lectures of James Barr.[21] That desire not to restrict unduly
the range of significance of Scripture has been continued in one of
von Rad's erstwhile pupils and eventual successor at Heidelberg,
Rolf Rendtorff, whose work has been notable for its concern to
take seriously the theological concerns of Jewish scholars. One
instance is his desire not to force the 'new covenant' of Jeremiah
into an attack on law (Jer. 31: 33).[22] One wonders, though,
whether in general the best strategy is really the search for a
common meaning in the same text, or whether the more realistic
option is not the recognition of the possibility of alternative trajectories, and the question then raised of what either can teach the
other. In the case of law this is particularly pertinent, as New
Testament scholars are now increasingly acknowledging the presence within the New Testament of parties who favoured continued observation of the Law and indeed, as we saw in *Tradition and
Imagination*, this may well have been the view of Jesus himself.

In that same volume we also observed that Paul's claim to find
in the story of Abraham an evaluation of faith over works may not
be nearly as securely grounded as Christian exegetes normally
suppose.[23] Even if it were shown that Paul's claim were not true
historically, though, it might be thought that his position would
be immeasurably strengthened by the now widely accepted recognition that the primary emphasis on law is really a post-exilic
development; for then it could be argued that, if elements of that
attitude are embedded in Abraham's story, they are really merely
a retrojection of later attitudes. But what grounds have we for
thinking later attitudes degenerate? As a Psalm like 119 makes
abundantly clear, law could be experienced as profoundly liberating. Moreover, if we reflect upon the later history of Judaism, it is
hard to deny that Christianity has been repeatedly guilty of carica-
turing what Judaism understood law to entail. One recent study
from a Jewish scholar has been at pains to emphasize how open
that later tradition in fact was. Not only did the Mishnah deliberately record two opposed interpretations, but also the later

---

[21] G. von Rad, *Wisdom in Israel* (Nashville: Abingdon Press, 1972); J. Barr,
Biblical Faith and Natural Theology (Oxford: Clarendon Press, 1993).

[22] R. Rendtorff, *Canon and Theology* (Edinburgh: T & T Clark, 1994),
196–206. For his involvement with Judaism, e.g. Ibid., 214.

[23] *Tradition and Imagination*, 213–37.

Talmud, while in theory offering a more strictly didactic approach, widened the options still further by arguing for reinterpretations of the Mishnah that transform its meaning.[24] Some rabbis sought closure, but the continued recording of minority views, as also the insistence on the relevance of philosophy or mystical experience as interpretative frames for understanding the Law, shows how wide in fact the options remained.[25]

That same scholar, Moshe Halbertal, observes that the modern Jewish return to the primary authority of the Hebrew Bible as against its interpretation through the lens of the Talmud has in fact led in some ways to a narrowing of options, and not their widening.[26] The process began with the eighteenth-century Enlightenment desire to see the particularity of Judaism as an instance of universal rational truths, while with the rise of Zionism this has been combined with the desire for a distinctively national epic that can attach itself to the value of the land. The result is that the Bible is now the almost exclusive focus of religious teaching in Israeli schools, whereas in earlier centuries study of the Bible would have been contextualized and focused through study of the Talmud. It is ironic to find those who would otherwise be highly critical of the consequences of the Enlightenment enthusiastic for this particular change. A more fundamental criticism, though, would be to ask whether it is really so self-evident that stress on the possession of a God-given land is a finer religious ideal than the attempt to conform one's life in every detail to obedient delight in God's service. Although all that Jews have suffered in the twentieth century makes attachment to the land natural, when due account is taken of all the ambiguities in the biblical elucidation of that notion,[27] one cannot help wondering whether the more profound critique of Christianity might not in some ways come from Judaism's later history rather than from the Old Testament on its own.

Different strands in contemporary Judaism operate with different

[24] M. Halbertal, *People of the Book* (Cambridge, Mass.: Harvard University Press, 1997), 45, 72–3.
[25] Ibid., 52, 59–72, 109–24. Maimonides played a key role for philosophy, Nachmanides in the Kabbalistic tradition.
[26] Ibid., 129–34.
[27] Not least with the *herem*. Its distinctively religious character as the 'sacred ban' makes it more offensive, not less: Barr, *Biblical Faith*, 207 ff.

notions of canon, and it is obviously not for me as a Christian to seek to determine on what basis adherents of Judaism might choose to begin dialogue. I make these remarks rather because of their relevance to Christianity's situation in the first century and how it might now be perceived. As Qumran reveals, at that time there was some fluidity in the Jewish canon,[28] and of course it only gradually emerged that Christianity would need to separate to form its own distinct faith community. Not that it was alone in this. Qumran itself could not be accommodated to rabbinical thought because of its insistence on a different liturgical calendar. Christology was one factor in Christianity's split, but so too was Paul's attitude to law. Neither religion will do adequate justice to the history of its developing tradition, so long as its own trajectories are seen as simple and obvious, and the creativity of other alternatives not fully acknowledged. The fact that certainly James, and possibly Peter, had a different view on law from Paul means that complex issues of authority are raised for Christianity no less than for Judaism. It is to these issues that I now turn.

Peter and Paul: law and authority

The final version of Christianity that was to emerge rejected both detailed observance of the Torah and any necessity for the Temple, reformed or otherwise. Yet, as I argued in *Tradition and Imagination*, this was not the picture which the earliest Church inherited from its Lord.[29] Jesus had certainly been critical of both, but the critique appeared to be combined with continuing respect, and thus to indicate a desire for reform rather than necessarily their abolition.[30] That would then explain why the first Christians continued to attend the Temple (e.g. Acts 2: 46; 3: 1; 5: 42) why too Paul's arguments for the abrogation of the Law were offered

[28] E.g. the book of *Jubilees* seems to have been treated as canonical.

[29] *Tradition and Imagination,* ch. 6.

[30] Various passages imply frequent attendance at the Temple: e.g. Mark 14: 49; John. 5: 1 and 7: 10. Jesus also urges lepers to observe the law, and he is described as regularly attending the synagogue: Mark 1: 44; Luke 4: 16. Again, though Mark places the cleansing of the temple between the two halves of the story of the cursing of the fig tree, the symbolism in itself as well as the words used (Mark 11: 17) surely suggest reform rather than destruction: for a different view, E. P. Sanders, *Jesus and Judaism* (London: SCM Press, 1985), 61–71.

with such heat and not always welcomed by his fellow-Christians. That very scenario, though, does open up the possibility of very opposed analyses and interpretations of how later developments are to be perceived. On the one hand, one might argue that Paul went in directions that Jesus himself would not have allowed, and so the more Jewish version of Christianity associated with James should be seen as his more natural inheritance. On the other hand, one might insist that Paul constitutes a legitimate trajectory from Jesus' less developed position. My own interpretation comes nearer to the second view. Where I differ from most of its advocates would be in insisting that the conflict was in itself valuable not only in terms of what finally emerged but also in the losing side continuing to offer us legitimate elements of critique with which to challenge what might otherwise be the unassailable dominance of Paul. To illustrate this, I would like to reconsider at this point first the relation between Peter and Paul on law, then their respective positions on authority, before concluding with some observations on how voices elsewhere in Scripture also offer a challenge to both.

The issue of Law   Before considering the rival theologies, some attempt must first be made to reconstruct that early history. While Luke in Acts makes the story of the transition to the new view more smooth than it could possibly ever have been, Paul's own evidence is also somewhat vitiated by his natural human desire to present himself in the best possible light. The result is the denigration of others and what are almost certainly exaggerated claims to independence.[31] For it is surely inherently unlikely that his integration into Christianity was little affected by the work of others, or that, initially at least, his authority would have been recognized without strong support from the Jerusalem church, and particularly from those who had known Jesus while alive. Indeed, it is not improbable that others than he were the first to have the ideas that are usually credited to him alone. One possibility is that he had already been anticipated in some respects by

---

[31]   Gal. 1–2 seeks to minimize any sense of dependence on others apart from God himself (e.g. 1: 16–17; 1: 19; 2: 2) while sarcastic language is used of others in positions of authority: e.g. 2: 6 and 9, a pattern repeated elsewhere: e.g. the 'superlative apostles' of 2 Cor. 11: 5.

the 'Hellenists' associated with Stephen.[32] Although other explanations are possible, the term 'Hellenists' is likely to have been a disparaging way of referring to Diaspora Jews, caricatured as speaking only Greek or adopting 'Greek' attitudes.[33] Therein may lie part of Stephen's reason for disparaging the Temple. For what is fascinating about the account of the history of God's people that he offers in Acts as part of his defence is that he makes the burden of this also an essentially Diaspora history (Acts 7: 2–53).[34] His argument seems to be that the covenant people did not always need the Temple in the past, and so by analogy it cannot be held to be indispensable for Diaspora Jews in the present. Scholars often argue that such a critique was combined with conservatism, and in particular a conservative attitude to the Law,[35] but, if one takes seriously the events surrounding the speech and to some extent the speech itself as an historical source,[36] then surely one must accord similar credence to the precise form of accusation laid against Stephen, which describes him as speaking 'words against this holy place and the law' (Acts 6: 13 RSV).[37]

None of this is to deny the considerable opposition that was ranged against Paul, not least from the circle round James. Ironically, it is only thanks to Paul that we know that it was probably as a result of an experience of the resurrection that James came to belief in his brother's ministry (1 Cor. 15: 7). Admittedly, the *Gospel of Thomas* appears to make him a disciple in Jesus' own lifetime, but on the other side must be weighed the canonical Gospels' consistent portrayal of opposition to his mission from

[32] Explored as one of several possible influences by H. Räisänen, *Paul and the Law* (Tübingen: Mohr, 1983), 229–63, esp. 251–6.

[33] M. Simon, *St Stephen and the Hellenists* (London: Longmans, 1958), 1–19, esp. 9–13; M. Hengel, *Between Jesus and Paul* (London: SCM Press, 1983), 4–11.

[34] Stephen recounts the early history of Israel, but in a way that focuses even with the patriarchs on their sojourn elsewhere, as with Abraham in Haran and Joseph in Egypt.

[35] 'Law . . . is at the very core of his thought': Simon, *St Stephen* 46. Cf. J. D. G. Dunn, *The Parting of the Ways* (London: SCM Press, 1991), 57–74, esp. 69.

[36] Although clearly adapted by Luke to his wider purposes, its content suggests some attempt on Luke's part to indicate Stephen's own distinctive view.

[37] Although the law is not specifically attacked in Stephen's speech, his last words are an attack on the manner of its observance (7: 53), and this may imply some further radicalization of Jesus' own limited critique.

Jesus' family and brethren.[38] In trying to explain why James so quickly assumed a position of leadership in the early Church, scholars sometimes appeal to traditional Jewish attitudes to the family,[39] but a better explanation would seem to me to lie in the dramatic change of position from his earlier hostility, combined presumably with his ability to claim detailed knowledge of his brother's life and views. It is often assumed that this went with strict Jewish orthodoxy and a very low Christology, but against is the need to explain why he was so quickly able to assume a role superior to the narrow band of disciples who had accompanied Jesus in his earthly ministry. That surely suggests a commanding figure of some insight, and so it is perhaps better to think of him as zealously guarding a rather literal transmission of the Jesus inheritance. Any suggestion of change would thus be met with the objection that it was this and not that which his brother had said or done.

The force of such an objection may perhaps receive its best illustration in the story of Paul's confrontation with Peter in Antioch (Gal. 2: 11 ff).[40] The incident is often used to tar Peter with a further instance of the inconstancy of purpose that he had already displayed at the time of the crucifixion. But it could also be read as indicative of neither inconstancy nor compromise but the real difficulty of determining in what direction Jesus' teaching should now be carried in the very different circumstances that have emerged subsequent to his death. Jesus had only occasionally directed his ministry towards Gentiles, whereas now significant numbers were joining the new community. Despite Paul's own attempt to confine Peter's mission to Jews in much the same way

---

[38] *Gospel of Thomas*, 10. It is implied rather than explicit, unlike the fragment of the *Gospel of the Hebrews* preserved by Jerome, where his presence at the Last Supper is accepted: *De viris illustribus*, 2. But both could be developments from the resurrection appearance, while if the canonical Gospels had really intended to attack James it is hard to understand why he is never mentioned by name. For a different view, P.-A. Bernheim, *James, Brother of Jesus* (London: SCM Press, 1997), 76–100.   [39] Ibid., 216–22.

[40] Though I find the argument implausible, it has been suggested that the common interpretation is wrong, and that Paul supported James's wish for the continuing imposition of the law on Jewish Christian communities, and that the real problem was Peter's failure to keep within one boundary or the other: W. Schmithals, *Paul and James* (London: SCM Press, 1965), esp. 63–78, 103–117.

as his own was to Gentiles, Acts, and indeed Paul's own letters, suggest a more complicated picture.[41] As the incident itself illustrates, Peter was willing to become involved with mixed congregations, and it may be that this reflected his own uncertainty about how far developments should go in the new situation. If we accept the view that Matthew's Gospel originated from Petrine circles, its teaching, and in particular the Sermon on the Mount, demonstrates how profound an intermediate position could be, with law not discounted but constant stress placed on the spiritual core at the heart of such observation.[42]

The Church did not of course finally accept the view that 'every jot and tittle' should be observed, but it did endorse the implicit Matthean (and thus Petrine) critique of aspects of the Pauline view as presented in Mark. For instance, whereas Paul had expressed indifference to the observance of holy days, Matthew carefully rewrites Mark to ensure, not that this message is drawn, but rather the conviction that such rules should remain except when overridden by more pressing needs.[43] So we should beware of characterizing the early conflict as resulting in an unqualified victory for Paul. The losing side is also present in the canon, helping to give a more nuanced overall position. Such supplements were in any case essential, if Paul's position was not in the end to be fundamentally undermined by the inadequacy of his own arguments. That may seem a strong judgement to make, but the difficulty with letting Paul have the exclusive final say is that we are then confronted with a bewildering number of arguments which one way or another either founder on the strangeness of the exegesis employed or on the arbitrariness of the picture thus gained of divine providence.

---

[41] For Paul's view, Gal. 2: 7–8; cf. Acts 18: 6. On the other side is not only the Cornelius incident in Acts (10: 1 ff.) but also Paul's own references to Petrine parties in his congregations: 1 Cor. 1: 12; 3: 22; and possibly 2 Cor. 11: 5.

[42] This is the most natural reading of the Sermon on the Mount, with the Law not abolished but reinterpreted as requiring a new level of commitment: e. g. 5: 20.

[43] Contrast Rom. 14: 5 ff.; Gal. 4: 10; Col. 2: 16, and especially Mark 2: 23–28, with Matt. 12: 1–8. Matthew omits 'the sabbath was made for man and not man for the sabbath' and adds other material in order to indicate that Jesus did not intend to oppose sabbath obligations, but wished rather to place them in a wider frame.

Galatians 3: 15–19 may be used as illustrative of the problematic character of Paul's exegesis of the Hebrew Scriptures. In that
short paragraph the use of the singular in the promise of 'seed' to
Abraham is presumed to require fulfilment in Christ, while the
fact that the Law was given through angels is taken as a sign of
disfavour and not importance.[44] This is not to deny that such
midrash could well have carried conviction at the time, nor that
revelation might work through such means, but it is to observe
that it makes the connections more problematic for our own
day.[45] This becomes still more obvious once we turn to the more
general pattern of Pauline arguments on this question. For so
concerned is Paul to present the Christian gospel positively that
by contrast the Law comes to be presented in crudely negative
terms. The gentler version is of the one outshining the other; the
more severe version of the Law's sole purpose being as a foil, in
bringing slavery and condemnation.[46] The great sweep of Jewish
history thus remains under God's charge, but at the puzzling price
of God instituting a form of religion that can only condemn.
Some scholars have attempted to reconcile such attitudes with
Paul's occasional more positive statements,[47] but it would seem to
me that not only do 'contradictions and tension have to be
accepted as constant features of Paul's theology', it is also in the
end the negative attitudes which predominate and which resist
easy integration:[48] in the words of one New Testament scholar,
'Paul's major explanation . . . was that the law was given to

[44] Contrast Stephen's laudatory reference on the same theme: Acts 7: 53; cf.
v. 38.

[45] As the history of its use in worship indicates. Set as the Epistle for the thirteenth Sunday after Trinity in the Book of Common Prayer, by the 1928 revision the rare expedient of an alternative reading (Heb. 13) was offered, while in
the 1980 Alternative Service Book it disappears altogether.

[46] For the gentler version, 2 Cor. 3; Phil. 3. For the more severe, Gal. 3–4;
Rom. 4–7. Romans 7 is often interpreted as Paul trying to draw back from the
full consequences of his earlier argument.

[47] E.g. C. E. B. Cranfield, *Epistle to the Romans* (Edinburgh: T & T Clark,
1979), 852–61. Though conceding Paul's 'regularly negative attitude . . . towards
the law' (129), this is also the direction of thought in J. D. G. Dunn, *The Theology
of Paul the Apostle* (Edinburgh: T & T Clark, 1998), 128–61.

[48] Räisänen, *Paul and the Law*, esp. 11. A similar view of irreconcilable inconsistencies is accepted by E. P. Sanders, *Paul, the Law and the Jewish People*
(Philadelphia: Fortress Press, 1983).

condemn'.[49] Admittedly, this Pauline emphasis on what was new
in Christianity was probably highly effective as a missionary strategy, but in the long term Paul's stress on radical discontinuity
could only undermine a religion that claimed a God so deeply
involved within the historical process as the incarnation implied.
It was no doubt for this reason that the later Church subtly modified Paul's claims. While there remained the negative side in the
claim that the Law had not been properly understood, the positive is the assertion that Christianity was in fact the true inheritor
of the whole sweep of Old Testament religion, including Law.

The issue of authority   One reason why Paul so often gets a much
better press than Peter is because we read both figures in the light
of later history. In other words, our imaginative grasp of them as
individuals is clouded by what later history made of them. So
because Peter became the primary symbol for the papacy, it is
assumed that he must have acted as a similar authority figure in
New Testament times. Likewise, because Luther found great
personal liberation in the writings of Paul, it is assumed that his
reactions to Peter constitute resistance to illegitimate claims to
authority, whereas the actual position seems immeasurably more
complex.[50] One notes, for instance, that Paul's normal practice is
not to substitute an alternative authority to himself, such as derivation from the teaching of Jesus or some wider principle of
consensus within the Christian community as a whole. Instead, he
insists that 'the "pillars" in Jerusalem could add nothing to his own
personal authority,'[51] and that this derives from God alone, in his
commissioning as an apostle and his role as founder of some of the
communities to which he writes.[52] That Paul was in no way a

[49]   E. Sanders, *Paul* (Oxford: Oxford University Press, 1991), 94. For Sanders,
Paul works 'in images and figures', but not as a 'systematic theologian' (127–8).

[50]   One needs to distinguish between Paul's explicit affirmations and what can
be deduced from elsewhere about the general church view at that time: B.
Holmberg, *Paul and Power* (Philadelphia: Fortress Press, 1980), 16–33.

[51]   The summary of the argument of Gal. 1: 16–2: 14 in W. A. Meeks, *The
First Urban Christians* (New Haven: Yale University Press, 1983), 116. The chapter on 'governance' is particularly helpful: 111–39.

[52]   Although his right to be called an apostle was contested (1 Cor. 9: 1–2), it
is the characteristic form of self-description that he uses to open his letters, and it
often functions elsewhere in the argument. For appeal to his role as founder, e.g.
1 Cor. 4: 14–16.

figure tolerant of views different from his own emerges with particular clarity when he is faced by challenges to his own position. Some highly pertinent examples are to be found in 2 Corinthians, where his own charismatic form of leadership is seen to have been subject to serious challenge. Although some have detected 'a pattern of authority that enabled a set of social relations through which there was new freedom, energy and mutuality',[53] that needs to be set against the denigration of opponents and the attempt to outdo them in revelations and charismatic powers.[54] Paul could even threaten 'a rod', which may be less metaphorical than is usually supposed, since some of the communities to which he writes do exhibit clear structures of authority and indeed in the case of the Corinthian church an excommunication is even proposed.[55] Certainly, his approach is more subtle than that found in the pastoral or catholic epistles, but that does not mean that it is necessarily any less authoritarian. None of this is to doubt Paul's sincerity, nor that he is in general, as it were, 'on the right side'. But being on the right side should not be allowed to blind us to how differently we might feel if such appeals to apostleship and so forth were being used to bolster James' very different understanding of the future of Christianity. Significantly, from Acts onwards later imaginative portrayals of the two principal apostles do not in general differentiate between the way in which either exercised his authority: Peter no less than Paul acts charismatically, and Paul no less than Peter is found relying on exercises of power such as miracles.

It is easy to be dismissive of the apocryphal *Acts of Paul* and *Acts of Peter* as worthless romantic fiction in which even a lion can end

---

[53] F. Young and D. F. Ford, *Meaning and Truth in 2 Corinthians* (London: SPCK, 1987), 207–34, esp. 220.

[54] If we knew who the opponents were in 2 Corinthians 11, we might be more sympathetic to them. Paul speaks of himself being granted 'abundance of revelations' and an ability to 'speak in tongues more than you all' (2 Cor. 12: 7; 1 Cor. 14: 18 RSV).

[55] 1 Cor. 4: 21 for 'rod'. The conclusion of that same epistle enjoins obedience to leaders whom Paul has baptized (16: 15–16; cf. 1: 16), while in 1 Thessalonians he urges the recipients 'to respect those who labour among you and are over you in the Lord and admonish you' (5: 12 RSV). For excommunication, 1 Cor. 5: 5.

up being baptized.[56] But dating as they do from the second century AD, they can be used to provide valuable evidence of what it was that popular Christian culture most valued and perceived in the lives and writings of the two saints. Facing the question of whether in any sense these stories can be described as 'true', one commentator opts for characterization of them as 'structure-maintaining narratives', in the sense that they embody values that the community of the time would have held to be true.[57] Another points out that this involved challenges to established social structures,[58] while yet another notes the way in which baptizing the lion can convey mythically the adoption of alternative strategies of power.[59] But most relevant here is the recognition that Paul and Peter alike become charismatic workers of miracles.[60] If to this it is objected that any such characterization is far from the Paul of the letters, in response it may be noted that on several occasions Paul appeals to demonstrations of 'power' using the same Greek word as is used elsewhere for 'miracle' (1 Thess. 1: 5; Gal. 3: 5; 1 Cor. 2: 4; 2 Cor. 12: 12; Rom. 15: 18–19). That being so, highly pertinent is the following question: 'Who more distorts the "genuine" Paul, the ancient writer who tried to imagine what these remarkably persuasive miracles were like, or the modern scholar who systematically de-emphasises something that is pervasive in Paul's thought and important to his self-understanding?'[61]

---

[56] For the text, W. Schneelmelcher (ed.), *New Testament Apocrypha* (Cambridge: James Clarke, 1992), II, 213–321. For the incident of the lion, 251–3. For a discussion of the once independent *Acts of Thecla*: S. E. McGinn in E. Schüssler Fiorenza (ed.), *Searching the Scriptures* (London: SCM Press, 1994), II, 800–28.

[57] A. Cameron, *Christianity and the Rhetoric of Empire* (Berkeley, Cal.: University of California Press, 1991), 89–119, esp. p. 93.

[58] Senators and patrons are deprived of the honour which they might have expected; so J. Perkins, *The Suffering Self* (London: Routledge, 1995), 124–41, esp. 133–9.

[59] T. Adamik, 'The baptised lion in the *Acts of Paul*' in J. N. Bremmer (ed.), *The Apocryphal Acts of Paul* (Kampen: Pharos, 1996), 60–74. The lion as symbol of power and sexuality yields to Christ and to virginity.

[60] Perkins notes that the miracles provide one answer to suffering, but martyrdom another—suffering can be valuable in itself: *Suffering Self*, 129–30.

[61] S. K. Stowers, 'What does unpauline mean?' in W. S. Babcock (ed.), *Paul and the Legacies of Paul* (Dallas: SMU Press, 1990), 70–77, esp. 72.

Indeed, Peter's action at Antioch may possibly suggest that of the two it was Peter and not Paul who was the more accommodating figure. Certainly, it looks as though it was Peter's influence that prevailed.[62] To respond that even so it was Paul who showed the greater loyalty to the gospel would be, in my opinion, grossly unfair to Peter, since such a critique in effect retrospectively applies categories, the applicability of which only became clear in the subsequent history of the Church. At that stage, it was still not at all obvious what was the correct course to pursue. The rejection of table-fellowship makes it sound as if only Paul could possibly be right, but it might be that James was worried about exposing the Jerusalem church to persecution, or that Paul was pressurizing converted Jews further than they wished to go.[63] Anyway, it looks as though as a result Peter no less than Paul paid a price in his missionary work, in his case losing leadership of the church at Jerusalem to James.[64] Again, although it is impossible to be certain that Matthew's Gospel originates from Antioch,[65] of the four it is undoubtedly the one most interested in Peter,[66] but yet not in a way that turns him into a highly authoritarian figure. That may seem belied by the famous passage (Matt. 16: 18–19) to which appeal is now so often made for the endorsement of papal authority, but not only does the history of its exegesis tell a different tale, but also both its

[62] Although one brief, later visit is recorded (Acts 18: 22), Paul never mentions Antioch again in his letters. Also in Galatians itself, he makes no mention of winning the debate.

[63] For a sympathetic portrayal from a Protestant of Peter's 'infinitely more difficult position' and 'particularly painful dilemma', O. Cullmann, *Peter Disciple—Apostle—Martyr* (London: SCM Press, 1953), 49–51, esp. 51.

[64] After his departure in Acts 12: 17, James assumes leadership (15: 13 ff.), and this appears confirmed by Paul, who places James' name first (Gal. 2: 9). Attempts to counter Cullmann's view fail to persuade. For a detailed response: O. Karrer, *Peter and the Church* (Edinburgh; Nelson, 1963). Though accepting the fluidity of elder/bishop (109), Karrer assumes that Peter's commission was unqualified.

[65] Accepted, for example, by John Meier in R. E. Brown and J. P. Meier, *Antioch and Rome* (London: Geoffrey Chapman, 1983), 45–72.

[66] Papias (Eusebius *Ecclesiastical History* 3.39.15) associated Mark with Peter, but this may have been to ensure direct contact with someone who had known Jesus while alive. Although Mark is a common name, the theology of that particular Gospel makes it quite likely that he is to be identified with John Mark, the companion of Paul: Acts 12: 25; Philemon, 24.

historical context and Matthew's Gospel as a whole argue for a quite different reading.[67]

Much depends on how early in his ministry Jesus envisaged the new order beginning without his personal presence, but the consensus seems to be that, though the saying requires a different context,[68] probably a resurrection appearance, its origins are early, and its meaning one which envisages Peter leading by personal example and confession.[69] Moreover, the way in which it was understood by the Petrine community can only properly be grasped once it is set against attitudes to authority elsewhere in Matthew's Gospel. Far from being authoritarian, these suggest a deep willingness on the part of the Petrine tradition to listen to the views of the community as a whole.[70] No doubt, to go too far in this direction would result in too seductively modern a portrait. That is not my aim. Rather, it is to suggest that in form of leadership neither apostle quite matched how the popular imagination now views the two figures. Peter almost certainly was far distant from the kind of authority figure that ultramontane Catholics would like, while Paul cannot be seen as quite the unqualified apostle of liberty that so many Protestants suppose him to be.

---

[67] Augustine took the passage to refer to Christ as the Rock: e. g. *Sermons* 76, 147, 149; for a detailed discussion of his various treatments, A.-M. Bonnardiere, 'La péricope "Matthieu 16.13–23" dans l'oeuvre de saint Augustin' *Irenikon* 24 (1961), 451–99. More commonly, as in Pope Leo (*Sermons* 4.2), the appeal is to Peter's personal faith. Despite the present prominence of the text in St Peter's at Rome, even in the Middle Ages it seldom formed the core of the argument for papal authority: K Froehlich, *Formen der Auslegung von Mt. 16.13–18 im lateinischen Mittelalter* (Tübingen: Präzis, 1963).

[68] Drawing on Luke 22: 31–2, Cullmann suggested the Last Supper (*Peter*, 178–84), but most commentators prefer a post-resurrection context: R. E. Brown et al. (eds.), *Peter in the New Testament* (London: Geoffrey Chapman, 1974), 85 ff.

[69] The Semitic character of the saying is widely accepted: e. g. Cullmann, *Peter*, 184 ff.; Brown, *Peter*, 90 ff. In considering the eschatological context, it has been suggested that 'Peter is the rock that will stand up to the storms of the last days, over which the gates of Hades, the power of death, will not prevail; James and John are the claps of thunder (Mk. 3.17) that herald the coming storm': Barrett, *Signs*, 27–8.

[70] Matt. 16: 18 needs to be balanced against 18: 15–20, where power of resolving issues is invested in the community as a whole. Nonetheless, to Peter alone is reserved the keys, which suggests some form of special standing: Brown, *Peter*, 96–8.

Indeed, there is a nice irony in the way in which Paul is so often used as a model with which to critique the papacy, for the charismatic authoritarianism of Pope John Paul II may in some ways have its closer analogue in his namesake than in Peter's communitarian church.[71]

The names of the two apostles were soon closely joined.[72] It is common to read that linking as little more than a strategy to give added weight to the authority of Rome, but the evidence for their martyrdom in Rome is in fact quite good, while it is not altogether impossible that they ended their lives engaged in a joint mission.[73] However, whether so or not, what we can say is that the gospel message is immeasurably enriched by such a combination. If the fundamental direction for the future of Christian doctrine was provided by Paul, we can also be thankful that there are countervailing tendencies in the New Testament which provide some useful correctives. On the subject of Law, Christianity had to hear more firmly what was good in its Jewish past, while on the issue of authority it had to move to a more consensual approach if something nearer the totality of God's revelation to humanity was to be heard.

Scriptural challenges from elsewhere The approach I have adopted thus far may sound like too neat a solution. Perhaps the internal conflicts ran much deeper,[74] and were in general as traumatic as

[71] Somewhat puzzlingly, Barrett takes Matt. 23: 8–10 with its rejection of titles such as 'teacher', 'father' and 'master' as indicative of 'the Pauline attitude to apostleship' (*Signs*, 81–2). Yet he does not postulate any direct influence from Paul, whereas elsewhere it is Paul that we find talking of himself as a 'father' prepared to use 'the rod': 1 Cor. 4: 14–21.

[72] Both alike characterized as giving commands, as early as Ignatius (d. *c.* 107): *Romans* 4.3.

[73] Although the tradition that they died the same day is probably an invention intended to 'catch the imagination', and it is unlikely that the three sites in Rome mark their place of burial (would an eschatological community have recorded such things?), the evidence for Rome being their place of martyrdom is strong: H. Chadwick, 'St Peter and St Paul in Rome', *Journal of Theological Studies* 8 (1957), 31–52. More recent excavations, though, do demonstrate how early there arose belief in Peter's association with the Vatican hill.

[74] For a more acerbic version, M. Goulder, *A Tale of Two Missions* (London: SCM Press, 1994). His account is hard to evaluate because so much is guesswork, as for instance his identification of Nicodemus as 'a successful Petrine missionary' (94).

the severance from Judaism must have been for many Jewish Christians.[75] Even so, I would stand by my claim that conflict is not necessarily a bad thing, since sometimes it is only in this way that the significance of what is at stake becomes clarified; it is also worth remembering that every difference of emphasis need not necessarily point to profound, or even irresolvable, conflict. Yet, contrary to any impression that may have been created thus far, I certainly did not intend to imply that all forms of disagreement find their creative resolution in a perfect balance between the two opposing factions. Even in the case of the Law, that was not my meaning. The greater weight it seems to me lies with Paul. But, however limited the qualifications are on any specific issue, it remains vital that they should be heard, given the constant Protestant temptation to create a canon within the canon, and suppose that Paul has most, if not all, of the answers. It would be a mistake, though, to think that such criticism could only come from within the Petrine tradition itself, or that it is only Paul who can be brought into creative conflict with Peter. Voices from elsewhere in the Bible have also their role to play.

Take the Gospel of John. One way in which to read the author's treatment of Peter is to surmise that it is the author's way of countering Petrine groups who remained resistant to changes in Christology. Not only is Peter no longer the first disciple to be called, he has a less honoured seat at the Last Supper. Moreover, he is presented as slow to comprehend the significance of both the foot-washing incident and the empty tomb, while it is only the beloved disciple who is to be found at the foot of the cross.[76] The aim may have been to place the primary emphasis on the living Lord as now imaginatively experienced, in preference to conservative appeals to the authority of the past. This would be particularly so if the beloved disciple is supposed to represent the reader, with us presenting ourselves at the foot of the cross and before the

[75] For an attempt to use deviance theory to explain why the conflict was so traumatic for both sides, J. T. Sanders, *Schismatics, Sectarians, Dissidents, Deviants* (London: SCM Press, 1993), esp. 82–151.

[76] For other examples and discussion, A. H. Maynard, 'The role of Peter in the Fourth Gospel', *New Testament Studies* 30 (1984), 531–48; A. J. Droge, 'The status of Peter in the Fourth Gospel', *Journal of Biblical Literature* 109 (1990), 307–11. A more conciliatory approach is offered in K. Quast, *Peter and the Beloved Disciple* (Sheffield: Sheffield Academic Press, 1989).

empty tomb and still believing (John. 20: 8), though we remain without the benefit of any direct contact with the past.[77] Yet, even in that instance there is something to be said in favour of the need for some counterweight to be allowed from the other side. For, if for me John in general represents the culmination of the gradual appropriation of the full nature of God's involvement in the life of Christ, there is also a negative side to be acknowledged in a certain docetic tendency in parts of his narrative. Christ goes too confidently to his death and with too much self-awareness. If that had been our only perspective, divine identification with our humanity would have seemed less than complete, but fortunately there are more 'primitive' Christologies in the New Testament to counter and balance any such presentation.

If John may be used to illustrate a challenge to Peter from elsewhere in Scripture, the possibility of a similar challenge to Paul may be approached more indirectly. The absence of the concept of a sacerdotal priesthood and related notions from the New Testament except as fulfilled in Christ is often thought to constitute a decisive argument against the return of such concepts in later Christianity, and indeed the Epistle to the Hebrews is commonly now used to construct a defining argument of this kind.[78] But matters are scarcely that simple. As with Paul on law, not only are the details of that particular epistle's appeal to Jewish history often strained,[79] there are unresolved tensions in what is usually thought to be its underlying philosophical argument: the Old Testament cult seen as a sort of Platonic shadow or image of what Christ has achieved in gaining direct access to the Father in heaven. There are at least two reasons for doubting whether this establishes dispensability. The first is that complete access still remains a heavenly reality, and so shadows are in some sense still the order of the day. Secondly, what the argument surely shows is the lack of complete congruence between Temple cult and

---

[77] Some readers will not wish to go that far, but it is hard to deny a mixture of the historical and the imaginative, given so may conflicts with the Synoptics, not least the placing of the beloved disciple at the foot of the cross.

[78] E. g. Dunn, *Parting*, 86–91, 270.

[79] Although they try to defend its 'enclosed world of meaning', many commentators cannot avoid admitting that to modern readers Hebrews' use of Scripture appears 'alien' and 'quite arbitary': B. Lindars, *The Theology of the Letter to the Hebrews* (Cambridge: Cambridge University Press, 1991), esp. 130–2.

heavenly reality rather than the illegitimacy of all such symbols under the new order. There should no longer be limited access confined to one person on one day of the year, but that hardly of itself argues the illegitimacy of something like a daily mass rich in symbolism, at which all may communicate.[80]

My point in raising such issues here is not to resolve them but rather to insist that they do not admit of as easy resolution as biblical scholars sometimes suppose. Certainly, Hebrews offers a trajectory that could have led to the Christian Church in general abandoning notions of priesthood, and, had it done so, it could well have claimed the authority of Paul. But that did not happen, not primarily because Hebrews was misunderstood, nor because of the influence of pagan practice (though both factors played their part).[81] More important was the way in which the problematic aspects of the book's argument opened up the possibility of an alternative approach that took the Old Testament dispensation with greater seriousness. In other words, just as the difficulties in Paul's presentation helped create a more positive attitude to moral law, so those in Hebrews allowed the ceremonial side of the Torah to be given new life. That could be seen as a retrograde step (and undoubtedly aspects were), but its positive side was to maximize the revelatory content of the canon as a whole. The early Church thus sought out its final view by working through the tensions between Hebrews and Leviticus, and not simply by jettisoning one in favour or the other. It was thus a notion of progress that continued to take the community's past with maximum seriousness.

But if reconsideration of the Hebrew Scriptures is one way in which modification occurs to what the community may initially have thought to have been revealed, another is the way in which

---

[80] Partly because he sees the epistle directed to former Jerusalem priests, C. Spicq has no difficulty in aligning the author's intent with a eucharistic liturgical frame: *L'Épitre aux Hébreux* (Paris: Librairie Lecoffre, 1952), esp. I, 316–24; II, 123. That could be true, though I think it unlikely. My point in the text, however, is that, even if the author's closest ally would have been a 'Protestant' Paul, the argument is by no means over.

[81] The patristic discussion of whether it was the humanity that was offered or the total reality of the eternal Word must also have played its part, since the latter lends itself more naturally to an eternal sacrifice being offered. For discussion of the argument (without its possible eucharistic implications), R. Greer, *The Captain of our Salvation* (Tübingen: Mohr, 1975).

the Church's changing cultural context across the centuries forces re-examination of particular perspectives. There is no need to repeat here any of my earlier examples. Suffice it to note my repeated emphasis that this need not entail simple conformity to one's surroundings, since it is the interaction between the deposit of faith and the cultural context that is important and not the social setting in itself. But it did mean that the closure of the canon could not put an end to the question of where trajectories might finally lead, nor where the balance of conflicting perspectives might finally fall. It is to that later history that I now turn.

The pattern repeated in church history

Two thousand years of Christian history can hardly be dealt with in a few pages. So what I propose to do here is illustrate the theme of this chapter in two ways, first by examining the question of heresy and secondly by considering the related issue of forms of authority. As we shall observe, the biblical pattern of conflict generating insight is one that we shall find repeated in the community of faith's later history. Nor should this turn out to be entirely unexpected, since disagreement is one of the most powerful pressures towards more careful formulation of one's own ideas.

Heresy and its teaching role

My subtitle may initially puzzle the reader, but the question of how heresy is to be evaluated is not nearly as simple a subject as it has been understood to be for most of the history of the Church. Conventional histories presented it as a quite alien root, whereas not only has its source often been found at the very heart of the living tradition, but also the way that tradition subsequently develops remains incomprehensible until due acknowledgement is made of how the heretic has helped shape both its course and its content. To illustrate that thesis, I propose to offer an all too brief survey of Christian history, noting first the impact of heresy in the patristic period, then possible ways of characterizing the reform movements that eventually culminate in Reformation and Counter-Reformation, before finally considering how my own communion of Anglicanism might be viewed from this perspective.

Patristic insight as parasitic   In assessing the role of the heretic, at least two major difficulties have to be faced. Not only has that history been written from the perspective of the victors, these victors have more often than not ensured the successful destruction of any adequate expression of the countervailing views. So for instance, if we take some of the major heretics of the patristic period, apart from fragments we are left to piece together how Arius might have defended himself from Athanasius' polemical *Contra Arianos*; of Apollinaris' extensive writings nothing would have survived had it not been for some cases of false attribution; while Nestorius' fortunes were only reversed in 1895 with the discovery of a Syriac translation of his long-lost defence of his position in the *Bazaar of Heracleides*.[82] Even the greatest Christian intellect of the earlier centuries before Augustine was to suffer a not dissimilar fate. In the fourth century, under pressure from Jerome, Rufinus in his Latin translation of Origen's Greek writings may have deliberately sought to modify Origen's views in order to make them more acceptable to the Church of his own day, while the condemnation of Origenism in 553 led to the loss of the great mass of his works.[83]

Much contemporary scholarship has been concerned to redress the balance. Admittedly, there are problems. The most obvious is an absolute lack of evidence or else a lack of balance in what has survived, and the consequent danger of reading too much into a few surviving sentences that in fact admit of a wide variety of differing interpretations.[84] Another is the romanticism of the modern world which prefers the rebel to the advocate of established institutions. That is an issue to which we will need to return when considering the issue of submission to authority at the end of this chapter. Yet another is the desire to find antecedents for a

[82]   In the case of Arius the position is complicated by the fact that he appears in any case not to have written much. Works that may be by Apollinarius are included in the corpus of Gregory Thaumaturgus, Athanasius and Pope Julius I.

[83]   The story is complicated both by the issue of how far later Origenism is to be identified with the views of Origen himself, as also by the extent to which it is true that Rufinus modified his views. For an attempt to defend his essential 'orthodoxy', H. Crouzel, *Origen* (Edinburgh: T & T Clark, 1989).

[84]   The wealth of post-war literature on Arius is perhaps the best example. Contrasting analyses have been offered, but it is hard to distinguish between 'possible' and 'probable'.

form of Christianity seen as more congenial to contemporary concerns. With Gnosticism, for example, Elaine Pagels has done much valuable work in demonstrating how its mythology may be understood in a more favourable light, but even so she moves with disconcerting speed in finding its attitudes congenial to modern feminism.[85] Again, in presenting Arius it is tempting to emphasize the more human Jesus that is on offer, but that needs to be carefully counterbalanced by due recognition of Arius' continuing stress on Christ's pre-existence.[86]

Yet, these limitations acknowledged, modern scholarship still, it seems to me, has its point, and indeed in some ways has not gone far enough. Take the issue of Arianism. Whatever consensus finally emerges, what cannot survive is a typical nineteenth-century judgement on the movement, that it was 'a lifeless system of unspiritual pride and hard unlovingness'.[87] Whether the concern was to defend the majesty of God or Christ as a properly salvific agent or some related variant, the intention was a genuinely religious one,[88] and this is probably as true of later stages of the movement as of earlier.[89] Moreover, its relative grading of the two

[85] A chapter that begins by admitting the negative side in the *Gospel of Thomas* ends by calling for the ordination of women. In the interim she has noted women consecrating among Gnostics, but failed to observe that this remained subordinate to the work of the presiding male. E. Pagels, *The Gnostic Gospels* (London: Weidenfeld & Nicholson, 1980), 48–69, esp. 59–60; Irenaeus, *Adversus Haereses* 1.13.2.

[86] Significantly, one account with such an emphasis leaves pre-existence to a third chapter, and then insists upon giving it a soteriological interpretation rather than its own independent rationale: R. C. Gregg and D. E. Groh, *Early Arianism* (London: SCM Press, 1981), esp. 77 ff.

[87] H. W. Gwatkin, *Studies of Arianism* (Cambridge: Cambridge University Press, 1882), 266.

[88] Unlike Gregg and Groh, Rowan Williams traces the origin of Arius' ideas to Neoplatonism, but unlike Gwatkin, he not only finds 'a thinker and exegete of resourcefulness, sharpness and originality', he also accepts his self-designation as a 'biblical theologian': *Arius* (London: Darton, Longman & Todd, 1987), 107, 116.

[89] For an intriguing attempt to transform 'the hair-splitting pseudo-Aristotelian dialectic' that John Kelly had found in Eunomius into an attempt to 'ensure . . . that our speech about God has a purchase on reality', see M. F. Wiles, 'Eunomius: hair-splitting dialectician or defender of the accessibility of salvation?' in R. Williams (ed.), *The Making of Orthodoxy* (Cambridge: Cambridge University Press, 1989), 157–72, esp. 160, 164.

persons, Father and Son, overwhelmingly reflects the Christian witness of earlier centuries, including that of the New Testament itself, even if its appeal to Scripture was not always as our intuitions might expect.[90] It was thus Nicaea and Athanasius that were the innovators, not Arius, who in some senses can be viewed as the biblical conservative in this debate. Indeed, had Athanasius lived longer, it might have been his turn to be condemned for heresy.[91] Not, though, that this means that Arius deserved to win. The question the Church faced was how the basic datum of God's total identification with humanity in the incarnation could best be preserved, and it saw that this could not be done without also asserting the complete equality of Father and Son. But it is important to observe that the Church came to see the necessity for such a declaration through being confronted with a far more explicit assertion of subordination than had hitherto been advocated. Arius offered superficially the more obvious trajectory, but it took its full expression before the Church came to realize the need for a different approach. In other words, it was the attempt to draw out one potential trajectory from the biblical revelation that led to the endorsement of another, quite different line. So in a sense orthodoxy needed heresy, in order for the deeper implications of revelation to be noted, with the Church now able to turn back to its classical texts and give them new meanings.[92]

Equally, one might argue that Gnosticism served a similar purpose. For although John's Gospel stands at a considerable remove from Christian Gnosticism as it formulated itself in the second century, in a more general sense there are elements in John that can be seen as pulling in similar direction, such as his dualism, his stress on knowledge and experience in the present and the very

[90] Although John 14: 28 was used by later Arianism, ironically in the earlier stages it was employed by orthodoxy, since it seemed at least to guarantee sameness of substance, if not equality: M. Simonetti, *Biblical Interpretation in the Early Church* (Edinburgh: T & T Clark, 1994), 129–30.

[91] While not denying a human mind to Christ, Athanasius fails to make any use of the notion, and so the development of a monophysite Christology by his friend, Apollinarius, might be regarded as a legitimate expansion of his own thought. For 'Apollinaris als Schüler des Athanasius', E. Mühlenberg, *Apollinaris von Laodicea* (Göttingen: Vandenhoeck & Ruprecht, 1969), 196–209.

[92] For the contrast and the required argument, *Tradition and Revelation*, ch. 6.

limited role assigned to Christ's humanity. Indeed, if Bultmann is right about sacramental additions to this Gospel, it is not inconceivable that it was part of the later redactor's aim to use eucharistic theology as a way of correcting any such perceived bias.[93] So, though the details of Bultmann's theories are now widely discredited, it remains the case that John could still be used to argue for the New Testament having a Gnostic trajectory.[94] But, what Gnosticism as a whole effectively did by exaggerating that trend was pull the Church towards a fuller recognition of counter-trends within the incipient Church and so towards recognition of a complementary canon of four Gospels.[95] None of this is intended to challenge the attractiveness of Gnostic religion,[96] nor to suggest that its advocates were insincere or bereft of religious sensibility, but it is to claim that, despite its no doubt often deep spirituality, where all Christian versions can be found wanting is in their one-sided focus in presenting revelation. In effect, the significance of Christ was dramatically lessened both through its elaborate mythology of intervening aeons and its strong assertion of personal initiative and responsibility over against divine grace.

If it be asked why logical argument or even exposition of Scripture could not of itself have sufficed, then we need to face firmly the openness of the biblical text which I have so often stressed across my two volumes. To talk of strict logical deduction is to speak of a tighter conceptual system than Christianity has in fact inherited. It is only in retrospect that certain options are seen as inadequate or illegitimate, but for this to be so they need first to have been lived fully as spiritual realities. It is after all a religion

[93] For a brief statement of Bultmann's ideas on Gnosticism, R. Bultmann, *Primitive Christianity* (New York: Meridian, 1957), 162–71; for Bultmann's own reasons for doubting that parts of chapter 6 were originally part of John's Gospel, *The Gospel of John: A Commentary* (Oxford: Blackwell, 1971), 218–37.

[94] For Gnostic use of John, M. F. Wiles, *The Spiritual Gospel* (Cambridge: Cambridge University Press, 1960), 96–111.

[95] As in Irenaeus' famous argument, significantly expressed in terms of a complementarity that reflects the four zones of the world, the four winds and so forth: *Adversus Haereses* 3.11.8.

[96] Apart from Pagels, two other useful books in trying to comprehend its attractiveness as a religious force are H. Jonas, *The Gnostic Religion* (Boston, Mass.: Beacon Press, 1963) and K. Rudolph, *Gnosis* (Edinburgh: T & T Clark, 1983). All, though, in my view tend to exaggerate the modernist side, Jonas the existentialist (320 ff.), Pagels the feminist, and Rudolph the Marxist (esp. 292–4).

with which we are dealing. So it is one thing to see something as a possible trajectory from the text; quite another to experience it as part of the daily practice of one's faith, in worship, ethical obedience, and apologetics: in short, for it imaginatively to become part of a lived reality.[97]

But if prepared to go this far in acknowledging a debt to heretics, why not go further and continue to allow the possibilities they raised as legitimate options within the Church? Is it not an accident that one side triumphed rather than another, if the opposition also had its appealing and effective religious content? Certainly, one strong modern trend is to treat all possible trajectories impartially, and this can be seen in the work both of some biblical scholars and of those who attempt to throw a bridge between biblical and systematic considerations.[98] One might also look back to the earlier arguments of Walter Bauer that non-orthodox positions were once in the ascendancy throughout the ancient world.[99] How much that was in fact true is now widely contested.[100] But let us for the sake of argument concede their wide dissemination, and ask what implications then follow. Surely it would be naïve to use success as a criterion for truth or legitimacy. My point perhaps can be put by contrasting two types of inclusivity, the modern tendency to treat all trajectories on a par as though fairness and equality demanded it, and the other (my own view) which maintains that, although heresy is usually sincere in its pursuit of truth, what its projections commonly

[97] The practical dimension of patristic argument is rightly stressed in M. Wiles, _The Making of Christian Doctrine_ (Cambridge: Cambridge University Press, 1967), esp. 62–113.

[98] For examples of the former, J. M. Robinson and H. Koester, _Trajectories through Early Christianity_ (Philadelphia: Fortress Press, 1971), H. Koester, _Introduction to the New Testament_ (New York: Walter de Gruyter, 1982), esp. 2, 147 ff; for an example of the latter, Schüssler Fiorenza, _Searching the Scriptures_, where the aim is 'to transgress canonical boundaries in order . . . to undo the exclusionary kyriarchal tendencies of the ruling canon': 2, 5.

[99] W. Bauer, _Orthodoxy and Heresy in Earliest Christianity_ (1934; London: SCM Press, 1972). His case is strongest with Edessa, the city with which he begins his analysis. For a limited defence in reaction to some of the criticism, see G. Strecker's Appendix 2: 286–316, esp. 310 ff.

[100] A good response was offered by H. E. W. Turner in his 1954 book _The Pattern of Christian Truth_. More recently, in _The Rise of Normative Christianity_ (Minneapolis: Fortress Press, 1994) A. J. Hultgren has attempted to identify a continuous normative tradition, though his stress on a number of shared features (e.g. 86) strikes me as less secure than it might initially appear.

reveal is a one-sidedness that needs correction if the overall balance of the Church's existing understanding of revelation is not to be fundamentally distorted.

In saying this I do not of course wish to endorse the practice of early Christian generations in persecuting heretics, but there is no escaping recognition that there comes a point when certain perspectives cannot be easily contained within the same worshipping community. This is not necessarily an argument for exclusion, but it will mean that expressions used in worship, exhortations in sermons and so forth will all inevitably reflect the ideology of the dominant grouping. Even so, it is worth noting that Nicaea did try to be as inclusive as possible, and not purely for pragmatic reasons. There was, for instance, a natural reticence not to proceed too quickly in the introduction of non-biblical language into the definition of Christian faith.[101] But there is also another way in which due note is taken of the heretic. Hitherto I have spoken of what is only a positive reaction to the heretic from the point of view of orthodoxy, of something learnt through conflict that might not otherwise have been clarified, but not of anything specifically adopted from heretics themselves. It is sometimes, however, possible to detect elements incorporated from the heretic's own position, and so to find its positive religious value acknowledged, however seldom such a debt is ever given explicit recognition. This may even be true of Arianism since later orthodox images of the Father as the source of the godhead certainly often retain in them, like Arianism, the notion of God as awesome and unfathomable ground, while an unkind critic might even detect in orthodox elucidation of trinitarian relations a continuing subordinationism. Likewise, not only did some of the language of Gnosticism find favour with Clement of Alexandria and Origen, but also orthodox interest in hierarchies of angels has some obvious parallels with Gnostic aeons; fourth century forms of baptismal practice could also be seen as deliberately intended to rival the sense of mystery that the Gnostic initiate had come to expect.[102]

---

[101] 'Essentially a formula of compromise'; so C. Stead, *Divine Substance* (Oxford: Clarendon Press, 1977), 223–66, esp. 242.

[102] Perhaps sufficiently indicated by titles of two books on the subject: E. Yarnold, *The Awe-Inspiring Rites of Initiation* (Slough: St Paul, 1971); E. Mazza, *Mystagogy* (New York: Pueblo, 1989).

Reform and heresy as mirror images   For a few centuries questions of
heresy seemed to become quiescent, but the problem was to
return once more in the Middle Ages with the revival of popular
heretical movements.[103] Although once thought to have been an
import from Eastern Christendom, explanations are now largely
sought in the wider changes that were taking place in society at the
end of the eleventh and beginning of the twelfth centuries, among
which were better living conditions and so more space for reflection, as well as a stronger sense of social identity that went with
greater readiness to identify threats to it.[104] But most relevant to
our discussion here is the role played by the Reform movement as
that began to emerge during the papacy of Gregory VII, and the
contemporaneous rise of heretical groupings. As with the patristic
period, what has come down to us is a story of 'them' and 'us', but
this needs to be treated with great caution. Gregory himself reinstated one condemned heretic, after his death, who had refused to
take the sacrament from 'unworthy' priests, and in the popular
mind it was not always easy to distinguish between such an officially endorsed policy of boycott and actually declaring the sacraments of suspect priests 'invalid'.[105] Likewise, there was often a
fine line between the behaviour of reformer and heretic, and how
far either was prepared to go in the rhetoric of critique.[106]

   More often than not, we are given 'a description not of what
happened but of the meaning of what happened', and so in effect
an inferred moral and physical corruption that was almost certainly

---

[103] Apart from isolated individual examples such as Gottschalk (d. 869), there
is a long gap in the appearance of more popular movements after the collapse of
Priscillianism. Although Priscillian was executed in 386, it was technically for
sorcery, and in fact capital punishment only became a key weapon against heresy
in continental Europe in the thirteenth century and in England not till 1401.

[104] For the notion of a continuous stream running from Manichaeism through
eastern Bogomils to Cathars, S. Runciman, *The Medieval Manichee* (Cambridge:
Cambridge University Press, 1947); for social change as explanation, R.
Morghen, 'Problèmes sur l'origine de l'hérésie au moyen âge', *Revue historique*
136 (1966), 1–16.

[105] The priest in question was Ramirhdus who was put to death in 1075, two
years into Hildebrand's pontificate.

[106] Illustrated by the career of Henry of Lausanne in A. H. Bredero,
Christendom and Christianity in the Middle Ages (Grand Rapids, Michigan:
Eerdmans, 1994), 211–24.

not there.[107] Valdès was even personally praised by Pope Alexander III at the Third Lateran Council in 1179, and it was only gradually that the Waldensians were turned into heretics.[108] Some commentators still wish to stress the contrasts, as for example between the lay emphasis of the heretics and the increasing sacralization of Church reformers, but this seems to me too simplistic.[109] The reformers also helped to introduce new forms of lay piety, and if some of these were essentially sacral such as eucharistic devotion, even among them were some that could enhance the status of the laity, such as the increased sense of marriage as a sacrament, now performed at the church door. The complex history of the Franciscans and in particular the role played by the Spirituals illustrates how easily a very different story might have been told. For it takes little historical imagination to envisage the Franciscan movement as a whole having been condemned, and so the necessity for a quite different account, with the movement now seen as essentially anticipatory of the more radical elements in the Reformation. Heretic and reformer are thus quite often on a continuous scale, rather than represented by some absolute division, as the later official view was to present them.

In considering the more substantial upheavals of the sixteenth century, historians are also forcing upon us a more complex picture. At the time each side saw the reform movement of the other as merely heresy in plausible guise, whereas now it is easier for us to detect strengths and weaknesses on both sides. For a start, the extent to which both emerged from a common heritage is now widely acknowledged. For, however much popular Protestant piety may continue to see its antecedents only in those duly condemned as heretics such as Wyclif and Hus,[110] historians

[107] The humours theory of mental health meant that leprosy could even be seen as one expression of heresy. Problems of interpretation are stressed in R. I. Moore, *The Birth of Popular Heresy* (Toronto: University of Toronto Press, 1975), 1–7, esp. 4–5.

[108] E. Peters, *Heresy and Authority in Medieval Europe* (London: Scolar Press, 1980), 139–63. This collection of documents also illustrates many other overlaps between reformers and those pronounced heretics.

[109] For such a contrast, P. Boglioni, 'La perception de l'hérétique au moyen âge' in M. Gourgues and D. Mailhiot (eds.), *L'Altérité* (Paris: Éditions du Cerf, 1986), 333–60.

[110] The views of both were condemned at the Council of Constance in 1415. Though both enjoyed royal protection, only Wyclif died a natural death (in 1384).

are increasingly forcing the recognition of how deeply the Protestant reformers were indebted to medieval Catholicism.[111] As part of that reappraisal, due recognition is also now being given to the religious vitality of much of what was swept away.[112] Moreover, many of the reforms initiated by one side have their parallel on the other. Thus, historians have not been slow to draw attention to a common pattern of increasingly individualistic piety, with private biblical study on one side matched by a regular pattern of confession and spiritual direction on the other. Likewise, both introduced private pews, and insisted on patterns of clerical training that tended to separate the clergy into a more obviously distinct and educated caste. Examples might be multiplied,[113] but there remains to be mentioned what is perhaps the most striking element in such mirror-imaging, the extent to which the pronouncements of Reformation and Counter-Reformation are virtually unintelligible without reference to what is being opposed.

Despite its lengthy deliberations, the Council of Trent is an obvious case in point. The exclusion of large areas of Catholic doctrine, such as the significance of the Virgin Mary,[114] clearly demonstrates that there was no real intention to produce an overall, balanced account,[115] and much the same could be said of many a corresponding Reformation settlement. The result was that until

[111] Particularly clear from some of the writings of Oberman and Ozment. E.g. H. Oberman, *Forerunners of the Reformation* (Philadelphia: Fortress Press, 1981); *Masters of the Reformation* (Cambridge: Cambridge University Press, 1981); *The Dawn of the Reformation* (Edinburgh: T & T Clark, 1992); S. Ozment, *The Age of Reform 1250–1550* (New Haven: Yale University Press, 1980); S. Ozment (ed.), *The Reformation in Medieval Perspective* (Chicago: Quadrangle, 1971).

[112] A view most widely disseminated by E. Duffy, *The Stripping of the Altars* (New Haven: Yale University Press, 1992). For presentation of the two sides of the debate, C. Haigh and A. G. Dickens in M. Todd (ed.), *Reformation to Revolution* (London: Routledge, 1995), 13–32 and 157–78

[113] For further examples, J. Bossy, *Christianity in the West 1400–1700* (Oxford: Oxford University Press, 1985), 115 ff.

[114] Otherwise, mentioned only incidentally.

[115] It is clear that the earlier sessions (1–8, in 1545–7) had as their primary aim 'to counter the Reformation understanding' and that when 'Protestant delegates arrives in January of 1552 . . . they were obviously too late to have any influence': C. Lindberg, *The European Reformations* (Oxford: Blackwell, 1996), 350–6, esp. 352, 354.

the arrival of the ecumenical movement, each side tended to regard
the other, if I may put it in this way, as wallowing in various depths
of heretical slime. Fortunately, attitudes have now changed significantly, but there is still little sense of how that past history may in
itself have been beneficial. To establish such a case convincingly, a
more detailed investigation would be required than I have space for
here, but one way to read subsequent history is to see each side
acting as a standing rebuke to the other, and, if it has taken a long
time for the message to sink in, the twentieth century does at least
offer quite a number of hopeful signs that this has indeed happened.
So, for instance, both Luther and Calvin thought of weekly
communion as the ideal,[116] but the Protestant churches have only
begun to move in this direction, at varying speeds, in modern
times. Again, Rome has witnessed a rediscovery of the importance
of Scripture. Not only did this find expression in the style and
reforms of the Second Vatican Council, it is now also the case that
some of the world's most outstanding biblical scholars are Roman
Catholics.[117] As a new millennium is entered, Protestant and
Catholic alike have been immeasurably strengthened by at last
taking into themselves the insights that have been better preserved
by the other. Had the Church remained united, this might still
have happened, but an alternative scenario is also worth pondering,
in which one side had triumphed but ossified, with, for example,
Rome never admitting the relevance of biblical criticism or Geneva
the importance of symbol and liturgy.

Anglicanism as a test case   If that is what can be said looking across
the great divide in Western Christendom, it is salutary also to
reflect upon what is often presented as its most divided church,
my own communion of Anglicanism. To an outsider it can seem
like a hopeless amalgam of irreconcilable tensions between
Catholic, Evangelical, and Liberal.[118] To some degree that reflects

---

[116] 'At least once a week': Calvin, *Institutes* 4.17. 43: 'administrari decentissime
poterat, si saepissime et singulis ad minimum hebdomadibus proponetur
Ecclesiae.'

[117] Most notably perhaps, Raymond Brown.

[118] 'Three churches within one,' which are 'as resistant to ecclesiastical
management as were the waves of the sea to king Canute's command': the
verdict of a Roman Catholic scholar, A. Nichols, *The Panther and the Hind*
(Edinburgh: T & T Clark, 1993), esp., 155, 177.

the accidents of history. As a recent biography of Cranmer observes, had Lady Jane Grey succeeded Edward VI a church firmly entrenched in a more uniform Protestant style might well have been the result.[119] Instead, the sympathies of Elizabeth I and Charles I ensured that the Oxford Movement would not seem a complete aberration when it began its campaign to push the Church of England in a more decisively Catholic direction. In the appearance of more Liberal thought in the eighteenth century, it of course reflects a wider European pattern. Even so, two quali-fications need to be noted. The caricature of English religion of the time has now been widely challenged by historians;[120] secondly, its characteristic method in appealing to reason had already been given a prominent place as early as Hooker.[121] So, while it is possible to tell a see-saw story of the ascendancy of now one group and now another, this needs to be qualified by recog-nition of the presence of underlying currents from each through-out that history, most obviously represented in the classical 'threefold cord not quickly broken', of seeing the essence of Anglicanism as shaped by Scripture, tradition, and reason.[122]

If that tells against any group claiming the monopoly or even core of its narrative history, it has still not been sufficient to prevent periodic outbursts of one faction setting itself against some other as heretical. If in the nineteenth century the object of venom tended to be Anglo-Catholic clergy, in recent years it has been

[119] D. MacCulloch, *Thomas Cranmer* (New Haven: Yale University Press, 1996), 618–20.
[120] The change of attitude began with N. Sykes, *Church and State in England in the Eighteenth Century* (1934), but has accelerated since. Influential has been J. Clark, *English Society 1688–1832* (Cambridge: Cambridge University Press, 1985). For a helpful survey, the 'Introduction' by J. Walsh and S. Taylor in J. Walsh, C. Haydon and S. Taylor (eds.), *The Church of England 1689–1833* (Cambridge: Cambridge University Press, 1993), 1–64.
[121] In his *Laws of Ecclesiastical Polity* of 1593, not only are the parallels with Aquinas' attitudes to reason and natural law evident (e.g. 1.8–10), but also some of his specific assertions might be said to lead naturally into later questioning, as, for instance, his declaration that 'Scripture is not the only law whereby God hath opened his will' (2.2) or his view that 'unless beside Scripture there were some-thing which might assure us that we do well, we could not think we do well' (2.4).
[122] Although perhaps most familiar in a transferred context in application to marriage, this use of Ecclesiastes 4: 12 (AV) in defining the essence of Anglicanism has a long history.

Liberal theologians. The diversity is now such, it is sometimes asserted, that the church lacks any common core. To such a critique various types of response are possible. Some would place the main emphasis on a shared liturgy and on common public reading of Scripture,[123] but, while not denying their indispensability, more important to my mind is the fact of shared doctrine,[124] and indeed even agreement that this can change.[125] Also relevant is the way that none of the groups has remained unaffected by the presence of other possibilities. In other words, I would claim that here too we have an example of the teaching role exercised by those whom others may deem heretics.

Currently, for instance, the Evangelical party is in the majority, but it is a quite different form of evangelicalism from that which predated the Oxford movement. To take one example, Bishop Edward King of Lincoln was the first bishop since the sixteenth century to wear a mitre.[126] He was also prosecuted for three liturgical offences: facing east at communion, having candles lit during daylight hours, and mixing water with wine.[127] A century later, and no Evangelical bishop is found objecting to wearing a mitre or to the non-functional use of candles, while old disputes about east versus north-facing have been resolved by the widespread practice of facing west. A new interest in symbolism had been learnt from 'heretical' coreligionists. Again, the Oxford Movement began in a concern for the recovery of the past, but it

---

[123] The main emphasis in S. W. Sykes, *The Integrity of Anglicanism* (London: Mowbray, 1978), as indeed also in his larger book on *The Identity of Christianity* (London: SPCK, 1984), esp. 262 ff.

[124] Despite his primary emphasis, a point also insisted upon by Sykes, who draws attention to a corporate insistence upon certain shared features such as episcopal ordination: *Integrity*, 43–4. One might also note the unanimity of recent reports from the Doctrine Commission: *We Believe in God*; *We Believe in the Holy Spirit*; *The Mystery of Salvation* (London: Church House Publishing, 1987, 1991, 1995).

[125] Hooker thought only practice could change, not doctrine (3.10), and viewed from the divine perspective he is of course right. But recent reports have significantly modified earlier perceptions, as, for instance, on the impassibility of God, or the existence of hell as a place of eternal punishment: hesitantly on the former, *We Believe in God*, 157 ff; emphatically on the latter, *Mystery*, 198–9.

[126] In the intervening period, though, bishops continued to be represented on tombs with mitres.

[127] For a brief outline of the affair which ran from 1888–90, O. Chadwick, *The Victorian Church* (London: 2nd edn, SCM Press, 1972), 2, 353–4.

developed later in the century, on the one hand, into evangelical zeal in slum parishes and, on the other, into a serious wrestling with the problems thrown up by liberal approaches to the Bible. For, if the new trend was set by *Essays and Reviews* and Catholics like Pusey and Liddon resisted to the end, a quite different reaction was soon being offered by *Lux Mundi* and the writings of Charles Gore.[128] Such mutual feeding is also found within the same individual. For instance, though Newman's stress on conscience could be traced exclusively to Butler in the previous century, the intensity of moral passion that goes with it suggests to me continuing impact from the Evangelical influences of his youth. Again, one of the great ironies of the twentieth century is the number of theological radicals who have clung to their more conservative liturgical roots in an Evangelical or Catholic past.

To all I have said in this section, it may be objected that I have been altogether too sanguine about the nature of conflict. Certainly, it would be absurd to pretend that it is always beneficial, or that there is always something to learn from the heretic. But I do think that there are grounds for being more positive than is commonly the case and that, more pertinent to our theme as a whole, this is not unconnected with questions of the imagination. The insidious temptation for all who have a deep religious commitment is to suppose that each belongs to a group that has all, or most of the, answers. Imaginations then cease to be fed with anything new, but instead run along well-worn tracks. The wider society is one way in which fresh stimuli can be produced, but more disconcerting and therefore more effective are the jolts caused by the realization that those claiming an equal commitment draw very different conclusions. To suggest that revelation advances through the imagination is thus in no way to suggest a gentle or smooth transition from one perspective to another.

Authority: conservative consensus and dynamic continuity

But to leave matters there with the Church divided in conflict is scarcely satisfactory for a community to whom is addressed the

---

[128] The hostility to *Essays and Reviews* (1860) was intense, eleven thousand clergy eventually signing a protest letter. Even so, the appearance of *Lux Mundi* in 1889 demonstrated that many of its lessons had been absorbed by Anglo-Catholics.

prayer 'that they may all be one' (John 17: 21).[129] In a world of accelerating change, it is perhaps too much to hope for the visible unity of all confessing Christians. Nonetheless, it remains an ideal towards which we should strive, and is indeed demanded by my analysis of the Church's conflicts, since without some reconciliation nothing will have been learnt. But it is also important to say something about the interim. That I shall do here under two heads. First, I want to draw attention to the inadequacy of claims to unity based on grounds of continuity alone, but then draw from this not the illegitimacy of all authority but rather the necessity for taking with maximum seriousness whatever degree of consensus may happen to exist in the present. Thereafter I shall return for one last time to Peter and Paul, this time to a consideration of what may be learnt on this topic of authority from the use to which their imagery has been put over the centuries.

Learning from history   It would be pleasant were we able to identify some simple type of continuity that establishes authority in the present, but, if my arguments over the two volumes hold any water at all, it seems to me that neither Catholic nor Protestant versions of continuity of authority can continue to be applied in their customary form. In the past the Protestant churches would have argued that identity with the New Testament was what was worth preserving. But, while Scripture is there to continue to challenge us, any attempt at a literal identity would be to ignore the transformations which the Holy Spirit has been seeking to effect since. So, if Peter was not in any meaningful sense the first pope, neither was Paul the first defender of justification by faith, the equality of the sexes or egalitarian forms of government. Peter's nearest equivalent in our own day may well be a Jewish Christian still devoutly observing the major Jewish feasts, while Paul's could be an authoritarian pastor in some charismatic house-church where miracles of healing are regularly proclaimed. In saying this I do not intend to decry either type of Christian, only to acknowledge the strength of their antecedents while challenging their failure to move with a changing world. The problem for the Protestant, though, is not significantly lessened, even if the

---

[129] Though the prayer is addressed to the Father, John's intention is clearly that it should be appropriated by his readers.

benchmark is set at some point nearer to our own times. Barth may have insisted that Schleiermacher was an aberration in relation to the Reformation, but Schleiermacher himself had no doubt that the more dynamic continuity lay with his own thought.[130]

Yet, equally, there is little to be said for Catholic claims for literal continuity, whether these be based on papal chair or in an episcopacy guaranteed by apostolic succession. Certainly, the symbolism is right, expressing as it does the desire to pass something on, but that of itself can provide no absolute guarantee of correctness. Anglicanism went through a brief period of toying with such guarantees,[131] but, as the Porvoo agreement has recently acknowledged, there can be other ways of striving for the same continuity.[132] Rome too exhibits some signs of a changing attitude.[133] One additional advantage it has in such debates is that since at least the nineteenth century it has sought to defend continuity of authority in terms of a more dynamic capacity for change. Even so, such openness has come at a price. Old Protestant jibes about heretical popes have been replaced, even among Catholics, by more substantial problems: not only the difficulty of sustaining any obvious biblical roots to the idea of a continuing central role for Peter and his successors but also discovery of a subsequent history in which any notion of development along one single path becomes hard to sustain. The papacy of the first millennium offers little by way of anticipation of the infallibility at the end of the second,[134] while, should its teaching on

[130] B. A. Gerrish, *The Old Protestantism and the New* (Edinburgh: T & T Clark, 1982), 179–95.

[131] It remained a dominant strain in Anglo-Catholic thinking until K. E. Kirk (ed.), *The Apostolic Ministry* (London: Hodder & Stoughton, 1946) met with a number of robust responses, among them K. Carey (ed.) *The Historic Episcopate* (London: Dacre Press, 1954).

[132] That underlying continuity might be preserved despite breaks in episcopal succession is accepted in the *Porvoo Common Statement* (London: Church House Publishing, 1993), paras. 46–54. The relevance of this point to the agreement (between the Church of England and the Scandinavian and Baltic churches) is that not all these churches have preserved a continuous chain of episcopacy.

[133] Vatican II makes it clear that the issue is not just a matter of uninterrupted transmission in the laying on of hands: *Lumen Gentium*, paras. 22–3; cf. J. Ratzinger, *Principles of Catholic Theology* (San Francisco: Ignatius Press, 1987), 245–6.

[134] Even juridical interventions were rare, with popes on the whole responding rather than themselves taking the initiative.

contraception ever be abandoned, this would join many another piece of moral detritus, once firmly held.[135] The problem with evidence from the past is that it is so easy to distort its significance by reading it in the light of modern assumptions, and so what was only ever intended at the time to imply a primacy of honour or jurisdiction is expanded into something very much wider. For instance, had not Cyprian in the third century rewritten his key paragraphs to exclude more than a primacy of honour quite different inferences might now be drawn,[136] while the fact that a lay pope could even have been considered is one key indicator of how far medieval arguments centred on juridical power rather than on theology and sacramental order.[137]

One could of course speak of the conciliarism of Vatican II balancing the absolutism of Vatican I,[138] but against are Pope John Paul II's covert attempts to extend the notion of papal infallibility even further.[139] Conciliarism, though, is, I believe, the way ahead. It has of course a long and venerable history in both the patristic

[135] For examples from a Catholic, B. Hoose, *Received Wisdom?* (London: Geoffrey Chapman, 1994). He argues for a more radical view of development: 151–81.

[136] For text and Jesuit editor's comments, M. Bévenot, *De Ecclesiae Catholicae Unitate*, 4 (Oxford: Clarendon Press, 1971), xi–xv, 61–5.

[137] For how Ockham's proposal could be seen as congruent with the long history of Catholic thought, M. Wilks, 'The *Apostolicus* and the Bishop of Rome', *Journal of Theological Studies* 13 (1962), 290–317; 14 (1963), 311–54. As an early example he quotes the seventh-century *Liber Pontificalis* which states that *gubernandum* was given to Clement but *omne ministerium sacerdotale* to Linus and Anacletus: (1963), 327.

[138] Easier to sustain for the collegiality of bishops than for the role of the laity. The continued hierarchical view of *Lumen Gentium* leaves unclear how much significance is really being assigned to the laity in *Apostolicam Actuositatem*.

[139] As in his apostolic letter, *Ordinatio Sacerdotalis*, issued in May, 1994, where the language of infallibility is used to rule out the ordination of women: 'to be definitively held by all the Church's faithful'. More recently, there has been *Ad Tuendam Fidem* (30 June, 1998), which emended Canon 750 to require all Catholic theologians to assent to the following: 'All that is contained in the written word of God or in tradition, that is, in the one deposit of faith entrusted to the church and also proposed as divinely revealed either by the solemn magisterium of the church or by its ordinary and universal magisterium must be believed with divine and Catholic faith': *Origins* 28 (1998), 114–19, esp. 115. Included in the 'ordinary and universal magisterium' would be rejection of the ordination of women; so Dulles, ibid., 117.

and the medieval church.[140] Although it could be read as a pale religious aping of the secular move towards democracy, that is not, I think, the point.[141] In its history Anglicanism has struggled with what kind of respect was properly due to the early ecumenical councils, and if such respect was due, to how many.[142] If those erred who assumed that an early ideal of visible unity guaranteed truth, so too did those who thought that no greater respect was due than what was justified by perceived conformity with Scripture. For individual distortions of truth are inevitable, and so the wider the range of voices heard the more successfully we can guard against what might otherwise be the likely consequences of our prejudices,[143] or, putting it in more religious terms, the more likely it is that God's present word to humanity will be heard.

This does not mean, though, that that word will necessarily prevail immediately. The innate conservatism of the religious mind means that, initially at least, few are likely to accept the need for change, and by way of confirmation one could point to numerous instances in history of what is now orthodoxy beginning with what looked like an insignificant minority.[144] Indeed, notoriously Arianism remained in the ascendancy long after the Council of Nicaea. Even so, that still does not mean that the heretic is entitled to regard his or her own views as on a par with those of the majority, as though that was what respect for truth required. Instead, those canvassing for change should see themselves as prophets, charged with a mission, but set within a context where the possibility of themselves being wrong requires due submission to the will of the majority. For the Church cannot flourish without shared patterns of worship and a common proclamation. I began this

[140] In the medieval period particularly associated with the Councils of Constance (1414–18) and Basle (1431–49). For the theology behind the latter, A. Black, *Council and Commune* (London: Burns & Oates, 1979).

[141] The theology of the principal intellectual figure behind Constance, Jean Gerson, was in fact thoroughly hierarchical: D. Luscombe, 'John Gerson and Hierarchy' in I. Wood and G. A. Loud (eds.), *Church and Chronicle in the Middle Ages* (London: Hambledon, 1991), 194–200.

[142] For a brief resumé and bibliography, H. Chadwick and F. H Striver in S. Sykes and J. Booty (eds.), *The Study of Anglicanism* (London: SPCK, 1988), 91–105, 188–93.

[143] For a secular parallel, J. Habermas, *The Theory of Communicative Action* (London: Heinemann, 1984).

[144] As in the history of attitudes to hell or contraception.

chapter by noting Newman's views on the different roles of theologian ('prophet') and ecclesiastical authority ('king'). As it draws to its close, let me offer a specific case, what happened during the 1980s in my own diocese of Durham. As a result of the new bishop, David Jenkins, expressing his controversial opinions on the virgin birth and resurrection, the House of Bishops of the Church of England issued a paper, carefully distinguishing the private views of a theologian and the official position of the Church as represented through its bishops.[145] Though the distinction has been much criticized, it seems to me valid and important. If bishops are to be symbols of unity and indicative of the catholicity of the Church, then the public dimension of their role cannot be otherwise than fundamentally conservative. But this does not mean that the theologian or prophet is left free to sit loosely to the Church's rules and conventions, for he or she is also part of that same corporate body, even if less centrally placed within it. So, the duty remains to be respectful of authority and mindful of the fact that one might well be wrong. That is why there is no necessary incongruity in a theologian speaking more cautiously in church than might be the case in the study, though integrity of course requires that, so far as possible, the one should be informed by the other. But that is still to put the matter altogether too weakly. For what that stress on guarding oneself from error (though right and proper) ignores is the extent to which the Church is itself the source of the Christian's life and inspiration, theologian or otherwise. This is not to deny the personal action of God, but it is to insist that even so it comes mediated, through the words and symbols that the Church provides.[146] So listening to, and obeying the wider community is a necessary mark of gratitude for one's communal enrichment, however trying such dependence may at times be.

Images of Peter and Paul   Authority then lies in the dynamic continuity of tradition as this is gradually and consciously (or implicitly)

---

[145] *The Nature of Christian Belief* (London: Church House, 1986).

[146] A high doctrine of the Church has so often gone with authoritarianism that it is refreshing to find already in the early nineteenth century an impressive, alternative ecclesiology from the Catholic theologian, J. A. Möhler. For a helpful study, M. J. Himes, *Ongoing Incarnation* (New York: Crossroad, 1997).

embraced by the Christian community as a whole.[147] Certainly, true discipleship must answer the divine call when it is heard to urge the Church towards new directions as these are generated by fresh circumstances, but such a response needs always to be set in the context of recognizing that the Church involves mutual inter-dependence and not arrogant self-assertion over against the cares and concerns of others. The imagination of some is naturally tempted towards the past, that of others into an openness towards the future, but being part of the same community enjoins on each a willingness to enter imaginatively into what the other sees as the implications of the gospel, however 'heretical' these insights may initially appear. It is important that this should be said, because the imagination can trap as well as create. To illustrate how, I want to conclude by briefly considering how the images of Peter and Paul have in fact functioned imaginatively across the centuries. Inevitably, here Paul takes a secondary place. In respect of Peter, what I suggest we find is, on the one hand, a papacy increasingly entering into his story as though it had already reached its comple-tion, and, on the other, a hugely rich image and complex narra-tive that subvert any such claim to completion. As we shall see, though, the image of Paul was also not entirely immune from such problems.

The tensions are already there in the early period. Two types of image are common.[148] One makes use of a cockerel to present Peter, either in the actual act of hearing the reminder of his betrayal or else simply there as a reminder of how he had once behaved. Although a number of interpretations are possible, most plausible is the notion that the image was intended to speak at once of human frailty and fallibility and of its overcoming in the forgiveness of Christ. Its potential as a universal image in this sense is well illustrated by one particular catacomb scene, which has no other human figures present except Christ but two cockerels on either side looking up to him in expectation. Peter has thus become a symbol for any and every Christian, used, as he thus is,

---

[147] 'Or implicitly' because, as earlier chapters illustrate, change is often read back into Scripture and so treated as though it had not happened.

[148] L. de Bruyne, 'L'iconographie des apôtres Pierre et Paul dans une lumière nouvelle' in B. M. Apollonj Ghetti et al. (eds.), *Saecularia Petri et Pauli* (Vatican: Pontificio Istituto di Archeologia Cristiana, 1969), 36–84.

to speak of discipleship as a continuing struggle for us all, with promise of complete fulfilment only at the end of our pilgrimage rather in the immediate here and now.[149] Quite different, though, is the other major image. This places Christ in the centre with Peter and Paul on either side. Peter is being handed the new Law.[150] Only gradually does this give way to the presentation of the keys, just as only gradually does Paul acquire his own distinctive emblem of a sword and characteristic features such as balding head and pointed beard.[151] If the latter has the tendency to make Paul appear the more severe of the two, whether he is depicted with the keys or being handed the new law the implication for the appropriation of Peter were profoundly troubling. For it suggested an image of authority that could put the ambiguities of Peter's earlier career firmly behind it in the past.

Although their joint representation was never entirely to die out, and indeed in the Middle Ages took some unusual forms,[152] Peter clearly becomes more common on his own, and, sadly, in a way that seemed to imply a Church that had ceased to perceive the need to learn. It is not necessary to reiterate here the repeated appeal to Peter in the writings of successive popes, except to note the extraordinary extent to which his image inspired the pope most responsible for setting the papacy in an authoritarian direction. For there is no doubt that Gregory VII not only had a strong personal devotion to Peter but also wholly identified himself with him.[153] He speaks of himself as having been nurtured from infancy

---

[149] 'Comme symbole du simple croyant' (ibid., 84). For illustration (from catacomb of Priscilla), 83.

[150] The sarcophagus of Junius Bassus (d. 359) is among the best known examples of the *Traditio Legis*.

[151] For the view that the *Acts of Paul* deduced Paul's appearance from his own writings, J. Bollók, 'The description of Paul in the *Acta Pauli*' in Bremmer (ed.), *Apocryphal Acts* 1–15.

[152] A seal of Innocent IV (1243–54), found at Coldingham Priory in southeast Scotland, has on it the faces of both Peter and Paul, but for some reason Paul is identified by his pre-Christian name of Saul.

[153] M. Maccarone, 'I fondamenti petrini del primato romano in Gregorio VII', *Studi Gregoriani* 13 (1989), 55–128, esp. 96 ff. Note Maccarrone's opening sentence: 'Il nome di San Pietro è omnipresente nelle lettere di Gregorio VII . . . e la sua idea domina nella mente e nell'azione di questo papa, come in nessun altor né prima né dopo' (55).

under Peter's wings,[154] and while it is clear that his devotion to Peter antedates his elevation to the papacy, this undoubtedly strengthened his sense of identification. Not only are prayers to Peter frequent in his letters, there are also ejaculations that suggest the pope now sees himself as Peter's mouthpiece.[155] He even speaks of the acceptance of papal commands as if the person concerned 'had received them from the mouth of the apostle himself'.[156] The other major pope in shaping the papal monarchy, Innocent III, may have lacked the same intensity of devotion, but the image of Peter was likewise directed to similar ends.[157] It was as though it was Peter as he now was, living and perfected in heaven, who guided his earthly counterpart, not the ambiguous story of how he had reached those heights. The certainty of the present dissolved the reality of what had brought him to that point.

Yet even in the medieval period there were some who protested that the same troubled story must also be told of the papacy in their own day. Two examples will suffice. In Dante the image of the keys in the hands of an ideal confessor is contrasted with how in fact they have been used by the papacy; the threat of excommunication should be seldom used:

> Da Pier le tegno; e dissemi ch' i'erri
> anzi ad aprir ch'a tenerla serrata.[158]

[154] 'Me ab infantia mea sub alis suis singulari quadem pietate nutrivit et in gremio suae clementiae fovit': quoted in ibid., 78.

[155] E. g. 'Utinam beatus Petrus per me respondeat': quoted in ibid., 97.

[156] 'veluti si ab ore ipsius apostoli accepisset': quoted in G. Tellenbach, *The Church in Western Europe from the Tenth to the Twelfth Century* (Cambridge: Cambridge University Press, 1993), 234. Note also his death-bed remark, that excommunicates were absolved 'provided only that they believe without doubt that I have this spiritual power as representative of St Peter' (252).

[157] 'Christ left to Peter, not only the whole church but also the whole world, to govern': Innocent's remark is placed on an opening page (unnumbered) as the clue to the period as a whole in C. Morris, *The Papal Monarchy: the Western Church from 1050 to 1250* (Oxford: Clarendon Press, 1989). Cf. also 431–2.

[158] *Purgatorio* IX, 127–8; 'From Peter, I hold them; and he told me that I should err towards opening rather than in keeping bolted' (my trans.). For further references and discussion, P. Armour, *The Door of Purgatory* (Oxford: Clarendon Press, 1983), 76–99, esp. 83 ff.

That was perhaps an expected critique. More pertinent, therefore, is how the conciliar movement also generated a painting of Peter that expresses an attitude quite different from the conventional views of the papacy. Probably attracted to Basle by the Council sitting there, Conrad Witz was commissioned to paint his famous painting of the draught of fishes.[159] But, not content with that post-resurrection scene, he also has Peter once more sink as Christ walks on the water to him. The intention seems to have been deliberate, to invoke at once present perils and future hope. Thereby was expressed both the reluctance of the former Duke of Savoy to serve as pope and the hope of the conciliarists for the future.[160] If these are rare examples of different imaginative perspectives on Peter from the Middle Ages, both Reformation and Counter-Reformation were to open up new possibilities.

If we begin with the Catholic side, pertinent to note is Michelangelo's two great paintings of the conversion of St Paul and the crucifixion of St Peter.[161] The latter incident derives from the *Acts of Peter*, and shows Peter crucified upside down.[162] The former with all its dramatic details, including a quite splendid horse, could be read as little more than a piece of Renaissance humanism. But that would, I think, be unfair. Both paintings in fact complement one another, and both speak of the overturning of values and the severe requirements of an adequate *imitatio Christi*. Peter even looks out from the canvas, interrogating us. It is sometimes suggested that the way Peter is portrayed was Michelangelo's own choice, while the less severe version for Paul was influenced by the then pope, Paul III.[163] If so, Caravaggio's more famous version of the same incident made the necessary modifications that would ensure that the same message was taken

[159] Painted *c.* 1444, and now in Musée d'art et d'histoire, Geneva. Its fame derives not from its theme, but because it is one of the earliest examples of a naturalistic landscape.

[160] A devout man, Duke Amadeus was elected antipope in 1440 as Felix V, and abdicated in 1449.

[161] Painted *c.* 1545–50 for the Pauline Chapel. For illustration and discussion, H. Hibbard, *Michelangelo* (London: Octopus, 1979), 174–95.

[162] There are occasional medieval examples; for one from Rouen illustrated, E. Mâle, *Religious Art in France: the Thirteenth Century* (Princeton, N. J.: Princeton University Press, 1984), 297.

[163] The 1550 version of Vasari's *Lives* informs us that the subject was to be the Keys. The Pope, though, died late in 1549 with the Petrine fresco still unfinished.

in each case. Gone is the heavenly host, gone too is the splendid
steed, and in their place has come a more human reality, with the
horse struggling to avoid stepping on the fallen Paul.[164] Likewise,
Michelangelo's Peter was to be given a simpler form in Zurburán's
mystical version, in which all that is left is Peter Nolasco contem-
plating his upturned namesake as he emerges out of an unadorned,
red background.[165] That went well with another Counter-
Reformation image, that of the penitent and weeping Peter, so
poignantly expressed by El Greco.[166] What these images surely
suggest is not confidence in power but a Church that must struggle to be loyal to its Lord and which discovers that obedience in
humility, and not self-assertion.

One of the earliest Reformation images of Paul comes from
Dürer in his *Four Apostles*.[167] Paul is to the fore, as is John, Luther's
favourite Gospel writer. Behind are Peter and Mark. As one might
expect from the Reformation, it is Paul who dominates. Almost
certainly present too are underlying assumptions about the four
basic types of character and their correspondence to the four
humours. The net result is that Paul is made melancholic and thus
the one, according to the theories of the time, most disposed to
genius. Peter, by contrast, is pressed to the back, and made to look
a broken man—old, tired, and downcast. All the new confidence
of the Reformation is there, but also, sadly, it seems to me, quite
the wrong image of Peter and Paul. Peter's keys are now made an
empty boast, but that is combined with a new danger, the cult of
the romantic individual genius that Paul's fiery look is so clearly
meant to represent. That could end up (and often did) as authoritarian as its predecessor. It is fortunate, therefore, that the

---

[164] In the Cerasi Chapel, Santa Maria del Popolo in Rome. By contrast, its
companion piece of Peter's crucifixion, seems to me much less successful than
Michelangelo's. For illustrations, A. Moir, *Caravaggio* (London: Thames &
Hudson, 1989), nos. 19 and 20.

[165] Now in the Prado, Madrid; illustrated in J. Brown, *Zurburán* (London:
Thames & Hudson, 1991), 58–9.

[166] In Bowes Museum, Barnard Castle; for a reproduction and brief discussion, Plate 8 of this book. The image was widely used to replace the now historically suspect, penitent Magdalene.

[167] Painted *c.* 1525 in Nuremberg and now in Munich. For discussion, E.
Panofsky, *The Life and Art of Albrecht Dürer* (Princeton, N. J.: Princeton
University Press, 4th edn, 1955), 232–5; for further comments on my part, Plate
7 of this book.

Reformation was to produce another, quite different image of Paul, Rembrandt's.[168] He painted the saint a number of times, once in his own likeness. What, though, is remarkable about these images is their quietly reflective character. Instead of arrogance, there is an implicit call to meditation and prayer.

In our own day, beginning with a critical discussion of Schelling's treatment of Peter, Paul, and John as symbols or types, Balthasar has developed an account of the nature of the Church that speaks of the necessity of all three, but significantly Peter is still characterized as the one to whom unquestioning obedience is due.[169] With the long history of the kind of papacy that developed from Gregory VII onwards, it is easy to suppose that no other conception of Christian leadership and authority is possible. It is therefore salutary to recall that the first papal Gregory was made of quite different metal. Not only did Pope Gregory the Great (d. 604) speak of full authority existing in the college of bishops as a whole, he also explicitly objected to the 'ecumenical patriarch' usurping such a title to himself, not because he wanted himself designated 'universal pope' (the two terms are equivalent), but because the very use of the title implied a different conception of authority to that which he wished to endorse.[170] Again, however we read the biblical Paul, in practice the Reformation which he was seen to inspire often ended up no less authoritarian than what it opposed, and thus very far from the model of *servus servorum Dei* that Gregory I had himself espoused.

Certainly, issues of authority cannot be ignored in a religion whose essence requires a life of shared values and common worship, but at least the competing history of the images of Peter and Paul remind us that there is more than one alternative. Peter

---

[168] For Rembrandt's general approach to Paul, and illustrations, W. H. Halewood, *Six Subjects of Reformation Art* (Toronto: University of Toronto Press, 1982), 107–20.

[169] With the love of John ideally inhering the Petrine office, and the 'teacher' Paul receiving 'a not unfriendly but reserved official attitude': H. U. von Balthasar, *The Office of Peter and the Structure of the Church* (San Francisco: Ignatius Press, 1986), 160–1. For obedience, esp. 60–4; for the apostles as symbols, 145–61, 308–31.

[170] R. A. Markus, *Gregory the Great and his World* (Cambridge: Cambridge University Press, 1997); 72–5 for his conception of the episcopate; 91–6 for his disagreement with the Bishop of Constantinople.

and Paul have been presented as seekers as well as finders. It is by giving each their due weight that authority in the Church of our own day will be most appropriately exercized, with an insistence that the past be heard but also equally openness to the further transformations in Christian self-understanding that are undoubtedly yet to come. In the past, as we have seen, those transformations have often come through the imagination in contributions which, from one point of view, are purely 'fictional'. Why, nonetheless, truth can sometimes be seen to be their deeper content is the subject of my final chapter.

7
Posing Pilate's question: Truth and fiction

' "WHAT is truth" said jesting Pilate, and would not stay for an answer;' thus the familiar opening words of the first of Francis Bacon's essays.[1] Quoting from John's version of Jesus' trial before Pilate, he ends with a ringing endorsement of the value of truth, but not before he had conceded some of the counter-attractions. So, for instance, though 'poesy . . . filleth the imagination . . . with the shadow of a lie', 'a mixture of a lie doth ever add pleasure'. Had he been more self-reflective, he might also have seen some parallels to Pilate in the pragmatism and deceptiveness of his own life.[2] Bacon's response to Pilate's question is set at the beginning of our final chapter, however, not because of any specific interest in Bacon but rather because of the way in which his treatment of Pilate is so effective in exposing the major issues that must now be confronted, as I seek to draw together the argument of my two volumes as a whole. Essentially, these are of two kinds. First, there is the question of what we are to make of non-historical narratives and images. In common with many others, Bacon denies that 'poesy' can lay claim to truth. But is he right, and, if not, what sense of truth attaches to the various developing narratives that have been defended in earlier chapters? Then, secondly, there is the question of criteria for legitimate developments. Bacon talks of a 'jesting Pilate', and there are some who would follow him, but there is also an alternative tradition that has resulted in Pilate's

---

[1] Quotations from *Essays* ed. M. J. Hawkins (London: Everyman, 1994), 3.
[2] He prosecuted his former patron, Essex, and he is found elsewhere endorsing Machiavelli: ibid: viii, xxv–xxviii.

canonization. Is it a matter of indifference which version we
follow, or, if not, in this as in related cases what criteria might be
held to make the decisive difference? These later developments
and the general question of criteria I shall consider in the second
half of the chapter. I shall begin, though, with the issue of types of
truth, and in particular what form of truth might attach to imaginative and non-historical writing.

Types of truth

Here I shall proceed by four stages. First, I shall examine the
contribution of Scripture, both in its own right, in the way in
which it treats truth and the role of the imagination, and in some
objections to what follows that some might claim to be biblically
based. Thereafter, consideration will be given to what kind of
truth is conveyed imaginatively through fictional narrative, poetry,
and the visual arts. Each will be tackled separately, not only
because they raise significantly different issues, but also because
they function differently both in relation to Scripture and in the
applications to which they have been put in my earlier chapters.

Biblical concepts and imagination's role

Pilate's question is set in the context of a dialogue that is highly
unlikely to be historically true. Even if there was some kind of
personal exchange between Jesus and Pilate, there is no way in
which the evangelists could have gained access to its contents.
What Christ says is in any case resonant, not of the Synoptics, but
of John's own distinctive Christology. Within that context,
though, 'truth' is a key term. The opening section of his first chapter had already concluded with the ringing declaration that 'the
Word became flesh and dwelt among us, full of grace and truth'
(1: 14 RSV); there are repeated references to truth throughout;
then, finally, comes Pilate's question, but in response to Christ's
own statement: 'For this I have come into the world, to bear
witness to the truth. Everyone who is of the truth hears my voice'
(18: 37–8). So, in considering whether the dialogue might in any
sense be said to be true, it would seem sensible to begin with the
Bible's own understanding of the term.

The strangeness in such verses of the application of truth to persons will already have alerted us to the fact that biblical usage and modern English are not in complete alignment. It is tempting to find simple synonyms such as sincerity, but that scarcely captures the meaning. The Hebrew Bible is at a particularly far remove. Only occasionally in the Septuagint is it found necessary to use an expression unrelated to the Greek word for truth.[3] Even so, the difference in meaning is marked. 'Reliability', it is proposed, is 'the best comprehensive word in English to convey the idea.'[4] Unfortunately, to the philosophical mind that could easily suggest modern pragmatic theories of truth,[5] whereas the primary notion seems to be of the faithfulness of God and thus of the reliability of his promises. Human beings are then expected to be reliable in turn, giving their 'amen' as a commitment to work towards the fulfilment of that for which they had prayed.[6] While some New Testament expressions, such as 'to do the truth' are inexplicable except in relation to this Hebrew background,[7] there seems general agreement that the different Hellenistic background and usage are influential, and particularly so in John.

That a new linguistic frame should be more decisive than the inheritance of the Hebrew Scriptures may seem surprising, but it is apparently equally true for some Jewish writers, such as Philo.[8] Although the literal meaning of 'non-concealment'

[3] For examples, G. Quell s.v. '*aletheia*: the OT term' in G. Kittel (ed.), *Theological Dictionary of the New Testament* (TDNT) (Grand Rapids, Michigan: Eerdmans, 1964), I, 232–7, esp. 233.

[4] A. Jepsen, s.v. '*emeth* in G. J. Botterweck and H. Ringgren (eds.), *Theological Dictionary of the Old Testament* (Grand Rapids, Michigan: Eerdmans, 1977), I, 309–16, esp. 313.

[5] The philosophical term 'reliabilism' is a theory about belief rather than truth as such. For the pragmatic approach to truth, W. James, *The Meaning of Truth* (New York: Longmans Green, 1909); D. Papineau, *Reality and Representation* (Oxford: Blackwell, 1987); R. Rorty, *Truth and Progress* (Cambridge: Cambridge University Press, 1998).

[6] Stressed by R. W. L. Moberly s.v. '*mn* in W. A. Van Gemeren (ed.), *New International Dictionary of Old Testament Theology and Exegesis* (Carlisle: Paternoster, 1997), I, 427–33, esp. 428.

[7] The AV retains ' he that doeth truth' for John 3: 21, but in most translations (e. g. RSV) this is modified to 'he who does what is true'; for Hebrew background, cf. Gen. 32: 10; 47: 29.

[8] C. H. Dodd, *The Interpretation of the Fourth Gospel* (Cambridge: Cambridge University Press, 1970), 170–8, esp. 173–4.

seldom exercises a role, the ability of the Greek word to speak of the 'real' as well as of the 'true' does provide material for some powerful contrasts. In John it becomes allied with what is 'of the Spirit', 'of God' and 'from above' over against 'the flesh', 'the world', 'the Devil' and what is 'from below'. The Devil thus does not simply 'tell lies'; he is the opposite of eternal reality, just as Christ does not simply speak the truth; he is that reality itself, or, at the very least, the revelation of it.[9] The demand for worship 'in spirit and in truth' then becomes a demand, not for sincerity, but for a right relationship with that ultimate reality, just as in the specific passage in John with which we began the point cannot simply be about the ability of sincere individuals to hear Christ's message. On John's presentation, Pilate is shown as sympathetic to Jesus, and makes a series of attempts to extricate him from what will follow, but that in itself, John is telling us, is not enough.[10] Another point to note is that in Greek one can use the same word for 'idol' as is used elsewhere for 'image' or 'appearance' where this is contrasted with reality;[11] so religious considerations can be seen to be at the heart of the Greek usage no less than is the case with the Hebrew.

For most of Christian history the relation between these two types of truth, the Hebrew and the Greek, would have been seen as essentially unproblematic: the Bible is our best guide to reality, and because it always speaks what is the case, there is no difficulty in relying on its words.[12] Ever since the rise of biblical criticism, however, the reader has been confronted by a potential rift and even divorce. What are presented as facts often turn out to be no such thing. In response, a rearguard action has often been fought, with the intention of insisting that, appearances notwithstanding,

---

[9] Cf. for Devil, John 8: 44; for Christ as truth, 14: 6. The account in the text is supported not only by Dodd but also by Bultmann: s.v. *aletheia* in Kittel, TDNT, 238–51, esp. 245–7.

[10] C. K. Barrett, *The Gospel according to St John* (London: SPCK, 2nd edn, 1978), 538.

[11] For an example of *eidolon* as 'image' contrasted with *aletheia* as reality: Plato, *Symposium* 212A.

[12] In the past the literal truth of narratives was sometimes denied on moral or theological grounds, but such denials do not afford good parallels for my subsequent discussion since the narrative was then generally transformed into something else, such as allegory. For an example, Gregory of Nyssa, *Life of Moses*, e.g. 2.89–101.

what is on offer still remains essentially a matter of factual information. In previous chapters, however, I have been concerned to highlight the way in which the imagination can give us an alternative access to truth, and what I now wish to note is the way in which the Bible's own attitude might be used to reinforce that contention. My later discussion of truth in fiction will in due course elaborate what I mean, but a few brief indicators might be helpful at this point. Take first the Hebrew notion of reliability. While facts can play their part, it is surely false that they are the only or best guarantor of the reliability of another. We trust another most deeply when certain kinds of relationship have been established, and in the case of discipleship reliance on what God has alleged to have done in the past is one thing, quite another experiential confirmation in the present. But could the latter be conveyed through what is not true? Obviously not, if the means employed are not true in any sense, but from this it by no means follows that the relevant sense must be the narrowly factual. To see why, we need only think of the New Testament sense of truth and John's identification of it with the real. Correspondence theories of truth tend to isolate particulars, whereas assessment of reality as a whole may require quite a different estimate. In short, issues of significance may take us down quite a different track, with the 'false' story telling us what is most true about ourselves and about God as the ultimate source of all reality.

Standing in the way of such an estimate, though, is continuing suspicion of the imagination, and so doubts whether it can really fulfil the role I am claiming for it. Nowadays, the word is most usually found used in a positive sense. This is part of our inheritance from the Romantic movement during which the imagination of the artist came to be closely associated with individual genius, but the longer history of the term indicates a more common attitude of continuing suspicion, not least because of the root association of the meaning of the word with images, and so with what merely appears to be so as contrasted with what is real.[13]

[13] The derivation of the English word 'fantasy' from the Greek word for the imagination (*phantasia*) well illustrates the problem. It is thanks to Augustine that 'imagination' and its equivalents became the normal term in many modern European languages. Although used to support the doctrine of the resurrection of the body, it is assigned a modest role: e.g. *Epistle* 7.5 ff.; *De Genesi ad litteram* 12.

So it is easy to reproduce a long litany of complaints about its character being wild and undisciplined,[14] and it was in this sense that it entered early English versions of the Bible.[15] More modern translations in general eliminate the term, since the references are for the most part to deliberative mental planning rather than to anything particularly to do with the imagination as we now understand the term.[16] Nonetheless, doubts that would claim biblical precedent continue to arise from both the modernist and postmodernist sides of current debates.[17] I shall, therefore, examine each in turn.

Postmodernist doubts is where I shall begin, since, given postmodernism's rejection of any overarching account of truth, one might have thought that its advocates would exhibit a basic sympathy towards the imagination, if only because on such an approach the imagination must surely be allowed as much right to speak as any other attempt to define our situation. Somewhat surprisingly, however, the old connection between images and imagination has pulled many of its exponents in a quite different direction. In a world that bombards us with its images and can so easily establish its own tyranny of conformity, our most basic need, they argue, is to revolt against any image or narrative as having decisive significance.[18] Instead, high art has to be undermined through exposure of its parallels with the ordinary and conventional, just as narrative structure has to be challenged by other possibilities being continuously brought to the attention of the

---

[14] E.g. although Hume thinks that sometimes we have no option but to yield, he speaks of the promptings of the imagination as 'often contrary to each other', and as generating 'errors, absurdities and obscurities': *Treatise of Human Nature* 1.4.7, ed. Selby-Bigge, (Oxford: Clarendon Press, 1888), 267. Samuel Johnson speaks of 'a licentious and vagrant faculty': quoted in H. Osborn, *Aesthetics and Art Theory* (New York: Dutton, 1970), 217.

[15] Examples would include the following : Gen. 6: 5; Jer. 23: 17; Luke 1: 51; Rom. 1: 21.

[16] The clearest example of difference of usage is 2 Cor. 10: 5, where AV's 'imaginations' has become RSV's 'arguments'.

[17] For how I understand these terms, see *Tradition and Imagination*, ch.1, esp. 9–11, 32–44.

[18] For an excellent discussion of this aspect of postmodernism, R. Kearney, *The Wake of the Imagination* (London: Routledge, 1994), 251–358.

reader.[19] Rather than pattern being imposed by the creative writer, symbols welling up from the unconscious should then be allowed their free play, to challenge any ultimate standard of representation or truth.[20]

That is of course to draw attention to the more extreme elements in the postmodern approach. Even so, it might be thought to indicate how dangerous any unqualified alliance with postmodernism could be for theology. Apart from the positive features of postmodernism already noted in my earlier book,[21] the explanation why no immediate resultant retreat is evident on the part of theologians may, I suspect, be put down to two key factors. The first is general support for the questioning of the authority of images, as underlining religious objections to idolatry. The second is dislike of the terminology of imagination as suggestive of an essentially human project. The Romantic notion of the artist comes immediately to mind, where in effect the artist takes over the creative role once assigned to God himself.[22] But both points can, I think, be answered. To the first, a brief response may be made. It is that constant suspicion of images almost inevitably tends to be self-destructive. For either it will mean failure to engage with the world at all, or else, more probably, the substitution of some alternative image which is not even acknowledged to be such. So in the theological case, in the rush to castigate later images, it is often forgotten how the Bible can itself establish its

---

[19] Thomas Pychon is a good example of a novelist who rejects narrative coherence. How much artists see themselves as issuing a challenge to established conventions is of course a moot point. Despite support from Saatchi and Saatchi, that might be one way in which to read the 1997 'Sensation' exhibition at the Royal Academy of Arts in London. Yet Andy Warhol, doing much the same thing, intended his works as a celebration of mass culture.

[20] E. g. Lacan, *Écrits* (Paris: Éditions du Seuil, 1966), esp. I, 111 ff. ; G. Deleuze and F. Guattari, *Anti-Oedipus* (London: Athlone, 1984). For a brief exposition of their ideas, D. Brown, *Continental Philosophy and Modern Theology* (Oxford: Blackwell, 1987), 160–66.

[21] *Tradition and Imagination*, ch. 1, esp. 54–9.

[22] Coleridge at least still shows due subordination, in speaking of 'the primary imagination . . . as a repetition in the finite mind of the eternal act of creation in the infinite I AM': *Biographia Literaria* 13 (London: Dent, 1975 edn.), 167. What Shelley says in his *Defence of Poetry* is more typical, and this finds plenty of twentieth-century parallels; for examples, N. Wolterstorff, *Art in Action* (Grand Rapids, Michigan: Eerdmans, 1980), 50–8.

own tyranny of images, with the narrative in effect treated as sacrosanct and so not allowed to open up new ways of hearing God's present address to humanity.

The other objection, that imagination suggests a purely human project, takes us back to Kant, and illustrates once more how implausible are any sweeping generalizations about Enlightenment or modernity, despite their frequency in contemporary theological discussion. Is Kant a late Enlightenment thinker, an early Romantic, or to be placed somewhere in between? Something can be said in favour of each account, depending on the question being addressed. Certainly, in respect of his treatment of the artist it is plausible to identify him as a Romantic, and thereby the source would be effectively identified of what is particularly problematic in modern treatments of creativity: that it is seen as self-determined rather than the product of a reality that is external to oneself. Thus the success of the artist is assessed in the third *Critique* by ability to produce an order or purpose that is measured by no eternal referent.[23] But if that is one side of the Kantian inheritance, another is the centrality given to the imagination, in making comprehension and understanding of our world possible at all. Kant can be seen as offering a mediating course between the two opposed earlier approaches to philosophy, the rationalist and empiricist. Both mental concepts and perceptual data are needed, but they are brought into intelligible relation with one another only through the work of the imagination. The ability of the mental to order the raw data of the perceptual is achieved through the imagination sharing something of each, and it is the imagination that unifies such activity into the sense of a united consciousness.[24] So far, therefore, from being the sole prerogative of the

---

[23] The imagination (*Einbildungskraft*) when applied to art in Kant's famous phrase produces 'purposiveness without purpose' (*Zweckmässigkeit ohne Zweck*), and because not subject to any universally accessible rules is therefore a work of 'genius': *Critique of Judgement*, sec. 46.

[24] For the first task, *Critique of Pure Reason* A138; B 177; for the second, unifying role, A 123–4. For a helpful exposition, M. Johnson, *The Body in the Mind* (Chicago; University of Chicago Press, 1987), 147–66. Heidegger was responsible for highlighting the key, wider role of the imagination for Kant in *Kant and the Problem of Metaphysics* (1929). For an attempt to carry the argument a stage further in assigning a stronger hermeneutical role, R. A. Makkreel, *Imagination and Interpretation in Kant* (Chicago: University of Chicago Press, 1990).

artist, the imagination has thus become basic to the understanding of our world for each and every one of us. So one way of answering the postmodernist objection is to observe that the work of the imagination is not a wholly human creation, far less a matter of native artistic genius. In its role it mediates objectivity and subjectivity, and so could be said to fit quite nicely into the limited notions of objectivity which some postmodernists at least are prepared to allow.

That response, however, immediately casts us up against the objection from the other side, from modernism, that the imagination can never afford us the same degree of objectivity as reason. For it is reason, such an objector might claim, that takes us nearest to the mind of God. How plausible that last contention is as an analysis of Scripture we need not pursue here.[25] More important is the objection in its own right. Ironically, that too can be made to focus in the writings of Kant, since his definition of reason precluded both theology and art from the possibility of knowledge. While it would be grossly unfair to suggest that Kant intended thereby to demean the importance of art and theology (both remain indispensable), there is no doubt that the net effect of his philosophy was to demote both in relation to the exalted standards which he set for reason. But we are not compelled to draw the same inference. The standards of reason and imagination can be brought more closely together by noting on the one hand that Kant's overconfidence in reason can be challenged,[26] and on the other the various ways in which residual suspicion of the imagination may be undermined. As one indicator of the latter, consider the case of Plato, often portrayed as the philosopher most hostile to the imagination. So familiar are his negative judgements on art in the *Republic* that it is frequently forgotten that not only does his concern with literary effect and image in that work tell a

---

[25] An adequate treatment would need to consider at length the long history of identifying the *imago Dei* in human beings with reason, as also the way in which Christ as the divine Logos came to be seen as the embodiment of Reason. Though neither are directly scriptural, there is no doubt of their scriptural roots, not least in the Wisdom tradition.

[26] As a small example, Kant is confident that the exceptionless character of keeping promises and the prohibition of suicide can be demonstrated: *Groundwork of the Metaphysic of Morals*, (421–2), 52–5. They cannot, but it by no means follows from this that his argument is therefore without worth.

different tale,[27] but also elsewhere in his writings there are several more positive assessments of the contribution that the imagination makes to our lives. It is thanks to an internal 'artist' that our perceptions are preserved and ordered in the memory, while such knowledge of ultimate reality as we have will contain an irreducible mythic element.[28] In later Platonism, some have even found anticipations of the larger role accorded by Kant.[29]

My point in noting this more complicated picture is to alert the reader to the possibility that there need not be any necessary conflict between the resources of reason and of the imagination, just as earlier we noted no good grounds for following those post-modernists who see in the imagination only a tyranny of images rather than the freedom that they seek. There can therefore be no insuperable objection to thinking of the imagination as itself one form of access to the truth. It is a claim made by various Romantic poets,[30] which in itself may be one reason why those sympathetic to the Enlightenment and to modernism continue to regard it with suspicion. But where the imagination has one undoubted advantage over either reason or ordinary perception is in its ability, as it were, to think laterally, to allow combinations that are not themselves necessarily already present either in the mind or in nature. Of course, the result will not always make sense, but image and metaphor can help detect connections that had not previously been identified. To this it may be objected that all such links will be located merely in the mind, and cannot therefore provide any independent access to external reality. Even if this were so, they could still be illuminating, as the work of the Hebrew prophets well illustrates, with their frequent resort to apparently arbitrary wordplay.[31]

---

[27] As in the Myth of Er with which the work ends.

[28] For the former, *Philebus* 39; for the latter, *Timaeus* 29. Summarizing the latter, F. M. Cornford declares that for Plato 'there remains an irreducible element of poetry': *Plato's Cosmology* (London: Kegan Paul, 1937), 32.

[29] So J. Dillon, 'Plotinus and the transcendental imagination' in J. P. Mackey (ed.), *Religious Imagination* (Edinburgh: Edinburgh University Press, 1986), 55–64.

[30] In *The Marriage of Heaven and Hell* (*c.* 1790) Blake offers various aphorisms called 'Proverbs of Hell' which he intends provocatively but positively. Included is the following: 'What is now proved was once only imagined.' Wordsworth speaks of 'imagination which in truth/ Is but another name for absolute strength/ . . . / And reason in her most exalted mood': *The Prelude*, 14, 189–92.

[31] For some examples, J. Lindblom, *Prophecy in Ancient Israel* (Oxford: Blackwell, 1978), 137–41.

But increasing recognition of a symbolic field in the unconscious can alert us to other options, in particular that not everything that is 'known' has necessarily already been conceptualized.[32]

How far the discovery of such connections will be necessarily disruptive is a hard question to answer. For some who take imagination as central to the process of revelation it is essential to think of an exercise that seeks 'to dismember the self's history'.[33] While not disputing that element, no less important to my mind is the way in which it becomes possible to think of growth in knowledge through a deepening understanding within tradition of the possible range of reference of images and stories.[34] Symbols and metaphors acquire unexpected new allusions, while stories are reordered into narratives indicative of a deeper truth. But how exactly? Philosophers are temperamentally inclined to favour prose as a vehicle for truth.[35] In what follows, I shall argue that story, poetry, and the visual arts have each their distinctive contribution to make in deepening our perception of divine reality.

Fictional narrative

Before outlining the three principal ways in which in my view fictional narrative typically tries to convey truth and the kind of parallels that exist with Scripture, I want first to pursue a little further that debate between modernists and postmodernists to which allusion has already been made. What strikes me about the debate in its Christian context is that as yet neither side seems to have fully entered into the complexity of the issues, and so noted the degree to which, whether we are dealing with fact or fiction, similar issues arise. Not all issues, though, are of this kind; hence

---

[32] The idea is found in modernists and postmodernists alike, e.g. Eliade, Jung, Lacan, Lévi-Strauss.

[33] R. L. Hart, *Unfinished Man and the Imagination* (New York: Seabury, 1979 edn), 217. Disequilibrium is caused 'by metaphors putting "unlikes" in contact with one another': 184, cf. 235.

[34] Hart does plead for a dynamic view of tradition: 283.

[35] Even Sartre insisted that prose was essentially concerned with communication of truth in a way that poetry because of its form was not. For a discussion of his argument, C. Altieri, 'Jean-Paul Sartre: the engaged imagination' in O. B. Hardison (ed.), *The Quest for Imagination* (Cleveland: Case Western Reserve, 1971), 167–89.

the reason for highlighting in what follows three ways of appropriating truth that are especially characteristic of fiction.

Modernist and postmodernist   For some the sense in which the biblical narrative is true is uncontentious, for simply in virtue of becoming part of the Christian community it is thought one thereby accepts its own definitions as authoritative. Accepting the Gospel narrative as true thus becomes part of what it means to be a Christian. As one writer puts it, 'imaging the world according to the biblical story, they find themselves persuaded that the story is true'.[36] That is to identify with a group of theologians which includes Lindbeck and who are, following his usage, commonly called postliberal, though the term postmodern is almost as appropriate.[37] Despite the huge differences in methodology, the philosopher Alvin Plantinga could also be included in this group, inasmuch as he insists that faith of itself offers 'a reliable source of true and warranted belief', which is taken to entail, in respect of biblical criticism, that one 'need feel no obligation, intellectual or otherwise, to modify . . . beliefs in the light of its claims and alleged results'.[38] What is puzzling about his argument is not the high value placed on faith, but the supposition that it can always trounce any considerations put forward by biblical criticism because of the uncertainty of its conclusions. Are not most philosophical and theological arguments likewise subject to varying degrees of plausibility and persuasiveness? Hans Frei at least concedes a problem when he acknowledges that in some ways the biblical text behaves more like a fictional narrative, but then appears to block off any other approach as significant for faith when he insists that what matters is that the narrative be treated as a unity.[39] The obvious alternative

[36] G. Green, *Imagining God: Theology and the Religious Imagination* (San Francisco: Harper & Row, 1998), 142–3.
[37] As he himself notes: G. A. Lindbeck, *The Nature of Doctrine* (London: SPCK, 1984), 135, n. 1.
[38] 'Two (or more) kinds of scripture scholarship', *Modern Theology* 14 (1998), 243–78, esp. 266, 273.
[39] For his comparison with the novel, *The Eclipse of Biblical Narrative* (New Haven: Yale University Press, 1974), 142–54. His insistence on reversing 'the great reversal' (130) and making the world fit the biblical story, though, is modified elsewhere by his recognition that sometimes at least 'about certain events in the gospels we are almost bound to ask, Did they actually take place?': *The Identity of Jesus Christ* (Philadelphia: Fortress Press, 1975) , 132.

might seem to lie in the self-styled revisionists, who like the term's originator, David Tracy, see the Bible functioning like a 'classic' that is creative of a particular culture and so open to public debate and dispute.[40] But, if the danger for the postliberal is retreat from what are real difficulties, the problem for the revisionist is a failure to recognize the possibility of any distinctive contribution from God at all.[41] In effect, this is what has happened in the thinking of Gordon Kaufman, for whom religion has become entirely a work of the human imagination.[42]

But is either side quite right in the way in which it is presenting the issues? On the one side, we appear to be told that all that matters is membership of the Christian community; on the other, that we cannot do otherwise than acknowledge our membership of the wider culture and academic community. But is not the situation immeasurably more complicated? Not only are we all members of a number of different intellectual communities, some coextensive with church membership and others not, but also there exists considerable pluralism in the Church, and indeed even within ourselves. Few of us have completely integrated our intellectual beliefs, and so they are often held together, imperfectly resolved. Moreover, these various realms of discourse and aspects of ourselves interact, and indeed should interact, since God as the creator and source of all knowledge is also source of this complexity, and it is therefore he who can give the apparent conflict some kind of overarching unity. So, for example, revelation can give us warrant for believing in miracles but biblical research may make us suspicious of the historicity of some as against others, as in the way in which explanation of the crossing of the Red Sea appears to

[40] D. Tracy, *The Analogical Imagination* (London: SCM Press, 1981). For a philosophical assessment of the strengths and weaknesses of Tracy's position in relation to foundationalism, F. Schüssler Fiorenza, *Foundational Theology: Jesus and the Church* (New York: Crossroad, 1985), 249–321.

[41] For a valuable attempt to identify the defects in both positions when taken to extremes, W. C. Placher, *Unapologetic Theology* (Louisville, Kentucky: Westminster Press, 1989), esp. 154–74.

[42] For a critique that assumes Kaufman's own Kantian presuppositions, yet argues that he has failed to take seriously enough the fact that 'Kant views the imagination as both constructive and receptive', D. J. Bryant, *Faith and the Play of the Imagination* (Macon, Georgia: Mercer University Press, 1989), *passim*, esp. 80. For Kaufman's most recent views, G. Kaufman, *In Face of Mystery: A Constructive Theology* (Cambridge, Mass.: Harvard University Press, 1993).

have developed gradually from natural account to supernatural.[43] Recognizing that a purely historical approach also carries presuppositions need not thus mean a retreat to alternative presuppositions, but rather creative interaction between the different assumptions and so a 'faith . . . open to revision in the light of the evidence'.[44] Similarly, recognizing the authority of Scripture cannot mean that it becomes exempt from all critique. For, as Schleiermacher rightly saw, there can be no change or development in religion except from what begins as heterodox opinion.[45] Authority has thus first to be contested before it can be reinstated in a new form. Of course, the temptation is to say that the only legitimate dissenter is the one who finds the dissenting voice within Scripture itself, but, if such a claim distorts the text's most obvious sense, it is not at all clear how this differs from a more explicit challenge that also appeals to the voice of God. All of course depends on what questions it is that we are addressing to the text. The historical are only one type, but it is essential to insist upon their legitimacy as part of the Christian's wider pursuit of truth. This seems essential, not only because historical research is one important form of access to the truth and Christians must surely be concerned with the historical grounding of their faith, but also because that historical dimension, so far from undermining faith, can in fact deepen it. Thus it was one of the principal contentions of my earlier book *Tradition and Imagination* that through historical criticism the doctrine of the incarnation has emerged as more significant, and not less, because of the extent of divine involvement now implied. Of course, the secular historian cannot be expected to endorse that latter view, but the Christian who is willing to take historical analysis seriously could.

But if interaction between our normal historical assumptions and the recognition of the Bible's unique authority can generate

[43] Cf. G. B. Caird, *The Language and Imagery of the Bible* (London: Duckworth, 1980), 209–10.

[44] For the point applied to the resurrection, A. G. Padgett, 'Advice to religious historians: on the myth of a purely historical Jesus' in S. T. Davis et al. (eds.), *The Resurrection* (Oxford: Oxford University Press, 1997), 287–307, esp. 305.

[45] For a persuasive presentation of Schleiermacher on development, J. E. Thiel, *Imagination and Authority* (Minneapolis: Fortress Press, 1991), 33–62; for the role of heterodoxy, 48–50.

one form of creative dialogue both in the wider Christian community and within ourselves, yet another becomes possible when we discover that fiction sometimes has very similar aims to accounts that present themselves as purely factual or historical. For, if the acknowledgement of the fictional character of a narrative cannot of itself be said to mark the end of discussion of its potential truth content, then any comparison of aspects of Scripture to the novel ceases to be automatically demeaning to the former, as though 'fiction' had necessarily to be contrasted with truth. Certainly, there are no shortage of novelists who have seen their role as conveyors of truth. Although one might perhaps expect a novelist to declare that 'no one can ever believe this narrative, in the reading, more than I believed it in the writing', Dickens sometimes goes much further in some of his prefaces, claiming not only careful consultation of records, where available, but also that in some deeper sense even the life of a fictional character can be true: 'It is useless to discuss whether the conduct and character of the girl seems natural or unnatural, probable or improbable, right or wrong. It is true.'[46] Again, Henry James objects to Trollope's admission that he is engaged only in 'making believe' on the grounds that 'it implies that the novelist is less occupied in looking for the truth . . . than the historian, and in doing so it deprives him at a stroke of all his standing room.'[47]

In response philosophers have often been dismissive. Bertrand Russell, for example, declares bluntly of *Hamlet* that 'the propositions in the play are false because there was no such man', while John Urmson says of the opening sentence of *Persuasion* that 'Jane Austen writes a sentence which has the form of an assertion beginning with a reference, but is in fact neither asserting or referring'.[48]

---

[46] First quotation from Preface to *David Copperfield*, second from *Oliver Twist* ('it is true' in bold in original). For an example of his attitude to historical detail, see the Preface to *Barnaby Rudge* on the Gordon Riots.

[47] 'The Art of Fiction' in *The Art of Fiction and Other Essays* (New York: Oxford University Press, 1948), 3–23, esp. pp. 5–6. The essay draws an extended analogy with painting. Somewhat surprisingly, 'closeness of relation' (16) with the reader's existing experience is stressed, rather than the possibility of imaginative engagement with new ways of viewing the world.

[48] B. Russell, *An Inquiry into Meaning and Truth* (London: Routledge, 1962), 277.; J. Urmson, 'Fiction', *American Philosophical Quarterly* 13 (1976), 153–7, esp. 155.

The latter view (which follows Frege) is now the more common position among philosophers, in part perhaps because of the obvious advantage it has in being less paradoxical than Russell's stance. The question of truth or falsity is thus held not to arise in the absence of any direct reference to the external world. It is the line taken in the most recent extended discussion of the issues, where the authors take the view that, though related questions of truth can arise, these are incidental to issues of literary merit, and so it simply muddies the waters if the novelist is depicted as involved in any essential way with the pursuit of truth.[49] In one sense the authors are clearly right: 'true' or 'true to life' can hardly of itself turn a piece of fiction into a work of art. Yet that hardly precludes of itself the author from also being engaged in the pursuit of truth.[50] Part of what Dickens may have meant was that because of his care in his research his novels convey the way the world is no less accurately than an historical analysis, the deficit side of which could be lack of liveliness in presentation because of insufficient factual information available. The test of the novelist's effectiveness in that aim would still be crucially dependent on the extent to which further historical research supported his general approach, but that cannot alter the fact that he might still have offered a more accurate portrayal of the situation than a professional historian, perhaps unduly swayed by some particular bias in his selection and interpretation of purely factual material.

   I. A. Richards is typical of many a literary critic for whom issues of truth are always minor and who thus find the *raison d'être* of fiction elsewhere, in his case in its ability to influence our affective and conative life.[51] He is of course right that historical accuracy could never of itself make a work of fiction a great novel, but even

   [49] P. Lamarque and S. H. Olsen, *Truth, Fiction, and Literature* (Oxford: Clarendon Press, 1994), e.g. 334, 368.
   [50] For a philosophical treatment prepared to make questions of truth more central, N. Wolterstorff, *Works and Worlds of Art* (Oxford: Clarendon Press, 1980). His analysis is conducted in terms of the projection of worlds: 198 ff., esp. 238–9.
   [51] I. A. Richards, *Principles of Literary Criticism* (London: Routledge & Kegan Paul, 2nd edn, 1926), esp. 272–87. Truth is confined to reference, 'acceptability' (internal coherence), and 'sincerity': 268–71. For an example of religous 'vision' placed more highly than truth, D. N. Morgan, 'Must art tell the truth?' in J. Hospers (ed.), *Introductory Readings in Aesthetics* (New York: Free Press, 1969), 225–41.

so matters are not quite so easily resolved. For, even if we were to pursue Richards' own suggestion about where the value of literature lies, questions of truth can still present themselves. Reacting against the late Tolstoy's attempt to impose stern moral criteria,[52] he failed to note that using literature to make sense of life's possibilities also raises the question of truth: Is it true of this character? Could it be true of me, if not, for others? So, while fully acknowledging that the main import of literary evaluation must lie elsewhere, I want now to direct attention to three areas where the 'fictional' narratives of Scripture and novel can be seen to raise important and distinctive issues of truth that cannot be reduced to the narrowly factual.

Truth and significance The first concerns questions of significance. Here some might wish to argue that such issues should be sharply distinguished from questions of realistic portrayal, with realism the more basic form of correspondence with truth, but it would seem to me that realism, exaggeration and caricature can all be seen as different means of bringing about the same effect: the reader regarding what happens to the characters in the narrative as interesting and significant. This is perhaps more obvious where social issues are addressed. Balzac, for instance, in introducing his novel series *La Comédie humaine* as a 'history of moral behaviour', muses: 'in order to deserve the praises to which every artist must aspire, am I not bound to study the causes or central cause of these social facts, and discover the meaning hidden in the immense assembly of characters, emotions and events?'[53] It is an aim that has been criticized as more appropriate to sociology, and as in any case incapable of realization since the analysis cannot be tested against further information about the individuals involved.[54] But that is surely to ignore the possibility of truth being perceived through more than one medium. Thanks to novelists such as Balzac or Dickens our imagination can be compelled into a different mapping of a reality with which we are already familiar. When

---

[52] Tolstoy in *What is Art?* (sec. 16) rejects Shakespeare, Dante and Goethe in favour of Dickens, Eliot and Hugo. For Richards' reaction, *Principles*, 63–6.

[53] My trans.: *La Comédie humaine* (Paris: Gallimard, 1976), I, 7–20, esp. 11. The Preface as a whole identifies a number of tensions, including that between 'type' and 'detail' (10, 15).

[54] Lamarque and Olson, *Truth*, 315–20.

this leads to acknowledgement of the injustice or inappropriateness of certain forms of social practice or individual behaviour, it is important to recognize that this can come not only through realistic portrayal of social conditions, but also sometimes through a heightened or exaggerated sense of their impact. So it matters not whether there was ever a school quite as bad as Dotheboys Hall under Wackford Squeers but that it imprints on our imagination what can go wrong with boarding education, just as Balzac in general makes us recoil from a society dominated by self-interest and money, even if he exaggerates the degree to which early nineteenth-century France was like this.[55] Some philosophers have responded by trying to separate out the truth and falsehood, suggesting that we speak of the details of the novel as a combination of truth and falsehood, with the truth whether of particulars or generalities being seen to correspond with reality in the conventional manner.[56] But what I think this ignores is the way in which our attitude to reality is not just a matter of its discrete elements but also about how these are placed in relation to one another, and that what the novelist can in effect do is force a remapping of that reality.

Certainly, this is by no means always so. Sometimes realism or invention is enough of itself for us to appreciate the author's literary skill. Yet worth noting is the way in which this power to focus or refocus our perceptions can sometimes play a much larger role in defining great literature than is commonly acknowledged. Take the case of Jane Austen. She is often criticized for dealing with mundane issues while the Napoleonic wars were convulsing Europe, but therein surely lies her power, in her ability to endow with significance the perennial, ordinary issues of life despite that larger backdrop. By contrast, Victor Hugo's *Les Misérables* offers us a larger, if less realistic, stage in the contrast between the exaggerated goodness of Jean Valjean and Javert's deadening commitment to duty, but thereby he too effectively brings to the centre of our focus important questions, this time of moral conversion and

[55] For Squeers, *Nicholas Nickleby*. Perhaps inevitably, Balzac has been seen as corroboration of a Marxist analysis of bourgeois society, but that would be to take the question of the truth or otherwise of his perceptions one stage further than the novels themselves.

[56] E.g. G. D. Martin, 'A new look at fictional reference', *Philosophy* 57 (1982), 223–36.

change.[57] Of course, that means that novelists can pull us in different directions, but the same is no less true of the different emphases of the four evangelists.

In theory the nearest analogy to the work of the evangelists should presumably be the historical novel, but this genre is so often affected by romantic notions of the past that it is hard to think of any serious parallels. Indeed, where the medium is applied directly to biblical stories, often it is the disanalogies that are the more striking, since promotion of personal ideology can tend to overwhelm any sense of historical context, though of course failure in historical realism does not preclude success in other terms.[58] So, the better parallel may after all lie in the more general type of fiction and its attempt to impose a pattern of significance. In Christ's case the key issue is the retelling of his life story in the light of the resurrection, and so what actually happened is now refocused in order that the whole narrative may naturally lead to its presently perceived final conclusion. We witness a related phenomenon in more conventional biography, whenever the writer selects what is to be recorded so that the narrative more naturally anticipates what is to come, and indeed we do this with our own lives, as our memories selectively impose on our data bank what seems of most continuing significance for our lives in the light of later events. But the Gospel narratives go much further, in engaging not only in selectivity but also in the imaginative creation of events. It is unlikely, for instance, that the Sermon on the Mount was ever delivered in that form,[59] but in being presented thus it allows Matthew to convey not only the

---

[57] Intriguingly, the 1992 film version, starring Richard Jordan and Anthony Perkins, intensified the contrasts still further, Valjean, for instance, committing no further crime after his encounter with Monseigneur Myriel.

[58] An illuminating contrast is provided by two novels on the life of King David. Although his decision to make David a practising homosexual seems dubious, Allan Massie's *King David* (London: Hodder & Stoughton, 1995) is undoubtedly the more successful historically. Yet Joseph Heller's *God Knows* (London: Jonathan Cape, 1984) is in my view the greater novel , because of the way David is used to tackle difficult moral and religious issues, with the comic very effectively used to highlight those issues.

[59] Film versions well illustrate the implausibility of any such uninterrupted piece of discourse. In Nicholas Ray's *King of Kings* (1961) the problem is solved by questions being constantly thrown by the crowd, but to achieve this material from all four Gospels is utilized.

power of Jesus as teacher but also his authority as that of the new and greater Moses that he is now conceived to be. Thereby, despite due respect being shown to what Jesus taught, considerable liberties were taken with the form in which that teaching is presented.[60]

More controversially, though, the Scriptures probably also contain some wholly invented incidents, content included. Aristotle tells us that fiction is concerned with type rather than particular,[61] and that is one possible way of understanding how an evangelist might have legitimated such a way of proceeding. Take the miracle at Cana. It is hard not to find it improbable historically, not merely because the quantities involved are so absurd, but more importantly because it would seem to turn Christ into the sort of wonder worker which the Synoptic Jesus' refusal of a sign is precisely intended to refute (John 2: 1–11; contrast Matt. 12: 38–40).[62] But one can easily envisage John arguing that this is precisely the sort of thing Jesus could so easily have done (it is no more miraculous than the feeding of the five thousand), while symbolically it perfectly fits the bill for the opening of his Gospel, with Jesus presented as the new wine of freedom and love emerging out of the old water of the past. Thus it is not implausible to claim that of all Jesus' miracles, this is the one which best expresses his significance, and is thus at one level the most 'true'. Over the course of my two volumes quite a number of other examples have been given. My point here, though, does not hang on the plausibility of specific instances. Rather, what I am seeking to do is challenge the view that because something is wholly unhistorical, it is therefore less significant, or even untrue. On the contrary, like the work of the novelist, such evangelistic invention can act as a way of restructuring our mapping of reality, and thus help show us where true significance lies.

---

[60] For some helpful modern parallels, and the recognition that in the Gospels' case this could involve 'going beyond and even against the available chronicle', N. Wolterstorff, *Divine Discourse* (Cambridge: Cambridge University Press, 1995), 252–60, esp. 259.

[61] Strictly speaking, he is contrasting 'historian' and 'poet'. The latter, he suggests, is concerned with 'a kind of thing that might be': *Poetics* 1451b.

[62] In modern measures, 120 gallons is produced! For the symbolic content of the miracle, D. Brown, *The Word To Set You Free* (London: SPCK, 1995), 128–31.

Truth and experiential insight The second area where the fictional can, it seems to me, make an important contribution to truth is on the issue of moral and experiential insight. I treat this under a different heading for two reasons: first, because here commonly we are concerned with the specificity of particular situations, not with general issues of significance; secondly, because such situations can even be remote from our own concerns and experience, and so not even significant in the narrower sense of personal reference. To give a couple of examples from my own recent reading, I think that I now understand better two contrasting lifestyles, the mind-set of a New York rentboy and that of a London Jewish entrepreneur, but this has been gained wholly from two well crafted novels, not from personal experience or encounter.[63] There is of course a potential danger in reading too widely, in the corruption of the heart, but against that needs to be set the need and desire to understand motivations very different from one's own.[64] A purely externalist perspective can very quickly lead to condemnation; an internalist will not necessarily lead to a different verdict, but at least it will not be based on false assumptions about the logic of that particular lifestyle.

These remarks may suggest that the narrative is only useful when the experience is relatively remote from one's own. That was not my intention. There is a marvellous chapter in *Adam Bede* where George Eliot challenges the view that the role of the novelist is to offer an exalted account of human nature.[65] Instead, she suggests, one of her key purposes is to disclose how 'things may be lovable that are not altogether handsome', and so how we 'should tolerate, pity and love' the 'more or less ugly, stupid, inconsistent people' around us. It is the exalted image, the 'griffin' that is easy to make attractive ('falsehood is so easy, truth so difficult'), but 'that marvellous facility which we mistook for genius is apt to forsake us when we want to draw a real unexaggerated lion'. In one of her letter she observes: 'Freethinkers are scarcely wiser than

---

[63] For the former, M. Merlis, *Pyrrhus* (London: Fourth Estate, 1998); for the latter, J. Rayner, *Day of Atonement* (London: Black Swan, 1998).

[64] For a debate on this issue, K. Walton and M. Tanner, 'Morals in fiction and fictional morality', *Proceedings of the Aristotelian Society,* Supp. 67 (1994), 27–66.

[65] Chapter 17: ' In which the story pauses a little.' For quotations, *Adam Bede* (Edinburgh: Nelson, n. d.), 191–201, esp. 192, 193.

the orthodox in this matter—they all want to see themselves and their opinions held up as the true and the lovely.'[66] That sounds exactly right. Novelists can thus be no less useful in forcing a different perception of those in our immediate context than they are in enabling us to enter imaginatively into the longings and aspirations of those who differ markedly from ourselves. In Chapter 3 I noted the evil consequences of the common human tendency to project evil onto the near-Other. If so, the need for imaginative aid in comprehending those nearest to us may possibly be the greater.

Certainly, there is a natural human temptation to organize one's convictions into some relatively simple code. Fiction can often successfully challenge such longings, and, indeed, may even call into question the very possibility of such an overall pattern.[67] In recent years Martha Nussbaum has been prominent in arguing for the relevance of the novel in helping one choose a particular form of life. The aim of the reader should thus not simply be understanding, but even the possibility of conversion. So, for instance, Henry James' *Ambassadors* is read as indicating the inadequacy of a Kantian ethic as opposed to a more Aristotelian approach.[68] But as she herself admits, some attitudes to life are easier to present sympathetically through story than others.[69] So, while in general she is right about the insights that can be derived in this way, some caution would seem advisable. An attractive character can still be a moral scoundrel.[70] Perhaps a more typical contribution from the novelist in furthering moral perception, therefore, is the way in which he or she, rather than determining a conclusion, can help highlight what is at stake either way. An illustration of this is the

---

[66] Letter to Charles Bray, 5th July 1859: text in J. W. Cross (ed.), *George Eliot's Life* (Edinburgh: William Blackwood, 1885), II, 117–18, esp. 118. She describes one of her principal aims as being to 'enlarge men's sympathies'.

[67] The conclusion which M. Weitz draws from *Anna Karenina* and *The Brothers Karamazov* in 'Truth in literature' in Hospers *Readings*, 213–24, esp. 222.

[68] M. C. Nussbaum, *Love's Knowledge: Essays on Philosophy and Literature* (New York: Oxford University Press, 1990), 168–94. Mrs Newsome is taken to represent the Kantian viewpoint, Strether the alternative.

[69] Ibid., 185: 'No narrative dealing in empirical particulars *could* see Kant's conception in a fully sympathetic way' (her italics).

[70] For example, Long John Silver in *Treasure Island* or Becky Sharp in *Vanity Fair*. One has also to reckon with how difficult it is to portray goodness effectively except in situations of extreme challenge.

manner in which Iris Murdoch has pursued across several novels various possible relations between sexual love and religious vision, now appearing to endorse a Dantean complete transcendence and now a Platonic insistence on continued mediation.[71] In the end we are left to choose, but that does not mean that exploration of the rejected alternative has been a waste of time, any more than reading Proust is only worthwhile if one endorses his basic thesis that love can only lead to unhappiness. One better understands the logic of the position, and indeed how in some ways it is self-fulfilling.

One way of reading Jesus' parables is to see them as Jesus himself endorsing this way of proceeding, though with this difference, that there is often a sting in the resultant perception, not infrequently involving us in some element of self-critique.[72] For example, one discovers oneself as the resentful elder brother in the parable of the prodigal son. A critique is most effective when it is self-made, and this no doubt explains in part Kierkegaard's use not only of story in his philosophy but also of multiple voices. The reader is left in doubt as to who represents Kierkegaard's real view, and so we find ourselves endorsing a position only to find it later being undermined because it is not in fact Kierkegaard's own. No less important than parable is the question of how the gospel narrative as a whole functions. In earlier chapters I have already indicated my belief that the evangelists adapted figures like Mary Magdalene, Peter, and the Beloved Disciple in order to help the reader appropriate the gospel's meaning. Christian readers would naturally identify with the disciples in the story, but to ensure that the gospel is not too easily accommodated to their existing perspective Mark may well have made Peter more obtuse than he really was, and John even invented the Beloved Disciple to set up a different kind of ideal from too narrow a preoccupation with

---

[71] For an analysis in these terms from Nussbaum herself, 'Love and vision: Iris Murdoch on eros and the individual' in M. Antonaccio and W. Schweiker (eds.), *Iris Murdoch and the Search for Human Goodness* (Chicago: University of Chicago Press, 1996), 29–53.

[72] The older view was that the parables had one essential point and were not originally allegorical: J. Jeremias, *The Parables of Jesus* (London: SCM Press, 8th edn, 1970), esp. 66–89. This is now widely challenged: e.g. J. Drury, *The Parables in the Gospels* (London: SPCK, 1985); P. L. Culbertson, *A Word Fitly Spoken* (Albany, NY: SUNY, 1995).

historicity.[73] The result is of course in one sense then false, but in another not so, since the reader emerges chastened and challenged. The insight gained in fact makes possible a new kind of relationship with Christ, and thus a new type of relation with the truth.

Truth and paradigm   The third area where we may see fictional narratives aspiring to truth is in the notion of paradigm. Here the non-Christian equivalent form of story is to be found in the defining character of myth for ancient peoples and civilizations, and indeed not for them alone.[74] Given the New Testament understanding of truth it might have seemed best to have begun here, since it is in this notion that we come closest to the idea of the biblical narrative being the measure of divine reality. But note that the Bible does not itself make this claim but one markedly different, that divine reality is itself the measure against which all other claims should be assessed, including presumably the story or text itself. That is just as well, since there seem to be a choice of possible narrative structures against which Christians might measure themselves. Are we, for example, to take Mark on his own, or as the Church has read him with the interstices filled by the other three evangelists? Or is even that right, since, as earlier chapters illustrated, there is many another covert assumption hidden beneath the Church's way of appropriating the text, from Mary Magdalene as penitent sinner to the shepherds as representative of the poor and the magi as rich kings.[75]

   That is not a conclusive argument against the biblical narrative as unchanging paradigm. It could be answered, for example, by legislating that the final canonical shape should be regarded as definitive. But there are, it seems to me, two decisive objections to any such view. The first is that it all depends on what question we are asking, and in fact each stage of the development of the narrative can be illuminating and helpful. Questions of history require

---

[73] That is, with the Beloved Disciple intended to represent the contemporary disciple as distinct from Peter, symbolic of those who insist too strongly on dependence on past history. The issue is discussed in Ch. 6.

[74] 'Myth' and 'symbol' are difficult terms to apply in modern secular contexts. For a discussion of attempts by Barthes and Ricoeur to do so, cf. my *Continental Philosophy and Modern Theology*, 62–6, 174–84.

[75] For Mary Magdalene, Ch. 1; for shepherds and kings, *Tradition and Imagination*, Ch. 2.

one form of address; the most appropriate interpretation for today perhaps another. Moreover, even where the same issue is to the fore, it is not always the same form of narrative that is most beneficial to each and every one of us. Take the issue of discipleship. Some of us who love problems and issues to be resolved may need most to hear the enigmatic Christ of Mark's account, while others who are naturally inclined to love of paradox and puzzlement would benefit most by hearing the insistence on progress in understanding that starts to echo from his Gospel only once it is contextualized by the other three. Secondly, as we see from science, paradigms only function in relation to a wider field, and in fact change or even collapse as they are adapted to meet that changing field. So, for instance, scientific explanation as mechanistic or uniform has had to be adjusted as random particle behaviour or the 'butterfly effect' has thrown up demands for new ways of viewing the paradigm. Likewise, then, in the religious case. As I argued in Chapter 2, the narrative of Jesus has seldom worked on its own, but either explicitly or implicitly with the help of supplementary stories in which the appropriate form of its application has been tested for circumstances nearer to the believer's own. Whether these subsidiary stories have taken the form of the Lives of saints, novel reading, or a personal exercise of the imagination, the point is that they do not stand on their own but feed back into how the paradigm is itself understood. It in turn thus by no means stands alone. So, while it seems basically correct to talk of the gospel narrative of Jesus as paradigmatic for the Christian, there remains the danger that, unless qualified, this will only disguise the complexity of how its normative truth is in fact appropriated.

Poetry

If we turn now to poetry, many of the issues simply repeat themselves. So, for instance, it is not hard to think of examples where poetry seeks through fictional narrative to highlight the significance of historical events, or where it is intended to interpret the poet's own experience, or where insight is offered into forms of life unfamiliar to the reader.[76] The most obvious difference, apart from

[76] Perhaps even unfamiliar to some degree to the poet himself; so Valéry as quoted in M. Hamburger, *The Truth of Poetry* (London: Anvil Press, 1968), 68–9.

metre, lies in the greater density of simile and metaphor. So it behoves us to consider here how that affects questions of truth.[77] In a rash moment in the course of his multi-volume work *Modern Painters* Ruskin pronounced against metaphors on the grounds that, unlike similes, they asserted what is false, an identity that does not exist. As an objection it has had a surprisingly long history. In his *An Apology for Poetry* Sir Philip Sidney tackles the issue head on, and argues on the contrary for the superiority of poetry to both history and philosophy. The former fails to offer any general truths, while the latter delivers its judgements in a cold style that fails to inspire. By contrast, the poet 'coupleth the general notion with the particular example' into 'a perfect picture' which 'yieldeth to the powers of the mind an image of that whereof the philosopher bestoweth but a wordish description, which doth neither strike, pierce, nor possess the sight of the soul so much as that other doth.'[78] Significantly, Plato is himself placed on the side of the poets because his style is seen as being closer to that of poetry.[79]

In these general judgements Sidney shows himself clearly a child of the Renaissance, which sought to place rhetoric above philosophy as a means of discovering truth.[80] One way of reading the dispute might be to see it as an earlier run of the contention later made by Kierkegaard that truth is subjectivity, that the issue of truth cannot be separated from our relation to, and involvement with, it.[81] But,

---

[77] The appositeness of the comparison may be the most obvious way in which questions of truth are raised: cf. R. Elliott, 'Poetry and truth', *Analysis* 27 (1967), 77–85.

[78] Ed. G. Shepherd, *An Apology for Poetry* (Manchester: Manchester University Press, 1973), 104–7, esp. 107. The *Apology* was first published posthumously in 1595.

[79] 'Though the inside and strength were Philosophy, the skin as it were and beauty depended most on Poetry': ibid., 97. For such considerations applied to the *Phaedo*, M. Warner, *Philosophical Finesse* (Oxford: Clarendon Press, 1989), 67–104.

[80] Shepherd suggests that the real contrast came to be, not between Plato and Gorgias, but between Aristotle and Isocrates: *Apology*, 19–21. For the key role played by rhetoric in the Renaissance, and its degree of continuity with what had gone before, P. O. Kristeller, *Studies in Renaissance Thought and Letters* (Rome: Edizioni di Storia e Letteratura, 1956), 553–83, esp. 561 ff.

[81] What is shared is the stress on engagement, not Kierkegaard's insistence on the impossibility of establishing objective truth. For a helpful discussion of Kierkegaard's views on truth, A. Hannay, *Kierkegaard* (London: Routledge & Kegan Paul, 1982), 122–39.

while that was undoubtedly part of what was under review, there is another dimension, of which note needs to be taken, more relevant to our present discussion. It is the question of whether connections are not disclosed by the use of metaphor and symbolism that might otherwise be concealed by the philosopher's more direct line of argument. One popular Renaissance theme, for example, is the parallels between macrocosm and microcosm, but the general notion goes back much further, and is particularly evident in what has been called 'the symbolist mentality' of the Middle Ages.[82] Not only were numbers, colours, and names held to possess additional meanings, but that potential, it was thought, lay inherent in every object in the world. This meant that, although the images of poetry might appear to offer only the 'shell' of falsehood, in fact at the centre the 'nut' contained the truth itself.[83] Indeed, one way of regarding invented symbols from this period might be to think of them as functioning as a means of opening new avenues of thought, without thereby incurring the censure that almost certainly would have followed, had a more literal approach been adopted.[84]

It is not difficult to determine what general metaphysical underpinning such views might have been given. If the world has indeed been created by God, then it would seem not unreasonable to suppose that everything that comes from the same source must be interconnected, even if these connections are not always immediately apparent. Again, because all things share in the same divine purpose in creating, even if one realm of discourse appears adequately to encapsulate a particular object or idea, it would be wrong to suppose on that basis that other, very different forms of connection are therefore precluded. Metaphorical language is thus of special importance in identifying truth, since it offers not only the possibility of unexpected connections, but also a plurality of possible discourses. That might be one possible way of interpreting the so-called 'conceits' in John Donne's poetry, not as irrelevant

---

[82] M.-D. Chenu, *Nature, Man and Society in the Twelfth Century* (Chicago: University of Chicago Press, 1968), 99–145.

[83] 'Cortex' and 'nucleus' in Alan of Lille's Latin: *De planctu naturae* (PL 210. 451C).

[84] Might, for example, the inclusion , as at Vézelay , of mythological creatures in the procession of those receiving salvation from Christ at the Last Judgement not have been a covert way of challenging the Church's official, very narrow constraints?

digression from their supposed central theme but as recognition of how illumination can in fact come from apparently quite unrelated areas.[85]

That is one reason why it seems to me a mistake to suppose that any except the simplest metaphors can ever be adequately translated into more literal language, so integrally related is their truth content to their density.[86] W. H. Auden once advised his fellow poets:

> Be subtle, various, ornamental, clever,
> And do not listen to those critics ever
> Whose crude provincial gullets crave in books
> Plain cooking made still plainer by plain cooks.[87]

In context the advice is a witty piece of self-mockery. Nonetheless, despite his hilarious examples of so little said by image, the poem ends with the recognition that it is often only 'the luck of verbal playing' that discloses the truth. Elsewhere, he protests against those who see poetry as the imposition of meaning, and instead insists upon its 'gratuitous' character as 'a game of knowledge, a bringing to consciousness' in which 'the poet is the father who begets the poem which the language bears'.[88] Certainly, metaphor has the capacity to disclose hitherto unrealized possibilities. Take such basic Christian images as water and blood. Both immediately open up two quite different realms of discourse: in the case of water, cleansing and refreshment; with blood, the giving up of life and the opposite, its sustaining. Yet no sooner is the attempt made to integrate these two aspects into a single comprehensive and literal discourse than new possibilities begin to emerge. Water, for instance, can also suggest threat and drowning. Although that too can once more be integrated, as in

---

[85] Cf. L. Lerner, *The Truest Poetry* (London: Hamish Hamilton, 1960), 204–18.

[86] For a critique of the assumption that translation necessarily means clarification, and for the identification of some parallel issues in religion and music, D. Fuller, 'Poetry, music and the sacred' in D. Fuller and P. Waugh, *The Arts and Sciences of Criticism* (Oxford: Clarendon Press, 1999), 180–96.

[87] 'The truest poetry is the most feigning' in W. H. Auden, *The Shield of Achilles* (New York: Random House, 1955), 44–6, esp. 44.

[88] W. H. Auden, 'Squares and oblongs' in R. Arnheim et al., *Poets at Work* (New York: Harcourt, Brace & Co., 1948), 163–81, esp. 167, 168, 173.

the parallel for baptism with the Red Sea, where threat and deliverance were also combined, closure still does not occur. One might think, for example, of the implications of water as a basic element, or again of what is suggested by water as 'flowing' or 'living'.

But, if that is to underline the power of metaphor, one must also consider its other side, its seductiveness. The range and potential of some metaphors means that, unlike more literal usage, they can sometimes entice readers, or even poets themselves, along avenues of thought which they would prefer not to travel. Indeed, the use of powerful imagery may even result in writers in effect endorsing attitudes which in their more prosaic moments they would have emphatically rejected.[89] This is an issue that worried T. S. Eliot. One of his essays opens with the recommendation that 'literary criticism should be completed by criticism from a definite ethical and theological standpoint', and he goes on to recommend the consistent application of specifically Christian criteria.[90] Yet, another essay shows the danger in such an approach. Virgil and Dante are taken as his two defining examples of poets, but it is hard to disentangle aesthetic elements in his evaluation from his conception of these two poets as marking key moments in the growth of Christian civilization.[91] Fortunately, despite continuing occasional attempts to identify him with Christianity, it is here that Shakespeare can act as a standing rebuke to any easy assumption that truth and beauty necessarily go close in hand in poetic writing. Auden wisely observed that Keats' famous equation was meant to entail the opposite: the Grecian urn failed to reveal anything of the dark side of life.[92]

That still, though, leaves us with our problem unresolved. For few would want to deny that Shakespeare helps to reveal aspects of truth, even if these remained unintegrated with Christian

---

[89] For an example (of a Puritan poet overwhelmed by eucharistic imagery), D. Brown and D. Fuller, *Signs of Grace* (London: Cassell, 1995), 64–5.

[90] 'Religion and literature' in F. Kermode (ed.), *Selected Prose of T. S. Eliot* (London: Faber & Faber, 1975), 97–106, esp. 97.

[91] 'What is a classic?', ibid., 115–31. Contrast, though, 'Dante', where 'philosophical belief' and 'poetic assent' are carefully distinguished: ibid., 205–30, esp. 221–2.

[92] 'Beauty is truth, truth beauty': *Ode on a Grecian Urn*; W. H. Auden, 'Robert Frost' in *The Dyer's Hand* (London: Faber & Faber, 1963), 337.

orthodoxy.[93] But is the problem any more serious than the partial disclosure of truth in more explicitly religious writing? The despair in some of Hopkins' poems is as absolute as what we find in Psalm 88, but the latter is part of the Christian canon.[94] What this suggests to me is that we need to follow what Eliot urged in theory in respect of the relation between literary and theological criticism rather than what in practice he sometimes allowed to happen to his judgements, with the latter in effect determining the former. That is to say, we need first to permit such insight as a poem offers fully to emerge of its own accord, and only then as a wholly separate exercise consider how such truth as it conveys might be integrated into our religious beliefs. The danger otherwise is that we will either reject the images and ideas contained in the poetry or else make them too easily conform to what we already believe.[95] Resistance to integration also need to be acknowledged. Theologians are very ready to admit the challenge that the Book of Job offers to any attempt to 'solve' the problem of evil, but they are surprisingly resistant to accepting the presence of equally powerful experiential challenges from outside the canon, whether it be Greek tragedy on the capriciousness of the divine, or Romantic poets' hesitancy to label their encounter with the numinous personal.

Because previous chapters have focused on how biblical narratives were changed over the centuries, it is easy to suppose that my remarks on poetry here must be of limited relevance. But any such supposition would be to ignore the extent to which the Old Testament is poetic in form, not just Psalms and Proverbs, but most of Job, much of the prophets, and portions even of the

---

[93] For a sustained critique of Christian analyses of *King Lear:* W. Empson, *The Structure of Complex Words* (London: Chatto & Windus, 1952), 125–57.

[94] Note 'No worst, there is none', 'Thou art indeed just, Lord', and especially 'I wake and feel the fell of dark, not day': W. H. Gardner, *The Poems of Gerard Manley Hopkins* (London: Oxford University Press, 4th edn, 1970), 100, 106–7, 101.

[95] The need for a delicate balance on the part of the poet is well argued by M. H. Abrams, 'Belief and the suspension of disbelief' in Idem (ed.), *Literature and Belief* (New York: Columbia University Press, 1958), 1–30. Dante's success is in part to be explained by the way in which 'he repeatedly misapplies his sympathy', in order first to share our doubts about divine punishment before then attempting to undermine them: 21–4, esp. 23.

Pentateuch. There is thus, it seems to me, a question mark over
the extent to which the Christian tradition has correctly appropriated its poetic heritage. Not only does its metaphorical, as distinct
from doctrinal, character needs to be more fully recognized, also
to be faced is the nature of the text as something from which we
should not necessarily expect any immediate integration into our
religious perceptions as a whole. A number of writers suggest that
poetry is most like painting, and so concerned with the presentation of images rather than any overall account of where truth
lies.[96] The comment may be more applicable to some forms of
poetry than others. How far painting itself is essentially a matter of
images is the final issue to which we turn in this section.

Visual arts

Painting as narrative is where I want to end, but I shall begin with
the more familiar context of the visual work of artists as images.
Revelation, I have maintained, continued to be communicated
throughout the history of the Church by means of fresh narratives
and new images. Since many of the latter were in the most obvious historical sense not 'true', the question that forces itself upon
us at this point is how then they can defended as contributing parts
of a continuing revelation. I shall begin by using some modern
secular examples to illustrate how truth in art need not be closely
tied to historical fact. Thereafter I shall note the way in which
symbolic indicators within a painting can pull in competing directions, and the importance of distinguishing the different kinds of
question that can be addressed to a painting. My contention will
be that the visual arts need to be granted their own distinctive
integrity, and so questions of truth must not be immediately fused
into those of beauty or of theology. Only then will the meditative
or revelatory character of art be allowed full play, and thus the
non-idolatrous way in which it points beyond itself be disclosed.
That way the power of narrative painting to initiate and develop
new ways of perceiving the Christian inheritance will be better
understood.

I begin then with some modern secular examples, to illustrate

---

[96] 'A speaking picture': Sidney, 101. Cf. Horace, 'ut pictura, poesis' *Ars
Poetica*, 361.

how complex the relation between what appears on the canvas and correspondence with reality can sometimes be. The history of the official commissioning of war paintings in Britain goes back to the First World War. Paul Nash, Stanley Spencer, and John Singer Sargent were among those who so acted in that war, while during the Second World War there were about forty artists, including Graham Sutherland. However, here I wish to focus on two more recent painters, John Keane and Peter Howson, the former so acting in the Gulf War and the latter in the Bosnian conflict.

Keane gained some initial experience of war through working in Northern Ireland during 1989–90. His initial reaction was that 'I had no fixed sympathies. I was baffled and wanted to get underneath it.'[97] Lack of religious commitment was, he held, an advantage, since it allowed him greater impartiality and objectivity, and his verdict was a world of entrenched positions, well captured by what is perhaps his best known painting from this period, *Other Cheek*. This shows no one turning the other cheek, but instead each of the three parties to the conflict (Republican, Unionist, and the British Army) in separate sections of the canvas, and each either looking out at us or in the opposite direction rather than towards one another. Keane's confidence in what he saw as a realistic approach, with a heavy reliance on photographs, was, however, to receive a serious shock when he accepted a commission from the Imperial War Museum to be its official artist for the Gulf War in 1991–2. His *Mickey Mouse at the Front* was reproduced and attacked by an editorial in Britain's best-selling daily newspaper, where the presence of excrement beneath the figure of Mickey Mouse was taken as a commentary on the attitude of the United States and its allies to the native population. In fact, his intention had been quite otherwise, to refer to the use by the invading Iraqis of an amusement arcade as a latrine.[98] That was a case of depiction of reality being turned by viewers into a symbol of its apparent opposite. In that same war Keane also experienced the reverse, with an intended symbol turned into 'fact'. In *Looking for Evidence*, in the course of portraying the Nayef Palace which the

---

[97] M. Lawson, *John Keane: Conflicts of Interest* (Edinburgh: Mainstream, 1995), 45.

[98] Ibid., 69 (illus., 70). The newspaper in question was the *Sun*, 15th January 1992.

Iraqis had used to interrogate prisoners, accustomed as he was to using photographs rather than initial sketches, Keane decided to place an anonymous photograph among the debris to symbolize the uncertain fate of those who entered the building. Suspiciously, however, within a couple of days a journalist has turned the anonymous photograph into a story of rape and torture for one of the Sunday newspapers.[99] To his bitter cost he had thus discovered that the relation between truth and reality is more complex than that offered by any simple adherence to strict representation as our guide.

Peter Howson's approach to art is quite different, but his experience in the Bosnian War may be used to illustrate how even those who start from symbol rather than representation must in the end face the same kind of issue, the complexity of the relation between any truth conveyed by painting and the nature of reality. In 1994 a lively debate took place as to which of his paintings best represented the war. The Imperial War Museum as the commissioning body was entitled to select at least one painting for its future ownership. *Cleansed* was chosen, but a minority preferred *Croatian and Muslim*, a depiction of a brutal rape that was eventually bought by David Bowie. In defending the choice of the committee, Alan Borg, Director of the Imperial War Museum, pointed out that no such scene had been personally witnessed by the artist.[100] The justification contrasts interestingly with the decision of the Tate to buy *Plum Grove*, for it too portrayed an incident not witnessed by the artist—children playing round a corpse that had been castrated.[101] Yet there is little doubt that both types of incident did take place during the war, and that, though Howson saw neither, he did hear tales of such atrocities and witnessed some of their effects, such as the blank faces of the children shown in *Plum Grove*. So one question raised is whether the less literal, symbolic approach did not in fact express a deeper estimate of the war than the more anodyne *Cleansed*, a simple portrayal of refugees. Indeed, the claim could still be maintained even if no rapes or castration had taken place, since,

[99] A. Weight, *John Keane: Gulf* (London: Imperial War Museum, 1992), 17, 24; illus. 5.

[100] For the history and illustrations of both paintings, A. Jackson, *A Different Man: Peter Howson's Art from Bosnia and Beyond* (Edinburgh: Mainstream, 1997), 70–3. [101] Illus., ibid., 78.

incontestably, the rape of a people was what was occurring. Although there is no explicit religious message in these paintings, it is also fascinating to observe that it was this war that brought Howson to acknowledgement of a wider symbolic reality, in a return to the Baptist faith of his youth.[102]

The conclusion I draw from this recent history is that representative realism is not necessarily the best way of conveying truth, and that an historically false symbol can indeed sometimes offer a more accurate assessment of our world. Some may wish to place on the other side of such a debate the contention that paintings cannot of themselves assert anything at all since they involve no statements in words or language, and that everything is dependent on how the viewer chooses to receive the work. But this is not quite true. Language itself is only a system of signs that also has no meaning outside a given social context. So, while the symbolism in painting may differ, the problems do not. Like authors, artists work within contexts, and so there remains a limited range of acceptable interpretation that can be given to their works, just as attaching modern meanings to words that bore a different sense in the period in which a particular text was written cannot be justified, unless due acknowledgement is first made. Indeed, painters may be at an advantage since it is often claimed that some of the signs they use are, unlike words, not arbitrary in their associations.

So, for instance, much of Kandinsky's work is premised on the assumption that colours in themselves bear meanings. Yellow, he suggests, has 'an insistent, aggressive character', while 'the ultimate feeling' that blue creates 'is one of rest'. He also maintains some colours are more naturally allied with some forms rather than others: 'on the whole, keen colours are well suited by sharp forms (e.g. a yellow triangle), and soft, deep colours by round forms (e.g. a blue circle).'[103] At the most basic, it has been observed that it can be no accident that human beings speak of 'a bright hope', since as 'a phototropic creature' we seek the light.[104] Since at least the

---

[102] For his own comments, ibid., 112; for a rare religious allusion, *Ustazi* (with three crucifixions), ibid., 74.

[103] W. Kandinsky, *Concerning the Spiritual in Art* (New York: Dover, 1977), 27–45, esp. 37–8, 29.

[104] 'If the termites had a language they would have to speak of "dark joy", of a "gloomy hope", and of "night descending on their antennae", for they shun the light': E. H. Gombrich, *Topics of our Time* (London: Phaidon, 1991), 44.

time of Goethe research has been taking place into the phenomenon known as synaesthesia, the habit of our minds regularly to
connect the same phenomena across different kinds of discourse,
including vision and sound. Not only has much empirical
evidence been accumulated, the phenomenon may also help
explain the effectiveness of metaphor.[105] So convinced was
Kandinsky of such underlying currents of meaning that he was
normally reluctant to provide any clues to meaning in the titles of
his paintings. Certainly, titles can sometimes function as the lazy
person's option, or even exclude possibilities that might otherwise
have been present.[106] So we must never think that the use of
language, as in a title, is necessarily the best route towards comprehending the truth in a painting. Equally, though, they can sometimes help our focus, even in controversial cases such as Marcel
Duchamp's *Fontaine*, his notorious exhibit of a urinal, signed and
dated 'R. Mutt, 1917'. The date, cartoon-character signature and
title all combine to speak of the terrible tragedies of Passchendaele
and Ypres that took place in 1917 and the possibility that it was the
culture that built impressive fountains such as those at Versailles
which brought them about.[107]

Some may be tempted to deny the relevance of someone like
Duchamp to our topic, and indeed the artist himself in some of his
moods described his work as 'anti-art'. But there are at least two
important factors to be considered on the other side. The first is
that the artefact has clearly been given a symbolic value, and, while
this is not sufficient to make it art, it clearly brings it close to such
a conception. A flag is not a work of art; a design for a flag is.
Secondly, and more importantly, irrespective of whether we want
to declare *Fontaine* a work of art or not, as I have tried to indicate,
it does bear a truth value in a way an ordinary urinal would not.
In short, the danger is that we confuse questions of truth with

---

[105] For discussion of some of the empirical data, and an attempt to identify the
aesthetic criterion of 'fittingness' with such 'cross-modal similarity', cf. N
Wolterstorff, *Art in Action* (Grand Rapids, Michigan: Eerdmans, 1980), 96–121.

[106] Gombrich observes that Klee's *In Angel's Keeping* is by its very title transformed from something potentially 'demonic and uncanny' to what is seen as
'protective and reassuring': *Topics*, 180.

[107] For a more detailed commentary, together with some helpful comments
on similar problematic works by Josef Beuys and the composer, John Cage: C.
Lyas, *Aesthetics* (London: UCL Press, 1997), 105–9.

other considerations. Defining a work of art, identifying the criteria that might make it a great work of art, asking what might allow
us to call it 'beautiful', and the question that concerns us here, that
of truth, seem to me four quite distinct, though interrelated, issues.
The temptation on the part of theologians has been to fuse too
quickly each of these elements into one. Thus, for example, in
both Augustine and Aquinas there had been the desire to see art as
a reflection of the divine order,[108] and this is a trend that has
continued into the twentieth century in some of the most influential attempts among Reformed theologians to establish a more
positive appreciation of the arts within their own tradition.[109]
Even in someone like James Joyce we find a continuing desire to
assert the fundamental identity of truth and beauty in ordered relationships,[110] but the recognition of disorder can surely also be a
form of truth. If that points to one of the strengths of Balthasar's
aesthetics, his insistence on speaking of the crucifixion as a form of
beauty raises once more the issue of too easy an integration of
opposed facets of reality.[111] It is as though theology is being
allowed to determine what is beautiful, bereft of any independent
criteria of assessment. Yet, precisely the factors that might make us
prepared to speak of beauty in some painted crucifixions are likely
to make us hesitate in respect of a painting like Grünewald's

---

[108] For Augustine, R. J. O'Connell, *Art and the Christian Intelligence in
Augustine* (Oxford: Blackwell, 1978); C. Harrison, *Beauty and Revelation in the
Thought of Saint Augustine* (Oxford: Clarendon Press, 1992). For Aquinas, U. Eco,
The Aesthetics of Thomas Aquinas (Cambridge, Mass.: Harvard University Press,
1988), esp. 64–121. Aquinas' three criteria for beauty, *integritas, proportio*, and *clar-
itas* are actually introduced in the context of his discussion of the perfection and
beauty of God the Son (*Summa Theologiae* 1a, 39, 8c).

[109] For a helpful introduction, J. S. Begbie, *Voicing Creation's Praise*
(Edinburgh: T & T Clark, 1991), 81–163. The stress on harmony is particularly
marked in Dooyeweerd.

[110] 'The true and the beautiful are akin. Truth is beheld by the intellect which
is appeased by the most satisfying relations of the intelligible; beauty is beheld by
the imagination which is appeased by the most satisfying relations of the sensible.': *A Portrait of the Artist as a Young Man* (London: Paladin, 1988), 212. The
influence of Aquinas is marked, with a good exposition of Aquinas' views offered
a few pages later: 216–17. For further elucidation, E. Mason and R. Ellmann
(ed.), *The Critical Writings of James Joyce* (New York: Viking Press, 1959), 141–8.

[111] E.g. *The Glory of the Lord* (Edinburgh: T & T Clark, 1982), I, 124.
Augustine, more weakly, speaks of the deformity of the cross making us beautiful: *Sermons* 27.6 (*PL* 38.181).

Isenheim altarpiece.[112] That does not make it any less a great work of art, nor its assertions untrue, but it does explain why we might recoil from too extended a gaze.

What seems most required of us is that we allow the work of art to function first in its own right. That does not mean abstracting all background information. The human eye in any case cannot avoid imposing patterns of meaning, as in the way in which we automatically supply what we think should be there, for example, a glow for reflecting water, even where the artist has used matt paint. But some types of additional information are more immediately pertinent than others. It is the grand theories that, initially at least, need most to be avoided. Instead, I suggest that the same policy should be pursued as I urged elsewhere in respect of our initial approach to the meaning of Scripture: that the work of art should first be placed, so far as possible, in its own historical integrity, and only then, if it is thought appropriate, be measured against some wider alternative backdrop.[113]

Perhaps some examples might help. Titian's *Venus of Urbino* and Gainsborough's *Mr and Mrs Andrews* are two relatively straightforward paintings which assert, in the one case the beauty of the woman concerned, and in other the pride of the family in their land. It remains a further, separate question whether we then follow someone like John Berger in seeing such paintings as making us complicit, on the one hand, in woman as sexual object and, on the other, in the rightness of a particular economic order. If so, that might lead us to welcome Manet's revision of the woman's gaze in his *Olympia*, or Adriaen Brouwer's realistic depictions of poverty, as offering a way to a more satisfactory overall view.[114] It is not that our earlier estimate was 'untrue', but

---

[112] One might contrast Grünewald's crucifixion with a painting like that by Fra Angelico: C. Lloyd, *Fra Angelico* (London: Phaidon, 2nd edn, 1992), no. 48. Not only is the suffering restrained, there are also various attempts at balance and harmony, including the skull at the foot of the cross nicely balanced at its apex by a tree of life, with a pelican perched on its branches, suggestive of the transformation that the cross can bring.

[113] This point is well made against Tillich's treatment of Giotto and Mark Taylor's of van Eyck's *Rolin Madonna* in J. Dillenberger, *A Theology of Artistic Sensibilities* (London: SCM Press, 1987), 221–4.

[114] J. Berger, *Ways of Seeing* (Harmondsworth: Penguin, 1972), 46–64, 83–112.

that Manet reveals through his subject's challenging gaze her independent reality, just as Brouwer discloses the other side of prosperity, in its purchase at others' expense. Equally, then,
Grünewald's painting needs first to be assessed as an assertion about
God's identification with us in suffering before any thought is
given to what it might say, for example, about atonement, far less
about God's beauty.[115]

Inevitably, of course, some paintings will better repay extended
attention than others, and it is here in their role as dense symbols
that the parallel with metaphor is perhaps closest. That is not to
say that they are simply equivalent. Metaphors sometimes make
sense visually, and sometimes not.[116] Equally, visual symbols do
not necessarily translate well as metaphors.[117] Rather, what I am
suggesting is that symbolic elements in paintings are perhaps most
usefully seen as the analogue of metaphors in the written
language, and so to be treated with similar consideration when
the question of truth arises. We would not dream of claiming a
complete assessment of some passage of prose without some
attempt at decoding its metaphorical elements, and yet works of
a painter like Raphael are commonly assessed entirely in terms of
the quality of his figurative portrayals without regard to the
symbolic elements often lurking just beneath the surface.
Triangular structures, for instance, are not incidental to the meaning of his Nativities.[118] Again, to understand why in the Sistine
Chapel Michelangelo gave the flayed skin of Bartholomew his
own face, it is not sufficient to talk of personal unhappiness.
Indeed, it is downright misleading, since Renaissance Platonism

[115] For some remarks on the painting's significance, *Tradition and Imagination*,
351–2.
[116] A much quoted example of the latter is Milton's 'blind mouths': *Lycidas*
119.
[117] For a helpful discussion, A. Harrison, *Philosophy and the Arts* (Bristol:
Thoemmes, 1997), 103–47. He suggests that Picasso's distorted faces offer a new
visual metaphor for grief that only really makes sense in its own medium: 145–7.
[118] For triangular symbolism, e.g. *The Canigiani Holy Family*, *The Virgin in the
Meadow* and *The Madonna of the Goldfinch* (the bird is of course also symbolic),
where not only the security of the group is implied, but also the underlying
support of a trinitarian God.

assumed a happy implication, and used the symbol as a sign of a soul purged through pain to new life.[119]

My two examples may suggest rummaging about in reference books, but, though that may now be necessary for most of us, that is not my point. Viewers reflecting on canvas and wall at the time would not have taken long to make the appropriate inferences, for the clues were already present within their existing culture, just as today we sometimes need learned commentaries to explicate biblical metaphors whose meaning would once have taken only a little effort to comprehend.[120] Even small alterations, though, in our perceptual field through such metaphors and symbols can work to produce major changes in our consciousness. Browning notes:

> we're made so that we love
> First when we see them painted, things we have passed
> Perhaps a hundred times nor cared to see;
> And so they are better, painted—better to us,
> Which is the same thing. Art was given for that.[121]

So, reflection on Michelangelo's Bartholomew and its implicit allusion to the Marsyas myth can lead us to see discipleship in a new light, not merely as a call to suffer on behalf of others but equally as a demand for costly, internal transformation. Again, paintings of the Trinity are often criticized for allowing too much stress to fall on the distinctiveness of the three persons, but further reflection can often discloses symbolic indicators of mutual

---

[119] Largely through connecting the image of Bartholomew's martyrdom with the classical legend of Marsyas: the story of Marsyas being flayed alive on the orders of Apollo was read as a symbol of the need for costly purgation of earthly desires in order to achieve identification with God. In Titian's version an ethereal, almost vanishing background leaves us with the distinct impression that Marsyas is in the process of being sucked into another world. His Spanish follower Ribera seems to have painted Marsyas and Bartholomew with equal frequency. The image has even survived into the twentieth century in Iris Murdoch's *Black Prince*, and this is reflected in her portrait in the National Portrait Gallery.

[120] E.g. 'Put thou my tears in thy bottle' (Ps. 56: 8 RSV); a metaphor for divine action drawn from actual mourning practice in Palestine and Egypt, where tears were collected in glass bottles as part of the ritual.

[121] From *Fra Lippo Lippi*, 300–4, in I. Jack (ed.), *Browning: Poetical Works 1833–64* (London: Oxford University Press, 1970), 576.

indwelling that suggest a quite different agenda.[122] If I may give a personal example, a painting of Christ's baptism by Giovanni Bellini had for long puzzled me.[123] It had the usual pattern of the Father looking down from heaven, with the dove winging its way to the Son being baptized. Three angels stood by assisting with his clothes, but puzzling was the presence of a parrot at the front of the frame. Despite showing the slide on a number of occasions, the best explanation that was ever offered was that it must be emblematic of the person who commissioned the painting. Then suddenly one day the light dawned, and I saw the point. The colours of the parrot reflect those of the Father and of Christ's clothes as held by the angels, and so what Bellini has done is provide us with, as it were, a substitute dove, where the mixture of his colours too can be allowed to complement those of the other two persons.

Bellini's freedom with dove as symbol, I think, well indicates that art brings the temptation to idolatry not when its symbols are taken seriously, but when they are not taken seriously enough. Idolaters, as it were, stop too soon, and thus fail to allow the work of transformation to occur in their consciousness. The medieval church was particularly worried by the openness of statuary to idolatrous abuse.[124] This was not merely because it looked real, but because if it stood in isolation from other artefacts there was nothing to draw the eye and mind beyond its immediate context. So it would seem not altogether implausible to suggest that idolatry is the product of a poor imagination, rather than of imagination being allowed to roam free and untrammelled.

That also indicates why narrative painting has potential advantages over its linguistic equivalent. In the latter the writer has already done most of the work, whereas the artist appears to offer only one small temporal segment, and then leaves the rest up to

---

[122] There are also numerous indicators of invitations to deepen discipleship. For a discussion, cf. D. Brown, 'The Trinity in art' in S. Davis, D. Kendall and G. O'Collins (ed.), *The Trinity* (Oxford: Oxford University Press, 1999), 329–56.

[123] In the Garzadori Chapel, Santa Corona, Vicenza; illustrated in R. Goffen, *Giovanni Bellini* (New Haven: Yale University Press, 1989), 164.

[124] Two responses in the later Middle Ages were the promotion of monochrome over polychrome and their incorporation into carved altarpieces: B. Decker, 'Reform within the cult image: the German winged altarpiece before the Reformation' in P. Humfrey & M. Kemp (ed.), *The Altarpiece in the Renaissance* (Cambridge: Cambridge University Press, 1990), 90–105.

us. Initially, that might tempt one to say that only a reminder of a narrative is offered, rather than a narrative in itself, but that must be judged unfair, since commonly there are prompts within the canvas that require us to embark upon just such a narrative. A woman reading a letter in a Vermeer painting, for example, invites us to reflect upon both its source and her reaction. Others draw us into the narrative more directly. In Titian's *Bacchus and Ariadne*, for example, Bacchus' inviting arc in the air is counterpoised by one of Ariandne's own which, while it matches that of Bacchus, also points to her past with Theseus' ship in the distance. The strong sense of movement thus almost forces us to engage with one possible version of the story.[125] Paintings of religious narratives often go one stage further, in the scene being placed at such an angle to compel some sense of personal presence, and so, when narrative is involved, the effect is to make the viewer one of the participants in the story.[126] Historically, this could not of course be the case, but it opens up an alternative way of assessing the truth of the narrative: its significance for the present. But there could be a price for that engagement. Julia Kristeva has suggested that it was essential for Giotto to break his narrative sequences if any serious possibility of the transcendent was to be indicated.[127] Whether that is so or not in the particular case, what we may note is how frequently even a single narrative painting succeeds in breaking the earthly, temporal mode simply by its position in the context of an altar, since frequently the setting in and of itself implies a strong vertical thrust.[128] In assessing the truth claims made by a painting it is thus sometimes important to consider its intended setting no less than the canvas itself. Religious narrative painting has thus in some ways greater revelatory potential than its linguistic equivalents. Not only is the narrative more open in terms of how its story may be told, but

[125] For a helpful analysis of the painting (in the National Gallery, London) by a professional artist, M. James, *Engaging Images* (London: Menard Press, 1992), 39–48.
[126] Very effectively argued in J. Shearman, *Only Connect* (Princeton, N. J.: Princeton University Press, 1992).
[127] J. Kristeva, 'Giotto's joy' in idem, *Desire in Language* (Oxford: Blackwell, 1980), 210–36, esp. 213–15.
[128] Stressed in D. Rosand, ' "Divinità di cosa dipinta": pictorial structure and the legibility of the altarpiece' in Humfrey and Kemp, *Altarpiece*, 143–64.

also both the external and the internal presentation of the painting can themselves invite the participation of the viewer and so
compel a more contemporary version of what may have
happened and its significance.[129]

The visual arts, then, no less than imaginative writing, can be
seen as laying claims to truth. Earlier chapters noted some of the
ways in which such claims might also be said to be innovative. In
the course of defending these innovations, various criteria were
implicitly employed. It is fitting, therefore, that we should
conclude this chapter on truth by attempting to identify these
criteria more formally. First, however, I want to set an appropriate context by once more returning to Pilate and his question.

Criteria and creative tradition

Pilate, history and change

Bacon speaks of a 'jesting Pilate', and thus of a government official indifferent to Jesus' fate. There are no shortage of historians
who would agree,[130] and indeed such external evidence as there is
regarding his character would seem amply to confirm such an
hypothesis.[131] Yet, there is also something to be said on the other
side. That is not in general how the Gospels present him,[132] and
in particular Bacon constitutes a travesty of John's intentions, since
that evangelist in particular takes great pains to underline various
actions of Pilate that were intended to extricate Jesus from the final
penalty. A common response is that all this amounts to is indication of increasing alienation from Judaism, combined with the

---

[129] 'External' in the sense of where and how the painting is hung; 'internal',
in the sense of the angle of vision set by the painter by which he tries to draw us
within the frame, or the gaze of some of the participants designed to effect the
same purpose.

[130] But for an attempt to rehabilitate Pilate's reputation, S. G. F. Brandon,
'Pontius Pilate in history and legend', *History Today* 18 (1968), 523–30.

[131] Philo, *Legatio ad Gaium* 38; Josephus, *Antiquities*, 18.3–4; *Jewish War*, 2.8 ff.
For a discussion, E. Schürer, *History of the Jewish People in the Age of Jesus Christ*
(Edinburgh: T & T Clark, 1973), I, 357–62.

[132] Mark's Pilate displays the least reluctance to sentence Jesus, but even Mark
shows Pilate attempting to have Jesus released: Mark 15: 6–15. Contrast Matt. 27:
19 and 24–5; Luke 23: 4, 14 and 22.

desire not to antagonize the Roman authorities, but even with a callous tyrant it is of course not impossible that dismissal of the charges would in any case have been the line of thought he chose to pursue.[133] For he might well have deemed Jesus a harmless idiot or, alternatively, much less dangerous to release than Barabbas. My point is not that this must be the case, but rather that we need to be on our guard against supposing that historical truth is a relatively simple matter compared to the complexities of the types of truth which we considered in the previous section. Nor is the danger of bias necessarily removed with the passage of time.[134] The wish of present-day Christians to dissociate themselves from the dreadful wrongs done to Jews over the centuries makes the desire to extricate them from any hand in the death of the faith's founder natural,[135] but the very location of that death would also appear to make some involvement in that death likely. Again, it is noticeable how easily fresh modern distortions are created, with Arabs now villains in the place of Jews.[136]

So, when we turn to consider imaginative developments in the story beyond Scripture, we should not think that we are moving to a quite different world. At the beginning of this chapter I tried to make clear how John was concerned with a notion of truth that is wider than the narrowly historical and that it is only in these terms that his construction of this fictional dialogue between Jesus and Pilate can properly be understood. Numerous illustrations of similar practices in later church history have been considered in

---

[133] For this line of thought, R. Brown, *The Gospel according to John XIII–XXI* (New York: Doubleday, 1970), 860.

[134] Although presented as historical analysis, the notion of a joint plot by Sejanus and Pilate to provoke the Jews to rebellion and subsequent destruction would now generally be seen as more symptomatic of a world conditioned by fears of Nazism. For the view, e.g. E. Stauffer's influential *Christ and the Caesars* (German, 1948; London: SCM Press, 1955), esp. 118–20.

[135] Although he claims to offer us an historical investigation in his attempt to restore the reputation of Judas, Klassen's repeated references to anti-Semitism likewise suggest a different agenda: W. Klassen, *Judas: Betrayer or Friend of Jesus* (London: SCM Press, 1996). This is not to deny the justice of some aspects of his critique; cf. e. g . his remarks on Barth, 182–91, esp. 190–1.

[136] E.g. Nicholas Ray's film *King of Kings* (1961) introduces Herod thus: 'But Caesar could find no Jew to press Rome's law . . . so Caesar named one Herod the Great, an Arab of the Bedouin tribe, as the new, false and maleficent King of the Jews.'

earlier chapters. With some, I have offered enthusiastic endorsement; with others, I expressed caution, or even rejected them outright. To make such distinctions criteria are clearly necessary, and, though various have been applied, as our discussion draws to its conclusion it is important that these should now be made fully explicit. But before doing so, let me briefly illustrate some of the issues once more by considering what happened in the specific case of Pilate. A galloping tradition of increasing exoneration can be detected that culminates in him being declared a saint in the Coptic and Ethiopian churches.[137] More widely within Eastern Christianity, this is applied only to his wife, but, as in the Western tradition, there are no shortage of legends of subsequent contrition and conversion. Precisely because the developments are so often read in purely negative terms it is a good example to take. My own view is that depending on the precise version of later developments very different evaluations become possible.

Admittedly, a brief reference like Tertullian's might well make one believe that all that is at stake is that imperial Rome should be brought on side,[138] but it is in fact possible to detect a richer strain of intention and meaning, and one which argues for alignment with a more religiously motivated and more deeply grounded trajectory. For there can be little doubt that, especially once Christianity became the official religion of the empire but even before then, Pilate's story is adjusted and expanded in order that he may elicit an appropriate response from the reader. In other words, the intention is to interrogate the reader, especially those endowed with power, as to the appropriate exercise of that power.[139] That, though, does not mean that the development is an altogether happy one. On the contrary, it is often profoundly flawed. For later writers in general fail to accept the tension, and so either Pilate is made entirely the victim of circumstance or else his guilt is not integrated into a new vision of forgiveness. On the

[137] In the Coptic church his feast day is the 25th of June; in the Ethiopian, the 25th day of their month of *sané*.
[138] *Apology*, 21. Pilate is described as already secretly a Christian: 'ipse iam pro sua conscientia Christianus'.
[139] A process that continues into the twentieth century, as in Mikhail Bulgakov's moving portrayal of a Pilate flawed by moral cowardice against the backdrop of Stalin's Russia: *The Master and Margarita* (1938; London: Fontana, 1969), esp. chs. 25–6.

latter score, particularly disappointing is Gerard Manley Hopkins' unfinished poem 'Pilate'.[140] Pilate simply becomes another Judas, though with his suicide much delayed.

More satisfactory are those versions that make some kind of real contrast between Pilate at Jesus' trial and his subsequent life and so speak of the possibility of transformation. One way of involving the reader can be seen in the instantaneous reaction evinced in the words credited to the centurion at the foot of the cross.[141] Luke's account that speaks of him simply declaring Jesus a good or innocent man seems intrinsically more probable, if only because the Jewish meaning of 'Son of God' would not have come naturally to a Gentile, while its pagan significance is far removed from what the Gospel writers hope to convey. The sentence is thus surely there in Mark and Matthew, not primarily to record history, but rather to shock us as readers into a proper perception of the strangeness and paradox of divine involvement in such a scene. Ironically, modern translations which make the centurion speak of '*a* son of God' rob the passage of much of its immediate impact, even while they render it historically more plausible.[142]

But precisely because conversion is not always immediate, that is why the more ambiguous Pilate of the Gospels can also function as a figure of engagement. He can reflect our own inner uncertainties, as also the complexities and ambiguities involved in the exercise of power, both human and divine. The refusal of the biblical narratives to present Pilate in exclusively black or white terms allows readers who themselves exercise power to feel that the complexities of their situation have thereby been acknowledged, while at the same time deeper appropriation of the issues is encouraged as they discover the contrast with the use to which the divine power is put in the situation. That to me explains the great success of the narratives as they are, whether or not Pilate is accurately portrayed. But something can also be said in favour of post-biblical developments, particularly where those initial ambiguities have also been accepted. For, if those versions which

---

[140] For the text, Gardner, Poems, 116–19.

[141] 'Truly this man was the Son of God' (AV): Mark 15: 39; Matt 27: 54. 'Certainly this was a righteous man': Luke 23: 47.

[142] The Greek allows either translation, but RSV and NEB are among those which opt for 'a son'.

whitewash Pilate's conduct or at the other extreme make him end in suicide produce merely a cardboard character, other accounts which speak of a later conversion from conduct now judged wrong can be seen to function in an way analogous to the centurion at the foot of the cross. But, whereas the latter's conversion was instantaneous, Pilate's would speak of the gradual change that is perhaps more typical of human nature. More importantly, it would also provide acknowledgement within Christ's story that divine forgiveness is after all available even for the most heinous of crimes. It would thus counter the limitations of the biblical narrative, in suggesting that the fate that met Judas is not after all the only possibility even for those deeply implicated in Christ's own death. Christ's words from the cross, 'Father, forgive them for they know not what they do', would thus be given clear priority in the final version of the narrative over the Gospels' view of Judas.[143] One Ethiopian poem even declares of Pilate: 'By thy repentance thou wert equal to the repentance of Peter.'[144]

What these brief comments are intended to indicate is my view that, because the same kind of literary techniques are employed both in the Bible and beyond, there can be no automatic assumption that the palm should always be accorded to the scriptural version of tradition. Later imaginative rewriting sometimes shares the same non-historical objectives as the biblical writers had, and so can legitimately be assessed on the same basis. Sometimes too distance allowed an implication of the gospel to be more clearly seen. So we must not automatically jump to the conclusion that the biblical narrative should always be pronounced best, whether we are thinking of historical or of more theological issues. All will depend on the questions with which we choose to approach the competing narratives. Often it will be the biblical narrative that will turn out to be the most significant, but dogmatically to assert this always to be so would be to ignore the sometimes conflicting

---

[143] The synoptics declare that 'it would be better for that man if he had never been born:' Mark 14: 21 (NEB); cf. Matt. 26: 24; Luke 22: 22. John's verdict is, if anything, even more negative, since it suggests the complete invasion by evil of Judas' soul: 'Satan entered into him' (13: 27 AV).

[144] Though sadly coupled with continuing condemnation of the Jews. For the complete poem, together with a brief outline of Ethiopian traditions, E. Cerulli, 'Tiberius and Pontius Pilate in Ethiopian tradition and poetry', *Proceedings of the British Academy* 59 (1973), 141–58.

trajectories that emerge from the existing text as a whole. In determining which should prevail I am conscious, though, that throughout both volumes I have allowed the criteria I am using to emerge implicitly. I want therefore to end with that issue addressed more directly.

Criteria and revelatory truth

No doubt some readers will be reluctant to arbitrate in this way. It will be seen as presumptuous, with human beings daring to judge the actions of God, and thoroughly disrespectful of the power of divine revelation to challenge each and every age. But what I see happening in such comparative judgements is not the triumph of human judgement but the Church fully acknowledging that revelation needs to be heard in new ways in new social and cultural contexts. Just as the incarnation was a real accommodation to the situation of first-century Palestine, so the way in which narrative, image, and doctrine are heard in our own day must take full account of how God has spoken to his Church in the intervening two thousand years. What I shall do is describe nine types of criteria which I have in effect been applying. More often than not, more than one has been in use at any one time. As befits the project as a whole, I shall conclude with the more imaginative.

It is worth noting at the outset that the criteria are intended to apply no less to priorities within the scriptural text as to modifications made subsequently. It is all too easy to pretend that questions of criteria only become difficult or problematic once we step beyond the canon, but in actual fact all Christians, however conservative their stance, not only frequently allow the teaching of one biblical text to determine the revelatory status of another, but also, either explicitly or covertly, apply criteria drawn from their wider experience and knowledge. It would be comforting were we able to say which criteria should always take priority, but unfortunately matters seem more complex than that. Indeed, even what is meant by some of the criteria can itself be affected by religious belief. So, for example, I have already indicated earlier in this chapter the way in which the relevance of historical issues cannot always be divorced from wider conceptual frames. That example, together with others to follow, will illustrate well why I want to locate myself on both sides at once, as it were, of the modernist–postmodernist debate. It also emphases, I hope, for the reader that, though the earlier criteria may sound purely external to the scriptural text, that is not how they are intended to function. It is a matter of interaction between text and new cultural context: fresh insights can arise from one side or the other or through the interaction itself that necessitate a re-ordering of existing biblical trajectories.

Historical criteria   To mention these at all might seem to some to make me unqualifiedly modernist in my approach. It is certainly true that I want to defend the continued usefulness of biblical criticism in its more conventional forms, but that is only because I wish to give it the first and not the final say. There are two key respects in which history continues to be relevant.

The first concerns the importance of locating how the text has in fact functioned both in relation to its point of origin, and with every significant new application. Where historical claims are made in the text, attempting to check their conformity with the facts will be part of this exercise, but by no means necessarily the most significant task, for loss of historicity carries no automatic implications for loss of revelatory value. To give what I presume is an uncontroversial example, the book of Jonah has for most of the past two millennia been regarded as historical, but the modern Church's abandonment of any such claim has done nothing to reduce the effectiveness of its message. Whether any prophet even behaved in this way matters little compared to the book's substantial claim, that God's concern has always been wider than the people of Israel.

Although in some cases such disjunction between text and fact could prove problematic, what is more likely to create trauma for today's Church is the discovery of discord between some original intended meaning and current theological assumptions. One cannot help suspecting that this explains the popularity of postmodernism in some unexpected quarters, since it would appear to dispense with the need to face alternative interpretations from those currently set by the community of faith.[145] Sometimes, of

---

[145] One notes with surprise its endorsement by some conservative writers (even some not far removed from fundamentalism) because that endorsement sits ill with postmodernism's acceptance of pluralism.

course, such a disjunction could come as a salutary challenge for the Church to change its perspective to the earlier view, but on other occasions there will no escaping the recognition that the text's most obvious meaning is one which a contemporary Christian ought rightly to disown as never properly part of the divine will.[146] Quite a number of examples have been offered in earlier chapters. It is important to note, though, that even such a discovery should not be taken as excluding altogether the text under view from questions of revelatory truth, for it is important that as a community the Church be confronted by its own history and so by the key role played throughout by its own distortions of the divine will. There is no more insidious trap than a self-deception that works in support of one's own prejudices and self-interest. Recognition that this befell even the greatest of prophets, psalmists, evangelists, and saints can act as a powerful restraint in controlling any present desire to distort the divine purpose in our own contemporary situation. The Bible can scarcely be used to manipulate or browbeat others if there is full consciousness, no less of the degree to which it is embedded in the world's corruption, than of its capacity to transcend that world. So, however unpalatable, the original sense needs to continue to be heard, even where a more fruitful meaning was assigned by later developments in the tradition.

Secondly, in addition to establishing how revelation in fact worked, there must remain core historical questions which cannot be discounted by any religion that claims a decisive revelation at a certain point in time. In discussing the patriarchal narratives, I observed that, even though I still thought it quite likely that they had some basis in fact, nothing much seemed to hang on whether they were historical or not.[147] At most, the story of the developing tradition would then need to begin later, whenever such legends were first invented. Matters are quite otherwise, though, on some other matters. Thus for anything like orthodox Christianity to survive, it would seem to me indispensable that the

---

[146] Expressing it thus, if anything, increases the obligation to identify the good motives as well as the bad that may have led to the adoption of the earlier perspective in its original context. Nothing could be more dangerous than a facile superiority to an earlier age.

[147] *Tradition and Imagination*, Ch. 5, esp. 220–2.

incarnation occurred. Yet, as I tried to indicate in the relevant chapter, for that to be historically grounded much less is required than is often supposed.[148] This, though, is not the place to renew that argument. Instead, let me draw attention to only one aspect of any such discussion, the extent to which the secular historian might be relevant.

Because the religious believer and secular historian reach different conclusions, it is often argued by postmodernists that it would be best if each went their own way. Certainly, it is important to recognize the way in which wider conceptual frameworks help shape how we read the evidence. It would be absurd, for example, to expect the key role played by the resurrection in my argument to be allowed except by someone already committed to a religious framework. Even so, that should not be taken to imply that the two frameworks can never profitably meet. People do change their conceptual frames, and one way in which this happens is through interaction between their existing perspectives and recalcitrant forms of evidence. The resistance of the resurrection to any easy naturalist explanation would be an example that pulls in one direction; the frequency of records of miracles in narratives from the ancient world, an example of pull the other way. But it is also important to note that there are also many instances where conceptual frame exercises a less powerful control, and here I think it does become possible fully to assimilate interpretations of the evidence from all sides, non-Christian no less than Christian. On my view, it is this scenario which has compelled an understanding of Jesus' life and teaching significantly different from what has been believed throughout most of the history of the Church.

Bultmann and Tillich thought that only the preached Christ mattered.[149] I cannot agree. One factor which motivated them in this view was a desire for certainty, but the fact that historical understandings of Jesus will require periodic revision surely need in principle be no more undermining of faith than any of the

---

[148] *Tradition and Imagination.* Ch. 6.

[149] Though Tillich tried to have it both ways. For, while rejecting the relevance of historical research, he still thought it appropriate to speak of what he calls an *analogia imaginis* 'between the picture and the actual personal life from which it has arisen'. *Systematic Theology* (London: SCM Press, 1978), 2, 101–17, esp. 115.

numerous other changes in the Church's understanding of him that have occurred across the centuries. The only difference now is that in our own more historically conscious age we tend to make such changes explicit to ourselves, and herein surely lies an advantage. It may also one day be an advantage shared by Islam, should it ever come to terms with a more developmental view of the Qur'an and Hadith.[150] Of the three monotheistic faiths, superficially at least it is Judaism that seems the least secure in its foundations, since few scholars would now any longer wish to claim that much of the Pentateuchal legal system comes from Moses himself. But I wonder whether such admissions are really as harmful to Judaism as similar admissions would be for the other two faiths. Reform Judaism has in any case chosen to relocate its focus in the message of the prophets, while, even were Orthodoxy forced into the admission that its essential form derived from the post–exilic period and that its real founders were anonymous, the pattern of appropriate obedience to God would still have been set as the marking definition for subsequent developments of the tradition.

Empirical criteria   Only brief mention is required of scientific cosmology and evolution, to give one clear indication of what I have in mind here. The requirement that the opening chapters of Genesis should still state revelatory truth but in a way that is compatible with scientific discovery has in my view not only opened up a more profound reading of the passages concerned, but also, somewhat ironically, almost certainly one more in accord with the original intentions of the writers concerned. We now have a myth that speaks to the condition of each and every one of us, rather than a very distant piece of past history.

However, I have used the looser term 'empirical' because I think such concerns extend well beyond the narrowly scientific. Take the issue with which this second volume began, the equality of the sexes. I suggested that the reason why the sexes were treated differently over the centuries, including during the scriptural period, was not simply because of prejudice but also because there were assumed to be relevant differences between the sexes that justified such treatment. That is something which most people now no longer believe to be the case, but it is hardly a conclusion

[150] *Tradition and Imagination*, 151–67.

of science. Rather, it has been more a matter of empirical discovery, as experience has demonstrated women to be no less effective in positions of leadership, education, and so forth. The more fundamental New Testament principle of equality of regard could then be invoked to require equality of status, once deep-seated assumptions about underlying differences justifying differences of status had been undermined.[151]

In making such discoveries, though, it is important that we do not pretend that such truths were after all hidden in the scriptural text. That is why I protested against any unqualified use of Galatians 3: 28 that failed to acknowledge its more limited meaning in its original context. God has enabled a new meaning to be given to the text in a quite new situation. Again, to take another example not previously discussed, our understanding of homosexuality and its causes is in the process of transformation. What the final result will be I leave to others to reflect. It remains important, though, that, in trying to understand potential implications, pronouncements of Bible and modern period alike are set against the backdrop of the way the issue was experienced at the time.

As a final example, consider the changing attitudes to providence that we considered in Chapter 4. Much of the material in the historical and prophetic books of the Old Testament is dominated by a theology of corporate judgement upon nations. Because the notion is so prominent in the Bible, numerous attempts to apply the scheme have been made throughout history. Even as late as the nineteenth century Parliament voted a national fast day in response to the outbreak of cholera in England while many attributed the Irish Potato Famine to an act of divine judgement. Indeed, even as late as 1949 the distinguished historian, Herbert Butterfield was still wrestling with the possibility of such a theology and its application to the two world wars.[152] Theological arguments could in their turn be brought against such a picture, and we noted some of these in the relevant chapter. But that is not

---

[151] I argued in Chapter 1 that one could infer from Jesus' teaching a principle of equality of regard that requires us to value all human beings as of equal worth in the sight of God, irrespective of their status or capacities, but of course that does not require us to abolish distinctions of status unless they are found to lack justification.

[152] H. Butterfield, *Christianity and History* (London: Fontana, 1949), esp. 67–91.

in the end what I think proved decisive. It is that as our world shrinks in size, experience makes it harder and harder to isolate either natural or historical events for this corporate role. There seems no obvious pattern to famine or flood, while the fate of the two little nations of Israel and Judah is not conspicuously different from many another small nation wedged between major empires, whether we take the Poles in the eighteenth century, Afghanistan in the nineteenth, or Belgium or Poland once more in the twentieth. The trust or otherwise of their peoples in God had little or nothing to do with what befell them.

Conceptual criteria   Here I have in mind questions of coherence and intelligibility. Some are all too familiar from exercises in philosophy. Does continuing personal identity require resurrection of the body or not? Does it make sense to speak of God creating in time? And so forth. Pertinent to our concerns here are somewhat looser, though in some ways more important, conceptual issues. An example would be what I take to be the final pressure towards adopting the doctrine of the Trinity. The previous chapter suggested that Arianism was in fact nearer to the general force of the New Testament witness than the orthodox assertion of the equality of the three persons in one God.[153] Nonetheless, it would be my contention that such extensive powers are assigned to Christ in the New Testament that it is simpler to speak of his complete identity with God rather than use the language of subordination which so dominates the biblical text. Whether the specific example is accepted or not, the point is that the demand for conceptual clarity has sometimes the power to overthrow the obvious surface meaning of the text.

Another, quite different example would be the question of heaven which we considered in Chapter 3. In the New Testament the dominant picture is of our resurrection having to wait to the end of all things, with Christ the only human being declared here and now unqualifiedly to be alive and awake in heaven. Yet does this make sense? Are human beings not necessarily social animals, with interdependence the very essence of what we are? Even hermits, it may be observed, presuppose some relation with others.

---

[153] Also argued at greater length in *Tradition and Imagination*, Ch. 6.

So I argued that it looks as though the doctrine of the permanent exaltation of Christ's human nature to heaven at the ascension makes no sense unless it is supplemented by a claim that heaven is not otherwise empty. The tendency of much modern theology to return to the primary biblical image is thus, so far from being illuminating, actually a perversion of what it is to be human: Christ's human nature living in complete isolation from all others. If this is denied and coherence after all claimed, the question could then forcibly be put as to why a similar pattern might also not then be applicable to the rest of humanity, with all the potential that has to undermine the doctrine of the Church as an interdependent body. That is why I therefore argued that the Church should follow the minority New Testament witness, and envisage a community of saints already with Christ in heaven. A subsequent chapter then suggested that therein lay one suitable *raison de'être* for the story and doctrine of the assumption of the Virgin Mary.

Moral criteria   Although under the two previous criteria I did not mention the way in which their application might be modified by wider frames and presuppositions, I take it that this also applies no less than in the case of historical questions. Indeed, I observed in the opening chapter of the previous volume the way in which philosophy itself is affected even by assumptions that may be largely unknown to activists in the field at the time.[154] One might in any case have suspected as much from the dismissive way in which philosophers sometimes refer to those belonging to alternative schools, as, for instance, continues to happen today with some of the comments made by analytic philosophers on continental philosophy. However, matters are not quite as culture-relative as the existence of such attitudes might be taken to imply. For, though difficult, it remains possible to present the arguments that weigh with those of a different school in a way that even a hostile critic can begin to see the point, and sometimes fruitful interchange is the result.

That issue of location within a particular perspective or appeal to something more universal applies also to the use of moral criteria. Believer and non-believer alike have in the past in my view

---

[154] Well illustrated in E. Craig, *The Mind of God and the Works of Man* (Oxford: Clarendon Press, 1987).

been too quick to apply what are seen as universal values to their estimate of the moral teaching of Scripture without any regard to cultural context.[155] Equally, though, we must guard against the other extreme of supposing that there are no values to which we need to give heed beyond those internal to the canon. Consider Abraham's planned sacrifice of Isaac. In my earlier volume I argued that later tradition rightly moved the focus to Isaac as himself a responsible agent, whereas the biblical version still treats the child as the father's property. Morally, by that move self-sacrifice became the supreme ideal for both Christianity and Judaism, an account which was later to be reinforced by the view that any child must be treated as valuable in its own right.[156] Historically, it looks quite likely that these perceptions may have originated at definite points in human history and in response to specific triggers, in the former case perhaps during the Maccabean period, in the latter during the Gothic age. So one story one might tell is of a self-regulating tradition, the later developments of which supplement and correct earlier positions.

But it is important that this should not be all that is said. So let me add three caveats. The first concerns the morality of the original context, and the need to hear fully how the particular perspective under review would have been received at the time. I am not suggesting that this would lead us to regard the conduct as after all appropriate, but such reflection can sometimes make us considerably more sympathetic. To most of us the notion of treating children as property sounds quite repulsive, but clearly it could be combined, as in Abraham's case, with a real love of the child. Secondly, the fact that it took centuries for our present attitudes to develop does not mean that they are just as relative as what preceded them. That would only follow if we denied any element of progress in moral understanding. While with the history of the twentieth century behind us it would be absurd to claim progress in moral conduct, the ideas that go with it are quite another thing. Changing attitudes to children would in my view be one such example; another, the move to a more internalized view of morality, which in the chapter on Job I suggested was integral to under-

---

[155] An objection I made against Voltaire and the Enlightenment generally in *Tradition and Imagination*, 18.

[156] For Isaac, ibid., 237–60 ; for general value attaching to children, 75–85.

standing changed attitudes to suffering. A God envisaged as
concerned to enable us through grace to use positively whatever
suffering befalls us is substituted for the earlier view where it was
primarily a matter of the external engineering of events to bring
about our good. It is not revelation alone, though, that brings
about such progress. Triggers sometimes come from outside, and
with the plurality of traditions in the modern world there would
seem no reason why that pattern should not continue. Indeed, on
an issue like human rights, Christianity can be seen to be heavily
dependent on insights from elsewhere: it is simply not a biblical
perspective. Yet at other times the only possible response to a
contribution from outside will necessarily need to be negative, so
hostile is the view to the perceived fundamental direction of the
Christian tradition. This brings me to my third caveat. For, while
I do believe in progress in moral insights, regression is also possible, not only in horrendous ways such as the ideology of Nazism
but also more subtly where the secular world might even tempt us
back to earlier positions within the developing religious tradition.
If we continue with the *Akedah*—the binding of Isaac—as our
example, a case in point might be the way in which those who
argue for abortion or infant euthanasia often readily speak of the
acceptability of the notion of a substitute child.[157] Though
canvassed by non-believers, such views, it seems to me, offer a
morality not far removed from some of the approaches to Isaac's
death that earlier tradition had already decisively rejected.

Criteria of continuity   With these and subsequent criteria we now
move away from typically modernist criteria that still make some
claim to universality, and focus instead on the specifics of a particular tradition. Revelation, I have argued, builds upon earlier
versions of itself, and so that is one reason why it is important to
locate trajectories in the earlier tradition from which later insights
can be seen, partly at least, to stem. Such trajectories, though,
should not be too closely identified with any formal process of
derivation. Indeed, even where matters could be set out thus, as
seems to be possible in the case of the developing doctrine of the
Trinity, it would still be important to acknowledge that in prac-

[157] E.g. 'New-born babies, like foetuses, are replaceable': J. Glover, *Causing
Death and Saving Lives* (Harmondsworth: Penguin, 1977), 159.

tice the development proceeds intuitively rather than by means of the retrospective kind of argument which I sought to offer in my own discussion. In other cases, however, such a formal presentation could not be achieved even in principle. Thus with Job what I suggested happened was more a case of Scripture setting and legitimating an open agenda of issues that still required resolution rather than setting the course towards one specific attitude to suffering that should then be adopted by the community. If I am right about the latter, more informal pattern, it proves the Bible to be a more open text than it is usually acknowledged to be.

But that emphatically does not mean that anything goes. In each case that I considered I sought to identify features which, if they did not necessitate the trajectory, at least meant that subsequent developments appeared natural. So, for instance, in Chapter 1 I noted the way in which the evangelists were already experimenting with the story of Mary Magdalene as a means of deepening discipleship, and so the extension of that story in post-biblical legends cannot be deemed inappropriate. Indeed, that is to put matters altogether too weakly, since it was my contention that the post-biblical version did more effectively what the Bible had only begun to do. Likewise, to give an example this time more relevant to developments within Judaism and Islam, the beginnings of reflection on the nature of virtue that are to be found in the biblical story of Joseph were considerably deepened through imaginative expansions of key incidents.[158] But sometimes it is hard to detect any form of continuity, and, where that happens, questions of legitimacy and so of revelatory truth are inevitably raised. That is why I suggested that Paul's attitude to the law was so deeply problematic.[159] His more extreme comments implied an entirely negative role. Yet the move to a God in whom one could confidently put one's faith seems convincing only if there were clear signs of consistency of divine purpose across history, and for that one needs the whole legal tradition that Paul appeared to reject. In other words, because Paul in his more radical moments wanted to claim total discontinuity, I argued that any notion of a trajectory therefore failed, and that, though Paul could still be speaking the

---

[158] *Tradition and Imagination*, 260–71. Reflection within Christianity was inhibited by the desire to draw a direct parallel with Christ.

[159] Ch. 6 in this volume, chs. 5 and 6 in *Tradition and Imagination*.

truth, the presumption must be that he could only make such a claim from outside the developing Jewish tradition and not as part of it. Some have of course sought to endorse such a divorce between Christianity and its Jewish past, but fortunately Matthew, I suggested, offered an alternative approach that maintained continuity but also introduced significant development, and in a way that allows a modified Paul to be incorporated within such a picture.

Christological criteria   The comments just made about Paul may seem inconsistent with remarks made a number of times elsewhere that speak of the tradition turning back on itself to 'correct' earlier perspectives. For instance, in *Tradition and Imagination* I said this both of the nativity and of the proper role of art within Christianity.[160] I claimed that the infancy narratives had originally nothing to do with the valuing of Christ's childhood as such, but were legitimately now given this role in our Christmas celebrations. Just as we must turn to later tradition for the significance of the incarnation to be applied to childhood, so also a later chapter argued that it required church reflection on God having painted and defined himself in the incarnation before the biblical suspicion of the visual arts could be overthrown. But both examples seem to me quite different from the Pauline case.

The contrast is perhaps clearer in respect of the infancy narratives. I argued that their original intention was partly to assert the predetermined character of God's plan and partly to anticipate Christ's significance, particularly as this was worked through in cross and resurrection. Divinity made manifest in a child was not part of the agenda of Matthew or Luke. In making that perception integral to the way in which the narratives are now understood, though, the Church is not contradicting the evangelists' claims. Rather, it is imposing a subsequently learnt pattern, in order to give them a wider, more inclusive focus.[161] The situation is thus quite different from the case of Paul, where something appears to be rescinded. The arguments about art might therefore be judged a closer parallel, but again I doubt this, though for somewhat

---

[160]   The argument of Chs. 2 and 5 respectively.

[161]   'Correct', though, still seems the right terminology, since the historical thrust of the narrative is judged inadequate in the light of later perspectives.

different reasons. Idolatry remains condemned throughout. What changes is the perception of whether religious art must necessarily fall foul of that charge. Given the attitudes of their pagan neighbours, the biblical writers seem to have assumed that such art would necessarily be corrupting, whereas the incarnation demonstrated that this is not an automatic implication. Biblical suspicion is thus contexualized rather than overthrown completely. Admittedly, even Paul's approach to Law is sometimes of this more limited but positive kind, but the fact that he argues differently elsewhere means that we should not acquit ourselves from facing his more radical claims in all their starkness.

Theologians sometimes assert that all of Scripture should be read in the light of Christ. There are versions of that claim that are right and proper. The person and teaching of Christ lie at the heart of the Christian faith; so every attempt should be made to integrate what is read and heard with commitment as one of Christ's disciples. But that demand can very easily go wrong when it is interpreted as the requirement that every story within the tradition be required to bear a christological meaning. Admittedly, sometimes thinking in this way helps. Most obviously is this so with the Gospel narratives themselves, where much is to be gained by reading them in the light of later beliefs regarding Christ's full significance, provided, that is, this is done in a way that does not fight shy of any problems raised by the earlier meanings. Again, interpreting Isaac as type for Christ, whether present as an approach in the New Testament or not, certainly helped reinforce and accelerate the already existing Jewish pattern of treating Isaac as an voluntary agent going to his death. But one might contrast that case with what occurs in respect of the story of Joseph. The danger is that all that happens is that already existing meanings are imposed, and so nothing new is learnt. Unlike the creativity shown in the Jewish and Muslim traditions, this is in effect what happened within Christianity with Joseph, primarily, it seems, because of the desire to see him as anticipatory of Christ. A more fruitful approach therefore, in my view, is first to allow texts their own independent integrity, and only then let the risen Christ cast his own distinctive but separate light on the narrative concerned. That way the value of both is respected. Yet it is only fair to add that even the most arbitrary imposition can sometimes generate fresh insights, especially where strong metaphors have been produced as a result, as in the case of David or Samson as Christ figures. One need only think of the image of the crucifixion as a lyre perfectly strung, or Christ as Samson throwing open the gates of hell.[162]

Degree of imaginative engagement   Objection may be taken to listing this among criteria for revelatory truth on the grounds that what is really at stake here is the effectiveness of a story rather than its truth content. But, as the first part of the chapter sought to illustrate, it is impossible to demarcate the two issues quite so sharply. A less factually based story might still exhibit overall greater correspondence with reality. Indeed, I argued that this was pre-eminently so of the Gospel narratives themselves. By pointing to where his life and teaching would finally lead, the evangelists offered a more accurate portrait of who Christ was and is, and his relevance to ourselves, than if they had given us a literal record of what he did and said while on earth. So what I am trying to suggest by such a criterion is the range of issues addressed by such rewritings. It is not that the Gospels ignore questions of historicity; note, for instance, Luke's frequent detailed locating of events at particular points in time (e.g. 3: 1; cf. 1: 5; 2: 1–2). It is just that historical fact is by no means the only type of truth to which the narratives intended to lay claim.

But, precisely because that type of writing does not cease with the closure of the canon, we are entitled to ask whether, sometimes at least, later tradition did not do the job at least as well, if not better. The story of Mary Magdalene has already been mentioned when discussing criteria of continuity. One might also note the way later versions of her story introduce new or greatly expanded elements that might be said to afford greater imaginative engagement or fit, in terms of the issues raised by discipleship. So, for example, one finds a more realistic acceptance of the gradualism that is characteristic of discipleship, with each incident in the life of the composite figure being used to suggest development and growth in discipleship, while the mere hint in the Scriptures of her proclaiming the gospel is turned in later legend into her acting as a preacher in the south of France in her own right.[163] None of this

---

[162] For examples and discussion: of the former, *Tradition and Imagination*, 330–1; of the latter, this volume, 113–14.
[163] The hint is at John 20: 18.

is historical, but neither is every detail in the Gospels. So the key question becomes which version offers the more accurate portrayal of the nature of discipleship and its demands.

Effectiveness of analogical construct   The exercise of our imagination is no less context dependent than that of any of our other faculties. This means that, though some narratives will continue to have universal appeal, others will be more able to be heard as relevant at some junctures of history than others. Controversially, I claimed that this applied even to the story of Jesus, and that in appropriating his example for our own lives it has often proved easier for this to be mediated in a story of circumstances more like our own. That I suggested was one key function in the past of the Lives of the saints, though today it might perhaps be more effectively achieved through the novel.[164] Truth in such cases would therefore be a matter of the effectiveness of the analogy between the two worlds, that of Jesus and the new narrative. Some might argue that the relating principles would be enough to determine appropriate conduct under different circumstances, such as marriage, war, or whatever, but something vital would in fact be lost without the corresponding new narrative: the worked-through example. That is to put the matter somewhat pedantically, but the point is that we often have to see something lived through before we can form a realistic estimate of its truth, and the writer of fiction helps us to see such a possible life in the round.

But there is also another type of situation where such considerations apply. This can perhaps best be illustrated by some of the claims which I made in the relevant chapter on the Virgin Mary. I noted how virginity changed its imaginative significance during the patristic period, from the biblical 'instrument' to a sign of the empowerment of women, before being largely usurped by more negative notions of purity. Again, the medieval period witnesses a major expansion in the role of Mary's mother, Anne, which in some quarters of the world was to continue even as late as the twentieth century. What we seem to have in both cases are alternative analogical constructs of how Mary's significance was to be appropriated, in the one case with virginity as a sign for women of freedom from family constraints and in the other an indicator of

---

[164] This volume, Ch. 2.

the indispensable contribution made by the wider, or extended
family. The two pull into opposed directions, the one challenging
the family, the other endorsing it, even if in a more feminine
direction. One way of understanding such phenomena would be
to talk of analogical constructs relevant to particular periods and
social conditions. Here it is harder to identify permanent truth
content, but in order that the past should not be distorted it is
clearly important that we should try to understand what kind of
truth-claims were embodied in the imagery of the time.
Otherwise, a false reading will easily take its place: virginity seen
as something entirely negative, the expanded cult of Anne as
amounting to little more than the wishes of two queens who
happened to bear the same name. However, the very act of trying
to discover such contextualized truth can liberate it for wider relevance to our own day. Thus my suggestion in that chapter as a
whole was that through careful re-reading of history Mary could
be freed for a new role as model disciple, full of 'virgin promise'.
Not, of course, that such a rereading means that everything can be
salvaged (the doctrine of the Immaculate Conception was
subjected to a sustained critique), but it does at least mean that we
are not compelled to remain prisoners of the perspectives of our
own day.

Ecclesial criteria   The previous chapter dealt at length with problems of authority, and in particular pleaded for a more positive
estimate of the role of conflict in generating true belief. The
vagaries of church history both within the canon and beyond
convince me that no official pronouncements of the Church,
however conceived, can of themselves be said to carry an automatic seal of truth, any more than does Scripture itself. Even the
universal belief of centuries may fail. Hell as a place of eternal
punishment is fast disappearing from the Christian horizon,
though it is the belief of Scripture and almost the whole of
Christian history until the nineteenth century, with very few, rare
exceptions.[165] Belief in the immorality of contraception survived
as a universal belief within all the denominations even longer, until
the early twentieth century. So even the *consensus fidelium* is not an

---

[165] Though the number of dissenters increases significantly from the seventeenth century onwards.

absolute guarantor of truth. Yet that does not entail that the corporate Church has no role in determining revelatory truth, for it can act as a useful protection against individual arrogance and prejudice. The Spirit of God remains active throughout the entire body of the faithful, past no less than present, and so we are less likely to go wrong, the more we are prepared to take account of that full range of insight rather than relying wholly on our own efforts. In other words, talk about the indefectibility of the Church cannot be taken to mean that there is some shortcut to truth, but I do contend that the presumption must always be that truth is to be found somewhere within Christ's Church, for the Spirit is ever searching to correct the Church's inadequacies.

Conclusion

Both this volume and its predecessor had as their point of origin lectures delivered at Oxford and endowed by Hensley Henson, a former Fellow of All Souls, Oxford, who subsequently served as both Dean and Bishop of Durham. Responding in 1924 to Cardinal Bourne on the question of continuity with the church of the age of Bede (one of Durham's saints) he does not hesitate to concede that the greater formal similarity lies with Rome, but at the same time he is adamant that that is not the end of the argument. 'Continuity', he declares, 'does not mean identity of opinion, or of point of view, or of degree of knowledge, or of state of culture.'[166] None of us, he observes, can escape from 'the conditions of his time' and so the real question for continuity must be what becomes appropriate under new conditions of knowledge, new forms of culture.

There I would agree. I suspect that he would have been less happy with my stress on the role of tradition, but it does seem to me that this has been the imaginative motor that has ensured the continuous adaptation of God's revelation to the world under new circumstances and conditions. The process was a messy one since it entailed God's deep involvement with people like ourselves, and so a fallible Bible and a fallible Church interacting with a no less fallible wider world. That is why it has proved impossible to place any absolute priorities between the various

---

[166] H. H. Henson, *Continuity* (London: Hugh Rees, 2nd edn, 1927).

criteria except in relation to specific instances. But discipleship, if it is about anything, is surely not so much about instantaneous results as about a continuing process of transformation, as both as individuals and as a community we gradually learn more deeply of God's meaning and purpose for our lives. No doubt I have not always drawn the right conclusions. To some I will have appeared too liberal, to others too conservative. But, either way, pray God may that not inhibit the reader from engaging fully with the richness of this developing imaginative tradition, for its voice and vision remain the possession of us all.

Plates

Plate 1. Botticelli's *Saint Mary Magdalene at the Foot of the Cross* (*c.* 1500)

The influence of the reforming friar, Savonarola, on Botticelli is well known. A famous example (now in the National Gallery, London) is his *Mystical Nativity*. A first glance suggests an entirely lyrical composition, with angels dancing above and embracing beneath, so unrestrained is their joy at the significance of the birth that is taking place. But closer inspection reveals little devils scurrying away, while the painting's Greek inscription makes an apocalyptic connection between the year in which the artist completed the painting (1500) and prophecies from the book of Revelation (chapters 11–12). That same year also saw this painting, sometimes correspondingly labelled his *Mystical Crucifixion* (now in the Fogg Art Museum, Harvard). Although badly damaged, its essential structure is still easily discernible. Mary Magdalene clings to the foot of the cross, and gazes expectantly at an angel as he slays the treacherous animal in his grasp. Meanwhile God the Father sends other angels (their shields alone now visible) across the sky to drive away the black cloud on the right from which demons continue to fire black missiles. What the disappearing cloud reveals is the city of Florence, with its principal landmarks clearly visible, among them the Cathedral, Campanile, Baptistery, and Palazzo Vecchio, the seat of government. There seems little doubt that here Mary Magdalene is being used to represent all the citizens of Florence, summoned to penance at the foot of the cross and with the promise that, like Mary Magdalene, they too can be forgiven and the city's fortunes be restored. For further discussion of this and other examples of Mary as model or representative disciple, see Chapter 1, esp. p. 43 ff.

Plate 2. Parmigianino's *Mystic Marriage of Saint Catherine* (c. 1530)

As his name implies, Parmigianino came from Parma in the north of Italy. His slightly older contemporary, Correggio, (from a village nearby) painted a number of sentimental and quietly meditative versions of the mystical marriage, whereas Parmigianino in this painting of *c.* 1530 (now in the National Gallery, London) uses several devices to create a more active and dynamic scene. The onlookers at the rear of the painting help to give us a sense that we too are observing something significant, while the contorted body of the Virgin combines with the expectant eyes of her Son to suggest that both must soon rise to witness what will happen next. The wheel on which Catherine's hand rests gives us our answer, but, so far from being merely a wheel of torture, the dawn of a new day is promised, as the curtain drawn back to reveal a light-filled window of similar shape makes abundantly clear. All this could be read as no more than the typical martyrdom message, but there are at least two indicators in the painting that seem to imply something more. In the first place, Catherine's marriage is unmediated: her relation with Christ is direct and immediate. Secondly, the dramatic exclusion of the male figure's body in the bottom left is scarcely accidental. Whether he is intended to be the hostile emperor who sent Catherine to her death or one of the fifty male philosophers who challenged her wisdom is unclear. His appearance perhaps makes the latter more likely, but either way the curve of the features that survive suggest a smaller, less significant version of the wheel, and so Catherine's triumph over both male power and male wisdom. For further discussion of the significance of Catherine's legend, see pp. 85–9.

Plate 3. Anonymous sixteenth-century tapestry of the *Hunt of the Unicorn*

This early sixteenth-century representation of the Hunt (now in the Burrell Collection) well illustrates the ambiguities inherent in the image. Is Christ as the unicorn the hunter or the hunted? In this particular version he appears to be both. On the one hand, he is clearly the object of the hunt with the angel driving the unicorn before him with his yelping pack of hounds. Admittedly, only one single dog appears before us, but the blown hunting horn surely suggests the presence of many others in the rear. Yet, on the other hand, the unicorn is clearly also in hunt of safety, and this he has just found by trespassing the elaborately fenced medieval garden that has brought him to the security of the Virgin Mary's lap. Mary's virginity as an enclosed garden is of course a common theme, deriving ultimately from the Song of Songs (4: 12). The German text is perhaps intended to reconcile the two interpretations. It declares that 'from heaven's throne I have come hunting to announce much good for the pure maid' (von himelthron ich hab gejagt verkund vil guts der reinne magt). Its form suggests that the words are intended to be attributed to the hunting angel who is here treated as equivalent to the angel of the annunciation, but, if so, then hunting the hunter becomes all part of a single divine plan. For further reflections on artistic uses of other versions of this image, see pp. 168–70.

Plate 4. Panel from Dürer's *Jabach Altarpiece* (*c.* 1503–4)

This painting well illustrates later developments in the way the story of Job was told. In medieval times his sufferings came to be associated with the pains of those afflicted with various forms of illness, including sexual disease, and it is therefore no accident that the triptych which Frederick the Wise commissioned in 1503 at Wittenberg to mark the end of an outbreak of plague should include references to Job in both its side panels. The right-hand panel (now in Cologne, where the Jabach family owned the entire work until the end of the eighteenth century) depicts two musicians, a piper and a drummer, the latter bearing Dürer's own features, while on the left (this illustration from Frankfurt) Job's wife pours a bucket of water over him. In the distance his house is on fire, and many take this as evidence enough that Job's wife must also be adding to Job's torments (hence its common title *Job Mocked by his Wife*), but the presence of the musicians in the other panel argues for a different interpretation. Music was normally interpreted as one means by which Job was comforted (this is how the matter was later treated by Blake), and there is nothing to suggest animosity in his wife's face. So a more likely interpretation is that this is a further development of the move that began early (most obviously in *The Testament of Job*) towards a more compassionate wife, and that the water is therefore intended to soothe his boils. Note too that Job sits on the Vulgate's 'dunghill' and not on the Hebrew 'ash-pit'. Changing patterns in the literary and artistic treatment of the story of Job are discussed in Chapter 4.

Plate 5. *The Holy Kindred* by the artist known as Older Master of the Holy Kindred (*c.* 1410–40)

This is the central panel of a triptych, the two side panels of which offer us four traditional nativity scenes. What is striking about this central panel is the substitution for the male-dominated Jesse Tree of this female table of affinity for Jesus' ancestors. The theme became very popular in the fifteenth century, and there are several examples like this one at Cologne, but as a topic it was discouraged by the Counter-Reformation. In this version most of the figures are helpfully named. Mary sits in the middle with Jesus on her lap. Her mother, a young Anne, is to her right, and points to her three husbands behind her: reading out the way towards the edge of the panel, we find first Joachim, the father of Mary, followed by Cleophas and Salomas, also fathers of children called Mary; then nearest to the painting's edge, their two husbands, Alpheus and Zebedee. Nearer to us and on Anne's right, Anne's other two daughters then sit, each holding some of the apostles as children; for example, Mary Salome is nearest to us and holds on her lap James the Great and John the Evangelist. Meanwhile, behind Mary on her left is Joseph who is engaged in conversation with Zechariah, while his wife Elizabeth sits before him and his child John the Baptist on her lap points to his cousin, Jesus. The other remaining figures on our right are from the Baptist's side of the family, culminating in the little boy nearest our vision on the far right. A descendant of Elizabeth's sister, Hismeria, he is identified as Saint Servatius, important because he was believed to be buried at nearby Maastricht. To the reader all this may seem like medieval invention at its very worst. By way of extenuation one could note in any case the confused nature of the biblical narratives, where there are a bewildering number of 'cousins' and 'Marys'. This table of affinity at least tried to make some sense of the relationships. More significant, though, is the dominant place given to women, who unlike the men, including the apostles, are not even identified, so secure is their place. For a discussion of the wider implications of the key role once given to Anne, see pp. 246–50; for an example of an attempt to subvent such images, p. 247, n. 74.

Plate 6. Simone Martini's *Christ Discovered in the Temple* (1342)

Mary's open book indicates, even if we could not guess it already, that the scene is based on the precise point in Luke's narrative at which Mary asks of her twelve-year-old son: 'My son why have you treated us like this? Your father and I have been searching for you in great anxiety' (2: 48 NEB). Some wish to interpret the boy's gesture as one of resignation to his heavenly Father's will, but it seems more natural to me to see the response as that of a typical adolescent sulking or in the huff at such a reprimand. Certainly, Joseph's gesture suggest that Jesus has not quite seen the point, while Mary gently pleads from her position of humility on a low bench. It is perhaps unlikely that in the fourteenth century either artist or church authorities would have been willing to ascribe such an attitude to the young Christ, especially if it were thought to raise troubling issues about his perfection and sinlessness. So perhaps a more plausible explanation is to suggest that Martini has unconsciously borrowed the gesture to suggest resolve and commitment, whereas what in fact he opened up was the way towards a more human and natural reading of Jesus' early life. In chapter 5 a more dynamic way of understanding the relation between Mary and Jesus is explored, including the notion of Jesus also depending on Mary and Joseph for his development (e. g. pp. 284–7).

Plate 7. Albrecht Dürer's *Four Apostles* (1526)

Now in Munich, this was originally a gift in 1526 by the artist himself to the city of Nuremberg which had officially endorsed the Reformation in the preceding year. Various symbols help us immediately to identify the figures, Saint Peter, for example, in the background on the left with his keys or Paul to the front on the right with his fat writings and holding the sword that would mark his eventual martyrdom. The youthful John on the left is also quickly recognizable. With Mark we might have experienced more difficulty, had not Dürer added a wealth of texts beneath that make the identity of all four indisputable. The Protestant context is underlined by the way in which the selection from the four writers is introduced: a stern warning is given that nothing must be added or taken away from the Scriptures as God's Word. Protestant too is the distribution of the figures, with Paul firmly to the front and Peter rather squashed in the rear. Note too how Paul alone looks quizzically at the viewer, and in effect becomes the interpretative key for the other three, for Mark stares admiringly at him, while so absorbed are the other two in the book open before them that it seems left to Paul to preach its contents. More worrying for community and tradition, Paul's own book is closed, as though despite the small print below, personal inspiration was now seen as enough. There is also contemporary evidence from the calligrapher to suggest that Paul was deliberately given the features of a melancholic genius, melancholy not being viewed in the same negative way as it is today. For a general discussion of visual images of Peter and Paul across the centuries, including this one, see pp. 335–42, esp. 340.

Plate 8. El Greco's *Tears of Saint Peter* (early 1580s)

The penitence of St Peter became a popular Counter-reformation theme for a number of reasons. The traditional alternative, Mary Magdalene, was now deemed less satisfactory, partly for historical reasons (the composite character of her legend was widely acknowledged) and partly because she was now being increasingly usurped for purely sensual compositions. But there was also a positive reason: it allowed the life of the first pope to imply the absolute centrality of a sacramental system as over against any notion of justification by faith alone. El Greco painted no less than five versions of this theme, this one (now in the Bowes Museum) probably being the earliest and dating from the early 1580s. Peter's internal turbulence is reflected in the sky and landscape, but also his grounds for hope. On the rock on the right the outline of some ivy growing is just visible—a sign of immortality—and this is confirmed by the images in the background on the left, an angel in a blaze of light sitting on the lid of Christ's tomb with Mary Magdalene in front already hastening to tell the disciples the good news. In itself all this might be taken to suggest that faith in what Christ has done is sufficient. That is no doubt why El Greco makes Peter's hands clasped in prayer central to his composition: action on our part is no less requisite. As if to underline the point, El Greco adds his signature (in Greek) on the right edge exactly parallel with the top of those hands. Here, though, there are no keys unlike in Goya's version from the 1820s (now in the Phillips Collection, Washington, DC), where their presence might be taken to argue more explicitly for a different model of the papacy. For the whole question of authority in the Church, see Chapter 6; for what paintings like this might be taken to imply, especially pp. 339–40.

INDEX